Political Science
An Introduction

Twelfth Edition

Michael G. Roskin
LYCOMING COLLEGE

Robert L. Cord

James A. Medeiros

Walter S. Jones

Longman

Boston   Columbus   Indianapolis   New York   San Francisco   Upper Saddle River
Amsterdam   Cape Town   Dubai   London   Madrid   Milan   Munich   Paris   Montréal   Toronto
Delhi   Mexico City   São Paulo   Sydney   Hong Kong   Seoul   Singapore   Taipei   Tokyo

Senior Acquisitions Editor: Vikram Mukhija
Senior Marketing Manager: Lindsey Prudhomme
Assistant Editor: Corey Kahn
Editorial Assistant: Beverly Fong
Associate Production Manager: Scarlett Lindsay
Project Coordination, Text Design, and Electronic Page Makeup: Integra
Cover Design Manager: John Callahan
Cover Designer: Kay Petronio
Cover Image: RTIMAGES, © Veer, Inc.
Image Researcher: Connie Gardner
Senior Manufacturing Buyer: Dennis Para
Printer and Binder: RR Donnelley–Crawfordsville
Cover Printer: Lehigh-Phoenix Color Corporation–Hagerstown

For permission to use copyrighted material, grateful acknowledgment is made to the copyright holders on p. 376, which is hereby made part of this copyright page.

Library of Congress Cataloging-in-Publication Data

Political science : an introduction/Michael G. Roskin ... [et al.].—12th ed.
   p. cm.
  ISBN 978-0-205-07594-2
  1. Political science.   I. Roskin, Michael
  JA71.P623 2012
  320—dc22

                                         2010052277

Longman
is an imprint of

www.pearsonhighered.com

1 2 3 4 5 6 7 8 9 10—DOC—14 13 12 11

ISBN-13: 978-0-205-07594-2
ISBN-10:   0-205-07594-0

Brief Contents

Detailed Contents

PART II POLITICAL ATTITUDES 117

CHAPTER 7 Political Culture 118

CHAPTER 8 Public Opinion 136

CHAPTER 14   Executives and Bureaucracies   252

CHAPTER 15   Judiciaries   274

Preface

An apocryphal edition of *Pravda* during the Bolshevik Revolution is said to have headlined: "No News Today, Events Moving Too Fast." Authors of political science texts often feel the same. The election of Barack Obama amid the worst recession since the Great Depression gave us a feast of questions and examples that enliven classroom discussions. Obama's election and his healthcare and finance reforms in the face of massive fiscal deficits triggered a conservative backlash. Exaggerated belief in "change you can believe in" quickly turned into exaggerated disappointment over Obama's economic policies and high unemployment rates. An angry Tea Party pledged to undo everything Obama tried to accomplish.

The twelfth edition of *Political Science: An Introduction* tries to incorporate these waves. We include such recent events to show that ideology is alive and well in U.S. politics; indeed, ideological polarization has reached levels not seen in decades. The passage of healthcare reform ran into one of the profound instincts of U.S. political culture: big government is bad. Angry over the sluggish recovery, voters blamed the president personally and punished him at elections.

The good news for political science instructors is that the contentious atmosphere may get students interested in politics again. Bailouts, deficits, and the economic rise of authoritarian China provoke discussion. For some years, students have been rather apolitical, a trend this book has always tried to fight. Now we can ask, "Well, what kind of a country do you want? You'd better start developing your own rational perspectives now because soon you will have to make political choices."

Political Science: An Introduction blends scholarship and citizenship. It does not presume that freshmen taking an intro course will become professional political scientists. Naturally, we hope to pique their curiosity so that some will major in political science. This is neither a U.S. government text nor a comparative politics text. Instead, it draws examples from the United States and from other lands to introduce the whole field of political science to new students. Fresh from high school, few students know much of other political systems, something we attempt to correct.

The twelfth edition continues our eclectic approach that avoids selling any single theory, conceptual framework, or paradigm as the key to political science. Attempts to impose a grand design are both unwarranted by the nature of the discipline and not conducive to the broadening of students' intellectual horizons.

Instructors with a wide variety of viewpoints have no trouble using this text. Above all, the twelfth edition still views politics as exciting and tries to communicate that feeling to young people approaching the discipline for the first time.

NEW TO THIS EDITION

Instructor input, the rapid march of events, and insights from colleagues brought the following changes to the twelfth edition:

- We revised Chapter 5 and retitled it from "Constitutions" to "Rights" to emphasize how difficult it is to guarantee what many accept as universal values. They may be universal values, but building them is a long, hard undertaking.
- Democracy now faces some doubts and competition, we analyze in Chapter 6. Chinese authoritarianism could look down—at least briefly—on the Western financial meltdown, which seemed to show the weaknesses of democracy.
- The debate about healthcare reform neatly illustrates how American political culture is highly suspicious of government programs. It now leads our discussion of political culture in Chapter 7.
- The Tea Party's hatred of big government raises anew an old question—can we dispense with bureaucrats and bureaucracy?—that now leads us into Chapter 14.
- Chapter 16, "Political Economy," is updated to include the recession and the controversy over how to get out of it—spending or austerity? Our list of economic problems now contains consumer debt and income inequality.
- A new discussion in the final chapter on international relations posits the rise of China as the century's biggest problem.

FEATURES

The consolidation of 21 chapters into 18, now more rationally arranged, received very positive instructor feedback in the eleventh edition and so remains, as does the introduction of methodologies early in an undergraduate's career. This does not mean high-level numbers crunching—which I neither engage in nor advocate—but a reality-testing frame of mind that looks for empirical verifiability. Where you can, of course, use valid numbers. As an instructor, I often found myself explaining methodologies in the classroom in connection with student papers, so I decided to insert some basic methodologies as "How To" boxes. Each of these boxes make one methodological point per chapter, covering thesis statements, references, quotations, tables, cross-tabulations, graphs, scattergrams, and other standard points, all at the introductory level. Other boxes—Key Concepts, Comparing, and Classic Works—highlight important political science ideas, provide real world examples, and break up pages, making the text more reader friendly.

Each chapter begins with questions to consider and concludes with key terms and further references. The text also boldfaces important terms and defines them in running marginal glossaries throughout the chapters. As an instructor, I learned not to presume students understood the key terms of political science. The definitions are in the context under discussion; change that context, and you may need another definition. There is a difference, for example, between the governing elites discussed in Chapter 6 (a tiny fraction of 1 percent of a population) and public opinion elites discussed in Chapter 8 (probably several percent).

SUPPLEMENTS

Pearson Longman is pleased to offer several resources to qualified adopters of *Political Science* and their students that will make teaching and learning from this book even more effective and enjoyable. Several of the supplements for this book are available at the Instructor Resource Center (IRC), an online hub that allows instructors to quickly download book-specific supplements. Please visit the IRC welcome page at **www.pearsonhighered.com/irc** to register for access.

MyPoliSciKit for Political Science   This premium online learning companion features multimedia and interactive activities to help students connect concepts and current events. The book-specific assessment, video case studies, mapping exercises, comparative exercises, *Financial Times* newsfeeds, current events quizzes, and politics blog encourage comprehension and critical thinking. With Grade Tracker, instructors can easily follow students' work on the site and their progress on each activity. Use ISBN 0-205-07403-0 to order MyPoliSciKit with this book. To learn more, please visit **www.mypoliscikit.com** or contact your Pearson representative.

Passport for Introduction to Political Science   With Passport, choose the resources you want from MyPoliSciKit and put links to them into your course management system. If there is assessment associated with those resources, it also can be uploaded, allowing the results to feed directly into your course management system's gradebook. With over 150 MyPoliSciKit assets like video case studies, mapping exercises, comparative exercises, simulations, podcasts, *Financial Times* newsfeeds, current events quizzes, politics blog, and much more, Passport is available for any Pearson introductory or upper-level political science book. Use ISBN 0-205-10956-X to order Passport with this book. To learn more, please contact your Pearson representative.

Instructor's Manual/Test Bank   This resource includes learning objectives, chapter outlines, multiple-choice questions, true/false questions, and essay questions for each chapter. Available exclusively on the IRC.

Pearson MyTest   This powerful assessment generation program includes all of the items in the instructor's manual/test bank. Questions and tests can be easily created, customized, saved online, and then printed, allowing flexibility to manage assessments anytime and anywhere. To learn more, please visit **www.mypearsontest.com** or contact your Pearson representative.

PowerPoint Presentation   Organized around a lecture outline, these multimedia presentations also include photos, figures, and tables from each chapter. Available exclusively on the IRC.

The Economist   Every week, *The Economist* analyzes the important happenings around the globe. From business to politics, to the arts and science, its coverage connects seemingly unrelated events in unexpected ways. Use ISBN 0-205-00255-2 to order a 15-week subscription with this book for a small additional charge. To learn more, please contact your Pearson representative.

The Financial Times   Featuring international news and analysis from journalists in more than 50 countries, *The Financial Times* provides insights and perspectives on political and economic developments around the world. Use ISBN 0-205-10904-7 to order a 15-week subscription with this book for a small additional charge. To learn more, please contact your Pearson representative.

Longman Atlas of World Issues (0-205-78020-2)   From population and political systems to energy use and women's rights, the *Longman Atlas of World Issues* features full-color thematic maps that examine the forces shaping the world. Featuring maps from the latest edition of *The Penguin State of the World Atlas*, this excerpt includes critical thinking exercises to promote a deeper understanding of how geography affects many global issues. Available at no additional charge when packaged with this book.

Goode's World Atlas (0-321-65200-2)   First published by Rand McNally in 1923, *Goode's World Atlas* has set the standard for college reference atlases. It features hundreds of physical, political, and thematic maps as well as graphs, tables, and a pronouncing index. Available at a discount when packaged with this book.

ACKNOWLEDGMENTS

Several people reviewed this and earlier editions, and I carefully considered their comments. Corey Kahn at Longman pointed out many ambiguous wordings that I tried to clarify. For this edition, I wish to thank Anika Leithner, California Polytechnic State University; Lynn Mauer, Southern Illinois University–Edwardsville; and Jody Peterson, Centralia College.

Are further changes needed in the book, or have I got it about right? Instructors' input on this matter—or indeed on anything else related to the text or supplementary materials—is highly valued. Instructors may contact me directly by e-mail at maxxumizer@gmail.com.

MICHAEL G. ROSKIN

PART I

THE BASES OF POLITICS

Main Lessons to Be Learned

Ch. 1 Politics and Political Science   We study politics in a naturalistic mode, like a scientist studies bacteria, never getting angry at a fact but trying to understand how and why something happens. Although political science draws from all the other social sciences, it focuses on power—how A gets B to do what A wants. We do not confuse our partisan preferences with the scholarly study of politics.

Ch. 2 Theories   Political theories—which questions to ask and which to ask first—range from the classic theories of our founder, Aristotle, through Hobbes, Locke, Rousseau, and Marx to institutional theory. Contemporary theories—meaning post World War II—include behavioralism, systems, modernization, rational-choice, and the new institutionalism. We learn there is nothing so practical as theory.

Ch. 3 Political Ideologies   Ideologies, often rooted in political theories, are plans to improve society. The classic liberalism of Adam Smith and classic conservatism of Edmund Burke and the modern versions of the same are still with us. Marx led to both social democracy and, through Lenin, communism. Nationalism is the strongest ideology, at times turning into fascism. New ideologies include neoconservatism, libertarianism, feminism, environmentalism, and, currently a problem, Islamism. We study ideologies; we don't believe them.

Ch. 4 States   Not all states are effective; many are weak, and some are failed. Aristotle's division of states into legitimate and corrupt is still useful. Basic institutional choices can make or break a state. The territorial organization of states, unitary vs. federal, and electoral systems, single-member vs. proportional representation, are such basic choices. The degree to which the state intervenes in the economy may point to prosperity or stagnation.

Ch. 5 Rights   These institutionalized documents formalize the basic structure of the state, limit government's powers, and define civil rights. Judicial review, the great U.S. contribution to governance, has over the years curbed sedition laws and expanded freedom of speech and of press.

Ch. 6 Regimes   Democracy is complex and must include accountability, competition, and alternation in power. In even the best democracies, elites have great influence but do not always trump pluralistic inputs. Totalitarianism is a disease of the twentieth century and has largely faded, but there are still plenty of authoritarian states. Democracy is not automatic but can fail in unprepared countries like Russia and Iraq.

1

Politics and Political Science

President Barack Obama speaks to a New Hampshire town hall meeting in 2010. (Rick Friedman/Corbis)

A major healthcare reform, bailouts of big corporations, and massive federal deficits have revived interest in politics in the United States. Students and attentive citizens who a few years ago turned away from politics are paying attention again. U.S. electoral turnout, with aroused voters, is up several percentage points from a low of 50 percent in presidential elections. For political scientists, the uptick in interest is welcome, but many still worry that Americans (and many other nationalities) are becoming depoliticized. Why did interest in politics decline for many years? Is it disgust at politicians and their constant, empty struggle for partisan advantage? Is it a feeling of helplessness, a sense that individual citizens do not matter? Is it the perception that the nation's capital is the playground of rich and powerful interest groups who simply buy whatever they want, including politicians? Or is it a healthy sign that, in relatively good times, people naturally turn to other concerns? If the economy is not bad and world problems seem distant, why follow politics? A bad economy and a long war renew interest in politics.

QUESTIONS TO CONSIDER

1. Why did politics fall out of favor? Is it now back?
2. What does it mean to "never get angry at a fact"?
3. Why did Aristotle call politics "the master science"?
4. What did Machiavelli bring to the study of politics?
5. How are legitimacy, sovereignty, and authority different but similar?
6. Is the Iraqi government now legitimate? How can you tell?
7. Is politics largely biological, psychological, cultural, rational, or irrational?
8. How can something as messy as politics be a science?

It is the thesis of this book that politics matters. If you do not take an interest and participate, others will, and they will influence the decisions that govern your life. Will they take us to war in a foreign land? Who might have to fight in that war? You. Will they alter the tax code to favor certain citizens and corporations? Who will have to pay in taxes what others avoid paying? You. Will they set up government programs whose costs escalate far beyond what anyone had foreseen? Who then will have to pay these costs? You. One of the tasks of this book is to make you aware of what politics is and how it works so that you can look after yourself and prevent others from using you. The ignorant are manipulated.

discipline   A field of study, often represented by an academic department or major.

Many find politics distasteful, and perhaps they are right. Politics may be inherently immoral or, at any rate, amoral. Misuse of power, influence peddling, and outright corruption are prominent features of politics. But you need not like the thing you study. Biologists may behold a disease-causing bacterium under a microscope. They do not "like" the bacterium but are interested in how it grows, how it does its damage, and how it may be eradicated. Neither do they get angry at the bacterium and smash the glass slide with a hammer. Biologists first understand the forces of nature and then work with them to improve humankind's existence. Political scientists try to do the same with politics.

THE MASTER SCIENCE

Aristotle, the founder of the **discipline**, called politics "the master science." He meant that almost everything happens in a political context, that the decisions of the *polis* (the Greek city-state) governed most other things. Politics, in the words of Yale's Harold Lasswell (1902–1978), is the study of "who gets what." But, some object, the economic system determines who gets what in countries with free markets. True, but should we have a totally free-market system with no government involved? A decision to bail out shaky banks sparks angry controversy over this

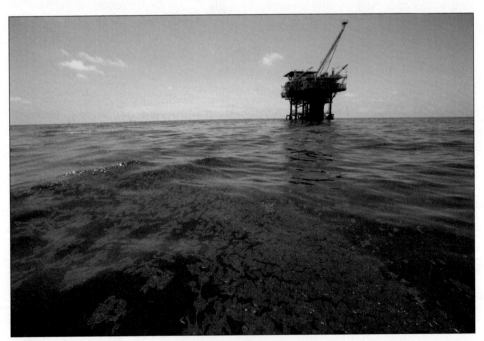

Oil from the BP spill in the Gulf of Mexico in 2010 raised political questions about deep-sea drilling. Should U.S. need for oil override environmental concerns? (Julie Dermansky/Corbis)

point. Few love the bankers, but economists say it had to be done to save the economy from collapse. Politics is intimately connected to economics.

Suppose something utterly natural strikes, like a hurricane. It is the political system that decides whether and where to build dikes and whether and which of the victims to aid. The disaster is natural, but its impact on society is controlled in large part by politics. How about science, our bacteriologists squinting through microscopes? That is not political. But who funds the scientists' education and their research institutes? It could be private charity (the donors of which get tax breaks), but the government plays a major role. When the U.S. government decided that AIDS research deserved top priority, funding for other programs was cut. Bacteria and viruses may be natural, but studying them is often quite political. In this case, it pitted gays against women concerned with breast cancer. Who gets what: Funding to find a cure for AIDS or for breast cancer? The choice is political.

Because almost everything is political, studying politics means studying nearly everything. Some students select "interdisciplinary majors." Political science already is one, borrowing from and overlapping with all of the other social sciences. At times, it is hard to tell where history, human geography, economics, sociology, anthropology, and psychology leave off and political science begins. Here, briefly, is how political science relates to the other social sciences.

History

History is one of the chief sources of data for political scientists. When we discuss the politics of the Third French Republic (1871–1940), the growth of presidential power under Franklin Roosevelt (1933–1945), and even something as recent as the Cold War (1946–1989), we are studying history. But historians and political scientists

---

KEY CONCEPTS ■ "NEVER GET ANGRY AT A FACT"

This basic point of all serious study sounds commonsensical but is often ignored, even in college courses. It traces back to the extremely complex thought of the German philosopher Hegel, who argued that things happen not by caprice or accident but for good and sufficient reasons: "Whatever is real is rational." That means that nothing is completely accidental and that if we apply reason, we will understand why something happens. We study politics in a "naturalistic" mode, not getting angry at what we see but trying to understand how it came to be.

For example, we hear of a politician who took money from a businessperson. As political scientists, we push our anger to the side and ask questions like: Do most politicians in

that country take money? Is it an old tradition, and does the culture of this country accept it? Do the people even expect politicians to take money? How big are campaign expenses? Can the politician possibly run for office without taking money? In short, we see if extralegal exchanges of cash are part of the political system. If they are, it makes no sense to get angry at an individual politician. If we dislike it, we may then consider how the system might be reformed to discourage the taking of money on the side. And reforms may not work. Japan reformed its electoral laws in an attempt to stamp out its traditional "money politics," but little changed. Like bacteria, some things in politics have lives of their own.

look for different things and handle data differently. Typically, historians study one episode in detail, digging up documents, archives, and memoirs on the topic. They have masses of data focused on one point but are reluctant to generalize. Political scientists, on the other hand, begin by looking for generalizations. They might take the findings of historians and compare and contrast them. A historian might do a detailed study of Weimar Germany (1919–1933); a political scientist might put that study alongside studies of France, Italy, and Russia of the same period to see what similarities and dissimilarities can be found. To be sure, some historians do comparative studies; they become de facto political scientists.

Human Geography

Human geography (as distinct from physical geography) has in recent decades been neglected by political scientists, although it influences politics more than many realize. The territorial components of human behavior—borders, regions, ethnic areas, trade flows, and centralization of power—have great political ramifications. Strife in Afghanistan, Iraq, India, and Turkey are heavily geographical problems, as is Canada's unsettled federalism, from which some Quebeckers wish to depart. French political scientist André Siegfried (1875–1959) pioneered the use of maps to explain regional political variations, a technique of today's electoral studies. The "red" and "blue" states in U.S. presidential elections show the relevance of political geography.

Economics

Economics, proclaim some economists, is the subject matter of politics. (Political scientists are apt to claim the opposite.) True, many political quarrels are economic: As Lasswell asked, "Who gets what?" Sufficient economic development may be the basis for democracy; few poor countries are democratic. A declining economy may doom democracy, as was the fate of Germany's Weimar Republic and recently of Russia. What policies promote economic development? How big a role should government have? Is the euro currency making Europe more united or ready to fall apart? When economists get into questions of policy, they become "political economists." A relatively new school of political science, "rational-choice theory," shares the economic perspective that humans pursue their self-interests.

Sociology

Sociology and political science overlap. Sociologist Seymour Martin Lipset (1922–2006) was equally renowned as a political scientist. He was among the first to demonstrate the close connection between democracy and level of wealth. As we shall consider in the next chapter, political science conventionally starts by looking at society to see "who thinks what" about politics. In demonstrating how political views vary among social classes, regions, religions, genders, and age groups, sociology gives an empirical basis to political-culture, public-opinion, and electoral studies.

Anthropology

Anthropology, which traditionally focused on preliterate societies, may seem of little relevance to political science. But the descriptive and interviewing techniques of anthropology have been heavily adopted by political scientists. The subfield of political culture can be viewed as a branch of anthropology. Japanese deference patterns, which we still see today, were laid down more than a millennium ago. Some current political systems are still run by traditionally influential families or clans. In Central Asia, the families of emirs who ruled under the Persians did so under the Russian tsars, the Communists, and now the newly independent states. In Africa, voting and violence follow tribal lines.

methodology The techniques for studying questions objectively.

political power Ability of one person to get another to do something.

Psychology

Psychology, particularly social psychology, contributes much to political science's understanding of which personalities are attracted to politics, why and under what circumstances people obey authority figures, and how people form national, group, and voting attachments. Studies of Hitler, Stalin, and Mao Zedong are often based on psychological theories. Psychologists are especially good with **methodology**; they devise ways to study things objectively and teach us to doubt claims that have holes in them. Asking questions in a "blind" manner and "controlling" for certain factors are techniques developed from psychology.

POLITICAL POWER

Political science often uses the findings of other social sciences, but one feature distinguishes it from the others—its focus on power: A gets B to do what A wants. Our second founding father (after Aristotle) is the Renaissance Florentine philosopher Niccolò Machiavelli, who emphasized the role of power in politics. You can take all the factors and approaches mentioned previously, but if you are not using them to study power—a very broad subject—you are probably not doing political science.

Some people dislike the concept of **political power**. It smacks of coercion, inequality, and occasionally of brutality. Some speakers denounce "power politics," suggesting governance without power, a happy band of brothers and sisters regulating themselves through love and sharing. Communities formed on such a basis do not last, or if they do last it is only by transforming themselves into conventional structures of leaders and followers, buttressed by obedience patterns that look suspiciously like power. Political power seems to be built into the human condition. But why do some people hold political power over others? There is no definitive explanation of political power. Biological, psychological, cultural, rational, and irrational explanations have been put forward.

legitimacy   Mass feeling that the government's rule is rightful and should be obeyed.

sovereignty   A national government's being boss on its own turf, the last word in law in that country.

Biological

Aristotle said it first and perhaps best: "Man is by nature a political animal." (Aristotle's words were *zoon politikon,* which can be translated as either "political animal" or "social animal." The Greeks lived in city-states in which the polis was the same as society.)

KEY CONCEPTS ■ LEGITIMACY, SOVEREIGNTY, AND AUTHORITY

These three related concepts—**legitimacy, sovereignty**, and **authority**—are basic to political science. Legitimacy originally meant that the rightful king or queen was on the throne by reason of "legitimate" birth. Since the Middle Ages, the term has broadened to mean not only the "legal right to govern" but also the "psychological right to govern." Legitimacy now refers to an attitude in people's minds—in some countries strong, in others weak—that the government's rule is rightful. Legitimacy in the United States is fairly high. Even Americans who do not particularly like the government generally obey it. We even pay taxes. One quick test of legitimacy: How many police are there? Few police, as in Sweden and Norway, indicates that little coercion is needed; legitimacy is high. Many police, as in North Korea or Iraq, indicates that much coercion is needed; legitimacy is low.

Where legitimacy is weak, few people feel obliged to pay their taxes and obey the law because the government itself is perceived as dirty and dishonest. Eventually, massive civil disobedience can break out, as it did in Serbia in 2000. Citizens rallied against the criminal misrule of President Slobodan Milošević; police batons and electoral rigging could not prevent him from being voted out of office. The Iraqi Governing Council of 2003–2004 was composed of highly educated Iraqis representative of all Iraqi groups, but it had little legitimacy because it had been installed by the U.S. occupiers. Arguably, the Council was the best government Iraq will ever have, but few valued it. Without legitimacy, governments are ineffective.

A government achieves legitimacy several ways. At the most elemental level, it must provide security, so that people feel reasonably safe. Many Iraqis complained that, bad as Saddam was, under him they could walk down the street. As Hobbes (see Chapter 2) saw, no security means no legitimacy. Related to security is "rule of law." Regimes that provide it gain legitimacy. Just existing a long time fosters legitimacy. Citizens generally respect long-established governments. The fact that the U.S. Constitution is more than two centuries old confers great legitimacy on the U.S. government. New governments, on the other hand, have shaky legitimacy; their citizens have little or no respect for them.

A government gains legitimacy by governing well. Ensuring economic growth and jobs so that people can feed their families builds legitimacy. The government of West Germany, founded in 1949 after defeat in World War II, had little legitimacy at first, but level-headed political leadership with sound economic policies gradually earned the Bonn government legitimacy. On the other hand, the German Weimar Republic that followed World War I faced a series of economic and political catastrophes that undermined its legitimacy and let Hitler take power.

The structure of government contributes to its legitimacy. If people feel they are fairly represented and have a say in the selection of their officials, they are more likely to obey. Finally, governments shore up their legitimacy by national symbols. The flag, historic monuments, patriotic parades, and ringing speeches aim at convincing people that the government

Aristotle meant that humans live naturally in herds, like elephants or deer. Biologically, they need each other for sustenance and survival. It is also natural that they array themselves into ranks of leaders and followers, like all herd animals. Taking a cue from Aristotle, a modern biological explanation would say that forming a political system and obeying its leaders is innate human behavior, passed on to future generations with

authority   Political leaders' ability to command respect and exercise power.

is legitimate and should be obeyed. Although they ended centuries of monarchy in 1975, in 2002 the Laotian Communist regime kneeled before a new bronze statue of the king who founded Laos's monarchy 650 years earlier. The Communists were trying to prop up their fraying legitimacy by tying themselves to the old kings, a symbol of legitimacy most Laotians could understand. When legitimacy has collapsed, however, the manipulation of national symbols may appear to be a hollow joke. A gigantic statue of dictator Marcos of the Philippines became an object of ridicule and a symbol of what was wrong with his regime. Symbols by themselves do not create legitimacy.

Sovereignty (from the Old French "to rule over") originally meant the power of a monarch over his or her kingdom. Later, the term broadened to mean national control over the country's territory, boss of one's own turf. Nations safeguard their sovereignty. They maintain armies to deter foreign invasion; they control their borders with passports and visas; and they hunt down terrorists. Disputes over sovereignty are among the nastiest: Palestine, Chechnya, and Iraq are examples.

Sovereignty is sometimes a legal fiction. Iraq regained nominal sovereignty in 2004 but was still under U.S. influence. Sovereignty and legitimacy are connected. Lebanese Muslims, for example, saw the Christian-dominated government as illegitimate. In 1975, civil strife broke out among a dozen politico-religious militias. Syria occupied eastern Lebanon from 1976 to 2005, and Israel occupied southern Lebanon from 1982 to 2000. Lebanon in effect lost its

sovereignty, which it is now slowly regaining. For decades, it could neither control its own territory nor repel foreign invaders. A loss of legitimacy led to a loss of sovereignty.

Authority is the psychological ability of leaders to get others to obey them. It relies on a sense of obligation based on the legitimate power of office. A private obeys a captain; a motorist obeys a state trooper; a student obeys a professor. But not all people obey authority. Some privates are insubordinate, some motorists are speeders, and some students neglect the assigned reading. Still, most people obey what they perceive as legitimate authority most of the time.

Some authority comes with the office, but it must also be cultivated. An American president gets much authority just because he is president. Gerald Ford was respected and obeyed even though he was not elected president or vice president. As minority leader of the House of Representatives, Ford became vice president when Spiro T. Agnew resigned and president when Richard Nixon resigned. Nixon, implicated in the Watergate scandal of 1972, suffered an erosion of executive authority so acute that he could not govern effectively. A president cannot rule by decree but must obtain the willing consent of Congress, the courts, the civil service, and important interest groups. When Nixon lost this consent, his power as president declined.

In short, legitimacy means respect for a government; sovereignty, respect for a country; and authority, respect for a leader. None are automatic; all must be earned. Where you find one, you find the others. Where one erodes, so usually do the others.

one's genes. Some thinkers argue that human politics shows the same "dominance hierarchies" that other mammals set up. Politicians tend to be "alpha males"—or think they are.

The advantage of the biological approach is its simplicity, but it raises a number of questions. If we grant that humans are naturally political, how do we explain the instances when political groups fall apart and people disobey authority? Perhaps we should modify the theory: Humans are imperfectly political (or social) animals. Most of the time people form groups and obey authority, but sometimes, under certain circumstances, they do not. This begs the question of which circumstances promote or undermine the formation of political groups.

Psychological

Psychological explanations of politics and obedience are closely allied with biological theories. Both posit needs derived from centuries of evolution in the formation of political groups. The psychologists have refined their views with empirical research. One is the famous Milgram study, in which unwitting subjects were instructed by a professor to administer progressively larger electric shocks to a victim. The "victim," strapped in a chair, was actually an actor who only pretended to suffer. Most of the subjects were willing to administer potentially lethal doses of electricity simply because the "professor"—an authority figure in a white lab smock—told them to. Most of the subjects disliked hurting the victim, but they rationalized that they were just following orders and that any harm done to the victim was really the professor's responsibility. They surrendered their actions to an authority figure.

Psychological studies also show that most people are naturally conformist. Most members of a group see things the group's way. Psychologist Irving Janis found many foreign policy mistakes were made in a climate of "groupthink," in which a leadership team tells itself that all is well and that the present policy is working. Groups ignore doubters who tell them, for instance, that the Japanese will attack Pearl Harbor in 1941 or that the 1961 Bay of Pigs landing of Cuban exiles will fail. Obedience to authority and groupthink suggest that humans have deep-seated needs—possibly innate—to fit into groups and their norms. Perhaps this is what makes human society possible, but it also makes possible horrors such as the Nazi Holocaust and more recent massacres.

Cultural

How much of human behavior is learned as opposed to biologically inherited? This is the very old "nurture versus nature" debate. For much of the twentieth century, the cultural theorists—those who believe behavior is learned—dominated. Anthropologists concluded that all differences in behavior were cultural. Cooperative and peaceful societies raise their children that way, they argued. Political communities are formed and held together on the basis of cultural values transmitted by parents, schools, churches, and the mass media. Political science developed an interesting subfield, *political culture*, whose researchers found that a country's political culture was formed by many long-term factors: religion, child rearing, land tenure, and economic development.

Cultural theorists see trouble when the political system gets out of touch with the cultural system, as when the shah of Iran attempted to modernize an Islamic society that did not like Western values and lifestyles.

culture Human behavior that is learned as opposed to inherited.

rational Based on the ability to reason.

The Iranians threw the shah out in 1979 and celebrated the return of a medieval-style religious leader who voiced the values favored by traditional Iranians. Cultural theories can also be applied to U.S. politics. Republicans often win elections by articulating the values of religion, family, and self-reliance, which are deeply ingrained into American culture. Many thinkers believe economic and political development depend heavily on **culture.**

The cultural approach to political life holds some optimism. If all human behavior is learned, bad behavior can be unlearned and society improved. Educating young people to be tolerant, cooperative, and just will gradually change a society's culture for the better, according to this view. Changing culture, however, is slow and difficult, as the American occupiers of Iraq discovered.

Culture contributes a lot to political behavior, but the theory has some difficulties. First, where does culture come from? History? Economics? Religion? Second, if all behavior is cultural, various political systems should be as different from each other as their cultures. But, especially in the realm of politics, we see similar political attitudes and patterns in lands with very different cultures. Politicians everywhere tend to become corrupt, regardless of culture.

Rational

Another school of thought approaches politics as a **rational** thing; that is, people know what they want most of the time, and they have good reasons for doing what they do. Classic political theorists, such as Hobbes and Locke, as we shall see in the next chapter, held that humans form "civil society" because their powers of reason tell them that it is much better than anarchy. To safeguard life and property, people form governments. If those governments become abusive, the people have the right to dissolve them and start anew. This Lockean notion greatly influenced the U.S. Founding Fathers.

The biological, psychological, and cultural schools downplay human reason, claiming that people are either born or conditioned to certain behavior, and individuals seldom think rationally. But how can we then explain cases in which people break away from group conformity and argue independently? How can we explain a change of mind? "I was for Jones until he came out with his terrible economic policy, so now I'm voting for Smith." People make rational judgments like that all the time. A political system based on the presumption of human reason stands a better chance of governing justly and humanely. If leaders believe that people obey out of biological inheritance or cultural conditioning, they will think they can get away with all manner of corruption and misrule. If, on the other hand, rulers fear that people are rational, they will respect the public's ability to discern wrongdoing. Accordingly, even if people are not completely rational, it is probably for the best if rulers think they are.

Irrational

Late in the nineteenth century, a group of thinkers expounded the view that people are basically **irrational**, especially when it comes to political power. They are
emotional, dominated by myths and stereotypes, and
politics is really the manipulation of symbols. A crowd
is like a wild beast that can be whipped up by charismatic leaders to do their bidding. What people regard
as rational is really myth; just keep feeding the people myths to control them. The
first practitioner of this school was Mussolini, founder of fascism in Italy, followed
by Hitler in Germany. A soft-spoken Muslim fundamentalist, Osama bin Laden,
got an irrational hold on thousands of fanatical followers. Believing the myth that
America was the enemy of Islam, some willingly ended their lives in terrorist acts.

irrational   Based on the power to
use fear and myth to cloud reason.

There may be a good deal of truth to the irrational view of human political
behavior, but it has catastrophic consequences. Leaders who use irrationalist
techniques start believing their own propaganda and lead their nations to war,
economic ruin, or tyranny. Some detect irrationalism even in the most advanced
societies, where much of politics consists of screaming crowds and leaders striking
heroic poses.

Power As a Composite

There are elements of truth in all these explanations of political power. At different times in different situations, any one of them can explain power. Tom Paine's
pamphlet *Common Sense* rationally explained why America should separate from
Britain. The drafters of both the U.S. Declaration of Independence and the Constitution were imbued with the rationalism of their age. Following the philosophers then
popular, they framed their arguments as if human political activity were as logical as
Newtonian physics. Historian Henry Steele Commager referred to the Constitution as
"the crown jewel of the enlightenment," the culmination of an age of reason.

But how truly rational were they? By the late eighteenth century, the 13
American colonies had grown culturally separate from Britain. People thought
of themselves as Americans rather than as English colonists. They increasingly
read American newspapers and communicated among themselves rather than with
Britain. Perhaps the separation was more cultural than rational.

Nor can we forget the psychological and irrational factors. Samuel Adams was
a gifted firebrand, Thomas Jefferson a powerful writer, and George Washington a
charismatic general. The American break with Britain and the founding of a new
order was a complex mixture of all these factors. The same complex mixture of factors goes into any political system you can mention. To be sure, at times one factor
seems more important than others, but we cannot exactly determine the weight to
give any one factor. And notice how the various factors blend into one another.
The biological factors lead to the psychological, which in turn lead to the cultural,
the rational, and the irrational, forming a seamless web.

One common mistake made about political power is viewing it as a finite,
measurable quantity. Power is a connection among people, the ability of one person

to get others to do his or her bidding. Political power does not come in jars or megawatts. Revolutionaries in some lands speak of "seizing power," as if power was kept in the national treasury and they could sneak in and grab it at night. The Afghan Taliban "seized power" in 1995–1996, but they were a minority of the Afghan population. Many Afghans hated and fought them. Revolutionaries think that they automatically get legitimacy and authority when they "seize power"— they do not. Power is earned, not seized.

Is power identical to politics? Some power-mad people (including more than a few politicians) see the two as the same, but this is an oversimplification. We might see politics as a combination of goals or policies plus the power necessary to achieve them. Power, in this view, is a prime *ingredient* of politics. It would be difficult to imagine a political system without political power. Even a religious figure who ruled on the basis of love would be exercising power over followers. It might be "nice power," but it would still be power. Power, then, is a sort of *enabling device* to carry out or implement policies and decisions. You can have praiseworthy goals, but unless you have the power to implement them, they remain wishful thoughts.

Others see the essence of politics as a *struggle for power*, a sort of gigantic game in which power is the goal. What, for example, are elections all about? The getting of power. There is a danger here, however. If power becomes the goal of politics, devoid of other purposes, it becomes cynical, brutal, and self-destructive. The Hitler regime destroyed itself in the worship of power. Obsessed with retaining presidential power, President Nixon ruined his own administration. As nineteenth-century British historian and philosopher Lord Acton put it, "Power tends to corrupt; absolute power corrupts absolutely."

KEY CONCEPTS ■ THE SUBFIELDS OF POLITICAL SCIENCE

Most political science departments divide the discipline into several subfields. The bigger the department, the more subfields it will likely have. We will get at least a brief introduction to all of them in this book.

U.S. Politics focuses on institutions and processes, mostly at the federal level but some at state and local levels. It includes parties, elections, public opinion, and executive and legislative behavior.

Comparative Politics examines politics within other nations, trying to establish generalizations and theories of democracy, stability, and policy. It may be focused on various regions, as in "Latin American politics" or "East Asian politics."

International Relations studies politics among nations, including conflict, diplomacy, international law and organizations, and international political economy. The study of U.S. foreign policy has one foot in U.S. politics and one in international relations.

Political Theory, both classic and modern, attempts to define the good polity, often focused on major thinkers.

Public Administration studies how bureaucracies work and how they can be improved.

Constitutional Law studies the applications and evolution of the Constitution within the legal system.

Public Policy studies the interface of politics and economics with an eye to developing effective programs.

quantify   To measure with numbers.

hypothesis   An initial theory a researcher starts with, to be proved by evidence.

IS POLITICS A SCIENCE?

If we cannot pinpoint which factors contribute what weight to politics, how can politics be a science? Part of the problem here is the definition of science. The original meaning of science, from the French, is simply "knowledge." Later, the natural sciences, which rely on measurement and calculation, took over the term. Now most people think of science as precise and factual, supported by experiments and data. Some political scientists (as we will consider later) have attempted to become like natural scientists; they **quantify** data and manipulate them statistically to validate **hypotheses**. The quantifiers make some good contributions, but usually they focus on small questions of detail rather than on large questions of meaning. This

HOW TO . . . ■ STUDY A CHAPTER

Read each chapter *before* class. And do not simply read the chapter; learn it by writing down the following:

A. Find what strikes you as the *three main points*. Do not outline; construct three complete sentences, each with a subject and predicate. They may be long and complex sentences, but they must be complete declarative sentences. You may find two, four, or six main points, but by the time you split, combine, and discard what may or may not be the main points, you will know the chapter. Look for abstract generalizations; the specifics come under point C, examples or case studies. Do not simply copy three sentences from the chapter. Synthesize several sentences, always asking yourself the following: What three sentences distilled from this chapter will most help me on the exam? These might be three main points from Chapter 1:

1. Study politics as a scientist studies nature, trying to understand reality without getting angry at it.
2. Political science combines many disciplines but focuses on power: who holds it and how they use it.
3. Politics can be studied objectively, provided claims are supported by empirical evidence.

B. List a *dozen vocabulary words*, and be able to define them. These are words new to you or words used in a specialized way. This text makes it easier with the boldfaced terms defined in the margins; for terms not in boldface, read with a dictionary handy. These are the key terms from Chapter 1:

authority	methodology
culture	political power
discipline	quantify
empirical	rational
hypothesis	scholarship
irrational	sovereignty
legitimacy	

C. Note specific *examples* or *case studies* that illustrate the main points or vocabulary words. Most will contain proper nouns (that is, capitalized). Examples are not main points or definitions; rather, they are empirical evidence that support a main point. The examples need not be complete sentences. These might be examples from Chapter 1:

Aristotle's "master science"
AIDS versus breast-cancer research
West Germany's success story
Communist regimes in Eastern Europe
Iraq's chaos
Shah's regime in Iran erodes

is because they generally have to stick to areas that can be quantified: public opinion, election returns, and congressional voting.

empirical Based on observable evidence.

But large areas of politics are not quantifiable. How and why do leaders make their decisions? Many decisions are made in secrecy, even in democracies. We do not know exactly how decisions are made in the White House in Washington, the Elysée in Paris, or the Zhongnanhai in Beijing. When members of Congress vote on an issue, can we be certain why they voted that way? Was it constituents' desires, the good of the nation, or the campaign contributions of interest groups? What did the Supreme Court have in mind when it ruled that laying off schoolteachers based on race is unconstitutional but hiring them based on race is not? Try quantifying that. Much of politics—especially dealing with how and why decisions are made—is just too complex and too secret to be quantified. Bismarck, who unified Germany in the nineteenth century, famously compared laws and sausages: It's better not to see them being made.

Does that mean that politics can never be like a natural science? Political science is an **empirical** discipline that accumulates both quantified and qualitative data. With such data, we can find persistent patterns, much like in biology. Gradually, we begin to generalize. When the generalizations become firmer, we call them theories. In a few cases, the theories become so firm that we may call them laws. In this way, the study of politics accumulates knowledge—the original meaning of science.

The Struggle to See Clearly

Political science also resembles a natural science when its researchers, if they are professional, study things as they are and not as they wish them to be. This is more difficult in the study of politics than in the study of stars and cells. Most political scientists have viewpoints on current issues, and it is easy to let these views contaminate their analyses of politics. Indeed, precisely because a given question interests us enough to study it indicates that we bring a certain passion with us. Can you imagine setting to work on a topic you cared nothing about? If you are interested enough to study a question, you probably start by being inclined

CLASSIC WORKS ■ CONCEPTS AND PRECEPTS

In the late eighteenth century, the great Prussian philosopher Immanuel Kant wrote, "Precepts without concepts are empty, and concepts without precepts are blind." This notion helped establish modern philosophy and social science. A precept is what you perceive through your sensory organs: facts, images, numbers, examples, and so on. A concept is an idea in your head: meanings, theories, hypotheses, beliefs, and so on. You can collect many precepts, but without a concept to structure them you have nothing; your precepts are empty of meaning. On the other hand, your concepts are "blind" if they cannot look at reality, which requires precepts. In other words, you need both theory and data.

scholarship   Intellectual arguments supported by reason and evidence.

to one side. Too much of this, however, renders the study biased; it becomes a partisan outcry rather than a scholarly search for the truth. How can you guard against this? The traditional hallmarks of **scholarship** give some guidance. A scholarly work should be *reasoned*, *balanced*, supported with *evidence*, and a bit *theoretical*.

Reasoned   You must spell out your reasoning, and it should make sense. If your perspective is colored by an underlying assumption, you should say so. You might say, "For the purpose of this study, we assume that bureaucrats are rational," or "This is a study of the psychology of voters in a small town." Your basic assumptions influence what you study and how you study it, but you can minimize bias by honestly stating your assumptions. Early in the twentieth century, German sociologist Max Weber (1864–1920), who contributed vastly to all the social sciences, held that any findings that support the researcher's political views must be discarded as biased. Few attempt to be that pure, but Weber's point is well-taken: Beware of structuring the study so that it comes out to support a given view.

Balanced   You can also minimize bias by acknowledging that there are other ways of looking at your topic. You should mention the various approaches to your topic and what other researchers have found. Instructors are impressed that you know the literature in a given area. They are even more impressed when you can then criticize the previous studies and explain why you think they are incomplete or faulty: "The Jones study of voters found them largely apathetic, but this was an off-year election in which turnout is always lower." By comparing and criticizing several approaches and studies, you present a much more objective and convincing

KEY CONCEPTS ■ POLITICS VERSUS POLITICAL SCIENCE

Political science ain't politics. It is not necessarily training to become a practicing politician. Political science is training in the calm, objective analysis of politics, which may or may not aid working politicians. Side by side, the two professions compare like this:

Politicians	Political Scientists
love power	are skeptical of power
seek popularity	seek accuracy
think practically	think abstractly
hold firm views	reach tentative conclusions
offer single causes	offer many causes
see short-term payoffs	see long-term consequences
plan for next election	plan for next publication
respond to groups	seek the good of the whole
seek name recognition	seek professional prestige

The two professions of politician and political scientist bear approximately the same relation to each other as do bacteria and bacteriologists.

case. Do not commit yourself to a particular viewpoint or theory, but admit that your view is one among several.

Supported with Evidence   All scholarly studies require evidence, ranging from the quantified evidence of the natural sciences to the qualitative evidence of the humanities. Political science utilizes both. Ideally, any statement open to interpretation or controversy should be supported with evidence. Common knowledge does not have to be supported; you need not cite the U.S. Constitution to "prove" that presidents serve four-year terms.

But if you say presidents have gained more and more power over the decades, you need evidence. At a minimum, you would cite a scholar who has amassed evidence to demonstrate this point. That is called a "secondary source," evidence that has passed through the mind of someone else. Most student papers use only secondary sources, but instructors are impressed when you use a "primary source," the original gathering of data, as in your own tabulation of what counties in your state showed the strongest McCain vote. Anyone reading a study must be able to review its evidence and judge if it is valid. You cannot keep your evidence or sources secret.

Theoretical   Serious scholarship is always connected, at least a little, to a theoretical point. It need not be a sweeping new theory (that's for geniuses), but it should advance the discipline's knowledge a bit. At a minimum, it should confirm or refute an existing theory. Just describing something is not a theory, which is why Google or Wikipedia are seldom enough. You must relate the description to another factor, supported, of course, with empirical evidence. The general pattern of this is as follows: "Most of the time X accompanies Y." Theory-building also helps lift your study above polemics, an argument for or against something. Denouncing al Qaeda, which we all may do with gusto, is not scholarship. Determining why people join al Qaeda (currently studied by several scholars) would have important theoretical and practical impacts.

What Good is Political Science?

Some students come to political science supposing it is just opinions; they write exams or papers that ignore all or some of the preceding points. Yes, we all have political views, but if we let them dominate our study we get invalid results, junk political science. Professional political scientists push their personal views well to one side while engaged in study and research. First-rate thinkers are able to come up with results that actually refute their previously held opinion. When that happens, we have real intellectual growth—an exciting experience that should be your aim.

Something else comes with such an experience: You start to conclude that you should not have been so partisan in the first place. You may back away from the strong views you held earlier and take them with a grain of salt. Accordingly, political science is not necessarily training to become a practicing politician. Political science is training in objective and often complex analysis, whereas the practice of politics requires fixed, popular, and simplified opinions.

Political science can contribute to good government, often by warning those in office that all is not well, "speaking Truth to Power," as the Quakers say. Sometimes this advice is useful to working politicians. Public-opinion polls, for example, showed an erosion of trust in government in the United States starting in the mid-1960s. The causes were Vietnam, Watergate, and inflation. Candidates for political office, knowing public opinion, could tailor their campaigns and policies to try to counteract this decline. Ronald Reagan, with his sunny disposition and upbeat views, utilized the discontent to win two presidential terms.

As far back as 1950, the American Political Science Association warned about the weaknesses of U.S. political parties; they were decentralized and uncontrolled. Political parties in the United States cannot force views on members, nor do the parties control who call themselves members. In 1989, David Duke, a former leader of the Ku Klux Klan with ties to Nazis, won a seat as a Republican in the Louisiana state legislature. The Republican National Committee tried to distance itself from Duke, but he continued to call himself a Republican, and there was no legal way to stop him. Parties in the United States are too weak even to control who uses their names.

Some political scientists warned for years of the weak basis of the shah's regime in Iran. Unfortunately, such warnings were unheeded. Washington's policy was to support the shah, and only two months before the end of the shah's reign did the U.S. embassy in Tehran start reporting how unstable Iran had become. State Department officials had let politics contaminate their political analyses; they could not see clearly. Journalists were not much better; few covered Iran until violence broke out. Years in advance, American political scientists specializing in Iran saw trouble coming. More recently, political scientists warned that Iraq was unready for democracy and that a U.S. invasion would unleash chaos. Washington deciders paid no attention to the warnings. Political science can be useful.

my**poliscikit** EXERCISES

Apply what you learned in this chapter on MyPoliSciKit (www.mypoliscikit.com).

Assessment   Review this chapter using learning objectives, chapter summaries, practice tests, and more.

Menu

Flashcards   Learn the key terms in this chapter; you can test yourself by term or definition.

Flashcards

Video   Analyze recent world affairs by watching streaming video from major news providers.

Videos

Comparative Exercises   Compare political ideas, behaviors, institutions, and policies worldwide.

Comparative
Exercises

KEY TERMS

authority (p. 9)
culture (p. 11)
discipline (p. 4)
empirical (p. 15)
hypothesis (p. 14)

irrational (p. 12)
legitimacy (p. 8)
methodology (p. 7)
political power (p. 7)
quantify (p. 14)

rational (p. 11)
scholarship (p. 16)
sovereignty (p. 8)

FURTHER REFERENCE

Almond, Gabriel A. *Ventures in Political Science: Narratives and Reflections.* Boulder, CO: Lynne Rienner, 2002.

Boulding, Kenneth E. *Three Faces of Power.* Newbury Park, CA: Sage, 1989.

Elster, Jon. *Alexis de Tocqueville: The First Social Scientist.* New York: Cambridge University Press, 2009.

Friedrich, Carl J., ed. *Authority.* Cambridge, MA: Harvard University Press, 1958.

Huysmans, Jeff. *What Is Politics? A Short Introduction.* New York: Columbia University Press, 2004.

Janis, Irving L. *Victims of Groupthink: A Psychological Study of Foreign-Policy Decisions and Fiascoes.* Boston: Houghton Mifflin, 1972.

Kagan, Jerome. *Galen's Prophecy: Temperament and Human Nature.* New York: Basic Books, 1994.

Lasswell, Harold. *Politics: Who Gets What, When, How.* New York: McGraw-Hill, 1936.

Lewellen, Ted C. *Political Anthropology: An Introduction,* 3rd ed. Westport, CT: Greenwood, 2003.

Milgram, Stanley. *Obedience to Authority: An Experimental View.* New York: Harper & Row, 1974.

Minogue, Kenneth. *Politics: A Very Short Introduction.* New York: Oxford University Press, 1995.

Shively, W. Phillips. *The Craft of Political Research,* 8th ed. Upper Saddle River, NJ: Prentice Hall, 2010.

Theodoulou, Stella, and Rory O'Brien, eds. *Methods for Political Inquiry: The Discipline, Philosophy, and Analysis of Politics.* Upper Saddle River, NJ: Prentice Hall, 1999.

Wilson, Edward O. *Sociobiology: The New Synthesis.* Cambridge, MA: Harvard University Press, 1975.

Zimbardo, Philip. *The Lucifer Effect: Understanding How Good People Turn Evil.* New York: Random House, 2007.

CHAPTER 2

Theories

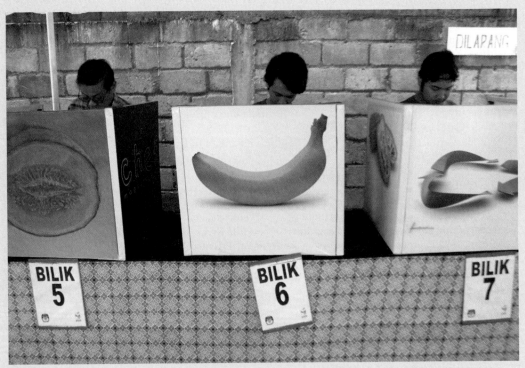

Indonesia struggles to stabilize its democracy in its 2009 legislative elections. Many of the 38 competing parties used fruits as symbols to aid illiterate voters. (Himawan/epa/Corbis)

Why bother with theories at all, wonder many students new to political science. Why not just accumulate facts and let the facts structure themselves into a coherent whole? Because they won't. Gathering facts without an organizing principle leads only to large collections of meaningless facts, a point made by Kant (see box on page 15). To be sure, theories can grow too complex and abstract and depart from the real world, but without at least some theoretical perspective, we do not even know what questions to ask. Even if you say you have no theories, you probably have some unspoken ones. The kind of questions you ask and which you ask first are the beginnings of theorizing.

QUESTIONS TO CONSIDER

1. Who founded political science?
2. What did Machiavelli, Confucius, Kautilya, and Ibn Khaldun have in common?
3. How did Hobbes, Locke, and Rousseau differ?
4. What is the crux of Marx's theory?
5. What is "positivism," and how does it underlie much of social science?
6. What is Easton's theory of the political system?
7. How does modernization theory borrow from Marx?
8. What is rational-choice theory?
9. Why must your paper have a "provable thesis"?

Take, for example, the structure of this book. We have adopted the view—widespread in political science for decades—that the proper starting point of political analysis is society. We assume that politics grows out of society. We start with people's values, attitudes, and opinions and see how they influence government. The subtitle of one influential book by a leading sociologist was *The Social Bases of Politics*. Its message: You start with society and see how it influences politics.

But that could stack the deck. If you assume that society is the basis of politics and that values and opinions are the important facts, you will gather much material on values and opinions and relatively little on the history, structure, and policies of government. Everything else will appear secondary to citizens' values and opinions. And indeed, political science went through a period in which it was essentially sociology, and many political scientists did survey research. This was part of the behavioral tide; survey research was seen as the only way to be "scientific" because it generated quantifiable data.

Most textbooks offered a "percolation up" model of politics. The first major bloc in most studies was concerned with the society and covered such things as how political views were distributed, how interest groups formed, who supported which political parties, and how people voted. That was the basis, the bottom part

Figure 2.1 ▶

Pyramid with social base and political superstructure. (Flow is from bottom to top.)

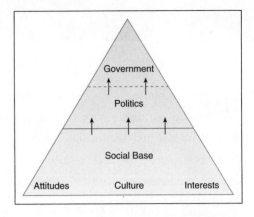

of the pyramid. The second major bloc was usually the institutions of government. They were assumed to be a reflection of the underlying social base. Legislatures and executives reacted to public opinion, interest groups, and political parties. The study of politics looked like Figure 2.1.

But just using the term social base assumes that society is the underlying element in the study of politics. Could it be the other way around? To use a coffee-making metaphor, instead of "percolating up," could politics "drip down"? Did healthcare reform percolate up from society or drip down from government officials? (Probably some of both.) One could imagine a book titled *The Political Bases of Society* that posits society as largely the result of political institutions and decisions made over the decades. Maybe politics leads society, in which case our model would look like Figure 2.2.

How can you prove which model is more nearly correct? It is possible (and very likely) that the flow is going both ways simultaneously and that both models are partly correct. Why, then, emphasize one model over the other? There is no good reason; it is simply the current fashion in political study, which began as a reaction against the emphasis on institutions that dominated political science before World War II. A seemingly simple matter of which topics to study first has theoretical implications. You cannot escape theory. We can only whet your appetite for political theories in our very brief discussion here. Consider further study of political theory; you will find that nothing is as practical as theory.

Figure 2.2 ▶

Pyramid with political institutions forming the social base. (Flow is from top to bottom.)

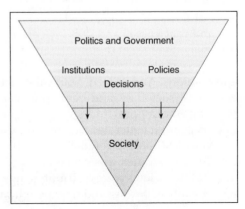

CLASSIC THEORIES

Some say Plato founded political science. His *Republic*, among other things, described an ideal polis, but his reasoning was largely speculative, and his ideal system ended up looking a bit like modern fascism or communism. Plato's student, Aristotle, on the other hand, was the first *empirical* political scientist. As noted in the previous chapter, he regarded politics as the "master science" and sent out his students to gather data from the dozens of Greek city-states. With these data, he constructed his great work *Politics*. Both Plato and Aristotle saw Athens in decline; they attempted to understand why and to suggest how it could be avoided. They thus began a tradition that is still at the heart of political science: a search for the sources of the good, stable political system. Aristotle was not shy about defining what was politically "best," as in this passage from *Politics*:

descriptive Explaining what is.

normative Explaining what ought to be.

realism Working with the world as it is and not as we wish it to be; usually focused on power.

> [T]he best political community is formed by citizens of the middle class, and those states are likely to be well administered in which the middle class is large ... in which the citizens have moderate and sufficient property; for where some possess much and others nothing there may arise an extreme democracy or a pure oligarchy, or a tyranny may develop out of either extreme. ...
> [D]emocracies are safer and more permanent than oligarchies, because they have a middle class which is more numerous and has a greater share in government, for when there is no middle class, and the poor greatly exceed in number, troubles arise, and the state soon comes to an end.

Even though *Politics* was written in the fourth century B.C., Aristotle could be describing why democracy succeeds or fails today: Much depends on the size of the middle class, a point confirmed by modern research. Do China and Iraq have a middle class strong enough to sustain democracy? Ancient can still be relevant. Aristotle was both **descriptive** and **normative**: He used the facts he and his students had collected to prescribe the most desirable political institutions. Political scientists have been doing the same ever since, both describing and prescribing.

Most European medieval and Renaissance political thinkers took a religious approach to the study of government and politics. They were almost strictly normative, seeking to discover the "ought" or "should" and were often rather casual about the "is," the real-world situation. Informed by religious, legal, and philosophical values, they tried to ascertain which system of government would bring humankind closest to what God wished.

Niccolò Machiavelli in the early sixteenth century introduced what some believe to be the crux of modern political science: the focus on power. His great work *The Prince* was about the getting and using of political power. Many philosophers peg Machiavelli as the first modern philosopher because his motivations and explanations had nothing to do with religion. Machiavelli was not as wicked as some people say. He was a **realist** who argued that to accomplish anything good—such as the unification of Italy and expulsion of the foreigners who ruined it—the Prince had to be rational and tough in the exercise of power.

Although long depreciated by American political thinkers, who sometimes shied away from "power" as inherently dirty, the approach took root in Europe and contributed to the elite analyses of Mosca, Pareto, and Michels. Americans became acquainted with the power approach through the writings of the refugee German scholar of international relations Hans J. Morgenthau, who emphasized that "all politics is a struggle for power."

The Contractualists

Not long after Machiavelli, the "contractualists"—Hobbes, Locke, and Rousseau—analyzed why political systems should exist at all. They differed in many points

CLASSIC WORKS ■ NOT JUST EUROPEANS

China, India, and North Africa produced brilliant political thinkers long before their European counterparts. Unknown in the West until relatively recently, it is unlikely that their ideas influenced the development of Western political theory. The existence of these culturally varied thinkers suggests that the political nature of humans is basically the same no matter what the cultural differences and that great minds come to similar conclusions on how to deal with politics.

In China, Confucius—a sixth-century B.C. advisor to kings—propounded his vision of good, stable government based on two things: the family and correct, moral behavior instilled in rulers and ruled alike. At the apex, the emperor sets a moral example by purifying his spirit and perfecting his manners. He must think good thoughts in utter sincerity; if he does not, his empire crumbles. He is copied by his subjects, who are arrayed hierarchically below the emperor, down to the father of a family, who is like a miniature emperor to whom wives and children are subservient. The Confucian system bears some resemblance to Plato's ideal republic; the difference is that the Chinese actually practiced Confucianism, which lasted two and a half millennia and through a dozen dynasties. Some claim it formed the cultural basis for East Asia's recent remarkable economic growth.

Two millennia before Machiavelli and Hobbes, the Indian writer Kautilya in the fourth century B.C. arrived at the same conclusions. Kautilya, a prime minister and advisor to an Indian monarch, wrote in *Arthashastra* (translated as *The Principles of Material Well-Being*) that prosperity comes from living in a well-run kingdom. Like Hobbes, Kautilya posited a state of nature that meant anarchy. Monarchs arose to protect the land and people against anarchy and ensure their prosperity. Like Machiavelli, Kautilya advised his prince to operate on the basis of pure expediency, doing whatever it took to secure his kingdom domestically and against other kingdoms. Kautilya thus could be said to have founded both political economy and the realist school of statecraft.

In fourteenth century A.D. North Africa, Ibn Khaldun was a secretary, executive, and ambassador for several rulers. Sometimes out of favor and in jail, he reflected on what had gone wrong with the great Arab empires. He concluded, in his *Universal History*, that the character of the Arabs and their social cohesiveness was determined by climate and occupation. Ibn Khaldun was almost modern in his linking of underlying economic conditions to social and political change. Economic decline in North Africa, he found, had led to political instability and lawlessness. Anticipating Marx, Toynbee, and many other Western writers, Ibn Khaldun saw that civilizations pass through cycles of growth and decline.

Notice what all three of these thinkers had in common with Machiavelli: All were princely political advisors who turned their insights into general prescriptions for correct governance. Practice led to theory.

but agreed that humans, at least in principle, had joined in what Rousseau called a **social contract** that everyone now had to observe.

Thomas Hobbes lived through the upheavals of the English Civil War in the seventeenth century and opposed them for making individuals frightened and insecure. Hobbes imagined that life in "the **state of nature**," before **civil society** was founded, must have been terrible. Every man would have been the enemy of every other man, a "war of each against all." Humans would live in savage squalor with "no arts; no letters; no society; and which is worst of all, continual fear, and danger of violent death; and the life of man, solitary, poor, nasty, brutish, and short." To get out of this horror, people would—out of their profound self-interest—rationally join together to form civil society. Society thus arises naturally out of fear. People would also gladly submit to a king, even a bad one, for a monarch prevents anarchy. Notice how Hobbes's theory, that society is based on rational self-interest, is at odds with Aristotle's theory that humans are born "political animals." Which theory is right? (Hint: Have humans ever lived as solitary animals?) But also notice that Hobbesian situations appear from time to time, as in Iraq, where Sunni and Shia murdered each other as if there were no government.

Another Englishman, John Locke, also saw the seventeenth-century upheavals but came to less harsh conclusions. Locke theorized that the original state of nature was not so bad; people lived in equality and tolerance with one another. But they could not secure their property. There was no money, title deeds, or courts of law, so ownership was uncertain. To remedy this, they contractually formed civil society and thus secured "life, liberty, and property." Locke is to property rights as Hobbes is to fear of violent death. Some philosophers argue that Americans are the children of Locke. Notice the American emphasis on "the natural right to property."

Jean-Jacques Rousseau lived in eighteenth-century France and, some say, laid the philosophical groundwork for the French Revolution. He accepted the theories of Hobbes and Locke but gave them a twist. Life in the state of nature, Rousseau theorized, was downright good; people lived as "noble savages" without artifice or jealousy. (All the contractualists were influenced by not-very-accurate descriptions of American Indians.) What corrupted humans, said Rousseau, was society itself. The famous words at the beginning of his *Social Contract*: "Man is born free but everywhere is in chains."

But society can be drastically improved, argued Rousseau, leading to human freedom. A just society would be a voluntary community with a will of its own, the **general will**—what everyone wants over and above the "particular wills" of individuals and interest groups. In such communities, humans gain dignity and freedom. Societies make people, not the other way around. If people are bad, it is because society made them that way (a view held by many today). A good society, on the other hand, can "force men to be free" if they misbehave. Many see the roots of totalitarianism in Rousseau: the imagined perfect society; the general will, which the

social contract   Theory that individuals join and stay in civil society as if they had signed a contract.

state of nature   Humans before civilization.

civil society   Humans after becoming civilized. Modern usage: associations between family and government.

general will   Rousseau's theory of what the whole community wants.

Zeitgeist   German for "spirit of the times"; Hegel's theory that each epoch has a distinctive spirit, which moves history along.

proletariat   Marx's name for the industrial working class.

bourgeois   Adjective, originally French for city dweller; later and current, middle class in general. Noun: *bourgeoisie.*

dictator claims to know; and the breaking of those who do not cooperate. Happily, the U.S. Founding Fathers were uninfluenced by Rousseau, but the architects of the French Revolution believed passionately in him, which perhaps explains why it ended badly.

Most of the U.S. Founding Fathers had studied Hobbes and Locke, whose influence is obvious. What is the Constitution but a social contract? Much of the Declaration of Independence reads as if it had been cribbed from Locke, which it had, by Jefferson. Please do not say political theories have no influence.

Marxist Theories

Another political theory that made a big difference was Marxism. A German living in London, Karl Marx, who was trained in Hegelian philosophy, produced an exceedingly complex theory consisting of at least three interrelated elements: a theory of economics, a theory of social class, and a theory of history. Like Hegel, Marx argued that things do not happen by accident; everything has a cause. Hegel posited the underlying cause that moves history forward as spiritual, specifically the **Zeitgeist**, the spirit of the times. Marx found the great underlying cause in economics.

Economics   Marx concentrated on the "surplus value"—what we call profit. Workers produce things but get paid only a fraction of the value of what they produce. The capitalist owners skim off the rest, the surplus value. The working class—what Marx called the **proletariat**—is paid too little to buy all the products the workers have made, resulting in repeated overproduction, which leads to depressions. Eventually, argued Marx, there will be a depression so big the capitalist system will collapse.

Social Class   Every society divides into two classes: a small class of those who own the means of production and a large class of those who work for the small class. Society is run according to the dictates of the upper class, which sets up the laws, arts, and styles needed to maintain itself in power. (Marx influenced the theory of elites, discussed in Chapter 6.) Most laws concern property rights, noted Marx, because the **bourgeoisie** (the capitalists) are obsessed with hanging on to their property, which, according to Marx, is nothing but skimmed-off surplus value anyway. If the country goes to war, said Marx, it is not because the common people wish it but because the ruling bourgeoisie needs a war for economic gain. The proletariat, in fact, has no country; proletarians are international, all suffering under the heel of the capitalists.

History   Putting together his economic and social-class theories, Marx explained historical changes. When the underlying economic basis of society gets out of kilter with the structure that the dominant class has established (its laws, institutions, businesses, and so on), the system collapses, as in the French Revolution. Prior to 1789, France's ruling class was the feudal nobility. This system was from the Middle Ages, based on hereditary ownership of great estates worked by peasants, on laws stressing the inheritance of these estates and the titles that went with them, and on chivalry

superstructure Marx's term for everything that is built on top of the economy (laws, art, politics, etc.).

leftist Favors social and economic change to uplift poor.

and honor. All were part and parcel of a feudal society. But the economic basis changed. Ownership of land and feudal values eroded with the rise of manufacturing, which brought a new class, the urban capitalists (or bourgeoisie), whose way of life and economy were quite different. By the late eighteenth century, France had an economy based on manufacturing but was still dominated by the feudal aristocrats of the past. The system was out of kilter: The economic basis had moved ahead, but the class **superstructure** had stayed behind. In 1789, the superstructure came down with a crash, and the bourgeoisie took over with its new capitalist and liberal values of a free market, individual gain, and legal (but not material) equality.

The capitalists did a good job, Marx had to admit. They industrialized and modernized much of the globe. They put out incredible new products and inventions. But they too are doomed, Marx wrote, because the faster they transform the economy, the more it gets out of kilter with the capitalist superstructure, just as the previous feudal society was left behind by a changing economy. This leads us back to Marx's theory of surplus value and recurring economic depressions. Eventually, reasoned Marx, the economy will be so far out of kilter from the bourgeois setup that it too will collapse. Socialism, predicted Marx, will come next, and we should aid in its coming. Marx was partly a theorist and partly an ideologist. We will consider Marxism as ideology in the next chapter.

Marxism, as applied in the Soviet Union and other Communist countries, led to tyranny and failure, but, as a system of analysis, Marxism is still interesting and useful. Social class is important in structuring political views—but never uniformly. For example, many working-class people are conservative, and many middle-class intellectuals are liberals or **leftists**. Economic interest groups still ride high and—by means of freely spending on election campaigns—often get their way in laws, policies, and tax breaks. They seldom get all they want, however, as they are opposed by other interest groups. Marx's enduring contributions are (1) his understanding that societies are never fully unified and peaceful but always riven with conflict and (2) that we must ask "Who benefits?" in any political controversy.

One of the enduring problems and weaknesses of Marx is that capitalism, contrary to his prediction, has not collapsed. Marx thought the Paris Commune of 1870–1871 was the first proletarian uprising. (It was not.) True, capitalism has gone through some major depressions, in the 1890s and 1930s and a big scare in 2008–2009, but it has always bounced back.

Marx erred in at least a couple of ways. First, he failed to understand the flexible, adaptive nature of capitalism. Old industries fade, and new ones rise.

institutions The formal structures of government, such as the U.S. Congress.

positivism Theory that society can be studied scientifically and incrementally improved with the knowledge gained.

Imagine trying to explain Bill Gates and the computer software industry to people in the 1960s. They wouldn't believe you. Capitalism rarely gets stuck at one stage; it is the system of constant change. Second, Marx failed to understand that capitalism is not just one system; it is many. U.S., French, Singaporean, and Japanese capitalisms are distinct from each other. Marx's simplified notions of capitalism illustrate what happens when theory is placed in the service of ideology: Unquestioning followers believe it too literally.

Institutional Theories

From the nineteenth century through the middle of the twentieth century, American thinkers focused on **institutions**, the formal structures of government. This showed the influence of law on the development of political science in the United States. Woodrow Wilson, for example, was a lawyer (albeit unsuccessful) before he became a political scientist; he concentrated on perfecting the institutions of government. Constitutions were a favorite subject for political scientists of this period, for they assumed that what was on paper was how the institutions worked in practice. The rise of the Soviet, Italian, and German dictatorships shook this belief. The constitution of Germany's Weimar Republic (1919–1933) looked fine on paper; experts had drafted it. Under stress it collapsed, for Germans of that time did not have the necessary experience with or commitment to democracy. Likewise, the Stalin constitution of 1936 made the Soviet Union look like a perfect democracy, but it functioned as a dictatorship.

CONTEMPORARY THEORIES

Some thinkers of classic bent dismiss contemporary theories as trivial, obvious, superficial, or simply restatements of classic ideas. One such scholar sniffed that everything he learned from modern theories could be written on the inside of a matchbook cover. We need not be so harsh. Contemporary—meaning post–World War II—theories have made some contributions. Even when they ultimately fail and are abandoned, they leave a residue of interesting questions. True, compared to classic theories, most are pretty thin stuff.

Behavioralism

The Communist and Fascist dictatorships and World War II forced political scientists to reexamine their institutional focus, and many set to work to discover how politics really worked, not how it was supposed to work. Postwar American political scientists here followed in the tradition of the early nineteenth-century French philosopher Auguste Comte, who developed the doctrine of **positivism**, the application of natural science methods to the study of society. Comtean positivism was an optimistic philosophy, holding that as we accumulate valid data by means of scientific observation—without speculation or intuition—we will perfect a science of society and with it improve society. Psychologists are perhaps the most deeply imbued with this approach. **Behavioralists**, as they are called, claim to concentrate on actual behavior as opposed to thoughts or feelings.

behavioralism The empirical study of actual human behavior rather than abstract or speculative theories.

postbehavioral Synthesis of traditional, behavioral, and other techniques in the study of politics.

Beginning in the 1950s, behaviorally inclined political scientists accumulated statistics from elections, public opinion surveys, votes in legislatures, and anything else they could hang a number on. Behavioralists made some remarkable contributions to political science, shooting down some long-held but unexamined assumptions and giving political theory an empirical basis. Behavioral studies were especially good in examining the "social bases" of politics, the attitudes and values of average citizens, which go a long way toward making the system function the way it does. Their best work has been on voting patterns, for it is here they can get lots of valid data.

During the 1960s, the behavioral school established itself and won over much of the field. In the late 1960s, however, behavioralism came under heavy attack, and not just by rear-guard traditionalists. Many younger political scientists, some of them influenced by the radicalism of the anti–Vietnam War movement, complained that the behavioral approach was static, conservative, loaded with its practitioners' values, and irrelevant to the urgent tasks at hand. Far from being "scientific" and "value-free," behavioralists often defined the current situation in the United States as the norm and anything different as deviant. Gabriel Almond (1911–2002) and Sidney Verba (1932–) found that Americans embody all the good, "participant" virtues of the "civic culture." By examining only what exists at a given moment, behavioralists neglected the possibility of change; their studies may be time-bound. Behavioralists have an unstated preference for the status quo; they like to examine established democratic systems, for that is where their methodological tools work best. People in police states or civil conflicts know that honestly stating their opinions could get them jailed or killed, so they voice the "correct" viewpoint.

Perhaps the most damaging criticism, though, was that the behavioralists focused on relatively minor topics and steered clear of the big questions of politics. Behavioralists can tell us, for example, what percentage of Detroit blue-collar Catholics vote Democratic, but they tell us nothing about what this means for the quality of Detroit's governance or the kinds of decisions elected officials will make. There is no necessary connection between how citizens vote and what comes out of government. Critics charged that behavioral studies were often irrelevant.

By 1969, many political scientists had to admit that there was something to the criticism of what had earlier been called the "behavioral revolution." Some called the newer movement **postbehavioral**, a synthesis of traditional and behavioral approaches. Postbehavioralists recognize that facts and values are tied together. They are willing to use both the qualitative data of the traditionalists and the quantitative data of the behavioralists. They look at history and institutions as well as public opinion and rational-choice theory. They are not afraid of numbers and happily use correlations, graphs, and percentages to make their cases. If you look around your political science department, you are apt to find traditional, behavioral, and post-behavioral viewpoints among the professors—or even within the same professor.

Systems Theory

A major postwar invention was the "political systems" model devised by David Easton (1917–), which contributed to our understanding of politics by simplify-ing reality but in some cases departed from reality. The idea of looking at complex entities as systems originated in biology. Living entities are complex and highly integrated. The heart, lungs, blood, digestive tract, and brain perform their functions in such a way as to keep the animal alive. Take away one organ, and the animal dies. Damage one organ, and the other components of the system alter their function to compensate and keep the animal alive. The crux of systems thinking is this: You cannot change just one component, because that changes all the others.

thesis   A main idea or claim, to be proved by evidence.

Political systems thinkers argued that the politics of a given country work as a feedback loop, a bit like a biological system. According to the Easton model (Figure 2.3), citizens' demands, "inputs," are recognized by the government decision mak-ers, who process them into authoritative decisions and actions, "outputs." These outputs have an impact on the social, economic, and political environment that

HOW TO . . . ■ MAKE THESIS STATEMENTS

You are assigned a paper in political science. Begin it with a clear, punchy **thesis**, a first sentence giving your main idea or claim, the thing you are going to prove. A thesis that cannot be proved with empirical evidence is just speculation, not solid research. An initial attempt at a thesis is a *hypothesis* (discussed on page 14). If your evidence does not sup-port your thesis, discard or change it. Your thesis paragraph should be about as long as this one.

The simplest thesis is that something is (or is not) happening: "More and more in-terest groups set up shop in Washington." Avoid trivial theses, anything well-known or established: "The president is inaugurated on January 20 following the election." An inter-esting thesis explains how one thing relates to another: "White Protestant males vote strongly Republican." Gathering examples or case studies (see page 14) is often the ini-tial step to developing a thesis. If you take the six counties in your state with the highest Obama vote, what generalizations can you make about them? Do not gently introduce your thesis (save that for your English class); move directly into it. A thesis is more definite than what the paper is "about." You left that behind in high school.

Indirect	**Direct**
Television has a big impact on politics, and many critics feel that it is not always a good impact.	U.S. television advertising makes viewers cynical and indifferent and leads to low voter turnout.

Unprovable	**Provable**
Democracy is gov-ernment of the peo-ple, by people, and for the people.	Better-off countries tend to be democracies, poor countries not.

Trivial	**Nontrivial**
Tea Party supporters were unhappy with both of the main parties.	Tea Party supporters were mostly Republican voters angry over Obama's programs.

Vague	**Clear**
This paper is about U.S. policy toward Iran over three decades.	U.S. policy toward Iran failed to notice rising discontent against the shah.

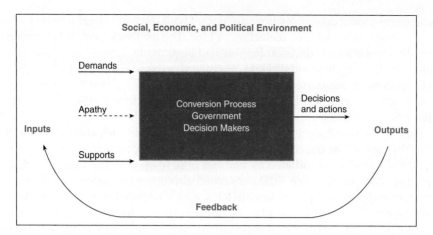

Figure 2.3
A model of the political system.

(*Adapted from David Easton*, A Systems Analysis of Political Life. *Chicago: University of Chicago Press, 1965, p. 32.*)

the citizens may or may not like. The citizens express their demands anew—this is the crucial "feedback" link of the system—which may modify the earlier decision. Precisely what goes on in the "conversion process" was left opaque, a "black box."

In some cases, the political systems approach fits reality. During the Vietnam War, feedback on the military draft was very negative. The Nixon administration defused youthful anger by ending the draft in 1973 and changing to an all-volunteer army. Recent lavish bonuses for executives of failed big companies—at that time propped up with billions of federal dollars—brought rage from citizens and Congress. The Obama administration saw healthcare reform as important and necessary, but roughly half the U.S. population opposed it, a point the Republicans used in the 2010 elections. In the 1980s, the socialist economics of French President François Mitterrand produced inflation and unemployment. The French people, especially the business community, complained loudly, and Mitterrand altered his policy away from socialism and back to capitalism. In these cases, the feedback loop worked.

But in other cases, the systems model falls flat. Would Hitler's Germany or Stalin's Russia really fit the systems model? How much attention do dictatorships pay to citizens' demands? To be sure, there is always some input and feedback. Hitler's generals tried to assassinate him—a type of feedback. Workers in Communist systems had an impact on government policy by not working much. They demanded more consumer goods and, by not exerting themselves, communicated this desire to the regime. Sooner or later the regime had to reform. All over the Soviet bloc, workers used to chuckle: "They pretend to pay us, and we pretend to work." In the USSR, (botched) reform came with the Gorbachev regime—and it led to system collapse.

How could the systems model explain the Vietnam War? Did Americans demand that the administration send half-a-million troops to fight there? No, nearly the opposite: Lyndon Johnson won overwhelmingly in 1964 on an antiwar platform.

The systems model does show how discontent with the war ruined Johnson's popularity so that he did not seek reelection in 1968. The feedback loop did go into effect but only years after the decision for war had been made. Could the systems model explain the Watergate scandal? Did U.S. citizens demand that President Nixon have the Democratic headquarters bugged? No, but once details about the cover-up started leaking in 1973, the feedback loop went into effect, putting pressure on the House of Representatives to form an impeachment panel.

Plainly, there are some problems with the systems model, and they seem to be in the "black box" of the conversion process. Much happens in the mechanism of government that is not initiated by and has little to do with the wishes of citizens. The American people were little concerned about the health effects of smoking. Only the analyses of medical statisticians, which revealed a strong link between smoking and lung cancer, prodded Congress into requiring warning labels on cigarette packs and ending television advertising of cigarettes. It was a handful of specialists in the federal bureaucracy who got the anticigarette campaign going, not the masses of citizens.

The systems model is essentially static, biased toward the status quo, and unable to handle upheaval. This is one reason political scientists were surprised at the collapse of the Soviet Union. "Systems" are not supposed to collapse; they are supposed to continually self-correct.

We can modify the systems model to better reflect reality. By diagramming it as in Figure 2.4, we logically change little. We have the same feedback loop: outputs turning into inputs. But by putting the "conversion process" of government first, we suggested that it—rather than the citizenry—originates most decisions. The public reacts only later. That would be the case with the Iraq War: strong support in 2003 but disillusion and discontent by 2006.

Next, we add something that Easton himself later suggested. Inside the "black box," a lot more happens than simply the processing of outside demands. Pressures from the various parts of government—government talking mostly to itself and short-circuiting the feedback loop—are what Easton called "withinputs." These two alterations, of course, make our model more complicated, but this reflects the complicated nature of reality. The systems model, like all models in political science, must be taken with a grain of salt.

KEY CONCEPTS ■ MODELS: SIMPLIFYING REALITY

A model is a simplified picture of reality that social scientists develop to order data, to theorize, and to predict. A good model fits reality but simplifies it, because a model that is as complex as the real world would be of no help. In simplifying reality, however, models run the risk of oversimplifying. The real problem is the finite capacity of the human mind. We cannot factor in all the information available at once; we must select which points are important and ignore the rest. But when we do this, we may drain the blood out of the study of politics and overlook key points. Accordingly, as we encounter models of politics—and perhaps as we devise our own—pause a moment to ask if the model departs too much from reality. If it does, discard or alter the model. Do not disregard reality because it does not fit the model.

Figure 2.4
A modified model of the political system.

Modernization Theory

Modernization theory, a broad-brush term, is rooted in Hegel, who argued two centuries ago that all facets of society—the economic, cultural, and political—hang together as a package, which changes and moves all societies in the same direction. Hegel thought the underlying cause of this process was spiritual, but Marx argued that it was economic: "Steam engines and dynamos bring their own philosophy with them." You cannot have a feudal society with a modern economy, at least not for long. Max Weber argued that the cause was cultural, specifically, the rise of Protestantism. Others have emphasized the growth of education, communications, and the middle class, but all agree it happens as a package. Today's modernization theorists see the process as complex, multicausal, and little amenable to outside guidance. We do not develop countries; they develop themselves, a point neglected in Iraq.

> **gross domestic product (GDP)** Sum total of goods and services produced in a given country in one year, often expressed per capita (GDPpc) by dividing population into GDP.

Most agree on the importance of industrialization. As a country industrializes, its economy, culture, communications, and politics also change. Giving new life to this theory was the remarkable second chapter of Seymour Martin Lipset's 1960 *Political Man*. Lipset classified countries as either "stable democracies" (such as Canada and Norway) or "unstable democracies and dictatorships" (such as Spain and Yugoslavia). With few exceptions, the stable democracies had more wealth, industry, radios, doctors, cars, education, and urban dwellers than the unstable democracies and dictatorships. In a word, they were more industrialized. And Lipset supplied an explanation: Industrialized countries have large middle classes, and they are the basis of democracy. Lipset combined Marx with Aristotle (see the quote from Aristotle earlier in this chapter).

More recent research tends to confirm a relationship between level of economic development and democracy. There is a dividing line between poor and middle-income countries, but it is not airtight. Lands with a per capita **gross domestic product (GDP)** of less than $5,000 are rarely democracies. If they attempt to found a democracy, it often fails, usually by military coup. Countries with a per capita GDP of more than $8,000, however, are mostly democracies. When they establish a democracy, it usually lasts. When South Korea and Taiwan were poor, they were dictatorships. As they industrialized, their middle classes and education levels grew, and by the 1990s both had turned into democracies. Much U.S. thinking on China is based on these hopeful examples. China's rapid economic growth suggests that it could soon become a middle-income country and hence be ripe for democracy. However, economic growth is rarely smooth, and China is a huge, complex nation ruled by a Communist Party that refuses to relinquish power. When Mexico topped $8,000 per cap, it was ready for its first democratic election, that of Vicente Fox in 2000. There is an interesting exception to this wealth-democracy connection: India, still with a per capita GDP of under $3,000, was founded and stayed democratic, likely the result of the age and authority of its founding Congress Party. For every theory, there are counterexamples.

Modernization theory also has some insights into the turmoil and instability that afflict many developing countries. It is because they modernize just one or two facets—often their economy and military—and leave the rest—such as religion and social structure—traditional. The two conflict; the traditional sectors resent and oppose the modern sectors. This helps explain the upsurge of Islamic fundamentalism in Iran, Egypt, Algeria, and Saudi Arabia. One must also note the high unemployment in these lands. If modernization theory is correct, if and when they reach middle-income levels, they should stabilize and democratize.

Rational-Choice Theory

In the 1970s, a new approach invented by mathematicians rapidly grew in political science—rational-choice theory. Rational-choice theorists argue that one

Shoppers in an upscale Beijing mall could watch 2010 World Cup soccer on a giant screen. Will China's rapid economic growth lead it to democracy? (AFP/Getty Images)

can generally predict political behavior by knowing
the interests of the actors involved because they rationally choose to maximize their interests. As U.S.
presidential candidates take positions on issues, they

paradigm   A model or way of doing
research accepted by a discipline.

calculate what will give them the best payoff. They might think, "Many people
oppose the war in Iraq, but many also demand strong leadership on defense.
I'd better just criticize 'mistakes' in Iraq while at the same time demand strong
'national security.'" The waffle is not indecision but calculation, argue rational-
choice theorists.

Rational-choice theorists enrage some other political scientists. One study of
Japanese bureaucrats claimed you need not study Japan's language, culture, or
history. All you needed to know was what their career advantages were to predict
how they would decide issues. A noted U.S. specialist on Japan blew his stack at
such glib, superficial shortcuts and denounced rational-choice theory. More modest
rational-choice theorists immersed themselves in Hungary's language and culture
but still concluded that Hungarian political parties, in cobbling together an extremely complex voting system, were making rational choices to give themselves
a presumed edge in parliamentary seats.

Many rational-choice theorists backed down from some of their more know-
it-all positions. Some now call themselves "neoinstitutionalists" (see following
section) because all their rational choices are made within one or another institutional context—the U.S. Congress, for example. Rational-choice theory did
not establish itself as the dominant **paradigm**—no theory has, and none is likely
to—but it contributed a lot by reminding us that politicians are consummate
opportunists, a point many other theories forget.

KEY CONCEPTS ■ POLITICS AS A GAME

Some rational-choice thinkers subscribed to a branch of mathematics called game theory, setting up political decisions as if they were table games. A Cuban missile crisis "game" might have several people play President Kennedy, who must weigh the probable payoffs of bombing or not bombing Cuba. Others might play Khrushchev, who has to weigh toughing it out or backing down. Seeing how the players interact gives us insights and warnings of what can go wrong in crisis decision making. If you "game out" the 1962 Cuban missile crisis and find that three games out of ten end in World War III, you have the makings of an article of great interest.

Game theorists argue that constructing the proper game explains why policy outcomes are often unforeseen but not accidental. Games can show how decision makers think. We learn how their choices are never easy or simple. Games can even be mathematized and fed into computers. The great weakness of game theory is that it depends on correctly estimating the "payoffs" decision makers can expect, and these are only approximations arrived at by examining the historical record. We know how the Cuban missile crisis came out; therefore, we adjust our game so it comes out the same way. In effect, game theory is only another way to systematize and clarify history (not a bad thing).

New Institutionalism

In the 1970s, political science began to rediscover institutions and, in the 1980s, proclaimed the "New Institutionalism." Its crux is that government structures—legislatures, parties, bureaucracies, and so on—take on lives of their own and shape the behavior and attitudes of the people who live within and benefit from them. Institutions are not simply the reflections of social forces. (Our discussion at the beginning of this chapter, on the importance of structures, is a neoinstitutionalist argument.) Legislators, for example, behave as they do largely because of rules laid down long ago and reinforced over the decades. Once you know these complex rules, some unwritten, you can see how politicians logically try to maximize their advantage under them, much as you can often predict when a baseball batter will bunt. It is not a mystery but the logic of the game they are playing. The preservation and enhancement of the institution becomes one of politicians' major goals. Thus, institutions, even if outmoded or ineffective, tend to rumble on. The Communist parties of the Soviet bloc were corrupt and ineffective, but they endured because they guaranteed the jobs and perquisites of their members.

The new institutionalism is a sound approach and popular in current research, and with it political science comes full circle, back to where it was before World War II, with some interesting new insights. It is, however, likely not the last model we shall see, for we will never have a paradigm that can consistently explain and predict political actions. Every couple of decades, political science comes up with a new paradigm—usually one borrowed from another discipline—that attracts much excitement and attention. Its proponents exaggerate its ability to explain or predict. Upon examination and criticism, the model usually fades and is replaced by another trend. Political science tends to get caught up in trends. After a few iterations of this cycle, we learn to expect no breakthrough theories. Politics is slippery and not easily confined to our mental constructs. By acknowledging this, we open our minds to the richness, complexity, and drama of political life.

 EXERCISES

Apply what you learned in this chapter on MyPoliSciKit (www.mypoliscikit.com).

Assessment Review this chapter using learning objectives, chapter summaries, practice tests, and more.

Menu

Flashcards Learn the key terms in this chapter; you can test yourself by term or definition.

Flashcards

Video Analyze recent world affairs by watching streaming video from major news providers.

Videos

 Comparative Exercises Compare political ideas, behaviors, institutions, and policies worldwide.

Comparative Exercises

KEY TERMS

behavioralism (p. 29)
bourgeois (p. 26)
civil society (p. 25)
descriptive (p. 23)
general will (p. 25)
gross domestic product
   (GDP) (p. 33)

institutions (p. 28)
leftist (p. 27)
normative (p. 23)
paradigm (p. 35)
positivism (p. 28)
postbehavioral (p. 29)
proletariat (p. 26)

realism (p. 23)
social contract (p. 25)
state of nature (p. 25)
superstructure (p. 27)
thesis (p. 30)
Zeitgeist (p. 26)

FURTHER REFERENCE

Almond, Gabriel A., and James S. Coleman. *Politics of Developing Areas.* Princeton, NJ: Princeton University Press, 1960.

Boesche, Roger. *The First Great Political Realist: Kautilya and His Arthashastra.* Lanham, MD: Lexington, 2003.

Colomer, Josep M. *The Science of Politics: An Introduction.* New York: Oxford University Press, 2010.

Easton, David. *A Framework for Political Analysis.* Englewood Cliffs, NJ: Prentice Hall, 1965.

Hardt, Michael, and Antonio Negri. *Commonwealth.* Cambridge, MA: Harvard University Press, 2009.

Lane, Ruth. *Political Science in Theory and Practice: The "Politics" Model.* Armonk, NY: M. E. Sharpe, 1997.

Laver, Michael. *Private Desires, Political Action: An Invitation to the Politics of Rational Choice.* Thousand Oaks, CA: Sage, 1997.

Lipset, Seymour Martin. *Political Man: The Social Bases of Politics*, rev. ed. Baltimore, MD: Johns Hopkins University Press, 1981.

———, ed. *Political Philosophy: Theories, Thinkers, and Concepts.* Washington, DC: CQ Press, 2001.

Losco, Joseph, and Leonard Williams, eds. *Political Theory: Classic and Contemporary Readings*, 2nd ed., 2 vols. Los Angeles: Roxbury, 2002.

Morgenthau, Hans J., Kenneth W. Thompson, and David Clinton. *Politics Among Nations: The Struggle for Power and Peace*, 7th ed. Burr Ridge, IL: McGraw-Hill, 2005.

Sen, Amartya. *The Idea of Justice.* Cambridge, MA: Harvard University Press, 2009.

Tannenbaum, Donald, and David Schultz. *Inventors of Ideas: An Introduction to Western Political Philosophy*, 2nd ed. Belmont, CA: Wadsworth, 2003.

Tinder, Glenn. *Political Thinking: The Perennial Questions*, 6th ed. New York: Longman, 2003.

White, Stephen K., and J. Donald Moon, eds. *What Is Political Theory?* Thousand Oaks, CA: Sage, 2004.

Political Ideologies

The FDR memorial in Washington, DC, shows his emphasis on helping poorer citizens, an example of modern liberalism. (William Manning/Corbis)

The theories of politics we discussed in the previous chapter lead to consideration of **ideologies**, which are often based on theories but simplified and popularized to sell to mass audiences, build political movements, and win elections. Ideologies might be called cheap theories. As is usual in U.S. politics, at least two of them contend.

Most Americans see themselves as **pragmatic**, but they can be quite ideological. Recently, for example, Republicans denounced the Democratic health-care and finance reforms as "liberal." Probably few Republicans knew it, but the basis of their opposition was actually *classic liberalism*, harkening back to Adam Smith's two-century-old admonition to get government out of the economy. Democrats, on the other hand, emphasized government solutions for financial crashes, poverty, health care, and home foreclosures. They were *modern liberals*, quite distinct from the classic variety. Ideology is alive and well in America.

QUESTIONS TO CONSIDER

1. Is it possible to be totally pragmatic, with no ideology?
2. How did classic liberalism turn into U.S. conservatism?
3. How close are modern liberalism and social democracy?
4. What changes did Lenin make to Marxism?
5. Why is nationalism the strongest ideology?
6. What are the main elements of fascism?
7. What is "Islamism," and why is it dangerous?
8. Do any ideologies attract today's students?
9. Could ideological politics die out?

WHAT IS IDEOLOGY?

An ideology begins with the belief that things can be better; it is a plan to improve society. As Anthony Downs put it, ideology is "a verbal image of the good society, and of the chief means of constructing such a society." Political ideologies are not political science; they are not calm, rational attempts to understand political systems. Rather, they are commitments to *change* political systems. (An exception is classic conservatism, which aimed to keep things from changing too much.) **Ideologues** make poor political scientists, for they confuse the "should" or "ought" of ideology with the "is" of political science.

In politics, ideology cements together movements, parties, and revolutionary groups. To fight and endure sacrifices, people need ideological motivation—something to believe in. Americans have sometimes not grasped this point. With their emphasis on moderation and pragmatism, they fail to understand the

ideology   Belief system that society can be improved by following certain doctrines; usually ends in *-ism*.

pragmatic   Using whatever works without theory or ideology.

ideologue   Someone who believes passionately in an ideology.

classic liberalism   Ideology founded by Adam Smith to keep government out of economy; became U.S. conservatism.

energizing effect of ideology in the world today. "Our" Vietnamese, the South Vietnamese, were physically no different from the Vietcong and North Vietnamese, and they were better armed. But in the crunch, the Vietnamese who had a doctrine to believe in—a mixture of Marx, Lenin, and Mao with heavy doses of nationalism and anticolonialism—won against the Vietnamese who didn't have much to believe in. We tend to forget that more than two centuries ago Americans were quite ideological, too, and—imbued with a passion for freedom and self-rule, via the pens of John Locke and Thomas Paine—beat a larger and better-equipped army of Englishmen and Hessians, who had no good reason to fight. Now we are aghast at the fanatics of a new ideology, Islamism.

Ideologies never work precisely the way their advocates claim. Some are hideous failures. All ideologies contain wishful thinking, which frequently collapses in the face of reality. Ideologues claim they can perfect the world; reality is highly imperfect. The **classic liberalism** of Adam Smith did contribute to the nineteenth century's economic growth, but it also led to great inequalities of wealth and recurring depressions. It was modified into modern liberalism. Communism led to brutal tyrannies, economic failures, and collapse. China quietly abandoned Maoism in favor of rapid economic growth. Ideologies, when measured against their actual performance, are more or less defective and should all be taken with a grain of salt.

THE MAJOR IDEOLOGIES

Classic Liberalism

Frederick Watkins of Yale called 1776 "the Year One of the Age of Ideology"— and not just for the American Revolution. That same year, Scottish economist Adam Smith published *The Wealth of Nations*, thereby founding classic laissez-faire economics. The true wealth of nations, Smith argued, is not in the amount of gold and silver they amass but in the amount of goods and services their people produce. Smith was refuting an earlier notion, called *mercantilism*, that the bullion in a nation's treasury determined its wealth. Spain had looted the New World of gold and silver but grew poorer. The French, too, since at least Louis XIV in the previous century, had followed mercantilist policies by means of government supervision of the economy with plans, grants of monopoly, subsidies, tariffs, and other restraints on trade.

Smith reasoned that this was not the path to prosperity. Government interference retards growth. If you give one firm a monopoly to manufacture something, you banish competition and, with it, efforts to produce new products and lower prices. The economy stagnates. If you protect domestic industry by tariffs, you take away incentives for better or cheaper products. By getting the government out of the economy, by leaving the economy alone (*laissez-faire*, in French), you promote prosperity.

CLASSIC WORKS ■ THE ORIGINS OF IDEOLOGIES

Many ideologies stem from the political theories discussed in Chapter 2. Classic liberalism traces back to the seventeenth-century English philosopher John Locke, who emphasized individual rights, property, and reason. Communism traces back to the early nineteenth-century German philosopher G. W. F. Hegel, who emphasized that all facets of a society—art, music, architecture, politics, law, and so on—hang together as a package, all the expression of an underlying *Zeitgeist* (see page 26).

The philosophers' ideas, however, are simplified and popularized. Ideologists want plans for action, not abstract ideas. Marx, for example, "stood Hegel on his head" to make economics the great underlying cause. Most ideologies have a large economic component, for it is economics that will improve society. Lenin later stood Marx on his head to make his ideas apply to a backward country where Marx doubted they should. Mao Zedong then applied Lenin's ideas to an even more backward country, where they did not fit at all. Ideologies become warped.

One ideology gives rise to others (see figure below). Starting with the classic liberalism of Adam Smith, we see how liberalism branched leftward into radical, socialist, and communist directions. Meanwhile, on the conservative side, it branched rightward.

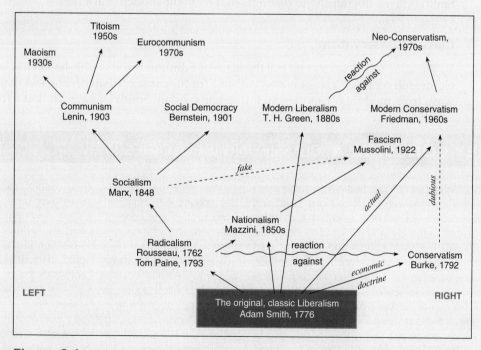

Figure 3.1
How political ideologies relate to one another: key thinkers and dates of emergence.

---
conservatism   Ideology of keeping systems largely unchanged.

But won't free competition unsupervised by government lead to chaos? No, said Smith; the market itself will regulate the economy. Efficient producers will prosper and inefficient ones will go under. Supply and demand determine prices better than any government official. In the free marketplace, an "unseen hand" regulates and self-corrects the economy. If people want more of something, producers increase output, new producers enter the field, or foreign producers bring in their wares. The unseen hand—actually, the rational calculations of myriad individuals and firms all pursuing their self-interest—micro-adjusts the economy with no government help.

This ideology took the name liberalism from the Latin word for "free," *liber*: Society should be as free as possible from government interference. As aptly summarized by Thomas Jefferson, "That government is best that governs least." Americans took to classic liberalism like a duck takes to water. It fit the needs of a vigorous, freedom-loving population with plenty of room to expand. Noneconomic liberty also suited Americans. Government should also not supervise religion, the press, or free speech.

But, you say, what you're calling liberalism here is actually what Americans today call conservatism. True. In the late nineteenth century, liberalism changed and split into modern liberalism and what we now call conservatism, which we will discuss next. To keep our terminology straight, we call the original ideas of Adam Smith "classic liberalism" to distinguish it from the modern variety.

Classic Conservatism

By the same token, we should call the ideas of Edmund Burke, published in the late eighteenth century, "classic conservatism," for his **conservatism** diverges in many ways from modern conservatism. Burke knew Adam Smith and agreed that a free

KEY CONCEPTS ■ CLASSIFYING IDEOLOGIES

Ideologies can be classified—with some over-simplification—on a left-to-right spectrum that dates back to the meeting of the French National Assembly in 1789. To allow delegates of similar views to caucus and to keep apart strong partisans who might fight, members were seated as follows in a semicircular chamber: Conservatives (who favored continuation of the monarchy) were on the speaker's right, radicals (who favored sweeping away the old system altogether in favor of a republic of freedom and equality) were seated to his left, and moderates (who wanted some change) were seated in the center.

We have been calling their ideological descendants left, right, and center ever since, even though the content of their views has changed. The left now favors equality, welfare programs, and government intervention in the economy. The right stresses individual initiative and private economic activity. Centrists try to synthesize and moderate the views of both. People a little to one side or the other are called center-left or center-right. Sweden's political parties form a rather neat left-to-right spectrum: a small Communist party; a large Social Democratic party; and medium-sized Center (formerly Farmers'), Liberal, Christian, and Conservative parties.

market was the best economic system. Burke also opposed crushing the rebellious American colonists; after all, they were only trying to regain the ancient freedoms of Englishmen, said Burke. So far, Burke sounds like a liberal.

But Burke strongly objected to the way liberal ideas were applied in France by revolutionists. There, liberalism turned into *radicalism*, influenced by philosopher Jean-Jacques Rousseau and, fresh from the U.S. revolution, Thomas Paine. As is often the case, an ideology devised in one place becomes warped when applied to different circumstances. Liberalism in America was easy; once the English and their Tory sympathizers cleared out, it fell into place without resistance. But in France, a large aristocratic class and a state-supported Roman Catholic Church had a lot to lose. The revolutionaries tried to solve the problem with the guillotine and swept away all established institutions.

This, warned Burke, was a terrible mistake. Liberals place too much confidence in human reason. People are only partly rational; they also have irrational passions. To contain them, society over the years has evolved traditions, institutions, and standards of morality, such as the monarchy and an established church. Sweep these aside, said Burke, and man's irrational impulses lead to chaos, which in turn ends in tyranny far worse than the old system. Burke, in his 1792 *Reflexions on the Revolution in France*, predicted that France would fall into military dictatorship. In 1799, Napoleon took over.

Institutions and traditions that currently exist cannot be all bad, Burke reasoned, for they are the products of hundreds of years of trial and error. People have become used to them. The best should be preserved or "conserved" (hence the name conservatism). They are not perfect, but they work. This is not to say that things should never change. Of course they should change, said Burke, but only gradually, giving people time to adjust. "A state without the means of some change is without the means of its conservation," he wrote.

Burke was an important thinker for several reasons. He helped discover the *irrational* in human behavior. He saw that institutions are like living things; they grow and adapt over time. And, most important, he saw that revolutions end badly, for society cannot be instantly remade according to human reason. Although Burke's ideas have been called an *anti-ideology*—for they aimed to shoot down the radicalism then engulfing France—they have considerable staying power. Burke's emphasis on religion, traditions, and morality has been taken over by modern conservatives. His doubts about applying reason to solve social problems were echoed by political scientist Jeane Kirkpatrick, President Reagan's UN ambassador, who found that leftists always suppose that things can be much better when in fact violent upheaval always makes things worse. In these ways, classic conservatism is very much alive.

Modern Liberalism

What happened to the original, classic liberalism of Adam Smith? By the late nineteenth century, it was clear that the free market was not as self-regulating as Smith had thought. Competition was imperfect. Manufacturers rigged the market—a point Smith himself had warned about. There was a drift to bigness

modern liberalism Ideology favoring government intervention to correct economic and social ills; U.S. liberalism today.

and fewness: monopoly. The system produced a large underclass of the terribly poor (which Dickens depicted). Class positions were largely inherited; children of better-off families got the education and connections to stay on top. Bouts of speculative investing led to recurring economic depressions—2008–2009 is just the most recent example—which especially hurt the poor and the working class. In short, the laissez-faire economy created some problems.

The Englishman Thomas Hill Green rethought liberalism in the 1880s. The goal of liberalism, reasoned Green, was a free society. But what happens when economic developments take away freedom? The classic liberals placed great store in contracts (agreements between consenting parties with no government supervision): If you don't like the deal, don't take it. But what if the bargaining power of the two parties is greatly unequal, as between a rich employer and a poor person desperate for a job? Does the latter really have a free choice in accepting or rejecting a job with very low wages? Classic liberalism said let it be; wages will find their own level. But what if the wage is below starvation level? Here, Green said, it was time for government to step in. In such a case, it would not be a question of government infringing on freedoms but of government protecting them. Instead of the purely negative "freedom from," there had to be a certain amount of the positive "freedom to." Green called this *positive freedom*. Government was to step in to guarantee the freedom to live at an adequate level.

Classic liberalism expelled government from the marketplace; **modern liberalism** brought it back in, this time to protect people from a sometimes unfair economic system. Modern liberals championed wage and hour laws, the right to form unions, unemployment and health insurance, and improved educational opportunities. To do this, they placed heavier taxes on the rich than on the working class. They also regulated banking and finance to dampen the boom-and-bust cycle. This is the liberalism of the United States over the last century—the liberalism of Woodrow Wilson, Franklin D. Roosevelt, and Barack Obama. One strand of the old liberalism remains in the new, however: the emphasis on freedom of speech and press.

Modern Conservatism

What happened to the other branch of liberalism, the people who stayed true to Adam Smith's original doctrine of minimal government? They are still very important, only today we call them conservatives. (In Europe, they still call them liberals or *neoliberals*, much to the confusion of Americans.) American conservatives got a big boost from Milton Friedman (1912–2006), a Nobel Prize–winning economist. Friedman argued that the free market is still the best, that Adam Smith was right, and that wherever government intervenes, it messes things up. Margaret Thatcher in Britain and Ronald Reagan in the United States applied this revival of classic liberalism in the 1980s with mixed but generally positive results.

Modern conservatism also borrows from Edmund Burke a concern for tradition, especially in religion. American conservatives would put prayer into public schools, outlaw abortion and same-sex marriage, and support private and church-related schools. Modern conservatives also oppose special rights for women and minority groups, arguing that everyone should have the same rights. Modern conservatism is a blend of the economic ideas of Adam Smith and the traditionalist ideas of Edmund Burke.

Marxist Socialism

Liberalism (classic variety) dominated the nineteenth century, but critics deplored the growing gulf between rich and poor. Unlike T. H. Green, some did not believe that a few reforms would suffice; they wanted to overthrow the capitalist system. These were the socialists, and their leading thinker was Karl Marx, whose complex theory we discussed in Chapter 2. Marx wrote not as a scholar but to promote revolution. He hated the "bourgeoisie" long before he developed his elaborate theories that they were doomed. An outline of his ideas appeared in his 1848 pamphlet, *The Communist Manifesto*, which concluded with the ringing words: "The proletarians have nothing to lose but their chains. They have a world to win. Workers of all countries, unite!" Marx participated in organizing Europe's first socialist parties.

Marx's *Capital* was a gigantic analysis of why capitalism would be overthrown by the proletariat. Then would come socialism, a just, productive society without class distinctions. Later, at a certain stage when industrial production was very high, this socialist society will turn into *communism*, a perfect society without police, money, or even government. Goods will be in such plenty that people will just take what they need. There will be no private property, so there will be no need for police. Because government is simply an instrument of class domination, with the abolition of distinct classes there will be no need for the state. It will "wither away." Communism, then, was the predicted utopia beyond socialism.

Marx focused on the ills and malfunctions of capitalism and never specified what socialism would be like. He only said that socialism would be much better than capitalism; its precise workings he left vague. This has enabled a wide variety of socialist thinkers to put forward their own vision of socialism and say it is what Marx really meant. This has ranged from the mild "welfarism" of social-democratic parties, to *anarcho-syndicalism* (unions running everything), to Lenin's and Stalin's hypercentralized tyranny, to Trotsky's denunciation of same, to Mao's self-destructive permanent revolution, to Tito's experimental decentralized system. All, and a few more, claim to espouse "real" socialism. These different interpretations of socialism caused first the socialist and then the communist movement to splinter.

Social Democracy

By the beginning of the twentieth century, the German Social Democrats (SPD), espousing Marxism, had become Germany's biggest party. Marx had disparaged conventional parties and labor unions; bourgeois governments would simply crush them. At most, they could be training grounds for serious revolutionary action. But the German Social Democrats started succeeding. They got elected to the Reichstag

This statue of Karl Marx and Friedrich Engels, key figures in the Communist movement, presides over a park in Berlin named in their honor. (Dallas and John Heaton/Corbis)

and local offices; their unions won higher wages and better working conditions. Some began to think that the working class could accomplish its aims without revolution. Why use bullets when there are ballots?

Eduard Bernstein developed this view. In his *Evolutionary Socialism* (1901), he pointed out the real gains the working class was making and concluded that Marx had been wrong about the collapse of capitalism and revolution. Reforms that won concrete benefits for the working class could also lead to socialism, he argued. In revising Marxism, Bernstein earned the name **revisionist**, originally a pejorative hurled at him by orthodox Marxists. By the time of the ill-fated Weimar Republic in Germany (1919–1933), the Social Democrats had toned down their militancy and worked together with Liberals and Catholics to try to save democracy. Persecuted by the Nazis, the SPD revived after World War II and in 1959 dropped Marxism altogether, as did virtually all social democratic parties. As social democrats in many countries moderated their positions, they got elected more and more. They transformed themselves into center-left parties with no trace of revolution.

revisionist Changing an ideology or view of history.

social democracy Mildest form of socialism, stressing welfare measures but not state ownership of industry.

What, then, do **social democrats** stand for? They have abandoned the state ownership of industry. Only about 10 percent of Sweden's industry is state-owned, and much of that conservatives did long ago to keep firms from going under and creating unemployment. Said Olof Palme, Sweden's Social Democratic prime minister, "If industry's primary purpose is to expand its production, to succeed in new markets, to provide good jobs for their employees, they need have no fears. Swedish industry has never expanded so rapidly as during these years of Social Democratic rule." Instead

> **communism**   Marxist theory merged with Leninist organization into a totalitarian party.
>
> **imperialism**   Amassing of colonial empires, mostly by European powers; pejorative in Marxist terms.

of state ownership of industry, social democrats use *welfare* measures to improve living conditions: unemployment and medical insurance, generous pensions, and subsidized food and housing. Social democracies have become welfare states: *Welfarism* would be a more accurate term than *socialism*.

There's one catch—there's always at least one catch—and that is that welfare states are terribly expensive. To pay for welfare measures, taxes climb. In Denmark and Sweden, taxes consume about half of the gross domestic product (GDP), exactly the kind of thing Milton Friedman warned about. With those kinds of taxes, soon you are not free to choose how you live. U.S. liberalism is tinged with social democratic ideas on welfare. The left wing of our Democratic Party resembles ideologically the moderate wings of European social democratic parties.

Communism

While the social democrats evolved into reformists and welfarists, a smaller wing of the original socialists stayed Marxist and became the Communists. The key figure in this transformation was a Russian intellectual, Vladimir I. Lenin. He made several changes in Marxism, producing *Marxism-Leninism*, another name for **communism**.

Imperialism   Many Russian intellectuals of the late nineteenth century hated the tsarist system and embraced Marxism as a way to overthrow tsarism. But Marx meant his theory to apply in the most advanced capitalist countries, not in backward Russia, where capitalism was just beginning. Lenin, in his 17-year exile in Switzerland, remade Marxism to fit the Russian situation. He offered a theory of economic imperialism, one borrowed from German revolutionary Rosa Luxemburg and English economist J. A. Hobson, who wondered why the proletarian revolutions Marx had predicted had not broken out in the advanced industrialized lands. They concluded that the domestic market could not absorb all the goods the capitalist system produced, so it found overseas markets. Capitalism had transformed itself, expanding overseas into colonies to exploit their raw materials, cheap labor, and new markets. Capitalism thus won a temporary new lease on life by turning into **imperialism**. With profits from its colonies, the mother imperialist country could also pay off its working class a bit to render it reformist rather than revolutionary.

Imperialism had to expand, Lenin argued, but it was growing unevenly. Some countries, such as Britain and Germany, were highly developed, but where capitalism was just starting, as in Spain and Russia, it was weak. The newly industrializing countries were exploited as a whole by the international capitalist system. It was in them that revolutionary fever burned brightest; they were "imperialism's weakest link." Accordingly, a revolution could break out in a poor country, reasoned Lenin, and then spread into advanced countries. The imperialist countries were highly dependent on their empires. Once cut off from exploiting them, capitalism would fall. World War I, wrote Lenin, was the collision of imperialists trying to dominate the globe.

Lenin shifted the Marxian focus from the situation within capitalist countries to the global situation. The focus went from Marx's proletariat rising up against the bourgeoisie to exploited nations rising up against imperialist powers. Marx would probably not have endorsed such a redo of his theory.

Organization   Lenin's real contribution lay in his attention to organization. With the tsarist secret police always on their trail, Lenin argued, the Russian socialist party could not be like other parties—large, open, and trying to win votes. Instead, it had to be small, secretive, made up of professional revolutionaries, and tightly organized under central command. In 1903, the Russian Social Democratic Labor party split over this issue. Lenin had enough supporters at the party's Brussels meeting to win the votes of 33 of the 51 delegates present. Lenin called his faction *bolshevik* (Russian for "majority"). The losers, who advocated a more moderate line and a more open party, took the name *menshevik* ("minority"). In 1918, the Bolsheviks changed the party name to Communist.

Lenin's attention to organization paid off. Russia was in chaos from World War I. In March 1917, a group of moderates seized power from the tsar, but they were unable to govern the country. In November, the Bolsheviks shrewdly manipulated councils (*soviets* in Russian) that had sprung up in the leading cities and seized control from the moderates. After winning a desperate civil war, Lenin called on all true socialists around the world to join in a new international movement under Moscow's control. It was called the Communist International, or *Comintern*. Almost all socialist parties in the world split; their left wings went into the Comintern and became Communist parties in 1920–1921. The resultant social democratic and Communist parties have been hostile to each other ever since.

How much Marxism-Leninism did the rulers of the Soviet Union really believe? They constantly used Marxist rhetoric, but many observers argued they were cynical about ideology and just used it as window dressing. The Soviets never defined their society as Communist—that was yet to come; it was what they were working on. It is we in the West who called these countries "Communist." In 1961, party chief Nikita Khrushchev rashly predicted "communism in our generation," indicating that utopia would be reached by 1980. Instead, it declined, and at the end of 1991, the Soviet system collapsed.

Maoism and Titoism   In the 1930s, Mao Zedong concluded that the Chinese Communist Party (CCP) had to be based on poor peasants and guerrilla warfare. This was a break with Stalin's leadership, and after decades of fighting, the CCP took over mainland China in 1949. Mao pursued a radical course that included a failed attempt at overnight industrialization (the Great Leap Forward of 1958), the destruction of bureaucratic authority (the Proletarian Cultural Revolution in 1966–1976), and even border fighting with the Soviet Union in 1969. After Mao's death in 1976, pragmatic leaders moved China away from his extremism, which had ruined China's economic progress. A few revolutionary groups stayed Maoist: Cambodia's murderous Khmer Rouge and India's Naxalites. **Maoism** is an ultraradical form of communism.

Maoism   Extreme form of communism, featuring guerrilla warfare and periodic upheavals.

Titoism   Mild, decentralized form of communism.

nationalism   A people's heightened sense of cultural, historical, and territorial identity, unity, and sometimes greatness.

Yugoslav party chief Josip Tito went the other way, developing a more moderate and liberal form of communism. Even though Tito's partisans fought the Germans in Stalin's name, Stalin did not fully control Tito, and in 1948 Stalin had Yugoslavia kicked out of the Communist camp. During the 1950s, the Yugoslav Communists reformed their system, basing it on decentralization, debureaucratization, and worker self-management. Trying to find a middle ground between a market and a controlled economy, Yugoslavia suffered economic problems in the 1980s. **Titoism** might have served as a warning to Communist rulers who wanted to experiment with "middle ways" between capitalism and socialism. The combination is unstable and worked only because Tito was undisputed ruler; when he died in 1980, Yugoslavia started coming apart until, by the early 1990s, it was a bloodbath.

Nationalism

The real winner among ideologies—one that still dominates today—is **nationalism**, the exaggerated belief in the greatness and unity of one's country. Nationalism is often born out of occupation and repression by foreigners. "We won't be pushed around by foreigners any more!" shout Cuban, Palestinian, Iraqi, Chinese, and many other nationalists. Nationalism has triumphed over and influenced all other ideologies, so that, in the United States, conservatism is combined with American nationalism, and, in China, nationalism was always more important than communism.

The first seeds of nationalism came with the Renaissance monarchs who proclaimed their absolute power and the unity and greatness of their kingdoms. Nationality was born out of sovereignty. *Nationalism,* however, appeared only with the French Revolution, which was based on "the people" and heightened French feelings about themselves as a special, leading people destined to free the rest of Europe. When a Prussian army invaded France in 1792, the "nation in arms" stopped them at Valmy; enthusiastic volunteers beat professional soldiers. The stirring "Marseillaise," France's national anthem, appeared that year.

Later, Napoleon's legions ostensibly spread the radical liberalism of the French Revolution but were really spreading nationalism. The conquered nations of Europe quickly grew to hate the arrogant French occupiers. Spaniards, Germans, and Russians soon became nationalistic themselves as they struggled to expel the French. Basic to nationalism is resentment of foreign domination, be it by British redcoats, Napoleon's legions, or European colonialists. Nationalism blanketed Europe in the nineteenth century and, in the twentieth century, spread to Europe's colonies throughout the world. It is in the developing countries that nationalism is now most intense.

By the mid–nineteenth century, thinkers all over Europe—especially in Germany and Italy—defined the nation as the ultimate human value, the source of all things good. Italian writer Giuseppe Mazzini espoused freedom not for individuals—that was mere liberalism—but for nations instead. One achieved true freedom by subordinating oneself to the nation. Education, for example, had to inculcate a sense of nationalism that blotted out individualism, argued Mazzini.

Nationalism arises when a population, invariably led by intellectuals, perceives an enemy or "other" to despise and struggle against. In the twentieth century, this has often been a colonial power such as Britain, France, or the Netherlands, against whom, respectively, Indians, Algerians, and Indonesians could rally in their fight for independence. Nationalism holds that it is terribly wrong to be ruled by others. Thus, Bosnian Serbs do not consent to be ruled by Bosnian Muslims, Palestinians by Israelis, and Lithuanians by Russians. Some Chinese and Iranians, feeling they have been repressed and controlled by outside powers, lash out with nationalistic military and diplomatic policies. Even some Canadians, fearful of U.S. economic and cultural dominance, turn nationalistic.

The big problem with nationalism is that it tends to lead to economic isolation. "We won't let foreigners take over our economy!" say nationalists, but rapid economic growth needs foreign investment and world trade. More than any of the previous ideologies, nationalism depends on emotional appeals. The feeling of belonging to a nation goes to our psychological center. What other human organization would we fight and kill for?

Regional Nationalism   In recent decades, the world has seen the rise of another kind of nationalism: regional nationalism, which aims at breaking up existing nations into what its proponents argue are the true nations. Militant Québécois want

HOW TO . . . ■ SUPPORT YOUR THESIS

"Well, that's what I think" isn't good enough. Writing a paper is like a lawyer making a case. Like a judge, your instructor decides if your evidence is valid and supports your point. In a short paper, you might back up your thesis with three to five supporting elements. You may wish to use subheads, little titles in the middle of your paper, to separate your supporting arguments. Subheads help you structure your ideas and make the paper easier to read and understand. If you cannot support your thesis with facts, numbers, quotes, or just plain reasoning, abandon or change it. As they say in the news business: "Back it up or back off."

Boldfaced and Centered

Boldface and center your subheads (like the above subhead) to make them stand out. A new subhead indicates you are moving on to another supporting element. A paragraph is one thought or point. Make about three of them per double-spaced page. A paragraph that rambles on for a whole page is hard to read. Have no more than one subhead per page. For example, if your thesis is that a sour economy hurts incumbent presidents in elections, you might make a subhead for each election: "The 2004 Elections," "The 2008 Elections," and so on. A five-page paper may have about three subheads, indicating you are supporting your thesis with three elements.

to separate from Canada, Basques from Spain, South Ossetians from Georgia, and Scots from Britain. It too is based on hatred of being ruled by unlike peoples.

fascism   Extreme form of nationalism with elements of socialism and militarism.

Fascism

In Italy and Germany nationalism grew into **fascism**, one of the great catastrophes of the twentieth century. One sign of a fascist movement is members in uniforms; they like military structure and discipline. Before World War I, Italian journalist Benito Mussolini was a fire-breathing socialist; military service changed him into an ardent nationalist. Italy was full of discontented people after World War I. "Maximalist" socialists threatened revolution. In those chaotic times, Mussolini assembled a strange collection of people in black shirts who wanted to end democracy and political parties and impose stern central authority and discipline. These Fascists—a word taken from the ancient Roman symbol of authority, a bundle of sticks bound around an ax (the *fasces*)—hated disorder and wanted strong leadership to end it.

Amid growing disorder in 1922, the king of Italy handed power to Mussolini, and by 1924 he had turned Italy into a one-party state with himself as *Duce* (leader). The Fascists ran the economy by inserting their men into all key positions. Italy looked impressive: There was little crime, much monumental construction, stable prices, and, as they used to say, "The trains ran on time." Behind the scenes, however, fascism was a mess, with hidden unemployment, poor economic performance, and corruption.

With the collapse of the world economy in 1929, however, some thought fascism was the wave of the future. Adolf Hitler in Germany copied Mussolini's fascism but had his followers wear brown shirts and added *racism*. For Hitler, it was not just Germans as a nation who were fighting the punitive and unfair Versailles Treaty and chaos of the Weimar Republic; it was Germans as a distinct and superior race. Hitler did not invent German racism, which went back generations, but he hyped it. The racist line held that a special branch of the white race, the Aryans, were the bearers of all civilization. A subbranch, the Nordics, which included Germans, were even better. (Actually, Germans are of very mixed genealogy.) Nazis argued that the superior Nordics were being subjugated to the sinister forces of Judaism, communism, world capitalism, and even Roman Catholicism. This doctrine was the basis for the death camps.

Hitler was named chancellor (prime minister) in 1933 in a situation of turmoil and, like Mussolini, within two years had perfected a dictatorship. Probably a majority of Germans supported Hitler. With Nazis "coordinating" the economy, unemployment ended and many working people felt they were getting a good deal with the jobs, vacations, and welfare the regime provided. The Nazis' full name was the National Socialist German Workers Party, but the socialism was fake. Hitler's true aim was war, as war builds heroes. For a few years, Hitler dominated Europe and started turning the Slavic lands of Eastern Europe into colonies for Germans—*Lebensraum* (living space). Nazi death camps killed some 6 million Jews and a similar number of Christians who were in the way. Was Hitler mad? Many of his views

neoconservatism   U.S. ideology of former liberals turning to conservative causes and methods.

were widely held among Germans, and he had millions of enthusiastic helpers. Rather than insanity, the Nazis demonstrated the danger of nationalism run amok.

The word *fascist* has been overused and misused. Some hurl it at everything they dislike. Spanish dictator Francisco Franco, for example, was long considered a fascist, but he was actually a "traditional authoritarian," for he tried to minimize mass political involvement rather than stir it up the way Mussolini and Hitler did. Brazilian President Getúlio Vargas decreed a fascist-sounding "New State" in 1937, but he was merely borrowing some fascist rhetoric at a time when the movement was having its heyday in Europe. Some right-wing American commentators denounce "Islamofascists."

The Ku Klux Klan in the United States is sometimes called fascist, and its members wear uniforms. The Klan's populist racism is similar to the Nazis', but the Klan strongly opposes the power of the national government, whereas the Nazis and Fascists worshipped it. Now some European anti-immigrant parties are tinged with fascism. Hungary's immigrant-hating Jobbik Party, for example, parades in uniform.

IDEOLOGY IN OUR DAY

The Collapse of Communism

By the 1980s, communism the world over was ideologically exhausted. Few people in China, Eastern Europe, and even the Soviet Union believed in it any longer. In the non-Communist world, leftists deserted Marxism in droves. Several West European Communist parties embraced "Eurocommunism," a greatly watered-down ideology that renounced dictatorship and state ownership of industry. Capitalism was supposed to have collapsed; instead, it was thriving in the United States, Western Europe, and East Asia. Many Communist leaders admitted that their economies were too rigid and centralized and that the cure lay in cutting back state controls in favor of free enterprise. Reform-minded Soviet President Mikhail Gorbachev (1985–1991) offered a three-pronged approach to revitalizing Soviet communism: *glasnost* (media openness), *perestroika* (economic restructuring), and *demokratizatzia* (democratization). Applied haltingly and half-heartedly, the reforms only heightened discontent, for now Soviets could voice their complaints. Starting in Eastern Europe in 1989, non-Communist parties took over. In the Soviet Union, a partially free parliament was elected and began debating change. Non-Communist parties and movements appeared. Gorbachev still could not make up his mind how far and fast reforms should go, and the economy, barely reformed, turned wildly inflationary. A 1991 coup failed, and, by the end of the year, the Soviet Union had ceased to exist.

Neoconservatism

In the 1970s, a new ideology emerged in the United States: **neoconservatism**, much of it from disillusioned liberals and leftists. As neoconservative writer Irving Kristol put it, "A neoconservative is a liberal who's been mugged by reality." Neoconservatives charged that the Democratic Party had moved too far left with unrealistic ideas on domestic reforms and a pacifist foreign policy. Neoconservatives reacted against the Great Society programs introduced by Lyndon Johnson in the mid-1960s that aimed to wipe out poverty and discrimination. Some liberals said the Great Society was never given a chance because funds for it were siphoned away by the Vietnam War. But neocons said it worked badly, that many of the programs achieved nothing. The cities grew worse; educational standards declined; medical aid became extremely costly; and a class of welfare-dependent poor emerged, people who had little incentive to work. Neocons spoke of negative "unforeseen consequences" of well-intentioned liberal programs. Especially bothersome to neocons: Affirmative action gave racial minorities preferential treatment in hiring, sometimes ahead of better-qualified whites.

> **libertarianism** U.S. ideology in favor of shrinking all government power in favor of individual freedom.
>
> **feminism** Ideology of psychological, political, and economic equality for women.

Many neoconservatives were horrified at the extreme relativism that had grown in the 1960s. Simplistic ideas—such as "It's all right if it feels good" and "It just depends on your point of view" and "multiculturalism"—drove many liberals to neoconservatism. Ironically, some neocons were college professors who had earlier tried to broaden their students' views by stressing the relativity of all viewpoints and cultures. Instead, students became vacuous. In the Bush 43 administration, highly placed neocons promoted war with Iraq both to protect the United States and to pull the Muslim world into democracy. Many old-fashioned Republican conservatives, who dislike overseas crusades, despised the neocons, and they faded from power and prominence.

Libertarianism

Slowly growing since the 1960s is an ideology so liberal that it became conservative, or vice versa. **Libertarians** would return to the original Adam Smith, with essentially no government interference in anything. They would deliver what Republicans only talk about. They note that modern liberals want a controlled economy but personal freedom while modern conservatives want a free economy but constraints on personal freedom. Why not freedom in both areas? Libertarians oppose subsidies, bureaucracies, taxes, intervention overseas, and big government itself. As such, they plugged into a very old American tradition and gained respectability. Although no Libertarian candidates won elections, their Cato Institute in Washington became a lively think tank whose ideas could not be ignored. (One Cato paper deplored cities building light rail systems when buses are better and cheaper. The paper's title: "A Desire Named Streetcar.") Some critics blame libertarian worship of unregulated markets for the reckless deals that produced the 2008–2009 financial meltdown.

Feminism

Springing to new life in the 1960s with a handful of female writers, by the 1970s the women's movement had become a political force in the United States and Western Europe. **Feminist** writers pointed out that women were paid less than men, were not

environmentalism   Ideology that environment is endangered and must be preserved through regulation and lifestyle changes.

promoted, were psychologically and physically abused by men, were denied loans and insurance, and were in general second-class citizens.

The root problem was psychological, argued feminists. Women and men were forced into "gender roles" that had little to do with biology. Boys were conditioned to be tough, domineering, competitive, and "macho," and girls were taught to be meek, submissive, unsure of themselves, and "feminine." Gender differences are almost entirely learned behavior, taught by parents and schools of a "patriarchal" society, but this could be changed. With proper child rearing and education, males could become gentler and females more assertive and self-confident.

Feminists joined "consciousness-raising" groups and railed against "male chauvinist pigs." Feminism started having an impact. Many employers gave women a fairer chance, sometimes hiring them over men. Women moved up to higher management positions (although seldom to the corporate top). Working wives became the norm. Husbands shared in homemaking and child rearing. With more women going to college than men, many male-dominated professions—medicine, law, business—saw an influx of women.

Politically, however, feminists did not achieve all they wished. The Equal Rights Amendment (ERA) to the Constitution failed to win ratification by enough state legislatures. It would have guaranteed equality of treatment regardless of gender. Antifeminists, some of them conservative women, argued that the ERA would take away women's privileges and protections under the law, would make women eligible for the draft, and would even lead to unisex lavatories. Despite this setback, women learned that there was one way they could count for a lot politically—by voting. In the 1980 election, a significant "gender gap" appeared, and now women generally vote more Democratic than do men.

Environmentalism

Also during the 1960s, **environmentalism** began to ripple through the advanced industrialized countries. Economic development paid little heed to the damage it did to the environment. Any growth was good growth: "We'll never run out of nature." Mining, factories, and even farms poisoned streams; industries and automobiles polluted the air; chemical wastes made areas uninhabitable; and nuclear power leaked radioactivity. To the credo of "growth," environmentalists responded with "limits." They argued, "We can't go on like this without producing environmental catastrophe." Love Canal, Three Mile Island, and Chernobyl seemed to prove them right. The burning of fossil fuels and rain forests increases CO_2 that may trap heat inside the earth's atmosphere and change climates.

The ecologists' demands were only partly satisfied with the founding of the Environmental Protection Agency (EPA) in 1970. Industrial groups argued that EPA regulations restricted growth and ate into profits; under Republican presidents, the EPA was rendered ineffective. Energy production had to take first place over pristine environments, they argued.

Regulation was only part of the environmental credo. Many argued that consumption patterns and life-styles in the advanced countries should change to conserve the earth's resources, natural beauty, and clean air

Islamism   Muslim religion turned into a political ideology.

and water. Americans, only about 4 percent of the world's population, consume a fourth of the world's manufactured goods and energy. In addition to being out of balance with the poor nations of the world, this profligate lifestyle is unnecessary and unhealthy, they argued. "Greens" urged public transportation and bicycles instead of cars, whole-grain foods and vegetables instead of meat, and decentralized, renewable energy sources, such as wind and solar energy, instead of fossil- or nuclear-fueled power plants.

Some environmentalists formed political parties, first the Citizens Party, then the Greens, but their main impact was within the two big parties, neither of which could ignore the environmental vote. In Western Europe in the 1980s, especially in Germany and Sweden, Green parties were elected to parliament, determined to end

COMPARING ■ ISLAMISM: A NEW IDEOLOGY WITH OLD ROOTS

Islamism illustrates how an ideology can suddenly arise by combining older elements. *Salafiyya*, or Islamic fundamentalism, started in the thirteenth century with a call to return to the pure ways of the Prophet and is the founding and current faith of Saudi Arabia. Al Qaeda is a *salafi* movement. Islamism exploded in 1979 with the Iranian revolution (see Chapter 17) and the Soviet invasion of Afghanistan.

Islamism is an angry blend of religion, nationalism, socialism, and a "rage against modernity" that had long been brewing in the Muslim world. With America in the lead, Islamists argue, the West erodes Islamic morals and culture, subjugates the region economically (oil), and steals Islamic holy land (Israel). Some of this traces back to centuries of antipathy between Christendom and Islam, some to the frustrations of modernization. Islamism grows with rapid population increases and high unemployment and in reaction to corruption and misrule in Muslim countries.

Islamism resembles nationalism, but in Islam the political was always intertwined with the religious. Mosque and state are to be one. The Prophet Muhammad founded Islam as one giant community, the *umma*, that

disdains nations as forms of idolatry. Accordingly, Osama bin Laden and his followers were uninterested in Palestinian or Iraqi nationalism except to use it on their march to a Muslim empire. Islamists seek to oust U.S. influence, destroy Israel, and take over all Muslim countries and eventually the world. Then a purified Islam will share the wealth now concentrated in the hands of a few corrupt rulers, a sort of socialism. Fanatic and uncompromising, Islamists jolted the world with terrorism. Some Muslim countries—Pakistan and Saudi Arabia among them—fearing Islamist overthrow, attempt to buy them off.

Islamism has several weaknesses. First, it is split between *Sunni* and *Shia* branches of Islam. Sunni is mainstream Islam, accounting for some 90 percent of the world's Muslims, but Shias dominate Iran and parts of Iraq, Saudi Arabia, Lebanon, and elsewhere. Sunnis despise and mistrust Shias. Second, Islamism, which has no economic plan, cannot put food on the table, something many Iranians now complain about. And most importantly, the Muslim extremists' indiscriminate murder of fellow Muslims has turned many Muslims against it, and Islamism has begun to fade.

nuclear power, toxic waste, and war. Many young Europeans found the Greens an attractive alternative to the old and stodgy conventional parties.

IS IDEOLOGY FINISHED?

In 1960, Harvard sociologist Daniel Bell argued that the century-long ideological debates were coming to a close. The failure of tyrannical communism and the rise of the welfare state were producing what Bell called the "end of ideology": There simply was not much to quarrel about. Henceforth, political debate would focus on almost technical questions of how to run the welfare state, said Bell, such as what to include under national health insurance. In 1989, political scientist Francis Fukuyama went even further: Not only had the great ideological debate ended with the victory of capitalist democracy, but also history itself could be ending. Widely misunderstood, Fukuyama did not mean that time would stand still but rather that the human endpoint propounded by Hegel—free people living in free societies—was now coming into view. Not only had we beaten communism, suggested Fukuyama, there were no longer any other ideologies to challenge ours. With the end of ideology would come the end of history in the sense of the struggle of great ideas. (Life could get boring, sighed the puckish Fukuyama.)

A glance at today's news makes one doubt the Bell and Fukuyama theses. First, the collapse of communism in Europe by itself did not disprove Marx's original ideas, although now Marxists carefully distance themselves from the Soviet type of socialism. (We use socialism here to mean state control of industry, not welfarism, which is just a variation on capitalist democracy.) Socialists still debate the possibility of a benign socialism. New and dangerous ideological challenges emerged just as communism collapsed: neofascism, breakaway nationalism, and Islamism. And within free democracy itself there are numerous ideological viewpoints: free market or government intervention, more welfare or less, a secular or religious state, and spreading democracy abroad or avoiding overseas involvement. Fukuyama need not worry about boredom.

 EXERCISES

Apply what you learned in this chapter on MyPoliSciKit (www.mypoliscikit.com).

Assessment   Review this chapter using learning objectives, chapter summaries, practice tests, and more.

Menu

Flashcards   Learn the key terms in this chapter; you can test yourself by term or definition.

Flashcards

Video   Analyze recent world affairs by watching streaming video from major news providers.

Videos

Comparative Exercises   Compare political ideas, behaviors, institutions, and policies worldwide.

Comparative
Exercises

KEY TERMS

classic liberalism (p. 40)
communism (p. 47)
conservatism (p. 42)
environmentalism (p. 54)
fascism (p. 51)
feminism (p. 53)
ideologue (p. 40)

ideology (p. 40)
imperialism (p. 47)
Islamism (p. 55)
libertarianism (p. 53)
Maoism (p. 49)
modern liberalism (p. 44)
nationalism (p. 49)

neoconservatism
   (p. 52)
pragmatic (p. 40)
revisionist (p. 46)
social democracy
   (p. 46)
Titoism (p. 49)

FURTHER REFERENCE

Baradat, Leon P. *Political Ideologies: Their Origins and Impact*, 11th ed. New York: Longman, 2012.

Beer, Jeremy, Bruce Frohnen, and Jeffrey O. Nelson, eds. *American Conservatism: An Encyclopedia*. Wilmington, DE: ISI Books, 2006.

Bernstein, Andrew. *The Capitalist Manifesto: The Historic, Economic, and Philosophic Case for Laissez-Faire*. Lanham, MD: University Press of America, 2005.

Blumenthal, Max. *Republican Gomorrah: Inside the Movement That Shattered the Party*. New York: Basic Books, 2009.

Cohen, G. A. *Why Not Socialism?* Princeton, NJ: Princeton University Press, 2009.

Edwards, Mickey. *Reclaiming Conservatism: How a Great American Political Movement Got Lost—and How It Can Find Its Way Back*. New York: Oxford University Press, 2008.

Farber, David. *The Rise and Fall of Modern American Conservatism: A Short History*. Princeton, NJ: Princeton University Press, 2010.

Flynn, James R. *Where Have All the Liberals Gone? Race, Class, and Ideals in America*. New York: Cambridge University Press, 2008.

Frank, Thomas. *The Wrecking Crew: How Conservatives Rule*. New York: Metropolitan, 2008.

Frum, David. *Comeback: Conservatism That Can Win Again*. New York: Doubleday, 2009.

Goldwag, Arthur. *'Isms and 'Ologies: All the Movements, Ideologies, & Doctrines That Have Shaped Our World*. New York: Vintage, 2007.

Grosby, Steven. *Nationalism: A Very Short Introduction*. New York: Oxford University Press, 2005.

Heilbrunn, Jacob. *They Knew They Were Right: The Rise of the Neocons*. New York: Doubleday, 2008.

Krugman, Paul. *The Conscience of a Liberal*. New York: Norton, 2007.

Micklethwait, John, and Adrian Wooldridge. *The Right Nation: Conservative Power in America*. New York: Penguin, 2004.

Phares, Walid. *The War of Ideas: Jihadism against Democracy*. New York: Palgrave, 2007.

Sandle, Mark. *Communism*. New York: Longman, 2006.

Schmitt, Richard, ed. *Toward a New Socialism*. Lanham, MD: Lexington, 2007.

Schumpeter, Joseph A. *Can Capitalism Survive? Creative Destruction and the Future of the Global Economy*. New York: HarperCollins, 2009.

Snyder, Louis L. *The New Nationalism*. New Brunswick, NJ: Transaction, 2003.

Starr, Paul. *Freedom's Power: The True Force of Liberalism*. New York: Basic Books, 2008.

Sullivan, Andrew. *The Conservative Soul: How We Lost It, How to Get It Back*. New York: HarperCollins, 2007.

Tanenhaus, Sam. *The Death of Conservatism*. New York: Random House, 2009.

Walzer, Michael. *Politics and Passion: Toward a More Egalitarian Liberalism*. New Haven, CT: Yale University Press, 2004.

Wolfe, Alan. *The Future of Liberalism*. New York: Knopf Doubleday, 2010.

CHAPTER 4

States

Mexican police patrol Nuevo Laredo with automatic weapons. War with the drug cartels illustrates the penetration of crime into politics. (Eduardo Verdugo/AP Photo)

A **nation** is a population with a certain sense of itself, a cohesiveness, a shared history and culture, and often (but not always) a common language. A **state** is a government structure, usually sovereign and powerful enough to enforce its writ. (Notice that here we use state in its original sense; the 50 U.S. states are not states in this sense of the word.) At last count, there were about 193 states in the world.

Which came first, states or nations? Many suppose nations did, but in most cases states created their nations. The Zulus of South Africa, for example, are an artificially created nation put together from many clans and tribes two centuries ago by a powerful warrior, Shaka. Paris united many regions, mostly by the sword, to create France and inculcated Frenchness by education, language, and centralized administration. The French nation is an artificial creation of the French state. The United States was put together by a few men in Philadelphia from 13 colonies. While assimilating tens of millions of immigrants, the United States developed a sense of nationhood based largely on the ideals of its founding documents. Nations do not fall from heaven but are created by human craftsmanship of varying quality.

QUESTIONS TO CONSIDER

1. What is the difference between a nation and a state?
2. What are *weak states* and *failed states*?
3. What were Aristotle's six types of government?
4. What is the crux of a political institution?
5. What are the problems of unitary and federal systems?
6. What are the two main electoral systems and their advantages and disadvantages?
7. What is the difference between socialism and statism?
8. Is the U.S. preference for minimal government shared worldwide?
9. Can or should government attempt to modernize society?

INSTITUTIONALIZED POWER

Political institutions are the working structures of government, such as legislatures and executive departments. Institutions may or may not be housed in impressive buildings, although that helps bolster their authority. The U.S. Supreme Court, even if it met in a tent, would be an important institution as long as its decisions were obeyed. As we will consider later, it was not clear what the powers of the Supreme Court were to be when it began, but forceful personalities and important cases slowly gave it power. Likewise, the Federal Reserve

59

nation   Population with a historic sense of self.

state   Government structures of a nation.

political institution   Established and durable pattern of authority.

weak state   One unable to govern effectively, corrupt and penetrated by crime.

failed state   One incapable of even minimal governance, with essentially no national government.

Board ("the Fed") evolved from calming bank panics, to fighting inflation, to arranging bailouts of financial giants. Congress could not do the job, so the Fed took on whatever new tasks were needed to stabilize the U.S. economy. Good institutions are flexible and evolve.

As we considered in Chapter 1, authority is a fluid thing and requires continual maintenance. A political institution is congealed or partly solidified authority. Over time, people have become used to looking to political institutions to solve problems, decide controversies, and set directions. Institutions, because they are composed of many persons and (if they are effective) last many generations, take on lives of their own apart from the people temporarily associated with them. This gives the political system stability; citizens know who is in charge.

Institutions are bigger than individual leaders. When President Nixon resigned under a cloud of scandal in 1974, the institution of the presidency was scarcely touched. If there had been a series of such presidents, and if they had refused to resign, the institution itself would have been damaged. Sometimes dictators try to

KEY CONCEPTS ■ EFFECTIVE, WEAK, AND FAILED STATES

Not all states really function as states; some hardly function at all. Just because a country has a flag and sits in the UN does not prove that it is a serious state. No world tribunal classifies states on the basis of their strength, but analysts see at least three categories:

Effective states control and tax their entire territory. Laws are mostly obeyed. Government looks after the general welfare and security. Corruption is fairly minor. Effective states tend to be better off and to collect considerable taxes (25 to 50 percent of GDP). Effective states include Japan, the United States, and Western Europe. Some put the best of these states into a "highly effective" category.

Weak states are characterized by the penetration of crime into politics. You cannot tell where politics leaves off and crime begins. The government does not have the strength to fight lawlessness, drug trafficking, corruption,

poverty, and breakaway movements. Justice is bought. Democracy is preached more than practiced and elections often rigged. Little is collected in taxation. Revenues from natural resources, such as Mexico's and Nigeria's oil, disappear into private pockets. Much of Asia, Africa, and Latin America are weak states.

Failed states have essentially no national government, although some pretend they do. Warlords, militias, and opium growers do as they wish. There is no law besides the gun. Territorial breakup threatens. Education and health standards decline (as in the increase of HIV/AIDS). Many count Afghanistan and Somalia as failed states. Pirates make their home in Somalia because there is no state power to stop them (and no jobs for young men). Only outside assistance and pressure keep these two countries from disappearing altogether. Some fear Yemen, home to Islamist fighters, could become a failed state.

make themselves into "institutions," but it fails; the institutions they tried to build unravel upon their deaths. Josip Tito ruled Yugoslavia for 35 years and attempted to ensure his system would survive him, but it was

institutionalize To make a political relationship permanent.

based too much on himself. Eleven years after his death, Yugoslavia split apart in bloody fighting. Dictators seldom build lasting institutions; they rarely **institutionalize** their personal power.

Powerful inhabitants of an office can sometimes put their personal stamp on the institution. George Washington retired after two terms, and until FDR no president tried to serve longer. Washington institutionalized term limits into the presidency that were not codified into law until the Twenty-Second Amendment in 1951. West Germany's first chancellor, Konrad Adenauer, offered such decisive leadership that the chancellorship has been powerful ever since.

One way to begin the study of institutions is to locate the most powerful offices of a political system: Who's got the power? Constitutions may help but do not tell the whole story. The U.S. Constitution indicates the executive and the legislative powers are equal and in balance, but over two centuries power has

CLASSIC WORKS ■ ARISTOTLE'S SIX TYPES OF GOVERNMENT

The earliest and most famous classification of governments was Aristotle's in the fourth century B.C. He distinguished among three legitimate kinds of government—where the ruling authority acts in the interests of all—and three corrupt counterparts—where government acts only in the interests of self.

A monarchy, according to Aristotle, is one person ruling in the interest of all. But monarchy can degenerate into tyranny, the corrupt form, under which the single ruler exercises power for the benefit of self. Aristocracy, Greek for rule of the best (*aristos*), is several persons ruling in the interest of all. But this legitimate rule by an elite can decay into oligarchy, the corrupt form, in which several persons rule in the interest of themselves.

Aristotle saw the *polity* (what we might call constitutional democracy) as the rule of many in the interests of all and the best form of government. All citizens have a voice in selecting leaders and framing laws, but formal constitutional procedures protect rights. Aristotle warned that polity can decay into the corrupt form, democracy, the rule of many in the interests of themselves, the worst form of government. Deluded into thinking that one person is as good as another, the masses in a democracy follow the lead of corrupt and selfish demagogues and plunder the property of the hardworking and the capable. Aristotle's classification, which reigned for nearly 25 centuries, is still useful and can be summarized like this:

Who Governs	Legitimate Forms *Rule in the Interest of All*	Corrupt Forms *Rule in the Interest of Selves*
One	Monarchy	Tyranny
A few	Aristocracy	Oligarchy
Many	Polity	Democracy

King Abdullah plays with a Saudi princeling at a festival. Saudi Arabia is one of the world's last working monarchies. (Saudi Press Agency/Reuters/Landov)

gravitated to the presidency. The French constitution, set up by Charles de Gaulle in 1958, seems to give the presidency near-dictatorial powers. But French legislative elections sometimes produce parliaments of one party facing a president of another—a "deadlock" in U.S. terms. The French president solved the problem by trimming his role and letting an opposed prime minister take a bigger role, what the French call "cohabitation." Constitutions (see next chapter) are themselves institutions, gradually evolving in practice if not in wording.

monarchy   Hereditary rule by one person.

republic   A political system without a monarch.

There are many ways to classify governments. One old question, now fading, is the "form of state," whether a country is a **monarchy** or **republic**. Most countries are now republics, but that does not necessarily mean "good" or "democratic." Figurehead constitutional monarchies still "reign" symbolically but do not actually rule in Britain, Norway, Sweden, Denmark, Spain, and Holland, which are happy with that status. Traditional, working monarchies are still found in the Arab world—Morocco, Saudi Arabia, Jordan, Kuwait—and may be doomed unless they can turn themselves into limited constitutional monarchies. Failure to do so has led to the overthrow of traditional monarchies and their replacement by revolutionary regimes in Egypt, Iraq, Libya, Ethiopia, and Iran.

UNITARY OR FEDERAL SYSTEMS

A really big and basic institutional choice is the territorial structure of the nation: unitary or federal. A **unitary system** accords its component areas little or no autonomy; most governance radiates from the capital city. The **first-order civil divisions**—departments in France, provinces in China, counties in Sweden, prefectures in Japan—are largely administered by national authorities with only small local inputs. The first-order civil divisions of **federalism**—U.S. and Brazilian states, German *Länder*, and Swiss cantons—have considerable political lives of their own and cannot be legally erased or easily altered by the central power.

unitary system Centralization of power in a nation's capital with little autonomy for subdivisions.

first-order civil divisions Countries' main territorial components, such as U.S. states or Spanish provinces.

federalism Balancing of power between a nation's capital and autonomous subdivisions, such as U.S. states.

center–periphery tension Resentment of outlying areas at rule by nation's capital.

regionalism Feeling of regional differences and sometimes breakaway tendencies.

devolution Shifting some powers from central government to component units.

Unitary Systems

Unitary governments control local authorities and citizens' lives more than federal systems do. France's education ministry in Paris draws up school curricula in order to reduce regional differences in language and culture, which at one time were very strong. Many decades ago, a French education minister looked at his watch and proudly told an interviewer which Latin verbs were being conjugated all over France. Unitary states have a national police force and one court system, whose judicial officers are appointed by the national government.

　　Center–periphery tensions or **regionalism** grew in several countries during the 1970s, and for several reasons. Economics was one. Local nationalists often claim that their region is poorer and shortchanged by the central government. The region may have a distinct language or culture that its people want to preserve. Many feel that important political decisions are not under local control, that they are made by distant bureaucrats. Often regions harbor historical resentments at having long ago been conquered and forcibly merged with the larger nation. Iraqi Kurds feel this way about rule by Baghdad. Several unitary systems grope for solutions to the regional problem.

Devolution in Britain　The Celtic Scots and Welsh, pushed to the peripheries of Britain centuries ago by the invading Angles and Saxons, retain a lively sense of their differences from England. Many Scots and Welsh resent being ruled by London. During the 1970s, the Scottish and Welsh nationalist parties grew until they won several seats in Parliament. In 1997, the new Labour government of Tony Blair passed **devolution** bills that gave home-rule powers to Scotland, Wales, and Northern Ireland. The Scottish parliament, first elected in 1999, now has a government of "Scot Nats" with the power to raise taxes and run Scotland's education, medical services, judicial system, and local government, somewhat quasi- Nearly or almost.

prefect Administrator of a French department.

department French first-order civil division.

decentralization Shifting some administrative functions from central government to lower levels; less than *devolution*.

autonomías Spanish regions with devolved powers.

like a U.S. state. Some say this makes Britain **quasi-federal**, but officially Britain is still unitary.

Decentralization in France France was historically much more unitary than Britain. Everything is—or, until recently, was—run from Paris, a pattern that began with the absolutist (see page 234) moves of Louis XI in the fifteenth century. In the seventeenth century, Cardinal Richelieu centralized power in Paris by a system of provincial administrators, *intendants*, who reported back to him. The French Revolution, Napoleon, and republics that followed increased centralization. Now **prefects** report back from the **departments** to the interior ministry.

Most of France's 96 *départements* were named after rivers to try to erase the historical memories of the old provinces. But France, like Britain, has distinctive regional subcultures: the Celtic Bretons (who fled from Britain centuries ago to escape the Saxons); the southerners of the Midi, whose speech is still flavored with the ancient *langue d'oc*; and the Corsicans, who still speak an Italian dialect. Breton and Corsican separatists sometimes promote their cause with violence.

In 1960, to better coordinate economic development, President de Gaulle decreed 22 regions consisting of two to eight departments each. Starting in 1981, President Mitterrand instituted genuine **decentralization** that gave the regions certain economic planning powers. The Paris-appointed prefects lost some of their powers to newly important departmental legislatures. France thus reversed five centuries of centralization.

Autonomy in Spain Spain, too, decentralized. Here the problem was more urgent, for regional resentments, long buried under the dictatorial rule of Francisco Franco (1939–1975), came out with anger. Spain's regional problems were among the most difficult in Europe, second only to Yugoslavia's. Basques and Catalans, in the north of Spain, have non-Castilian languages and distinctive cultures. Basques, for example, speak a language related to no other and are intensely proud of it. In addition, many areas of Spain were granted *fueros* (local rights) in medieval times, which they treasured for centuries. On top of great regional diversity, Spanish centralizers attempted to plant a unitary system on the French model. The result was great resentment that appeared whenever Spain experimented with democracy. Breakaway movements appeared in 1874 and in the 1930s, only to be crushed by the Spanish army, which regards the unity of the country as sacred.

With this background, Spain held its breath in the late 1970s and 1980s as the post–Franco Spanish democracy instituted 17 regional governments called **autonomías**. The big problem is still the Basque country in the northwest, where the terrorist ETA strives for complete Basque independence with murder and bombing. To appease regionalist feeling, which also appeared in more moderate forms in Catalonia, Galicia, Andalusia, and other areas, Madrid allowed regions to become autonomous, with regional parliaments, taxation power, language rights, and control over local matters. Most Spaniards approve of the *autonomías,* but *center-periphery tensions* (see page 63)—especially in Catalonia—continue over taxes and the sharing of revenues.

prefecture   Japanese first-order civil division.

Pros and Cons of Unitary Systems   Authority in unitary states can be absurdly overcentralized. Local government may not be able to install a traffic light or bus stop without permission from the capital. This leads citizens to ignore local affairs and produces political alienation. Centralization of power, however, can be an advantage in facing modern problems. Clear lines of authority without excess bickering among units of government can be useful. In unitary systems, the capital can marshal economic resources and coordinate planning and development. Taxation is the same nationwide, so firms and individuals cannot flee to low-tax states, as in the United States. Education standards can be high and uniform, as in Japan.

Japan gives a certain amount of autonomy to its subunits, but they, too, tug in a quasi-federal direction. An 1871 copy of the French system, Japan has 43 **prefectures** plus its three largest cities and the thinly populated northernmost island, each with its elected governor and unicameral assembly. Their activities are still overseen and limited by the home affairs ministry in Tokyo, and they collect only about 30 percent of the taxes they need, what Japanese call "30 percent autonomy." Colorful and outspoken prefectural governors have recently been demanding more autonomy.

Federal Systems

Federalism gives first-order civil divisions much autonomy while the central government runs areas that are inherently national. It is a difficult balancing act that varies among federal nations. Americans, with one of the first federal systems, sometimes urge federalism on other nations, including Iraq, where it may not work. The hostility among Iraq's Shia, Sunni, and Kurds could rip it apart. The ex–Soviet Union and Mexico became so centralized that some wondered if they were still federal. The crux of a federal system is that the component states have some powers that cannot be easily overridden by the central government.

The components of a federal system are typically represented in an upper house such as the U.S. Senate or German Bundesrat. (Unitary systems do not really need upper houses, but most have them.) In federal systems, the central government has exclusive control over foreign, defense, and monetary policy. The states typically control education, police, highways, and other close-to-home

confederation Political system in which components override *center.*

center Nation's capital and its powers.

affairs. Because the division of these powers is seldom clear or permanent, a federal government rests on a delicate balance between central power and local autonomy.

There are several reasons for starting a federal union. The first is national security; small and weak states cannot defend themselves against powerful aggressors. (This was one of the main arguments of *The Federalist*.) The pooling of diplomatic and military resources of the states made Bismarck's Germany a major power. Federal unions serve economic purposes. U.S. prosperity is based in large part on its continent-wide market without trade barriers, a feat the European Union has copied. Federalism is often the only way to protect national unity. As Britain freed India in 1947, New Delhi set up a federal system that allowed such states as Bengal and Punjab to maintain their own cultures while joining the Indian nation. Indian states would not have entered the federal union without a guarantee of local autonomy. Much of Latin America—especially the large countries of Argentina, Brazil, and Mexico—saw federalism as the only way to control their vast territories. Belgium in 1993 switched from a unitary to a federal system to give its two languages (French and Flemish) their own turf. The two still dislike each other, and Belgium could split apart.

Pros and Cons of Federal Systems   Citizens are closest to their local governments, where they can influence officials and see how decisions are made. U.S. states have been called "laboratories of democracy" because they can experiment with new programs. If they work, they can be copied nationwide; if they fail, not much harm is done. On the other hand, local governments may lack the money to finance programs, and their officials are sometimes incompetent and corrupt. Local decision making can lead to duplication of services and poor coordination.

COMPARING ■ THE SHAKY LIVES OF CONFEDERATIONS

Theoretically, a third alternative to unitary and federal systems is the **confederation**. In a unitary system, power is concentrated in the national capital. In a federal system, power is balanced between the **center** and the components. In confederations, the component parts can override the center. Confederations tend to have short lives; they either fall apart or become federations. This was the fate of the early United States under the Articles of Confederation. Similarly, in the Confederate States of America, the states had such independence that they could not effectively wage the Civil War. Switzerland still calls itself a confederation (*Confederatio Helvetia*)—which the Swiss proudly date to 1291—but it is now a federal system. The European Union (EU) started as a confederation, but with the growth of the powers of Brussels (its headquarters), especially with economic and monetary union (the euro currency), it is trying to become a federal system.

The relationship of the states or provinces to other levels of government varies among federal systems. In Germany, each of the 16 Länder has its own constitution and government for **Land** affairs. The Landtag (state legislature) can even affect the national policy because it elects members of the Bundesrat (the upper house of the national legislature). India is unique among federal states because New Delhi can proclaim "president's rule" during disorder in a state and take over its government.

Land   German federal first-order civil division; plural *Länder.*

republic   In Communist Soviet Union and Yugoslavia, federal first-order civil division.

glasnost   Gorbachev's policy of media openness.

Each of America's 50 states can legislate in any area not delegated to the federal government or to the people. Usually, education, welfare, civil law, property taxes, and licensing of professions are state functions. However, in the twentieth century, the federal government expanded in the areas of civil law, welfare, and economic regulation. Bush 43 moved education standards to the federal level with his No Child Left Behind Act—something that many states and traditional Republicans did not like. Dependent on federal grants and revenue sharing, the states must meet federal standards in many areas. Washington, for example, threatened to withhold federal highway funds if states did not make 21 the legal drinking age. Most quickly did.

From the beginning, the United States has debated the proper role of the federal government and worried that "sectionalism" could pull the Union apart, which it did. Southern insistence on "states' rights" led to a clash with President Lincoln over slavery and then to civil war. In the 1960s, controversial U.S. Supreme Court decisions prompted a campaign to curb the power of federal courts. Some insist that the concentration of power in Washington perverts American federalism and encroaches on individual freedoms. At the same time, local governments and citizens continue to rely on federal help in solving complex—and expensive—problems. Federalism is not an easy system to maintain and does not necessarily solve the problems of large and diverse countries. Consider the following.

Ex-Soviet Federalism   On paper, the Soviet Union was a federation: Its 15 **republics** were supposed to have the right to secede. In practice, under the tight control of the Communist Party—although usually staffed by local talent (Georgians ran Georgia, Uzbeks ran Uzbekistan, and so on)—they followed Moscow's orders. Beneath a centralized veneer, however, lurked disunion. Gorbachev underestimated the strength of local nationalism, and when he allowed **glasnost** in the late 1980s, many Soviet republics went for independence, led by the Baltic states of Lithuania, Latvia, and Estonia, which Stalin had brutally annexed in 1940. With the collapse of the Soviet Union at the end of 1991, all 15 republics proclaimed themselves independent, something Moscow always hated. Now Russia aims to regain what it calls the "near abroad" either by economic or by military means, as in Georgia.

The bulk of the old Soviet Union continued as the Russian Federation, which is composed of 89 autonomous republics, districts, regions, and even centrifugal   Pulling apart.

cities, most of which have signed a federation treaty with Moscow. Several areas, home to some of the hundred-plus ethnic groups within Russia, refused to sign and billed themselves as independent. The largely Muslim North Caucasus never liked being ruled by Moscow, and some areas now try to break away. Moscow, fearing that Chechen independence would encourage such demands elsewhere, brutally crushed Chechnya. Putin reinstituted central control over unruly governors by creating seven super-regions headed by former colleagues from the security police.

Could the three Communist federations—the Soviet Union, Yugoslavia, and Czechoslovakia—have devised a more genuine federalism that would not have fallen apart? Or were these federations of unlike components doomed from the start? The Communists, by pretending to have solved the "nationalities question," merely suppressed it until it came out later.

Ex-Yugoslav Federalism   Yugoslavia, founded only in 1918, was a new and somewhat artificial country whose components were rarely content. It fell apart once before, in World War II, when its German conquerors set up an independent Croatia with expanded territories. Croatian fascists murdered a third of a million Serbs and others who had lived among them for centuries, thus sowing the hatred that erupted in the 1990s. The Communist Partisans who fought the Nazis thought federalism was the answer. Under the maverick Communist Tito (see page 49), Yugoslav federalism let Yugoslavia's six republics run local affairs and sent equal numbers of representatives to both houses of parliament. Yugoslavia's collective presidency had one member from each republic.

This hyperfederal setup, however, did not calm local nationalism; it inflamed it. Each republic wanted its own railroads, steel mills, and control of its economy. Under Tito, the Communist Party and security police could hold Yugoslavia together, but after he died in 1980 the republics went their separate ways. Tito deserves blame for this, as he designed an unworkable system that had to fall apart. Yugoslavia is an example of poor institutional choices.

Slovenia and Croatia declared their independence in 1991, followed by Bosnia in 1992. Serbian forces brutally practiced "ethnic cleansing" and murdered thousands. A 1995 U.S.-brokered and NATO-enforced peace calmed Bosnia, but ethnic Albanians in Kosovo, a Serb province, moved for independence. In 1999, a U.S.-led bombing campaign prevented Serbia from wholesale massacre of Kosovars. Bosnia and Kosovo are in effect NATO protectorates. Even tiny Montenegro chose independence from Serbia in 2006.

Canadian Federalism   Canada is another federation with **centrifugal** tendencies. As we will consider in Chapter 7, the British allowed the French-speaking Québécois to keep their language, and francophones became second-class citizens, poorer than other Canadians and discriminated against because almost all private and government business was conducted in English. In the 1960s, the

Parti Québécois (PQ) sprang up, dedicated to Quebec's independence from Canada. To appease them, the federal government in Ottawa in 1969 made Canada bilingual, with French and English having equal rights. The PQ wanted more and made French the only official language of Quebec. Trying to hold the federation—which came to look a bit like a confederation as the provinces overruled the center—together, Ottawa and the provincial governments laboriously developed two new federal accords (Meech Lake in 1987 and Charlottetown in 1992), which were then rejected. The stumbling block was a separate status for Quebec as a "distinct society." Quebeckers said it did not go far enough; other Canadians said it went too far. Quebec's drive for sovereignty has receded, but Canadians still quarrel over federalism.

> **single-member district**   Electoral system that elects one person per district, as in the United States and Britain.

Federalism is difficult. These three cases remind us that federalism cannot cure everything. If the components are too different from one another—culturally, economically, linguistically, or historically—a federal system will not hold together. A shared political culture, as in the United States, Australia, Brazil, and Germany, is a big help. With that as a foundation, the right balance must be found between central and state governments. The United States is still searching for its correct balance.

ELECTORAL SYSTEMS

Electoral systems are also important institutional choices; they help determine the number of parties, the ease of forming a stable government, and the degree of citizen interest in politics. There are two general types of electoral systems with many variations.

Single-Member Districts

The simplest electoral system is the Anglo-American **single-member district**, wherein one member of Parliament or of Congress is chosen to represent the entire district by winning a plurality (not necessarily a majority) of the votes. Called "single-member districts with plurality win" or "first past the post" (FPTP), this system pushes interest groups and political factions to coalesce into two big parties. If there were, say, four parties who received 25, 25, 24, and 26 percent of the vote, respectively, the last would win. Losing parties that are not far apart ideologically quickly recognize that their advantage is to combine for the next election. Then this new party wins, forcing other small parties to combine. The message: Merge or lose. Woodrow Wilson won in 1912 only because Theodore Roosevelt split the Republican Party. FPTP countries tend to have two-party systems.

Third parties exist in such systems but without much hope of winning. They may have an impact as protest and pressure groups on the big parties. The British

majoritarian Electoral system that gives more than half of seats to one party.

proportional representation Elects representatives by party's percent of vote.

Liberal Democrats win nearly one vote in five, but because they are dispersed throughout the country, they win few seats. Single-member systems are unkind to third parties except in situations like Canada and India, where provincial and state concentration of parties permits many to win seats.

Advantages of Single-Member Districts   Politics in FPTP systems tend to the center of the political spectrum, for this is usually where the most votes are. This inhibits the growth of extremism. If leaders out of touch with mainstream views control the party, it will lose, and the losing leaders will likely be replaced. This is what happened with the Republicans after the conservative Goldwater in 1964, the Democrats after the liberal McGovern in 1972, and the British Conservatives after two ineffective leaders, William Hague in 2001 and Michael Howard in 2005. As we will see in Chapter 8, public opinion in most democracies forms a bell-shaped curve. Parties that depart too far from the center penalize themselves.

Most FPTP systems also give a clear parliamentary majority to one party—thus, they are called **majoritarian** systems—so coalitions are rarely necessary. Gains are magnified in single-member systems. In 2010, for example, the British Conservatives won only 36 percent of the vote but took 47 percent of the seats in Parliament. Remember, seats in FPTP systems are not proportional to votes. A relatively small swing of votes from one party to another can translate into many parliamentary seats, perhaps enough to form a parliamentary majority and a new government. The United States, with its constitutionally mandated separation of powers, muddies the advantage of this system by frequently giving the White House to one party and the Congress to another.

Disadvantages of Single-Member Districts   FPTP creates an artificial majority in parliament, which makes governing easier but does not fairly or accurately reflect public opinion or voting strength. In each district, the winner takes all. If there are two parties, the losing party, even if it received 49 percent of the vote, gets no representation. Thanks to computers, most U.S. states are now so perfectly gerrymandered—some of the districts have bizarre shapes—that close to 400 out of 435 House seats are "safe" for one party or the other with few close or unpredictable races.

Single-member districts teach parties a sort of golden rule about sticking to the political center, which makes politics safe but dull. The two big parties often sound alike, resulting in voter boredom and low turnout. The European multiparty systems have higher voter turnouts, partly because voters can choose from a more interesting menu of parties.

Proportional Representation

Proportional representation (PR) systems are based on multimember districts; that is, each district sends several representatives to parliament, not just one. In the small countries of the Netherlands and Israel, the entire country is one big district. In Sweden, the district is a county; in Spain, a province. If the district is entitled to ten seats, each party offers voters a *party list* of ten candidates. Each voter picks one list, and the party gets seats in proportion to the votes it receives. If the party won 30 percent of the votes in a ten-member district, it would send the first three names on its party list to parliament. A party with 20 percent would send its first two names.

majority More than half.

plurality The most, even if less than half.

mixed-member Hybrid electoral system that uses both single-member districts and proportional representation.

Rarely does the vote divide so neatly; one party might win 42 percent of 11 seats. Would it get 4.62 seats? How do you send a fraction of a person to parliament? The most common way to handle this is the d'Hondt mathematical formula, which slightly overrepresents the larger parties at the expense of smaller ones. Sweden "tops off" numerical discrepancies by using nationwide seats. Sweden's 28 districts elect only 310 of the Riksdag's 349 seats; the remaining 39 seats are parceled out to rectify variances from the parties' national percentages.

To minimize the problem of splinter, nuisance, or extremist parties, PR systems require parties to win a certain percentage of the vote in order to obtain any seats at all. These are called "threshold clauses." In Germany and Poland, a party must win at least 5 percent of the vote nationwide; in Sweden and Italy, 4 percent.

COMPARING ■ FRENCH AND GERMAN VARIATIONS

France uses single-member districts but with runoffs. Few candidates win a **majority** (more than 50 percent, not the same as the simple plurality in the Anglo-American system) on the first round, so those with at least an eighth of the vote go to a runoff a week later. Then a simple **plurality** suffices to win. By previous agreement between parties, some candidates withdraw and urge their supporters to vote for the candidate closest to them ideologically, so in most second-round contests there are only two or three candidates. The first round in France is somewhat like a U.S. primary election.

The German system is basically half FPTP and half proportional representation (PR). On a split ballot, Germans vote in one column for an individual to represent their district; here plurality wins. In a second column, they vote for a party to represent their *Land* (state) in proportion to the votes received. Overall strength in the Bundestag is set by the second vote—the one for parties—so seats are always proportional to votes. Half of the seats, though, are reserved for the 328 winners of the district contests. Germany's split representation system produced a two-plus party system (discussed in Chapter 11) and governing stability. The German system is a modification of the PR system and was designed after World War II to prevent a return to the weak and unstable Weimar system, which had proportional representation that treated the country as one big district. In the 1990s, Italy, New Zealand, and Japan adopted German-style **mixed-member** systems that combine single-member districts with PR for their parliamentary elections.

laissez-faire   French for "let it be"; economic system of minimal government interference and supervision; capitalism.

welfare state   Economic system of major government redistribution of income to poorer citizens.

Advantages of Proportional Representation   PR means that the country's legislature accurately reflects public opinion and party strength. Parties do not have to capture the big middle of the electoral spectrum as in Anglo-American systems and can thus articulate ideologies and principles more clearly because they do not try to please everybody. If a small part of the population—as low as 2 percent in Israel— really believes in something, they can run as a party and win seats. They are not forced to amalgamate into bigger parties and dilute their views, as in FPTP systems.

Disadvantages of Proportional Representation   PR systems do little to fight party splintering, so they often lead to multiparty systems. This tendency, however, is waning, and two-plus party systems have emerged, even in PR systems. Sweden and Spain have one or two large parties, plus a few smaller ones. Their political systems are not terribly splintered. Israel, on the other hand, is plagued by splinter parties; as many as 15 parties are elected to the Knesset. If the largest party falls short of half the seats in PR systems—usually the case—it must form a coalition with other parties. These coalitions are often unstable and unable to decide important issues. Where one party is big enough to govern alone, however, the system is quite stable. The Anglo-American systems mostly confer a majority and thus stability. When no party won a majority of seats in Britain in 2010, it too had to form a coalition (of Conservatives and Liberal Democrats).

STATES AND THE ECONOMY

Yet another way to classify governments is how they handle the economy. States face two questions: (1) How much of the economy should the state own or supervise? (2) How much of the nation's wealth should be redistributed to help the poorer sectors of society? The answers produce four basic approaches to promoting the general welfare: laissez-faire, statism, socialism, and the welfare state. These array themselves into a fourfold table (see Figure 4.1).

In a **laissez-faire** system, the government owns little or no industry and redistributes little in the form of welfare programs. As we explored in Chapter 3 on ideologies, these countries follow Adam Smith, seconded by Thomas Jefferson, who argued that government interference in the economy decreases growth and prosperity. The theory here is that private enterprise and individual initiative make a nation both free and prosperous.

A **welfare state** owns little or no industry but does redistribute wealth to the less well-off. Sometimes known as "social democracies," the welfare states of northwest Europe offer "cradle-to-grave" benefits in health insurance, child care, job training, and retirement funds. To pay for this, they charge the world's highest taxes—in Sweden and Denmark, about 50 percent of GDP. Industry, though, is private and moneymaking.

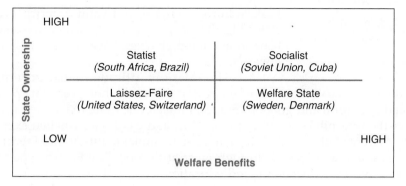

Figure 4.1
Statist, socialist, laissez-faire, and welfare-state approaches.

Statism is an old system that predates laissez-faire. In a statist system, the state (meaning the national government) is the number-one capitalist, owning and running much major industry but providing few welfare benefits. Statism began when the French kings founded a powerful, centralized state that supervised industry for the sake of French wealth and power. Sometimes called by its French name *étatisme*, it typically includes state ownership of railroads, steel mills, banks, oil, and other big enterprises. Small and medium business is left in private hands. Statism caught on in much of Europe and Latin America. France, Brazil, Chile, and Mexico were statist systems but reformed in a free-market direction. Many developing countries have followed statist models with the argument that only the government has the money, ideas, and talent to start up new industries. The economic results suggest state-owned firms are inefficient because they are run by bureaucrats and face no competition; often they operate at a loss and have to be subsidized by the national treasury.

statism Economic system of state ownership of major industries to enhance power and prestige of state; a precapitalist system.

socialism Economic system of government ownership of industry, allegedly for good of whole society; opposite of capitalism.

A **socialist** system practices both state ownership and extensive welfare benefits. Exemplified by the former Soviet Union, government owns nearly all the means of production, claiming it runs the economy in the interests of the society as a whole. However, the collapse of Communist regimes (which called themselves "socialist"; we called them "Communist") indicates they worked poorly. Today, only North Korea and Cuba remain as (negative) examples of socialism, and their systems seem ripe for change.

In actual practice, governments often combine elements of these four systems. Even the basically laissez-faire United States demands welfare measures and bailouts of financial giants deemed "too big to fail." Communist China and Vietnam, once strictly socialist, now have rapidly growing private, capitalistic economies. These questions are never settled, and countries often change their combinations. In our day, we have seen a massive shift away from state-owned industry in

strong state   Modern form of government, able to administer and tax entire nation.

Eastern Europe, France, and Latin America. Welfare states like Sweden, feeling the pinch of too-generous benefits and too-high taxes, have elected conservative governments.

A basic American attitude is that government should be kept small. In much of the rest of the world, however, state power is accepted as natural and good. In France, for example, Louis XI started a strong state in the fifteenth century, and Louis XIII and Cardinal Richelieu expanded it in the seventeenth century. This strong state implanted itself into French consciousness and later spread through most of Europe. The French-type **strong state** supervised the economy and education, collected taxes, built highways and canals, and fielded standing armies. A bureaucratic elite, trained in special schools, ran the country.

These attitudes lasted well into the twentieth century and are still present. Defeated by Germany in 1870–1871, the French elite used the state as an *agent of modernization*. Paris tried to build a unified and cohesive population, to turn "peasants into Frenchmen." A centralized school system stamped out local dialects, broke stagnant rural traditions, and recruited the best talent for universities. State-owned industries turned France into an economic power. Beaten by Germany again in World War II, the French elite again used state power to modernize France.

Did it work? France did modernize greatly, but was this the fastest or most efficient way? Britain and the United States advanced further with minimal government supervision; the competitive spirit of the free-market economy did the job faster and cheaper. (The comparison is not quite fair; Britain and the United States faced no powerful, expansionist Germany on their borders. If they had, the role of government would have been much bigger.)

Japan is another example of state-led modernization. With the Meiji Restoration of 1868, Tokyo assigned various branches of industry to samurai clans, provided funds, and told them to copy the best of the West. In one generation, Japan went from handicrafts to heavy industry under the slogan "Rich nation, strong army!" After World War II, the Ministry of Finance and Ministry of International Trade and Industry (MITI) supervised Japan's rapid economic leap by aiming bank loans to growth industries, keeping out foreign competition, and penetrating the world market with Japanese products. Before we say government supervision of the economy does not work, we must explain why it worked in Japan. The Japanese, of course, have an entirely different and more cooperative culture. An American MITI might not work in our economic and cultural context.

Should government attempt to supervise the economy by providing plans, suggestions, industry-wide cooperation, insurance, and loans? The traditional American answer is "No, it'll just mess things up." Europeans and Canadians are amazed that the United States had to go through bitter controversy to pass even a moderate healthcare reform, something they did decades ago. Even in America, however, the federal government has repeatedly pushed the U.S. economy forward by acquiring large territories, letting settlers homestead them, and giving railroads rights of way. In the 1930s, the Tennessee Valley Authority brought electricity and flood control to a backward part of America. Conservatives disliked the 2008 bailout of major financial institutions, but most agreed it was necessary. America, too, has used the state as an agent of modernization and now debates federal programs to reform healthcare. One of the great questions of modern politics is how much state intervention do we want?

HOW TO... ■ USE SOURCES

Sources—where you get your facts, data, quotes, and ideas—are very important and are the first things an instructor checks. Good sources are from specialized books, scholarly articles, or respected periodicals. Bad sources are ones that appear commonplace or dubious, such as textbooks (never use your current textbook as a source), encyclopedias (yes, even Wikipedia), dictionaries, and popular newsweeklies. To cite something, in parentheses and just before the period, put the author's last name followed (without comma) by the year (Smith 2010).

Google and Wikipedia are easy to use but seldom give a complete picture. They do not tell you what questions to ask. Many Web sites are advertising or propaganda. Most are so current or narrow that they fail to mention what happened last year or in another country; they lack historical and comparative perspective. For that, you still need books and articles.

Scholars divide sources into two types: primary and secondary. A primary source is direct material unfiltered through the mind of another. It might be a 2008 quote from presidential candidate Barack Obama (Jones 2009). It might be a statistical tabulation in a report (World Bank 2007, 274–275). It might be your own survey of college students.

A secondary source is another's synthesis, ideas, or opinions. It might be an article on a Web site about the U.S. occupation of Iraq (Berry 2006). It might be a scholar's reading of the World Bank figures (Adams 2007). To use a football analogy, which is better—your personal observation of the game (primary source) or the sportscaster's description of it (secondary source)? Instructors usually like primary sources.

A paper may include as a primary source numbers from official documents, such as EPA budget cuts under Bush (Williams 2005). Williams's comments on the cuts, on the other hand, would be a secondary source (Williams). Just noting the same source twice does not make it two sources. A source means a different book or article.

Instructors are impressed if you have many good sources, say, ten in a five-page paper. If you cite a specific fact or quote, include the page number (Thompson 2001, 247). In the library's reference section, there are ways to get started fast, most on computer.

New York Times Index

Reader's Guide to Periodical Literature

Social Sciences Index

Public Affairs Information Service

CIA World Factbook

Facts on File

LexisNexis

Academic Index

First Search

For anything to do with executive-legislative relations (Congress, the White House, new laws, budgets), there's something so good, it's almost cheating: *Congressional Quarterly*, which puts out a weekly, an annual, and a *Congress and the Nation* for each presidential term. For foreign countries, check the magazine *Current History* and the Country Study series of books published by the Library of Congress.

myposcikit EXERCISES

Apply what you learned in this chapter on MyPoliSciKit (www.mypoliscikit.com).

 Assessment   Review this chapter using learning objectives, chapter summaries, practice tests, and more.

Menu

 Flashcards   Learn the key terms in this chapter; you can test yourself by term or definition.

Flashcards

Video   Analyze recent world affairs by watching streaming video from major news providers.

Videos

 Comparative Exercises   Compare political ideas, behaviors, institutions, and policies worldwide.

Comparative
Exercises

KEY TERMS

autonomías (p. 64)
center (p. 66)
center–periphery
   tension (p. 63)
centrifugal (p. 68)
confederation (p. 66)
decentralization (p. 64)
department (p. 64)
devolution (p. 63)
failed state (p. 60)
federalism (p. 63)
first-order civil
   divisions (p. 63)
glasnost (p. 67)

institutionalize (p. 61)
laissez-faire (p. 72)
Land (p. 67)
majoritarian (p. 70)
majority (p. 71)
mixed-member (p. 71)
monarchy (p. 62)
nation (p. 60)
plurality (p. 71)
political institution (p. 60)
prefect (p. 64)
prefecture (p. 65)
proportional
   representation (p. 70)

quasi- (p. 64)
regionalism (p. 63)
republic (p. 62, 67)
single-member
   district (p. 69)
socialism (p. 73)
state (p. 60)
statism (p. 73)
strong state (p. 74)
unitary system (p. 63)
weak state (p. 60)
welfare state (p. 72)

FURTHER REFERENCE

Burgess, Michael. *Comparative Federalism: Theo-ry and Practice.* New York: Routledge, 2006.
Dahl, Robert A., and Bruce Stinebrickner. *Modern Political Analysis,* 6th ed. Upper Saddle River, NJ: Prentice Hall, 2003.
Doran, Charles. *Why Canadian Unity Mat-ters and Why Americans Care: Democratic Pluralism at Risk.* Toronto: University of Toronto Press, 2001.

Farrell, David M. *Electoral Systems: A Com-parative Introduction.* New York: Palgrave, 2001.
Gallagher, Michael, and Paul Mitchell, eds. *The Politics of Electoral Systems.* New York: Oxford University Press, 2006.
Hueglin, Thomas O., and Alan Fenna. *Com-parative Federalism: A Systematic Inquiry.* Decorah, IA: Broadview, 2006.

LaCroix, Alison L. *The Ideological Origins of American Federalism*. Cambridge, MA: Harvard University Press, 2010.

Lijphart, Arend. *Patterns of Democracy: Government Forms and Performance in Thirty-Six Countries*. New Haven, CT: Yale University Press, 1999.

Lindblom, Charles E. *The Market System: What It Is, How It Works, and What to Make of It*. New Haven, CT: Yale University Press, 2001.

McCabe, Neil Colman, ed. *Comparative Federalism in the Devolution Era*. Lanham, MD: Lexington, 2002.

Moreno, Luis. *The Federalization of Spain*. Portland, OR: F. Cass, 2001.

Stephens, G. Ross, and Nelson Wikstrom. *American Intergovernmental Relations: A Fragmented Federal Polity*. New York: Oxford University Press, 2006.

Van Creveld, Martin. *The Rise and Decline of the State*. New York: Cambridge University Press, 1999.

Zijderveld, Anton C. *The Waning of the Welfare State: The End of Comprehensive State Succor*. Piscataway, NJ: Transaction, 1999.

CHAPTER 5

Rights

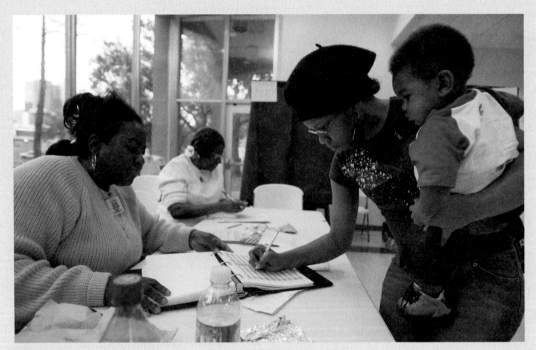

Voters sign to cast primary ballots in New Orleans in 2008. (Mario Tama/Getty)

The nation has suffered a terrible wound, and its enemies aim to do worse. Citizens demand both security and revenge. Can basic constitutional rights and guarantees be curbed in what many people believe is an emergency? Must the nation stand defenseless against terrorists who use our very freedoms against us? These were the questions the United States faced after 9/11 and the speedy—some say hasty—passage of the Patriot Act, which increased government surveillance of anyone deemed suspicious. The Constitution, as many have noted, "is not a suicide pact." Especially troubling were the "enhanced interrogation techniques" authorized by the Bush administration, which included "waterboarding," simulated drowning used by the Spanish Inquisition. Can rights be abrogated for national security?

QUESTIONS TO CONSIDER

1. What are constitutions and constitutionalism?

2. What makes something a "right"?

3. Should constitutions specify social and economic rights?

4. How can the very short U.S. Constitution still work in the modern age?

5. Do most constitutions have "checks and balances"?

6. How has the U.S. Constitution changed over time?

7. Should outlawing hate speech trump free speech?

8. Should terrorist suspects have any rights?

9. How did 9/11 alter the U.S. climate for rights? Has this happened before?

This was not a new problem in U.S. history, which has seen similar restrictions on freedoms in other tense situations. Every political system has a problem establishing and limiting power, especially in times of stress. A fair balance between government powers and civil liberties and between the wishes of the majority and the rights of the **minority** are not easy choices. For example, may states ban same-sex marriages, or does that deny homosexuals equal rights? And if one state allows such marriages, must other states recognize them as legal? May federal agencies survey telephone calls, e-mails, and the transfer of funds—without warrants—to try to detect terrorists?

These questions raise the issues of rights and political power. Most Americans would agree that a Supreme Court decision is law even if Congress dislikes it. We will probably disagree, though, over whether Muslims praying at the airport should be kicked off their flight on the suspicion that they might blow up the plane. Should special attention be paid to Middle Eastern–looking men who might, just might, be terrorists? And if they are not terrorists, do they have the right to sue their accusers? How do we determine the limits of political power and balance the needs of the majority with the rights of individuals and minorities? Some guidelines are provided by traditions, by **statutes**, and above all by national constitutions, which lay down the basic rules for governing.

CONSTITUTIONS IN THE MODERN WORLD

In common usage, a **constitution** is a written document outlining the structure of a political system. Political scientists define "constitution" as the rules and customs, either written or unwritten, legally established or extralegal, by which a government conducts its affairs. Almost all nations have constitutions because they operate according to some set of rules. In chaotic, corrupt, or dictatorial systems, constitutions may not count for much. Afghanistan, divided by armed tribes and warlords, has not been able to implement its new constitution. In Congo (formerly Zaire), Mobutu allowed nothing to limit his stealing of the country's wealth. And Stalin in 1936—precisely when he began his bloody purges—set up a Soviet constitution that looked fine on paper but was a trick to fool the gullible. A few countries like Britain and Israel have no single written document but still have constitutions. British customs, statues, precedents, and traditions are so strong that the British government considers itself bound by practices developed over the centuries. Thus, Britain has a constitution.

minority Subgroup distinct by background, viewpoint, or practice within the larger society.

statute An ordinary law passed by a legislature, not part of the constitution.

constitution Basic rules that structure a government, usually written.

Most constitutions now also specify individual rights and freedoms. Except for the U.S. Constitution, this has been a more recent thing. Canada got its Charter of Rights and Freedoms only in 1982. Britain got the equivalent only in 2000, when it adopted the European Convention on Human Rights. Before that, British rights and freedoms were not so clear.

Constitutions are supposed to establish the forms, institutions, and limits of government and balance minority and majority interests. Not all function that way. Political scientists study not only what is written but what is actually practiced. The Constitution of the United States, for example, is very short and leaves much unsaid. Its seven articles mostly define the powers of each branch of government; the subsequent 27 amendments broadly define civil rights but leave much open for interpretation.

In contrast, most constitutions written since World War II have remarkable detail. The postwar Japanese constitution, which was drafted by the U.S. military government in five days in 1946, contains 40 articles on the rights and duties of the people alone, among them the right to productive employment, a decent standard of living, and social welfare benefits—a sharp contrast to the general values of "justice...domestic tranquility...common defense...general welfare...liberty" outlined in the American Preamble. Article I of the postwar German constitution (the Basic Law) also has a long list of rights, including not only fundamental legal and political freedoms but also social and economic safeguards, including state supervision of the educational system and public control of the economy.

The 1988 Brazilian constitution enumerates many rights—40-hour workweek, medical and retirement plans, minimum wages, maximum interest rates, environmental protection, you name it—that Brazil's economy cannot afford. These rights can block needed economic reforms. Many now believe that detailed social and economic rights should never have been put into the constitution; they should have been passed as statutes or left to the workings of the market. Rights that cannot be fulfilled are common in newer constitutions, whose drafters thought they could fix social and economic problems.

Britain may be able to get by with no written constitution, although the British government is thinking about drafting one. The United States manages to function with a very general constitution. In both Britain and the United States, the details are filled in by usage over time. But most recently established nations commit themselves to long written constitutions that try to spell out everything in detail.

The Highest Law of the Land

Nations adopt constitutions for the same reason that the ancient Mesopotamian lawgiver Hammurabi codified the laws of Babylon: to establish a supreme law of the land. Constitutions state the fundamental laws of society and are not meant to be easily revised. They are yardsticks by which activities of the government or the people are measured. A legislature can pass a law one year and repeal it the next, but amending the constitution is made deliberately much harder. In Sweden, constitutional amendments must be passed by two successive legislatures with a general election in between. Amending the U.S. Constitution is even more difficult. The most common procedure requires the approval of two-thirds of both the Senate and the House of Representatives, then ratification by three-fourths of the state legislatures. The fact that our Constitution has been amended only 17 times since the adoption of the Bill of Rights in 1791 illustrates how difficult the amendment procedure is. (The last, the Twenty-Seventh Amendment of 1992, specified no congressional pay raises without an election in between.) The Equal Rights Amendment failed to pass in 1983 because fewer than three-fourths of the state legislatures voted to ratify it.

COMPARING ■ THE DANGERS OF CHANGING CONSTITUTIONS

Beware the country that keeps changing its constitution; it is a sign of instability and indicates that no constitution has rooted itself into the hearts and minds of the people. France since the Revolution has had 15 constitutions, not all of them put into practice. Brazil has had seven since independence in 1822. Yugoslavia under Tito came out with a new constitution every decade, each more dubious than the one before. The 1963 Yugoslav constitution provided for a legislature of *five* chambers. Such constant experimentation with the highest law of the land meant that no constitution was established and legitimate, one reason Yugoslavia fell apart in bloodshed in 1991. Constitutions are too important to experiment with.

judicial review Ability of courts to decide if laws are constitutional; not present in all countries.

judicial activism Willingness of some judges to override legislatures by declaring certain statutes unconstitutional.

judicial restraint Unwillingness of some judges to overturn statutes passed by legislatures.

Basic Law German *Grundgesetz*. Germany's constitution since 1949.

The General Nature of Constitutional Law Because constitutions, no matter how detailed, cannot cover every problem that may arise, many provide for a constitutional court to interpret the highest law in specific cases. This concept of judicial interpretation of a constitution is a fairly new thing worldwide; it was pioneered by the United States and has spread only in recent decades. Accordingly, many of our examples are American.

The U.S. Constitution says that "Congress shall make no law respecting an establishment of religion, or prohibiting the free exercise thereof" in Amendment I of the Bill of Rights. This is a very general statement, and how it is interpreted in a specific case (such as the question of prayer in school or a satanic cult that believes in animal sacrifice or illegal drugs) depends on those in power at the time. Does it mean that prayer in public schools breaches the separation of church and state? Or that prayer in schools is part of the free exercise of religion? Or that prayer in schools is permissible if that is what most people in a given school district want?

Constitutional law must be interpreted for specific incidents. Who has the authority to decide what the general wording of a constitution means? Starting with the United States, now more than 30 nations give the power of **judicial review** to the highest national court. Such courts rule on the constitutionality of government acts and declare null and void acts it considers unconstitutional. This power is controversial. Many critics have accused the Supreme Court (most notably when Earl Warren was chief justice from 1953 to 1969) of imposing personal philosophies as the laws of the land. To a large extent, a constitution is indeed what its interpreters say it is, but the possibility of too-subjective an interpretation is a necessary risk with judicial review.

The courts do not always interpret the constitution in a consistent fashion. The Warren Court exemplified **judicial activism**, which does not necessarily mean "liberal." It refers to a judge's willingness to strike down certain laws and practices. The opposite philosophy is **judicial restraint**, when a Supreme Court sees its job not as legislating but as following the lead of Congress. Justices Oliver Wendell Holmes and Felix Frankfurter, who counseled the Court on judicial restraint, are regarded as great liberals. The Roberts Court, on the other hand, struck down several laws but was considered conservative.

Likewise, Germany's Federal Constitutional Court is no stranger to controversy. Modeled after the U.S. Supreme Court—except that it has 16 justices—the German court is mandated to make sure all laws conform to the **Basic Law**. In 1975, the German court found that a law permitting abortions conflicted with the strong right-to-life provisions of the Basic Law—enacted to repudiate the horrors of the Nazi era—and declared abortion unconstitutional. After German unification in 1990, the court allowed some abortions in East Germany because it had been the established law and usage there. In 1979, the German court found there was nothing unconstitutional about "worker codetermination"—that is, employees having nearly the same rights as owners and managers in determining the long-term future of their corporations. Not all nations give their highest court the power of judicial review; some reserve that power for the legislature. The British Parliament alone determines what is constitutional.

political culture   The psychology of the nation in regard to politics.

constitutionalism   Degree to which government limits its powers.

Constitutions and Constitutional Government   A constitution depends largely on the way it is interpreted. Two separate nations could adopt very similar constitutions but have them work quite differently. Sweden and Italy have similar structures, but their **political cultures** (see Chapter 7) are quite different, so their written rules function differently. A constitution can be a fiction. The Soviet constitution set a government framework—a federal system with a bicameral legislature, with executive and administrative powers given to the cabinetlike Council of Ministers—and accorded to its citizens a long list of democratic rights. In actuality, the top command of the Communist Party controlled nearly everything, including individual rights.

Constitutionalism means that the power of government is limited. We see its beginnings in the Magna Carta, which England's nobles forced King John to sign in 1215. The Great Charter does not mention democracy; it merely limits the king's power and safeguards the nobles' rights. Over the centuries, however, it was used to promote democracy and individual freedom in modern Britain, the United States, and Canada. In a constitutionally governed nation, laws and institutions limit government to make sure that the fundamental rights of citizens are not violated. In contrast, a totalitarian or authoritarian government (see Chapter 6) is not limited by its constitution; individuals and minority groups have little protection against arbitrary acts of government, in spite of what the constitution may say. In the 1970s, the military regimes of Argentina and Chile "disappeared" (meaning tortured and killed) thousands of suspected leftists even though their written constitutions promised human rights.

The United States is no stranger to violations of minority rights. Perhaps the biggest was the 1942 internment of some 120,000 Japanese Americans on the West Coast under infamous Executive Order 9066, in the mistaken belief

COMPARING ■ CANADA'S NEW CONSTITUTION

Canada was in a curious situation. The British North America Act of 1867, passed by the British Parliament, gave Canada its independence, but as the British Dominion of Canada, it could amend its constitution only by approval of the House of Commons in London. Increasingly, this rankled Canadians, who demanded "patriation" of their constitution, that is, bringing it back to Canada. They got this only in 1982 along with something they had never had before: a Charter of Rights and Freedoms similar to the U.S. Bill of Rights.

that they were enemy aliens (most were born in the United States). Robbed of their homes, businesses, and liberty without due process of law, they were sent to ramshackle, dusty camps surrounded by barbed wire and guard towers—in some ways, similar to Nazi concentration camps. Not one case of disloyalty was ever demonstrated against a Japanese American; they were victims of racism and wartime hysteria.

Even Secretary of War Henry L. Stimson, who signed the order, feared it "would make a tremendous hole in our Constitution." It did, but not until 1983 did a federal court overturn the legality of internment. The incident shows that even a well-established democracy can throw out its civil liberties in a moment of exaggerated and groundless panic. (A similar reaction flared after 9/11, aimed at Muslims.) The 442nd Regimental Combat Team, recruited from Japanese Americans, was the most decorated U.S. unit of World War II.

The Purpose of a Constitution

If some nations pay little heed to what is written in their constitutions, why do they bother to write a constitution at all? Constitutions do several things: They put in writing national ideals, formalize the structure of government, and attempt to justify the government's right to govern.

A Statement of National Ideals   The Preamble of the U.S. Constitution proclaims its dedication to six goals: to form a more perfect union, to establish justice, to ensure domestic tranquility, to provide for the common defense, to promote the general welfare, and to secure the blessings of liberty. The 1977 Soviet constitution proclaimed the Soviet Union to be a "developed socialist society" dedicated to building a classless utopia. The constitution of the Federal Republic of Germany, seeking to repudiate the Nazis, states its determination to "serve the peace of the world" and expressly proclaims that no group of people can be stripped of their German citizenship—a reaction to Hitler's Nuremburg Laws, which made hundreds of thousands of Germans noncitizens.

Preambles and lists of rights are symbolic statements: They indicate the values, ideals, and goals of those who draft the documents. Preambles are by nature very general and have dubious legal force. How are they interpreted? What does the U.S. Constitution mean by a "more perfect union," "establish justice," or "promote the general welfare"? Constitutions state national ideals, but the interpretation of these goals and values requires some decisions.

Formalizes the Structure of Government   A constitution is also a blueprint, a written description of who does what in government, defining the authority and limiting the powers of each branch and providing for regularized channels through which conflict may be resolved. Articles I through III of the U.S. Constitution outline the duties of Congress, the president, and the judiciary. Congress may collect taxes and customs duties but is prohibited from taxing exports. The president is named commander in chief of the armed forces but must have the "advice and consent" of the Senate to conclude treaties. In a system in which there is **separation of powers**, the constitution divides authority and responsibilities among the various branches of government; it also limits the power of each branch.

separation of powers U.S. doctrine that branches of government should be distinct and should check and balance each other, found in few other governments.

No other constitution uses "checks and balances" like the American one; most, in fact, specify the unification of power, a point we will study in Chapter 13. Few other countries abhor the concentration of power the way the U.S. Founding Fathers did. Many observers think the 1993 Russian constitution gives the executive far too much power and the parliament, the **State Duma**, too little, an imbalance that bothers few Russians, most of whom prefer a strong hand at the top to prevent anarchy and stabilize the economy. Again, political culture counts for a lot in how a constitution actually works.

State Duma Russia's national legislature.

constituent assembly Legislature convened to draft new constitution.

As we considered in the previous chapter, constitutions also outline the division of power between central and regional or local governments. In a federal system, powers and responsibilities are divided between one national government and several provincial or state governments. In the U.S. Constitution, this division is a general one; any powers not accorded to the central government are reserved for the states or the people. This division of power has become less clear-cut, especially in recent years, as the federal government has taken on a greater share of financing the operations of education, health, welfare, housing, and much else.

Most nations are unitary systems; that is, they do not divide power territorially but concentrate it in the nation's capital. Unitary systems do not seek to "balance" powers between central and provincial, but they may give a little autonomy to counties (Sweden and Ireland) or prefectures (Japan). They may also remake and even erase existing states and localities; this is not true with federal systems, which cannot easily erase or alter their component states, each of which has a legal existence

Establishes the Legitimacy of Government   A constitution may also give a government the stamp of legitimacy, something both symbolic and practical. Many nations will not recognize a new state until it has established a written constitution, which is a sign of permanence and responsibility. The U.S. Articles of Confederation and, subsequently, the U.S. Constitution symbolized American independence.

Most constitutions were written shortly after major changes of regime and try to establish the new regime's right to rule. A **constituent assembly** is a legislature meeting for the first time after the overthrow of one regime to write a new constitution. The Spanish parliament elected in 1977 turned itself into a constituent assembly to repudiate the Franco system with the new 1978 constitution. That job done, it turned itself back into the Cortes, the regular parliament. In 1990, Bulgaria elected a 400-member Grand National Assembly to write a new, post-Communist constitution. That done, in 1991 Bulgaria elected a regular parliament, the 240-member National Assembly. After ousting the Taliban regime, Afghan factions met in a *loya jirga*, a traditional constituent assembly, to produce a new constitution in 2004. The warlords and Taliban who run much of Afghanistan, however, ignore it.

Can Constitutions Ensure Rights?

Civil Liberties and Civil Rights During World War II, Nazi concentration camps exterminated millions, and the Japanese army raped and pillaged China. In reaction, the world took steps to prevent such horrors. In 1948, the UN General Assembly adopted the Universal Declaration on Human Rights, a symbolic statement (with no real power of sanction) that establishes fundamental precepts and norms that most nations are reluctant to violate openly. Countries that do—Mao had tens of millions of Chinese killed; Saddam Hussein used poison gas against fellow Iraqis; Laurent Kabila condoned and covered up tribal massacres in the Congo—risk being isolated from world aid and trade. Charges of human rights violations try to persuade Sudan to cease killing in its Darfur region. Although not directly enforceable, the setting of norms for human rights made us more likely to seek them.

The Universal Declaration, patterned on the French Declaration of the Rights of Man and Citizen and on the American Declaration of Independence and the Bill of Rights, affirms the basic civil and human rights that government may not arbitrarily take away. These include the rights to life and freedom of assembly, expression, movement, religion, and political participation. The Universal Declaration also provides for many economic and cultural needs: the rights to work, to an education, to marry, to raise a family, and to provide for that family and the right to live according to one's culture. These rights are almost impossible to enforce, and few have tried. The fact is that rights and liberties are difficult to define, and all nations restrict civil liberties in some way. The problem of minority groups is worldwide. Europe's most serious civil rights problem is with Gypsies, who are despised nearly everywhere.

Minority Groups and Civil Liberties Few nations are homogeneous; most have citizens from several racial, ethnic, religious, cultural, or linguistic backgrounds, and their civil or cultural liberties are often compromised. Haitians living in Florida or Mexicans in California are at a disadvantage unless they speak English. Indians and Pakistanis in Great Britain, Algerians in France, and Turks in Germany are under pressure to conform to the dominant culture. But the Universal Declaration states that minorities have the right to preserve their cultural uniqueness. Can it—or should it—be enforced in these situations? The U.S. debate over "multiculturalism" hinges on this question. Should the United States abandon *e pluribus unum* in favor of preserving ethnic groups? Do the children of minority groups have the right to be schooled in their parents' language? In 1998, California voters—including a majority of Latinos—approved Proposition 227, ending bilingual education and making English the only and standard language of instruction. Were rights violated? Or were they improved? Most Spanish speakers want their children to master English *para ganar más dinero.*

THE ADAPTABILITY OF THE U.S. CONSTITUTION

Constitutions are modified by traditions, new usages, and laws. The U.S. Constitution does not mention political parties, yet our party system has become an established part of the American political process. Judicial precedents and government traditions, too, make up the fundamental laws of a society. Constitutions need some flexibility to adapt over time. The right to bear arms and freedom of expression illustrate the changing nature of the U.S. Constitution.

The Right to Bear Arms

In 2008, the Supreme Court ruled for the first time that the Second Amendment's "right to bear arms" is an *individual* right. The point has been and continues to be controversial. In 1939, the Court ruled in *United States v. Miller* against transporting sawed-off shotguns, and

human rights   Freedom from government mistreatment such as arrest, torture, jail, and death without due process.

civil rights   Ability to participate in politics and society, such as voting and free speech; sometimes confused with but at a higher level than human rights.

economic rights   Guarantees of adequate material standards of living; the newest and most controversial rights.

constructed   Something widely believed as old and hallowed but actually recent and artificial.

KEY CONCEPTS ■ WHAT IS A RIGHT?

Where do "rights" come from? Are they natural or artificial? Thinkers of a classic bent—including the U.S. Founding Fathers—took "natural rights" as a basis for **human rights**. Nature expresses God's intentions, which are not hard to discern. You know instantly and instinctively that it is wrong to crash a jetliner into a building. Life and liberty are natural; therefore, government may deprive people of these basic rights only for good cause. Human rights can generally be formulated in the negative as "freedom from," namely, from various forms of tyranny, the great concern of Thomas Jefferson.

Civil rights are newer and at a higher level; they grew up with modern democracy, in which citizens need the freedom to speak and vote. They are not as self-evident as human rights. Press freedom is probably a civil rather than a human right, although the two overlap. Those deprived of civil rights—such as the right to organize an opposition party—may soon also find themselves locked up by the dictatorial regime. In the United States, equal opportunity became a major civil rights issue.

Economic rights are the newest—appearing in the nineteenth century with the early socialists (see Chapter 3) and shifting rights into the material realm. Advanced by people like Franklin D. Roosevelt, they are usually formulated in the positive as "freedom to," namely, to live adequately, have a job, and get an education and health care. Many of them cost lots of taxpayer money in government programs. Conservatives say these are not rights at all, merely desirable things demanded by various groups, such as oldsters demanding prescription drugs as a "right." Some fear a "rights industry" creating dubious rights without limit.

"Right" said English philosopher Jeremy Bentham, "is the child of law." Something becomes a right only when it is put into a constitution or statutes. Before the Medicare law, senior citizens had no right to federally funded health insurance. Now it is a right. All rights are more or less artificial or "socially **constructed**." Is something good and desirable automatically a right? Is everything an interest group demands really its right? Beware of overusing the term "rights."

judges nationwide used Miller as the *precedent* (see page 278) to allow restrictions on gun ownership. But with *District of Columbia v. Heller* in 2008, the Court ruled that the District's strict gun law violated the Second Amendment. (Titles of U.S. court decisions are the italicized names of plaintiffs and defendants.)

The Founding Fathers wanted to prevent any concentration of power that might flow from a standing national army. The Constitution's "militia clauses" envisioned defense as largely in the hands of state "militias," which would disperse power among the states and citizen militia members. To bolster this, Amendment II of the Bill of Rights (adopted in 1791) says, "A well regulated Militia, being necessary to the security of a free State, the right of the people to keep and bear Arms, shall not be infringed." The militia concept of citizen-based defense never came to much (the states did not want to spend the money), so Washington turned the militias into the National Guard.

But is there also an *individual* right, apart from belonging to a militia, to have guns? Liberals and gun-control advocates claimed there is not, that the right pertains only to militias. Accordingly, states and municipalities can restrict gun ownership. Washington, DC, for example, in 1976 outlawed private handguns, something that conservatives charged was unconstitutional. The Supreme Court in *Heller* decided 5–4 that handguns in the home for defense were legal. That instantly became the law of the land, and the National Rifle Association immediately brought suits to strike down similar laws nationwide.

Heller opened the door to numerous Second Amendment questions that will drag on for years. Does it mean Americans can own any gun without restriction? Outside of the home? Concealed? Machine guns? Sawed-off shotguns? Cop-killer ammunition? How about suspected terrorists or deranged youths? Or do states and municipalities still have the power to impose reasonable restrictions? Both *Miller* and *Heller* illustrate that a two-century-old constitution will be reinterpreted in response to new conditions and specific cases.

Freedom of Expression in the United States

"Congress shall make no law…abridging the freedom of speech, or of the press; or the right of the people peaceably to assemble, and to petition the government for a redress of grievances." So says Amendment I of the U.S. Bill of Rights. We regard freedom of expression as a hallmark of any democratic nation. Citizens who think the government is bad or wrong may say so publicly. An antigovernment or anti-religion artwork should draw no interference or investigation from a government agency.

This is a peculiarly American problem, as most countries outlaw "hate speech" in the interests of domestic calm. In most of Europe, it is illegal to deny that the Holocaust happened. A 2008 British Columbia case accused Canada's leading news magazine of hate speech for an article warning that Muslims will take over the world. In the United States, this case would have been thrown out immediately. Shouted one Canadian spectator: "It's hate speech!" Shouted another: "It's free speech!" In 2010, the Supreme Court took up the case of a fringe pastor who called U.S. combat deaths divine punishment for a country that tolerates homosexuality. The Court considered the pain this inflicted on the family of the deceased and seemed ready to set a limit on hateful speech.

red scare Exaggerated fear of Communist subversion, as in World War I and McCarthy periods.

Free speech is not easy. Does it give a campus bigot the right to incite hatred of African American students? Does a newspaper have a right to publish information that might damage national security? Can a publicly funded museum reject artworks that offend some religious sensibilities? Americans believe in the right of free expression, but most agree that there are limits. As Justice Oliver Wendell Holmes argued, one cannot yell "Fire!" in a crowded theater unless there really is a fire. Does free speech include the right to spread dangerous or malicious falsehoods, for example, urging that political figures who support healthcare reform be "eliminated"? Suppose some fanatic acts on that suggestion.

According to Justice Holmes, freedom of expression must also be restricted in cases in which statements or publications present a "clear and present danger" of bringing about "substantive evils," which Congress has a right to prevent. The Supreme Court in its 1925 *Gitlow v. New York* decision upheld the conviction of a radical who called for the violent overthrow of the government on the grounds that his words had represented a "bad tendency," which could "corrupt morals, incite crime, and disturb the public peace." That decision, during a "**red scare**," would likely have come out differently in tranquil times.

First Amendment controversies are never-ending. In 1971 a multivolume, secret Defense Department study of the decisions that led to the Vietnam War was leaked to the *New York Times* and *Washington Post*, both of which started publishing a series of sensational articles based on them. The Nixon administration immediately got a court order blocking further publication on national-security grounds. In what became known as the Pentagon Papers case, the Supreme Court quickly and unanimously rejected the government's claim that official secrets had been compromised. By that time, most Americans were fed up with the war. The reasoning of Justice Hugo Black:

> *Only a free and unrestrained press can effectively expose deception in government. And paramount among the responsibilities of a free press is the duty to prevent any part of the Government from deceiving the people and sending them off to distant lands to die of foreign fevers and foreign shot and shell.... [T]he newspapers nobly did precisely that which the founders hoped and trusted they would do.*

Recently, some have argued that free speech has gone too far, especially if it deals in racism and pornography or if it throttles others' speech in the name of "political correctness." In 2010, the Supreme Court overturned portions of a campaign-reform law designed to curb the influence of big money, partly because campaign contributions are seen by many as a form of free speech. Dollars, they argued, are like words; both should flow without restriction to support candidates and causes. Now corporations can give freely and directly to political campaigns. Some critics fear rich corporations will simply buy elections. The Internet has opened vast new areas in this debate, as the Internet lends itself

Peace protesters tell the White House what they think of the Iraq and Afghanistan wars. (Kevin Lamarque/ Corbis)

sedition Incitement to public disorder or to overthrow the state.

to all manner of hate-filled, extremist causes. Should WikiLeaks be stopped from putting classified cables on the Internet for all to read?

Free Speech and Sedition

Sedition is criticism of the government or officials aimed at producing discontent or rebellion. The U.S. government has used sedition laws to suppress radical expression several times since the adoption of the Bill of Rights. Congress passed the first Sedition Act in 1798, after the XYZ affair. It was aimed at the "Jacobins," as American defenders of the French Revolution were called, at a time when the United States was in an undeclared naval war with France. The Sedition Act was supposed to expire the day that President John Adams left office (which indicates that its true purpose may have been to influence the election). The act was controversial, but it lapsed without any test of constitutionality in the Supreme Court. The next Sedition Act came during the Civil War, when President Lincoln used his war powers to suppress Northern opponents of the war. The matter came before the Supreme Court, which declined to judge the legality of his actions, so they went untested. After the Civil War, all "political prisoners" were pardoned.

Twentieth-Century Sedition Acts   As the United States entered World War I, many socialists and pacifists spoke against it, urging Americans to refuse military service and to disrupt the war effort. The 1917 Espionage Act aimed to silence the radicals, and several hundred, including Socialist Party leader Eugene Debs, were jailed under it. The Supreme Court upheld the law on the grounds that free speech could be restricted if it created, in Justice Holmes's words, a "clear and present danger" to national security. Most of those jailed were later released, and the 1917 act was little used thereafter because it was hard to prove that speech was dangerous. Recently, some wanted to silence and prosecute WikiLeaks under the Espionage Act.

In the 1940s and 1950s, sedition acts were directed against Communists. The 1940 Smith Act, the most comprehensive sedition act ever passed, made it a crime to advocate the violent overthrow of the government, to distribute literature urging such, or to knowingly join any organization or group that advocated such actions. The Smith Act aroused much controversy but was not put to a constitutional test

HOW TO ... ■ LIST REFERENCES

Whoever reads your paper should be able to look up your sources to make sure they are valid and in context. References are now usually put at the end of a paper. Shown here is the standard urged by the American Political Science Association, but this is not sacred. It is derived from the American Psychological Association ("psych style") and a variation of the *Chicago Manual of Style*. Your instructor may prefer the similar style of the Modern Language Association, and some may prefer the old-fashioned footnote style, which at least was consistent across disciplines. There is some variation in what is considered standard, especially with Web sites. In general, references give the reader a road map to your sources.

At the end of your paper, under the subhead "References" or "Works Cited," with hanging indents and in alphabetical order, give the author (last name first), the year, the article in quotation marks, the journal or book title italicized, and, if a book, the city and publishing house. If a journal, give the month and day at the end. Separate these elements with periods. If there is no listed author, use the article's title or, especially with Web sites, the sponsoring agency's name. Referring to the "How To... Use Sources" box on page 75, here is what they look like:

Works Cited

Adams, Jonathan. 2007. *Development and the Environment.* Washington, DC: National Ecology Association.

Berry, Nicholas O. 2006. "Wrong Turns in Iraq." *Foreign Policy Forum.* April 21. foreignpolicyforum@msn.com.

Jones, Robert. 2009. "Obama Announces Environment Program." *New York Press.* December 4.

Smith, Paul. 2010. "Obama and the Environment." *New Departure.* June 20.

Thompson, Earl. 2001. *George Bush and the Environment.* New York: Simple & Simon.

Williams, Charles. 2005. "The EPA Budget under Bush." *Ecology Quarterly* 17:417.

World Bank. 2009. *World Development Report 2008/2009.* New York: Oxford University Press.

---

habeas corpus   Detainee may
protest innocence before judge.

---

until 1951, when the Supreme Court upheld the convictions of the leaders of the American Communist Party
even though they had not been charged with any overt
acts of force against the government. "It is the existence
of the conspiracy which constitutes the danger," ruled Chief Justice Vinson, "not
the presence or absence of overt action." Since then, there have been other court rulings on the constitutionality of the Smith Act, and they have fluctuated. In *Yates v.
the United States* in 1957, the Warren Court reversed the conviction of the Communist leaders on the grounds that there was no overt action, only abstract advocacy
of rebellion. Four years later, in *Scales v. the United States*, the Court upheld the section of the Smith Act that makes membership in the Communist Party illegal—but
this ruling also specified that it is active membership, involving the direct intent to
bring about the violent overthrow of the government, that is criminal. The Court
was careful to point out that membership per se was not made illegal by the Smith
Act.

The most stringent legislation against Communist subversion was passed during the McCarthy era after World War II, another red scare. The McCarran Act of
1950 (the Internal Security Act) barred Communists from working for the federal
government or in defense-related industries, established a Subversive Activities
Control Board (SACB) to enforce the act, and required SACB-designated organizations to register with the attorney general. Critics of the McCarran Act charged
that the law not only encroached on the rights of free speech and free assembly but
also violated the self-incrimination clause of the Fifth Amendment. Although the
Internal Security Act in its entirety has never been declared unconstitutional, every
action by the SACB demanding specific organizational or individual registration
with the attorney general's office has been declared unconstitutional. Finally, with
the realization on all sides that the SACB accomplished nothing, it was abolished
in 1973. Interestingly, the U.S. government did essentially nothing to stop criticism
of the Vietnam War; opposition was too widespread, and there was no declaration
of war.

Rights for Terrorists?

After 9/11 the Bush administration invented a new category for terrorist suspects
who had been arrested: "unlawful enemy combatants." Evidence against them
was often vague. They were in a limbo between criminal suspects and prisoners
of war and lacked the rights of either. They were harshly interrogated by means
such as "waterboarding," simulated drowning. No one knows if valid information
was obtained. Some were held in Guantánamo—because it was not on U.S. soil—
without charge, trial, lawyers, or time limit. Unquestionably many of them—but
which?—were dangerous terrorists, but evidence against them was kept secret. In
effect, they got life sentences without a trial.

After the 9/11 panic subsided, many wondered if this was constitutional. In
2004, the Supreme Court ruled that Guantánamo is effectively under U.S. laws.
In 2006 and 2008, it ruled that suspected terrorists had **habeas corpus** rights.

The court did not free any detainees or order any trials, but it did push the administration to decide whether they were criminal suspects or war prisoners. If the former, they get a trial; if the latter, they get treated under the Geneva Conventions. The law did not sit easily with the new category of "unlawful enemy combatant."

The history of government actions to curb speech or arrest suspicious persons in the United States indicates that the guarantees of the Bill of Rights have been interpreted to mean different things over time. When Congress, the president, and the courts perceive danger and threat, they tend to be more restrictive; in other times, they are more permissive. Rights are highly context-dependent. After the 9/11 terrorist attacks of 2001, few Americans worried about detaining hundreds of suspicious people without due process. A few years later, with examples of panicked overreaction in mind, some worried that the Patriot Act, passed in haste, should be modified to make sure it does not infringe on the Constitution. Warrantless wiretaps of that period were ruled unconstitutional.

We should remember this context-dependency when we see legal restrictions on human and civil rights in other lands. Some regimes really are under siege; opponents want to overthrow them (often with good reason). And because elections are routinely rigged, the only way to overthrow such regimes is by extralegal means, which may include violence. In such situations, free speech may lead quickly to violent overthrow, which may be richly deserved. Governments of whatever stripe clamp down when they are scared, and they are scared because they know they may be overthrown. Myanmar (formerly Burma), South Korea, Indonesia, Egypt, Iran, South Africa, Argentina, and many other lands have imprisoned political opponents for speaking out. "Free speech" is not just a nice thing; it can be dynamite. Freedom of expression thrives best under long-established, legitimate governments in tranquil times. It is, in short, political.

 EXERCISES

Apply what you learned in this chapter on MyPoliSciKit (www.mypoliscikit.com).

Assessment   Review this chapter using learning objectives, chapter summaries, practice tests, and more.

Menu

Flashcards   Learn the key terms in this chapter; you can test yourself by term or definition.

Flashcards

Video   Analyze recent world affairs by watching streaming video from major news providers.

Videos

Comparative Exercises   Compare political ideas, behaviors, institutions, and policies worldwide.

Comparative
Exercises

KEY TERMS

Basic Law (p. 82)
civil rights (p. 87)
constituent assembly
  (p. 85)
constitution (p. 80)
constitutionalism (p. 83)
constructed (p. 87)

economic rights (p. 87)
habeas corpus (p. 92)
human rights (p. 87)
judicial activism (p. 82)
judicial restraint (p. 82)
judicial review (p. 82)
minority (p. 80)

political culture (p. 83)
red scare (p. 89)
sedition (p. 90)
separation of powers
  (p. 85)
State Duma (p. 85)
statute (p. 80)

FURTHER REFERENCE

Ackerman, Bruce. *The Decline and Fall of the American Republic.* Cambridge, MA: Harvard University Press, 2010.

Amar, Akhil Reed. *America's Constitution: A Biography.* New York: Random House, 2006.

Arkes, Hadley. *Natural Rights and the Right to Choose.* New York: Cambridge University Press, 2002.

Axelrod, Alan. *Minority Rights in America.* Washington, DC: CQ Press, 2002.

Cornell, Saul. *A Well-Regulated Militia: The Founding Fathers and the Origins of Gun Control in America.* New York: Oxford, 2006.

Dahl, Robert A. *How Democratic Is the American Constitution?* 2nd ed. New Haven, CT: Yale University Press, 2003.

Eisgruber, Christopher L., and Lawrence G. Sager. *Religious Freedom and the Constitution.* Cambridge, MA: Harvard University Press, 2007.

Exoo, Calvin F. *The Pen and the Sword: Press, War, and Terror in the 21st Century.* Thousand Oaks, CA: Sage, 2010.

Fagan, Andrew. *The Atlas of Human Rights: Mapping Violations of Freedom Around the Globe.* Berkeley, CA: University of California Press, 2010.

Fisher, Louis. *The Constitution and 9/11: Recurring Threats to America's Freedoms.* Lawrence, KS: University Press of Kansas, 2008.

Freeberg, Ernest. *Democracy's Prisoner: Eugene V. Debs, the Great War, and the Right to Dissent.* Cambridge, MA: Harvard University Press, 2009.

Goldsmith, Jack. *The Terror Presidency: Law and Judgment Inside the Bush Administration.* New York: Norton, 2007.

Howard, John. *Concentration Camps on the Home Front: Japanese Americans in the House of Jim Crow.* Chicago: University of Chicago Press, 2008.

Hunt, Lynn. *Inventing Human Rights: A History.* New York: Norton, 2007.

Lewis, Anthony. *Freedom for the Thought That We Hate: A Biography of the First Amendment.* New York: Basic Books, 2008.

Lichtblau, Eric. *Bush's Law: The Remaking of American Justice.* New York: Pantheon, 2008.

Maddex, Robert L., Jr. *Constitutions of the World,* 3rd ed. Washington, DC: CQ Press, 2007.

Mayer, Jane. *The Dark Side: The Inside Story of How the War on Terror Turned into a War on American Ideals.* New York: Doubleday, 2008.

Murphy, Walter F. *Constitutional Democracy: Creating and Maintaining a Just Political Order.* Baltimore, MD: Johns Hopkins University Press, 2007.

Nelson, Samuel P. *Beyond the First Amendment: The Politics of Free Speech and Pluralism.* Baltimore, MD: Johns Hopkins University Press, 2005.

Posner, Richard. *Not a Suicide Pact: The Constitution in a Time of National Emergency.* New York: Oxford University Press, 2006.

Raskin, Marcus, and Robert Spero. *The Four Freedoms Under Siege: The Clear and Present Danger from Our National Security State.* Westport, CT: Praeger, 2007.

Sabato, Larry J. *A More Perfect Constitution: 23 Proposals to Revitalize Our Constitution and Make America a Fairer Country.* New York: Walker, 2007.

Snyder, Timothy. *Bloodlands: Europe Between Hitler and Stalin.* New York: Basic Books, 2010.

Stone, Geoffrey R. *Perilous Times: Free Speech in Wartime from the Sedition Act of 1798 to the War on Terrorism.* New York: Norton, 2004.

Tushnet, Mark. *Why the Constitution Matters.* New Haven, CT: Yale University Press, 2010.

Wittes, Benjamin. *Law and the Long War: The Future of Justice in the Age of Terror.* New York: Penguin, 2008.

CHAPTER 6

Regimes

Venezuelan President Hugo Chávez, a classic demagogue, whips up a crowd in 2010 to march Venezuela away from democracy. (Carlos Garcia Rawlins/Landov)

As the millennium changed, democracy experienced some ups and downs. In the early 1990s, with the collapse of Soviet-style dictatorships, democracy was celebrated as the permanent winner of the great twentieth-century ideological struggle (see page 56). By 2010, however, in the wake of the financial meltdown, democracy faced criticism. Western democracies let themselves get into a severe economic downturn. They eventually handled the crisis, but every step was slow, contested, and angry. In comparison, China handled the crisis well; its economy continued to grow fast. Beijing's brainy nine-man **Standing Committee** quickly tripled bank lending, then throttled back to head off inflation. There were no delays, political fights, or backtalk. Some people, especially in the developing lands, began to wonder if Western democracy was the right model; maybe Chinese-style "market authoritarianism" was better and faster.

QUESTIONS TO CONSIDER

1. Why does modern democracy mean representative democracy?
2. Which are the defining characteristics of democracy?
3. Which is more accurate, the elite or pluralist theory?
4. Why is totalitarianism a twentieth-century phenomenon?
5. What is the difference between totalitarian and authoritarian?
6. Are totalitarian systems bound to fail? Why?
7. Why have many countries recently turned democratic?
8. Why does democracy sometimes fail? Will it work in Iraq?
9. Should the United States try to export democracy?

This was not the first debate over democracy. At the birth of the American Republic, many wondered if it would survive. They noted that Athenian and Roman democracy had both perished. (In 1831–1832, French visitor Tocqueville took a close look and concluded that U.S. democracy was amazing and viable.) The rest of the world moved only slowly and grudgingly to democracy in the late nineteenth and early twentieth centuries. Some countries tried democracy but slid backward. The Soviet, Italian, and German dictatorships evoked some admiration from Depression-wracked citizens of democracies.

The debate between dictatorship and democracy will likely continue. The two, however, are not simply black and white; in between are many variations. Classification is difficult; Table 6.1 is just an attempt. Some countries are pretend democracies, with controlled media, rigged elections, and obedient parliaments and parties, like Russia and Egypt. Many countries are in flux, shifting between

TABLE 6.1	Main Regime Types			
	Democratic *U.S., West Europe*	**Transitional** *Nigeria, Russia*	**Authoritarian** *Iran, China*	**Totalitarian** *N. Korea, Cuba*
Media	free	curbed	obedient	state-controlled
Parties	several	one dominant	none or one	one
Elections	competitive	flawed	rigged	fake
Power	alternates among parties	changes tumultuously	in hands of small group	concentrated in one leader
Ideology	many	limited range	none or pretend	one militant
Constitution	restrains government	selectively interpreted	restrains individuals	worships state
Civil Liberties	protected	vulnerable	few	none
Interest Groups	many and autonomous	few and cowed	state-supervised	no autonomous ones
Economy	market	partly market	partly state-run	state-run
Military	subordinate to elected officials	plays a political role	intertwined with regime	controlled by ruling party
Corruption	minor	widespread	pervasive	major

Standing Committee Top leadership of Chinese Communist Party, China's ruling elite.

democracy Political system of mass participation, competitive elections, and human and civil rights.

illiberal democracy Regimes that are elected but lack democratic qualities such as civil rights and limits on government.

more and less democratic and vice versa, what the table calls "transitional" regimes. Venezuela, Bolivia, and Peru have recently taken on authoritarian hues, but Indonesia and Nigeria have moved in a more democratic direction.

Freedom House annually ranks countries on a 1–7 scale and puts them into "free" (1 to 2.5), "partly free" (3 to 5), and "not free" (5.5 to 7) categories to indicate their degree of democracy (see Table 6.2). Note how several countries are borderline, some barely free (India and Mexico at 2.5), and others at the upper end of not free (Egypt and Russia at 5.5).

REPRESENTATIVE DEMOCRACY

Democracy has many meanings. Dictators misuse the word to convince subjects that they live in a just system. The Soviet Union used to claim it was the best democracy, and mainland China still calls itself the "People's Republic." Democracy does not always equal freedom. Elections, even free and fair ones, can produce regimes that ride roughshod over rights and freedoms, what is called **illiberal democracy**. Democracy is a complex and carefully balanced system that needs thoughtful citizens, limits on power, rule of law, and human and civil rights. Not every country that calls itself a democracy is one, and not every country is capable of becoming one.

Democracy (from the Greek *demokratía*; demos = "people" and kratía = "government") carried a negative connotation until the nineteenth century, as

TABLE 6.2 | **Select Freedom House 2010 Rankings**

United States	1	free
Canada	1	free
Brazil	2	free
India	2.5	free
Mexico	2.5	free
Philippines	3.5	partly free
Bosnia	3.5	partly free
Kuwait	4	partly free
Malaysia	4	partly free
Nigeria	4	partly free
Pakistan	4.5	partly free
Ethiopia	5	partly free
Iraq	5.5	not free
Russia	5.5	not free
Egypt	5.5	not free
Afghanistan	6	not free
Iran	6	not free
Zimbabwe	6	not free
China	6.5	not free
Cuba	6.5	not free
Burma	7	not free
North Korea	7	not free

Source: Freedom House

thinkers accepted the ancient Greeks' criticism of direct democracy as mob rule. A "true" democracy, a system in which all citizens meet periodically to elect officials and personally enact laws, has been rare: Athens's General Assembly, New England town meetings, and Swiss *Landsgemeinde* are among the few.

referendum A mass vote on an issue rather than for a candidate; a type of direct democracy.

representative democracy One in which the people do not rule directly but through elected and accountable representatives.

Some direct democracy continues in U.S. states through **referendums** on issues the legislature will not handle. Although referendums seem very democratic, their sponsors can oversimplify and manipulate issues, as Californians see with the scores of measures—some contradicting others—they face on every ballot. French President Charles de Gaulle called referendums to build his own power and bypass conventional politicians. Pakistan's former president—a general who seized power in a 1999 military coup—had himself confirmed in office by a 2002 referendum. Few were fooled.

Direct democracy is difficult to carry out because of the size factor. As the Englishman John Selden noted in arguing for a Parliament in London: "The room will not hold all." A national government that submitted each decision to millions of voters would be too unwieldy to function. **Representative democracy** evolved as the only workable system.

Modern democracy is not the actual setting of policy by the people. Instead, the people play a more general role. Democracy today is, in Lipset's words, "a political system which supplies regular constitutional opportunities for changing the governing officials, and a social mechanism which permits the largest possible part of the population to influence major decisions by choosing among contenders for political office." *Constitutional* means that the government is limited and can wield its authority only in specific ways. Representative democracy has several essential characteristics. Notice that it is not a simple system or one that falls into place automatically. It must be carefully constructed over many years. Attempts to thrust it onto unprepared countries like Russia or Iraq often fail.

Popular Accountability of Government   In a democracy, the policymakers must obtain the support of a majority or a plurality of votes cast. Leaders are accountable to citizens. Elected leaders who govern badly can be voted out. No one has an inherent right to occupy a position of political power; he or she must be freely, fairly, and periodically elected by fellow citizens, either at regular intervals (as in the United States) or at certain maximum time spans (as in Britain). Most systems permit reelection, although some specify term limits. Reelection is the people's means both of expressing support and of controlling the general direction of government policy.

Political Competition   Voters must have a choice, either of candidates or parties. That means a minimum of two distinct alternatives. In Europe, voters have a choice among several parties, each of which tries to distinguish its ideology and policies. One-party or one-candidate elections are fake. Americans are supposed to have a choice of two candidates, one for each major party, but most congresspersons run with little or no opposition, as campaign costs dissuade challengers from even trying. Gerrymandering by state legislatures guarantees most incumbents' reelection. Even the United States is less than fully democratic.

The parties must have time and freedom to organize and present their case well before elections. A regime that permits no opposition activity until shortly before election day has rigged the election. Likewise, denying media access—for example, by controlling television—stunts any opposition. Much of democracy depends on the political freedoms in the months and years before the actual balloting takes place. Physical balloting can still be a problem. In some places (such as Afghanistan in 2009 and in old Chicago), reliable people "vote early and often," and votes are miscounted. Defective voting systems, such as Florida's punch-card ballots, may negate the popular will. Elections by themselves do not equal democracy. Supposing they do is a common mistake.

Alternation in Power   The reins of power must occasionally change hands, with the "ins" becoming the "outs" in a peaceful, legitimate way. No party or individual should get a lock on executive power. A system in which the ruling party stays in power many decades cannot really be democratic. Such parties say they win on popularity but often tilt the rules. In 2006, Singapore's People's Action Party won its tenth election in a row; it allowed only a short campaign and redrew constituency boundaries. Mexico's Institutional Revolutionary Party (PRI) won

14 straight elections since the 1920s. In 2000, however, Vicente Fox of the National Action Party (PAN) won the presidency, and Mexico started looking democratic. Likewise, Kenya in 2002 voted out the party that had ruled for 39 years. Other African countries are also getting alternation in power, a good sign.

caste   Rigid, hereditary social class or group.

mandate   A representative carrying out the specific wishes of the public.

One unstated but important role of alternation in power is control of corruption. An opposition party that hammers incumbents for corruption is a powerful corrective to the human tendency to misuse public office. Systems without alternation are invariably corrupt.

Uncertain Electoral Outcomes   Related to alternation in power, democratic elections must have an element of uncertainty, fluidity, and individual vote switching. Voting must not be simply by groups, where 100 percent of a tribe, religion, social class, or region automatically votes for a given candidate or party. In such situations the country may get locked in bitterness and intolerance. Some fear the U.S. *culture wars* (see page 124) are leading in that direction. A certain percent of the electorate must be up for grabs to keep politicians worried and attentive to the nation as a whole.

In Iraq, voting follows religion too closely. Most Sunnis vote for Sunni parties and most Shias for Shia parties, making democracy difficult and violence frequent. African voting, closely tied to tribe, does not produce democracy. In Zimbabwe, Robert Mugabe's majority Shona tribe reelected him for decades; he used his dictatorial powers to kill members of the minority Ndebele tribe with impunity. What finally limited Mugabe was enough Shonas saying, "I don't care if he's a Shona; he has ruined this country," and voting against his ZANU-PF party. Indians jest that "in India you don't cast your vote, you vote your **caste**." Indian elections can be partially predicted by knowing which castes favor which parties. Fortunately, Indian individualism often overrides caste, making Indian elections democratic and unpredictable.

Popular Representation   In representative democracies, the voters elect representatives to act as legislators and, as such, to voice and protect their general interest. Legislators usually act for given districts or groups. But how should they act? Some theorists claim legislators must treat elections as **mandates** to carry out

KEY CONCEPTS ■ THE "TWO-TURNOVER TEST"

Harvard political scientist Samuel Huntington proposed a "two-turnover test" to mark a stable democracy. That is, two electoral alternations of government indicate that democracy is firmly rooted. Poland, for example, overthrew its Communist regime in 1989 and held free and fair elections (called "founding elections"), won by the Solidarity coalition of Lech Walesa. Some Poles, however, hurt by rapid economic change, in 1995 voted in a president from the Socialists, a party formed out of the old Communist Party. But after a while, they did not like the Socialists either and in 1997 voted in a right-of-center party. Poland thus had several turnovers and established its democratic credentials. Russia has never had a turnover.

trustee A representative deciding what is the public good without a specific mandate.

constituents' wishes: What the voters want is what they should get. Other theorists disagree; constituents often have no opinion on issues, so representatives must act as **trustees**, carrying out the wishes of constituents when feasible but acting in the best interests of the whole.

With opinion running against the 2008 and 2009 financial bailouts, U.S. congresspersons swallowed hard and voted for them, abandoning the mandate theory to act as trustees for the public good. As Joseph Schumpeter argued against the mandate theory: "Our chief problems with the classical (democratic) theory centered in the proposition that 'the people' hold a definite and rational opinion about every individual question and that they give effect to this opinion—in a democracy—by choosing 'representatives' who will see to it that the opinion is carried out."

Of course, few people hold definite opinions on every subject. If they were asked to vote on nitrous oxide limits or curbs on reckless lending, few would vote. Representative democracy, therefore, does not mean that the representative must become a cipher for constituents; rather, it means that the people as a body must be able to control the *general* direction of government policy. For example, the people may have a general desire to improve education, but they leave the means and details of achieving this goal to their legislators. It is this partnership between the people and the lawmakers that is the essence of modern democracy. E. E. Schattschneider summarizes the case succinctly:

> The beginning of wisdom in democratic theory is to distinguish between the things that the people can do and the things the people cannot do. The worst possible disservice that can be done to the democratic cause is to attribute to the people a mystical, magical omnipotence which takes no cognizance of what very large numbers of people cannot do by the sheer weight of numbers. At this point the common definition of democracy has invited us to make fools of ourselves.

Majority Decision   On any important government decision, there is rarely complete agreement. One faction favors something; another opposes. How to settle the question? The simple answer is that the majority should decide, the procedure used in the democracies of ancient Greece. However, our more modern and practical concept of democracy is that the majority decides but with respect for minority rights. To uphold such rights, an independent judiciary, one not under the thumb of the regime, is a necessity.

Minority views are important. Probably every view now widely held was once a minority view. Most of what is now public policy became law as a result of conflict between majority and minority groups. Furthermore, just as it is true that a minority view may grow over time until it is widely accepted, so may a majority view eventually prove unwise, unworkable, or unwanted. If minority views are silenced, the will of the majority becomes the "tyranny of the majority," which is just as foreboding as executive tyranny.

Right of Dissent and Disobedience   Related to minority rights, people must have the right to resist the commands of government they deem wrong or unreasonable. This right was invoked in 1776 in the Declaration of Independence.

Henry Thoreau, in his opposition to the 1846 war with Mexico, made probably the most profound American defense of **civil disobedience** when he declared, "All men recognize the right of revolution; that is, the right to refuse allegiance to, and to resist, the government, when its tyranny or its inefficiency are great and unendurable." The most celebrated advocate of civil disobedience was Indian independence leader Mahatma Gandhi, who was influenced by Thoreau. Both considered their method of resistance to be "civil"; that is, it was disobedience but it was nonviolent and did not exceed the general legal structure of the state. It was an attention-getting device that forced the authorities to rethink. Ultimately, Gandhi and his followers forced the British to leave India.

civil disobedience The nonviolent breaking of an unjust law to serve a higher law.

mass media Modern means of communication that quickly reach very wide audiences. (The word *media* is plural; *medium* is the singular form.)

Some look on civil disobedience as an individual act of conscience, but others seek to organize it and mobilize it. The most prominent American organizer was the Reverend Martin Luther King Jr., whose 1960s nonviolent civil rights campaigns deliberately challenged racist local laws. He and others in his Southern Christian Leadership Conference were often arrested, but once the charges were brought before a federal court, the discriminatory law itself was usually declared unconstitutional. The long-range consequence of their actions changed both the laws and the psychology of America. Without civil disobedience, minority claims would have gone unheard.

Political Equality In a democracy, all adults (usually now age 18 and over) are equally able to participate in politics: "one person, one vote." In theory, all are able to run for public office, but critics point out that it takes a great deal of money—and often specific racial and religious ties—to really enter public life. Under the pressure of minority claims and civil disobedience, however, democracies tend to open up over time and become less elite in nature. Barack Obama's 2008 victory is an example.

Popular Consultation Most leaders realize that to govern effectively, they must know what the people want and must be responsive to their needs and demands. Are citizens disturbed by foreign wars, taxes, unemployment, or the cost of gasoline? Intelligent leaders realize that they must neither get too far ahead of public opinion nor fall too far behind it. A U.S. public skeptical of healthcare reform cost President Obama support. Leaders monitor opinion on a continuous basis. Public opinion polls are closely followed. The media can create a dialogue between people and leaders. At press conferences and interviews with elected officials, reporters ask "hot" questions. Editorials and letters to the editor indicate citizens' views.

In recent years, several critics have noted that U.S. officials often rely heavily on the opinions of small segments of their constituencies because they are well-organized and highly vocal. Most Americans favor at least some gun control, but the National Rifle Association often blocks firearms legislation. In 2008, Washington listened to the finance community more than to ordinary citizens.

Free Press Dictatorships cannot tolerate free and critical **mass media**; democracies cannot do without them. One of the clearest ways to determine the degree of democracy in a country is to see if the media criticize government, tracked by Reporters Without elites The "top" or most influential people in a political system.

pluralism Theory that politics is the interaction of many groups.

Borders in its World Press Freedom Index. No criticism, no democracy. One current antidemocratic stunt: Use libel laws to block news reports of government corruption. The mass media provide citizens with facts, raise public awareness, and keep rulers responsive to mass demands. Without a free and critical press, rulers can disguise wrongdoing and corruption and lull the population into passive support. As China permitted a "democracy movement" in the late 1980s, the Chinese media became freer, more honest, and more critical. Beijing did not stand for that long; now critical journalists, medical doctors, lawyers, and activists are jailed. Even the Internet is controlled and thousands of blogs shut down every year.

Some Americans argue that the U.S. media go too far, that they take an automatic adversarial stance that undermines government authority and weakens the nation. In some cases, this may be true, but in a democracy there is no mechanism to decide what "too far" is. The checks on reckless reporting are competing journals, channels, and blogs that refute each other in what has been called "the marketplace of ideas." Then citizens, with no government supervision, can decide for themselves if charges are accurate. Only half in jest has the U.S. press been called "the fourth branch of government."

DEMOCRACY IN PRACTICE: ELITISM OR PLURALISM?

Even if all these democratic criteria are met—no easy feat—political power will still not be evenly distributed; a few will have a lot, and many will have little or none. Political scientists see this unevenness of power as normal and unavoidable: **Elites** make the actual decisions, and ordinary citizens, the *masses*, generally go along with these decisions. The key dispute is how much elites are accountable to masses. Those who argue that elites are little accountable are *elite theorists*; those who argue that elites are ultimately accountable are **pluralists**.

One of the early thinkers on elites, Italian political scientist Gaetano Mosca, argued that government always falls into the hands of a few.

> *In all societies—from societies that are very undeveloped and have largely attained the dawnings of civilization, down to the most advanced and powerful societies—two classes of people appear—a class that rules and a class that is ruled. The first class, always the less numerous, performs all of the political functions, monopolizes power, and enjoys the advantages that power brings, whereas the second, the more numerous class, is directed and controlled by the first, in a manner that is now more or less legal, now more or less arbitrary and violent.*

The German thinker Robert Michels argued that any organization, no matter how democratic its intent, ends up run by a small elite; he called this the "Iron Law of Oligarchy." More recently, Yale political scientist Robert Dahl held that "participatory democracy is not possible in large modern societies; government is too big and the issues are too complex.... The key political, economic, and social decisions...are made by tiny minorities.... It is difficult—nay, impossible—to see how it could be otherwise in large political systems." These three agree on the inevitability of elites,

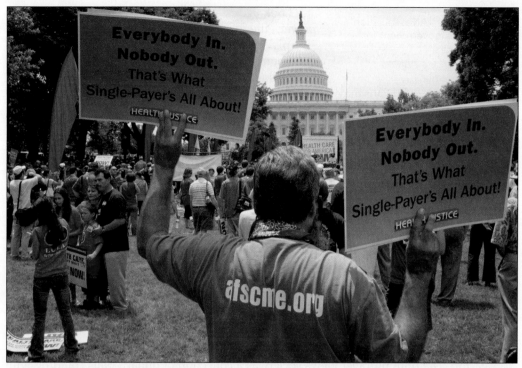

A union member works for a more radical healthcare reform in 2010. Interest groups such as trade unions are a key element in pluralist politics. (Scott Ferrell/Getty)

but Mosca and Michels, elite theorists, see elites as unaccountable, whereas Dahl, a pluralist, sees them as accountable.

Contrary to what one might suppose, modern elite theorists are generally not conservatives but radicals; they decry rule by elites as unfair and undemocratic. Columbia sociologist C. Wright Mills denounced the "Power Elite" in which big business gave money to politicians, politicians voted massive defense spending, and top generals gave lush contracts to big business. This interlocking conspiracy was driving the United States to war, Mills predicted.

Money and connections give elites access to political power, emphasize elite theorists. 2004 presidential candidates and Yale graduates Bush ('68) and Kerry ('66) are both members of the super-elite and secretive Skull and Bones society. Elite does not equal "rich." Few rich people run for office, but they influence those who do by contributions. In return, they get favorable laws, subsidies, and tax breaks. The Bush administration gave the biggest of its 2001 tax cuts to the richest 1 percent and gave special deals to the oil industry, in which both Bush and Vice President Cheney had been executives. Big corporation money controls both major parties, charged independent presidential candidate Ralph Nader. Massive campaign contributions make sure no important industry gets seriously harmed; witness the finance industry's ability to water down laws to regulate them. Critics detected a cozy club of top Wall Streeters and top federal officials. Elite theorists make their case with items like these.

interest group   An association that pressures government for policies it favors.

Look again, argue pluralists. The Cold War, not a power elite, drove defense spending, which declined sharply after the Soviet threat disappeared. Most politicians are of modest origins; few are from wealthy families (exceptions: both Roosevelts, JFK, and both Bushes). Politicians may take big contributions, but they are usually attuned to what wins votes. Big companies do get leaned on. The entire asbestos industry was closed down as a health hazard. Tobacco firms have paid millions in lawsuits and face continual government pressure. And Wall Street, much against its will, was regulated.

Politics functions, say pluralists, through **interest groups**, which we will explore further in Chapter 10. Just about any group of citizens can organize a group to protest or demand something, and politicians generally listen. To be sure, if the group is wealthy and well-placed, it gets listened to more, but nobody has a hammerlock on the political system. U.S. oil companies are among the richest firms in the world, and they are pro-Arab. Why then does U.S. policy usually tilt toward Israel? Most American Jews and fundamentalist Christians are pro-Israel, and politicians need their votes and contributions. According to pluralists, interest groups are the great avenues of democracy, making sure government listens to the people. Many argue that only a pluralist society can be democratic. Efforts to found democracies in societies without traditions of pluralism are like trying to plant trees without soil, as we have seen in Russia, where the long Communist rule erased most naturally occurring interest groups.

The pure elite theorist views society as a single pyramid—with a tiny elite at the top. The pure pluralist views society as a collection of billiard balls colliding with each other and with government to produce policy. Both views are overdrawn. A synthesis that more accurately reflects reality might be a series of small pyramids, each capped by an elite. There is interaction of many units, as the pluralists would have it, but there is also stratification of leaders and followers, as elitist thinkers would have it. (See Figure 6.1.) Robert Dahl called this a "polyarchy," the rule of the leaders of several groups who have reached stable understandings with each other.

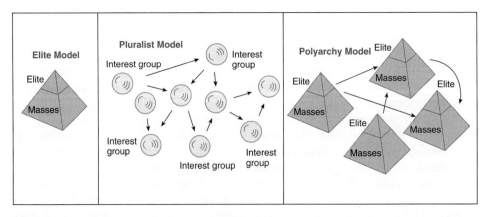

Figure 6.1
Elite, pluralist, and polyarchy models.

Arend Lijphart called it "consociational democracy." The elites of each important group strike a bargain to play by the rules of a constitutional game and to restrain their followers from violence. In return, each group gets something; no one gets everything. Lijphart's example

of where this has worked successfully is the Netherlands, where the elites of the Catholic, Calvinist, and secular blocs have reached an "elite accommodation" with each other. In Lebanon, by contrast, elite accommodation broke down, resulting in civil strife. Most stable countries have "conflict management" by elites. The United States shows an interplay of business, labor, ethnic, regional, and other elites, each delivering enough to keep their people in line, each cooperating to varying degrees with other elites. When elite consensus broke down, the United States, too, experienced a bloody Civil War.

TOTALITARIANISM

In **totalitarian** systems, elites are almost completely unaccountable; they lock themselves into power and are very difficult to oust, short of regime collapse, which we saw in Eastern Europe in 1989 and in the Soviet Union in 1991. There is now little totalitarianism left. Its emphasis on total control, brainwashing, and worship of the state and its leaders has proven mistaken and inefficient. Few people are now attracted to such political models. Only North Korea remains as a pristine example of totalitarianism, while China and Vietnam have opened up economically if not politically. Earlier in the twentieth century, though, with the regimes of Stalin, Mussolini, and Hitler, totalitarianism was riding high. Some thought it was the wave of the future, but it was a disease of the twentieth century. Most of our examples are historical, not current.

What Is Totalitarianism?

The twentieth-century phenomenon of totalitarianism is far removed from past autocracies. Peter the Great and Louis XIV were powerful despots but limited by the poor communications of the time. They could not closely control their subjects. Even Louis XIV, a kind of royal dictator, did not try to control everything in France; average citizens lived their private lives. In contrast, totalitarian states of the twentieth century attempted to remold and transform every aspect of human life.

Totalitarianism began with Lenin's 1917 seizure of power in Russia. Mussolini in Italy in 1922 and Hitler in Germany in 1933 did the same. Note that all three countries had been deranged by World War I. Totalitarianism—a word coined by outside analysts in the 1930s—is a system in which one party holds total power and attempts to restructure society in accordance with party values. Freedom disappears. The old autocratic rulers kept their subjects quiet, but the totalitarian state insists on mass enthusiasm. Carl J. Friedrich and Zbigniew Brzezinski identified six features of totalitarian states. Four of them would have been impossible in preindustrial countries.

An All-Encompassing Ideology   Totalitarians push an official theory of history, economics, and future political and social development. The ideology portrays the world in black-and-white terms and claims to be building a perfect, happy society,

---
hierarchy   Organized in a ranking of power from top to bottom, as if on a ladder.

---

so anyone against it is an "enemy of the people." All are supposed to believe and study the official ideology. Courses on Marxist-Leninist thought were required in all Communist states.

A Single Party   Only one party legally exists, led by one man who establishes a cult of personality. Mussolini, Hitler, Stalin, and Mao had themselves worshipped. Party membership is controlled—usually less than 10 percent of the population—and is supposed to be an honor. Membership brings privileges, and in return members strongly support the party. **Hierarchically** organized, the party is either superior to or tied in with the formal institutions of government. Party functionaries hold all important posts and impose at least outward conformity on all citizens.

HOW TO... ■ WRITE TIGHTLY

Hemingway urged writers "to strip language clean, to lay it bare down to the bone." If you make your written work half as long, typically you make it twice as clear. Throw out unnecessary words. Ripest targets: adverbs, adjectives, and specialized jargon. Combine sentences that have the same subject. Ask yourself, "By making it shorter, have I really left anything out?" Use active voice rather than passive. Whenever possible, use verbs instead of nouns. Stanley Walker, city editor of the old *New York Herald Tribune*, told budding journalists "to avoid adjectives and to swear by the little verbs that bounce and leap and swim and cut."

Loose	**Tight**
Persistent governmental indifference and bureaucratic obstructionism over a long period of time tend to foster a political culture of apathy and nonparticipation.	Distant government and do-nothing bureaucrats turn people away from politics.

Uses Nouns	**Uses Verbs**
German elections show a marked tendency to the casting of ballots along confessional lines, with Catholic Länder favoring the Christian Democratic party and Protestant Länder favoring the Social Democratic party.	German Catholics tend to vote Christian Democrat, Protestants Social Democrat.
take a leadership role	lead
achieve success	succeed

Same Subject, Two Sentences	**Combined Sentence**
The Federal Election Commission figures showed Gore with a small (half a percent) lead in the popular vote nationwide. But the same commission showed that Bush had won in the electoral college by four votes.	The Federal Election Commission gave Gore a small lead in the popular vote but found that Bush had won in the electoral college.

Passive Voice	**Active Voice**
The popular vote was won by Gore.	Gore won the popular vote.

Organized Terror   Security police use both physical and psychological methods to keep citizens cowed. The Nazi Gestapo, the Soviet NKVD under Stalin, and Mussolini's OVRA had no judicial restraints. Constitutional guarantees either did not exist or were ignored, thus making possible secret arrests, jailing, and torture. The security forces—sometimes called "secret police"—were often directed against whole classes of people, such as Jews, landlords, capitalists, socialists, or clergy. The threat of the "knock at the door" cows most of the population. Mass arrest and execution shows the state's power and the individual's helplessness. Not counting deaths in war, the Soviet Union killed an estimated 62 million civilians, Communist China 35 million, and Nazi Germany 21 million. Such terror doesn't work over the long run, however, and the Soviet Union abandoned the more ruthless tactics of Stalin, replacing them with more subtle forms of control and intimidation, such as loss of job or exile to a remote city.

Monopoly of Communications   The mass media in totalitarian states sells the official ideology and shows the system is working well under wise leaders. Only good news appears. Sinister outside forces, however, are trying to harm the system and must be stopped.

Monopoly of Weapons   Governments of totalitarian nations have a complete monopoly on weapons, thus eliminating armed resistance.

KEY CONCEPTS ■ IMAGE AND REALITY OF TOTAL CONTROL

Just as there is no perfect democracy, neither is there perfect totalitarian dictatorship. Often outsiders were overly influenced by the image of total control projected by these states. Visitors to fascist Italy were impressed by the seeming law, order, cleanliness, and purposefulness of what they thought was one-man rule. We know now that many Italians quietly disliked Mussolini, that his organizations and economic plans were a shambles, and that he wasn't even in firm command of the country. In 1943, as the British and Americans overran southern Italy, Mussolini's own generals—who had been disobeying and lying to him for years—overthrew him in a coup. Then the king of Italy—Italy was technically a kingdom until 1946—fired Mussolini as prime minister. What kind of total control is that?

Since Stalin's death, every Soviet party chief denounced the bureaucracy, the deadening hand of routine, and the economic irregularities that impeded Soviet growth. But Khrushchev, Brezhnev, and Gorbachev couldn't touch the problem. Much of Soviet economic life ran by means of under-the-table deals and influence that defied centralized planning. Soviet workers stole everything from radios to locomotives and often showed up to work drunk or not at all. Where was the total control? The pages of *Pravda* and *Izvestia* thundered against these problems, but the government was unable to fix them.

We should bear in mind that the model of totalitarianism presented earlier never matched reality. The model describes an *attempt* to impose total control, not the achievement of it. Starting in late 1989, as one country in Eastern Europe after another cast off its Communist system, we beheld how weak the system was. As to ideology, many citizens, even former Party members, detested communism. The single ruling parties collapsed and handed power over to non-Communists. Organized terror lost its punch. The official mass media, widely ignored for years, was simply discarded in favor of a free press. The controlled economies were turned, with much pain, into market economies. We now realize that these Communist regimes had never exercised total control.

authoritarian Nondemocratic government but not necessarily totalitarian.

Controlled Economy Totalitarian regimes control the economy. Stalin did so directly by means of state ownership and Hitler indirectly by means of party "coordination" of private industry. Either way, it makes the state powerful, for resources can be allocated to heavy industry, weapons production, or whatever the party wishes. Workers can be moved wherever labor is needed, and the needs or wants of the consumer are unimportant. The Soviet Union was the first to send men into outer space, for example, but non-Communist countries always had more and better consumer products. Economic backwardness proved to be the great weakness of the Soviet Union.

Right-Wing Totalitarianism

We tend to focus on communism, but right-wing totalitarianism—Italian Fascism and German National Socialism—was somewhat different. It developed in industrialized nations plagued by economic depression, social upheaval, and political confusion and weakness, and in which democracy was weak. Interwar Germany was in turmoil, saddled with an enormous reparations debt following World War I. In conditions of high unemployment, labor disputes, and inflation, Communists and Nazis slugged it out in elections and street fighting. Hitler promised to discipline the labor unions, to restore order, to renounce the humiliating Versailles Treaty, and to protect private property from the Communist menace to the east. His program appealed to industrialists, militarists, and middle-class people, who typically support a fascist state.

Right-wing totalitarianism does not want revolution; rather, it aims to block a leftist revolution by strengthening the existing social order and glorifying the state. It attempts to get rid of those deemed foreign or inferior, as Hitler strove to annihilate Jews and Gypsies. Citizens are also directed toward national glory and war. Private ownership is generally permitted, but obedient cartels and national trade associations carry out party wishes.

AUTHORITARIANISM

The terms *authoritarianism* and *totalitarianism* are often confused but have different meanings. **Authoritarian** regimes are governed by a small group—a party, a dictator, or the army—that minimizes popular input. They do not attempt to control everything. Many economic, social, religious, cultural, and familial matters are left up to individuals. Most of the six points of totalitarianism discussed earlier are diluted or absent. Authoritarian regimes, for example, rarely have a firm ideology to sell. Some called the Saddam regime in Iraq totalitarian, but it was closer to authoritarian. The main types of authoritarianism are shown in Table 6.3.

Authoritarian regimes limit individual freedoms in favor of a hierarchical organization of command, obedience, and order. Citizens obey laws and pay taxes that they have no voice in establishing. Some trappings of democracy may exist for appearance's sake. Elections confirm the rule of the dominant party; opponents have no chance, and some are arrested. Legislatures rubber stamp the dictator's

TABLE 6.3   **Types of Authoritarianism**

	Examples
1. Military	Burma, Niger
2. Personalistic	Libya, Venezuela
3. Traditional monarchy	Saudi Arabia, Kuwait
4. Dominant-party	Russia, Zimbabwe
5. Single-party	China, Cuba

laws, and puppet prime ministers and cabinets carry them out. Louis XIV of France showed an early form of authoritarianism with his famous phrase: *"L'état c'est moi"* (The state—that's me).

Spain under Franco (1939–1975) was "traditional authoritarian" rather than totalitarian, as the *caudillo* (leader) sought political passivity and obedience rather than enthusiastic participation and mobilization. Franco and his supporters had no single ideology to promote, and the economy and press were pluralistic within limits. Some observers now see a new model, the "authoritarian capitalist" regimes of China and Russia, which allow market economies but tightly retain political control. Their selling point is continual economic growth and rising living standards, and most citizens accept it and show no interest in democracy. But what happens when growth slows?

Jeane J. Kirkpatrick, a political scientist and President Reagan's ambassador to the United Nations, argued that there is a difference between authoritarian and totalitarian regimes. The former (such as Argentina, Chile, and Brazil) can reform, but once a totalitarian system (such as communism) takes over, the system cannot reform itself. Argentina, Chile, and Brazil did return to democracy in the 1980s. Kirkpatrick's thesis was borne out in the fact that the Communist regimes of the Soviet bloc never did reform themselves; they collapsed while trying to reform. The big question of

KEY CONCEPTS ■ DAHL'S "INFLUENCE TERMS"

One of Yale's Robert Dahl's many contributions is his explication of the varieties of power, which Dahl defines as A getting B to do what A wants. Dahl prefers the more neutral "influence terms," which he arranged on a scale from best to worst:

- *Rational persuasion*, the nicest form of influence, means telling the truth and explaining why someone should do something, like your doctor convincing you to stop smoking.
- *Manipulative persuasion*, a notch lower, means lying or misleading to get someone to do something, the way politicians do in elections.

- *Inducement*, still lower, means offering rewards or punishments to get someone to do something, like bribery.
- *Power* threatens severe punishment, such as jail or loss of job.
- *Coercion* is power with no way out; you have to do it.
- *Physical force* is backing up coercion with use or threat of bodily harm.

Thus, we can tell which governments are best: the ones that use influence at the higher end of the scale. The worst use the unpleasant forms of influence at the lower end.

Third World The developing areas: parts of Asia, Africa, and Latin America.

the twenty-first century: Will China's rapidly growing economy produce an educated middle class that starts demanding democracy? Or can the regime forever buy off its people with rising living standards plus Chinese nationalism? So far, Chinese support the regime.

Authoritarianism and the Developing Nations

One of the great changes after World War II was the breakup of colonial empires into independent nations, all of them proclaiming themselves "democratic." But democracy did not last long. The colonialists had always discouraged a democratic political culture. Democracy in the Western tradition grew out of individualism and a competitive market economy. The developing societies had preindustrial, traditional peasant economies that stress families and tribes. Levels of education and income were often low, and most people were absorbed in the struggle to survive. The leadership typically believed that political and economic survival and growth need centralized power. The leaders think they know what the people need and rig elections.

In this way, much of the **Third World** fell into authoritarianism under single parties. Such systems are usually terrible. Government officials push wasteful, unrealistic projects, stifle individual initiative by regulations and taxes, and crush critical viewpoints. Corruption is massive. In this way, such countries as Tanzania and Myanmar (formerly Burma) have impoverished themselves, ending up with neither democracy nor economic growth. Zimbabwe, for example, started democratic in 1980 but found that some parties opposed the dominant party and its leader, Robert Mugabe, who cracked down harshly with soldiers of his dominant tribe and created an authoritarian system, arguing that this was the only way to build unity and a socialist economy. In 2008, miscounted elections kept Mugabe in power as inflation topped 1,000,000 percent, most Zimbabweans were unemployed and hungry, and regime opponents were jailed or killed.

THE DEMOCRATIZATION OF AUTHORITARIAN REGIMES

Since 1974, dozens of countries have abandoned authoritarian or totalitarian systems in favor of democratic systems. Now, about half of the world's nations are at least somewhat democratic. The expansion of democracy from the previous two dozen countries, mostly in Western Europe and North America, became a major scholarly topic. An excellent new quarterly appeared in 1989, *Journal of Democracy*, explaining why democracy appears and what policies encourage it.

There seem to be two types of regimes that contributed to the latest wave of democracy: authoritarian regimes that enjoyed strong economic growth and collapsed Communist regimes whose economic growth lagged. The fast-growth systems—such as Chile, Brazil, South Korea, and Taiwan—were politically authoritarian but developed a private market economy. It was as if the dictator said, "I'll take care of politics; you just work on your various businesses." The pro-business regimes set macroeconomic policy (sound currency, low inflation, plenty of capital for loans) and exported to the world market. After a time, the growing economy transformed the whole society into a democracy. As countries improve from poor to middle income, they become ready for stable democracy. (See *modernization theory* in Chapter 2.) Democracy seldom lasts in poor countries—India is an exception, and Indonesia, after decades of dictators, now looks promising—but it mostly works in middle-income and richer countries.

whig democracy   Democracy for the few, typical of early stages of democracy.

demagogue   Politician who whips up masses with extreme and misleading issues.

Why should this happen? First, economic growth creates a large middle class, which has a stake in the system; the middle class may wish to reform it but not overthrow it. Second, education levels have risen; most people are high-school graduates, and many are college graduates. They are no longer ignorant and do not fall for demagogues, extremist ideas, or vote buying. Third, people increasingly recognize their interests and express them: pluralism. They voice business, professional, regional, and religious demands. They can spot cruel, corrupt, or inefficient governments and do not like being treated like children. Finally, the market itself teaches citizens about

KEY CONCEPTS ■ WHY DEMOCRACIES FAIL

Democracy can actually come too soon in the political life of a nation. Stable democracy has historically taken root in countries with large, educated middle classes. As Barrington Moore observed in 1966, "No bourgeoisie, no democracy." People in poor countries care more about survival than democracy. In a 2004 UN survey of Latin America, a majority said they preferred a dictator who puts food on the table to an elected leader who does not. Middle classes bring with them moderation, tolerance, and the realization that not everything can be fixed at once. Without that, elections can undermine democracy, as seen in Iraq, Russia, and Zimbabwe.

The transition to democracy is delicate and happens best slowly and gradually, as it did in Britain with a series of Reform Acts during the nineteenth century. Typically, during the first decades of democracy, only the better off can participate, a pattern called **whig democracy**. (In the United States, this ended with Jackson's election in 1828.) When the broad masses of citizens suddenly get the vote, the system can break down. Newly enfranchised and unsophisticated voters often fall for the extravagant or extremist promises of **demagogues**, who offer

simple solutions to get the votes of the gullible. They vow to "share the wealth" or advocate aggressive nationalism or religious fundamentalism. Chávez of Venezuela, Thaksin of Thailand, and Ahmadinejad of Iran are examples. Military coups often throw out demagogues. If Saudi Arabia had free elections, many Saudis would vote for Osama bin Laden. Attempting democracy too soon can lead to rule by demagogues, generals, or fanatics.

Several characteristics tend to block democracy:

1. Poverty
2. Major inequality
3. No middle class
4. Low education levels
5. Oil
6. Tribalism
7. Little civil society
8. No earlier democratic experience
9. No democratic countries nearby

Actually, the first four usually come as a package. Democracy in a country with all or most of these characteristics rarely succeeds.

petrostate   Country based on oil exports, such as Saudi Arabia.

self-reliance, pluralism, tolerance, and not expecting too much—all attitudes that sustain democracy. Gradually, if everything works right, the regime eases up, permitting a critical press, the formation of political parties, and finally free elections. Taiwan carried out this transition from 1984 to 2000 and is now a full-fledged democracy.

This does not work with **petrostates**. Oil exports, because they concentrate wealth and power in the hands of a few, retard democracy. None of the 23 countries that get 60 percent or more of their export income from oil or natural gas is a democracy. And that includes petrostates with high per capita GDPs. The oil industry does not employ many workers. Citizens depend on the government for jobs and handouts and do not form an autonomous, pluralistic middle class. Such countries, many around the Persian Gulf, are ripe for overthrow but not for democracy.

The collapse of Communist regimes shows the role of the economy in a negative sense. It was poor economic performance and slow growth—especially in comparison with the West and with the rapid-growth countries—that persuaded relatively liberal Communists, such as Mikhail Gorbachev, to attempt to reform their systems. They knew they were falling behind, especially in crucial high-tech sectors, and thought they could energize the system by bringing elements of the free market into

COMPARING ■ DEMOCRACY IN IRAQ?

Iraq was a new and artificial country the British put together in 1922 from three former Ottoman provinces. Its population groups do not like each other. Sixty percent of Iraqis are Shia Muslims, a repressed and suspect minority throughout the Arab world (see page 101). Saddam Hussein had ruled through his Sunni Arabs (20 percent of the population) and murdered hundreds of thousands of Shias. Freed in 2003, Shias won elections in 2005. Sunni extremists car-bombed Shias, who now controlled Iraq's police and army and retaliated by killing Sunnis. In the north of Iraq, Kurds (about 20 percent) who are Sunni but not Arab, rule themselves like an independent country.

Iraq's elections of 2010 were better. The narrow winner was a secular party headed by a Shia but supported by many Sunnis who were fed up with extremism. The United States welcomed this trend. But there was still much electoral violence as Al Qaeda in Iraq bombed mostly Shia targets. The second-place party, a militant Shia one with ties to Iran, put together a Shia coalition after nine months of haggling. The Sunnis felt excluded, and no one predicted a calm future for Iraq.

Elections do not automatically produce democracy, which requires stable countries with much economic, educational, and political development. Most of Iraq's neighbors are dictatorships, some more authoritarian than others. Saddam was not an accident but a product of a rebellious country that is ready to fall apart. In 2005, the United States launched a major promotion of democracy in the Middle East, but it made little headway. Dictators and monarchs were not prepared to relinquish their power, arguing that only they could keep their countries stable. Free elections in Lebanon and Palestine increased the power, respectively, of the extremist Hezbollah and Hamas. As Jeane Kirkpatrick observed: "No idea holds greater sway in the mind of educated Americans than the belief that it is possible to democratize governments, anytime and anywhere, under any circumstances." Iraq was an expensive lesson that taught Americans a more realistic view.

an otherwise socialist economy. But communism, like other brands of totalitarianism, doesn't tolerate reform. By attempting to control everything, as in Friedrich's and Brzezinski's six points, they have created a brittle system that can break but not bend. Once they started admitting that the system needed to be fixed, they admitted that they were wrong. The ideology was wrong,

kleptocracy Rule by thieves, used in derision and jest.

democratic peace Theory that democracies do not fight each other.

single-party control was wrong, the centralized economy was wrong, and so on. The reform attempt turned into system collapse.

Will the countries that emerge from the wreckage of dictatorship establish lasting democracies? Will Iraq? So far, the ex-Communist lands of Central Europe (Poland, Czech Republic, Hungary, and others) have done so. Farther east and south, however, democracy is incomplete or in retreat. Market systems are strange and frightening to Russians, Ukrainians, Uzbeks, and others, and indeed the transition from a controlled to a market economy inflicts terrible hardships. Some voters, never having known democracy, turn to authoritarian figures, who promise to restore stability and incomes. Vladimir Putin cowed or jailed opposition, and most Russians supported him. Russian political culture favors rule by one strong leader. The executive is extremely powerful and can rule by decree, the State Duma (parliament) is weak and obeys the executive, the entire energy sector (oil and gas) was brought back under state control, and most of the mass media again obeys the state. A favored few get very rich. Some call this a **kleptocracy**, and it is found in much of the world.

Democracy is not easy. It is a complex, finely balanced system that depends on a political culture that grows best under a market economy with a large, educated middle class and a tradition of pluralism. Centuries of religious and philosophical evolution prepare democratic attitudes. Iraq lacked all of these. Eventually, Iraq or any other country can turn democratic, but it may take decades. Most scholars look forward to it, as there is strong support for the theory of the **democratic peace**, that no two democracies have ever fought each other. If this is true, a more democratic world means a more peaceful world.

 EXERCISES

Apply what you learned in this chapter on MyPoliSciKit (www.mypoliscikit.com).

 Assessment Review this chapter using learning objectives, chapter summaries, practice tests, and more.

Menu

 Flashcards Learn the key terms in this chapter; you can test yourself by term or definition.

Flashcards

 Video Analyze recent world affairs by watching streaming video from major news providers.

Videos

Comparative Exercises Compare political ideas, behaviors, institutions, and
Comparative Exercises policies worldwide.

KEY TERMS

authoritarian (p. 110)
caste (p. 101)
civil disobedience (p. 103)
demagogue (p. 113)
democracy (p. 98)
democratic peace (p. 115)
elites (p. 104)
hierarchy (p. 108)

illiberal democracy (p. 98)
interest group (p. 106)
kleptocracy (p. 115)
mandate (p. 101)
mass media (p. 103)
petrostate (p. 114)
pluralism (p. 104)
referendum (p. 99)

representative
    democracy (p. 99)
Standing
    Committee (p. 98)
Third World (p. 112)
totalitarian (p. 107)
trustee (p. 102)
whig democracy (p. 113)

FURTHER REFERENCE

Acemoglu, Daron, and James A. Robinson. *Economic Origins of Dictatorship and Democracy.* New York: Cambridge University Press, 2005.

Bartels, Larry M. *Unequal Democracy: The Political Economy of the New Gilded Age.* Princeton, NJ: Princeton University Press, 2008.

Collier, Paul. *Wars, Guns, and Votes: Democracy in Dangerous Places.* New York: Harper, 2010.

Dahl, Robert A. *On Political Equality.* New Haven, CT: Yale University Press, 2006.

Diamond, Larry. *The Spirit of Democracy.* New York: Holt, 2009.

Dworkin, Ronald. *Is Democracy Possible Here? Principles for a New Political Debate.* Princeton, NJ: Princeton University Press, 2009.

Flathman, Richard E. *Pluralism and Liberal Democracy.* Baltimore, MD: Johns Hopkins University Press, 2005.

Halper, Stefan. *The Beijing Consensus: How China's Authoritarian Model Will Dominate the Twenty-First Century.* New York: Basic Books, 2010.

Linz, Juan. *Totalitarian and Authoritarian Regimes.* Boulder, CO: Lynne Rienner, 2000.

Lipset, Seymour Martin, and Jason M. Lakin. *The Democratic Century.* Norman, OK: University of Oklahoma Press, 2004.

McFaul, Michael. *Advancing Democracy Abroad: Why We Should and How We Can.* Lanham, MD: Rowman & Littlefield, 2010.

Peleg, Ilan. *Democratizing the Hegemonic State: Political Transformation in the Age of Identity.* New York: Cambridge University Press, 2007.

Przeworski, Adam. *Democracy and the Limits of Self-Government.* New York: Cambridge University Press, 2010.

Schedler, Andreas, ed. *Electoral Authoritarianism: The Dynamics of Unfree Competition.* Boulder, CO: Lynne Rienner, 2006.

Snyder, Timothy. *Bloodlands: Europe Between Hitler and Stalin.* New York: Basic Books, 2010.

Stepan, Alfred. *Democracies in Danger,* Baltimore, MD: Johns Hopkins University Press, 2009.

Tilly, Charles. *Democracy.* New York: Cambridge University Press, 2007.

Wedel, Janine R. *Shadow Elite: How the World's New Power Brokers Undermine Democracy, Government and the Free Market.* New York: Basic Books, 2009.

PART II

POLITICAL ATTITUDES

Ch. 7 Political Culture   Political culture searches for a given society's broad, general views on government and politics. A participatory and work-ethic culture sustains a free and prosperous society, but cynical culture can damage it. Political culture, once laid down, lasts a long time, but under the pressure of events can decay. Any society shows elite-mass and subcultural differences. Political culture is learned chiefly from the family, sometimes bolstered by overt socialization in schools.

Ch. 8 Public Opinion   Public opinion looks for specific views on leaders and problems; it is narrower and faster changing than political culture. The opinions of individuals are shaped by social class, education, region, religion, age, gender, and ethnicity. Scientific polling can be accurate, provided the sample is random and question is clear. U.S. presidents go through honeymoons and rally events but generally get less support over time. Polling is plagued by respondents' varying levels of interest and intensity, leading to great volatility.

CHAPTER 7

Political Culture

Activists of The National Confederation of Dalits (untouchables) rally for more economic aid from the Indian government. (Prakash Singh/AFP/Getty Images)

The Obama administration encountered a big problem with American political culture. It argued that healthcare reform was urgent and something most Americans wanted. But roughly half of Americans said they opposed the measure, and it barely squeaked through Congress in 2010. The Obama administration tried to make a rational case that the reforms were moderate and not too expensive, but it neglected a deep-seated part of American *political culture* (see page 11), namely, its visceral dislike of big government and high taxes. Europeans and Canadians, equipped with political cultures that have long accepted state supervision, including of medical plans, were perplexed at the U.S. debate. They were amazed that the United States, like any advanced democracy, did not have national healthcare. Political culture sets a country's norms and limits; it is not easily overridden.

QUESTIONS TO CONSIDER

1. What is political culture?
2. How does political culture differ from public opinion?
3. How do Russia and Iraq exhibit problems of political culture?
4. Explain the three types of political culture found by Almond and Verba.
5. If Americans are participatory, why do they vote so little?
6. What happened to U.S. attitudes starting in the 1960s?
7. How do elite and mass political cultures differ?
8. Why do some cultures lead to economic growth?
9. How can you tell if a group forms a distinct subculture?
10. What are the most potent agents of political socialization?

WHAT IS POLITICAL CULTURE?

Each society imparts its norms and values to its people, who pick up distinct notions about how the political system is supposed to work and about what the government may do to them and for them. These beliefs, symbols, and values about the political system are the political culture of a nation—and it varies considerably from one nation to another.

The political culture of a nation is determined by its history, economy, religion, and folkways. Basic **values**, laid down early, may endure for centuries. Political culture is a sort of collective political memory. America was founded on the basis of "competitive individualism," a spirit of hustle and looking out for oneself, which is still very much alive. The millennia-old Hindu emphasis on caste persists in

---

values   Deeply held views; key
component of political culture.

---

present-day India despite government efforts to abolish
it. The French, after centuries of *étatisme*, still expect a
big state to supervise the economy. Iraq, for centuries
part of Arab and Turkish empires, has known only
autocracy, recently under the brutal Saddam Hussein. Democracy has no roots in
Iraq's political culture.

As defined by political scientist Sidney Verba, political culture is "the system
of empirical beliefs, expressive symbols, and values, which defines the situation in
which political action takes place." Much of this goes far back. Americans always
liked minimal government. In Japan, where the vestiges of a traditional feudal
class system still exist, those who bow lower indicate they are of inferior status.
The Japanese still tend to submit to the authority of those in office, even when
they dislike their corruption and incompetence. Americans, who traditionally do
not defer to anyone, consider it their democratic birthright to criticize the way the
country is governed, even if they know little about the issues. In political culture,
Japan and the United States are vastly different.

Political Culture and Public Opinion

Political culture and public opinion overlap, for both look at attitudes toward
politics. Political culture looks for basic, general values on politics and government. Public opinion, on the other hand, looks for views about specific leaders
and policies. Political culture looks for the underpinnings of legitimacy, the gut
attitudes that sustain a political system, whereas public opinion seeks responses
to current questions.

The methodologies of political culture and public opinion also overlap: Random
samples of the population are asked questions, and the responses are correlated
with subgroups in the population. The questions, however, are different. A political
culture survey might ask how much you trust other people; a public opinion survey
might ask if you think the president is doing a good job. A political culture study
may ask the same questions in several countries to gain a comparative perspective.
Both may want to keep track of responses over time to see, in the case of political
culture, if legitimacy is gaining or declining or, in the case of public opinion, how a
president's popular support changes.

Political culture studies often go beyond surveys, however. Some use the
methods of anthropology and psychology in the close observation of daily life
and in the deep questioning of individuals about their feelings. Public opinion
studies rarely go beyond quantified data, whereas political culture studies can use
history and literature to gain insights. For instance, the observations of nineteenth-
century European visitors show continuity in American political and social values. Indeed, the brilliant observations of Frenchman Alexis de Tocqueville, who
traveled through the United States in the early 1830s, still generally apply today.
Tocqueville was one of the founders of the political culture approach in political
science.

It used to be assumed that political culture was nearly permanent or changed
only slowly, whereas public opinion was fickle and changed quickly. Recent

studies, however, have shown that political culture is rather changeable, too. Periods of stable, efficient government and economic growth solidify feelings of legitimacy; periods of indecisive, chaotic government and economic downturn are reflected in weakening legitimacy. Public opinion,

cynical Untrusting and suspicious, especially of government.

if held long enough, eventually turns into political culture. In the 1960s, public opinion on Vietnam showed declining support for the war. Over precisely the same time, confidence in the U.S. government also declined. Public opinion on a given question was infecting the general political culture, making it more **cynical** about the political system.

To be sure, a country's political culture changes more slowly than its public opinions, and certain underlying elements of political culture persist for generations, perhaps for centuries. The basic values Tocqueville found in America are largely unchanged. The French still take to the streets of Paris to protest perceived injustice, just as their ancestors did. Italians continue their centuries-old cynicism toward anything governmental. Russians, who have never experienced free democracy, still favor strong leaders and shrug off democracy. Although not as firm as bedrock, political culture is an underlying layer that can support—or fail to support—the rest of the political system. This is one reason Russia's attempt at democracy faded.

Participation in America

Even in America, not all citizens actively participate in politics. How, then, could Almond and Verba (see box on page 122) offer the United States as their model of a

KEY CONCEPTS ■ CIVIL SOCIETY

The concept of "civil society" is closely related to political culture. Hobbes used the term to indicate humans after becoming civilized; Hegel used it to designate associations bigger than the family but smaller than the state—churches, clubs, businesses, and so on. Edmund Burke called these the "little platoons of society" that form the basis of political life. They encourage cooperating with others, rule of law, restraint, and moderation—what Tocqueville called "habits of the heart." Without them, politics becomes a murderous grab for power.

With the fall of communism in Eastern Europe and the Soviet Union, the concept attracted new interest to explain the growth of democracy—or the lack of it. The Communist regimes had attempted to stomp out civil society and control nearly everything. When a totalitarian (see Chapter 6) regime collapses, it leaves a vacuum where there should be a civil society. Nothing works right; lawlessness sweeps the land. Americans supposed that, after Communism, Russia would quickly become like us, but Russia had no civil society and soon reverted to authoritarianism. Likewise, we supposed that, after Saddam Hussein, Iraq would become a stable democracy, but with little civil society Iraq degenerated into chaos.

A vibrant and developed civil society is the bedrock of democracy. Central Europe—especially Poland's strong Catholic Church, which always taught Poles to ignore communism—had some civil society and moved quickly to democracy. Without a civil society, democracy may not take root.

participatory Interest or willingness to take part in politics.

political competence Knowing how to accomplish something politically.

political efficacy Feeling that one has at least a little political input (opposite: feeling powerless).

"civic culture"? One of their key findings was that participation need only be "intermittent and potential." In effect, they offer a "sleeping dogs" theory of democratic political culture. Leaders in a democracy know that most of the time most people pay little attention to politics. But they also know that if aroused—because of scandal, unemployment, inflation, or unpopular war—the public can vote them out of office at the next election. Accordingly, leaders usually work to keep the public passive

CLASSIC WORKS ■ THE CIVIC CULTURE

Gabriel Almond and Sidney Verba did the pioneering study of cross-national differences in political beliefs and values. The researchers interviewed some 1,000 people each in five countries in 1959 and 1960 to measure underlying political views. From the data, Almond and Verba discerned three general political cultures: participant, subject, and parochial. Every country, they emphasized, is a varied mixture of all three of these ideal types.

Participant

In a **participant** political culture, such as the United States and Britain, people understand that they are citizens and pay attention to politics. They are proud of their country's political system and are willing to discuss it. They believe they can influence politics and claim they would organize a group to protest something unfair. Accordingly, they show a high degree of **political competence** and **political efficacy**. They say they take pride in voting and believe people should participate in politics. They are active in their communities and often belong to voluntary organizations. They are likely to trust other people and to recall participating in family discussions as children. A participant political culture is clearly the ideal soil to sustain a democracy.

Subject

Less democratic than the participant political culture is the **subject** political culture, predominant at that time in West Germany and Italy, in which people still understand that they are

citizens and pay attention to politics, but they do so more passively. They follow political news but are not proud of their country's political system and feel little emotional commitment toward it. They are uncomfortable discussing politics and feel they can influence politics only to the extent of speaking with a local official. It does not ordinarily occur to them to organize a group. Their sense of political competence and efficacy is lower; some feel powerless. They say they vote, but many vote without enthusiasm. They are less likely to trust other people and to recall voicing their views as children. Democracy has more difficulty sinking roots in a culture where people are used to thinking of themselves as obedient subjects rather than as participants.

Parochial

Still less democratic is the **parochial** political culture, where many people do not much care that they are citizens of a nation, as in Mexico at the time of the survey. They identify with the immediate locality, hence the term *parochial* (of a parish). They take no pride in their country's political system and expect little of it. They pay no attention to politics, have little knowledge of it, and seldom speak about it. They have neither the desire nor the ability to participate in politics. They have no sense of political competence or efficacy and feel powerless in the face of existing institutions. Attempting to grow a democracy in a parochial political culture is very difficult, requiring not only new institutions but also a new sense of citizenship.

and quiet. Following the **rule of anticipated reactions,** leaders in democracies constantly ask themselves how the public will likely react to their decisions. They are happy to have the public *not* react at all; they wish to let sleeping dogs lie.

This theory helps explain an embarrassing fact about U.S. political life, namely, its low voter **turnout,** the lowest of all the industrialized democracies. Until recently, only about half of U.S. voters cast ballots in presidential elections, although it is now somewhat higher. Even fewer vote in state and local contests. In Europe, voter turnout has been about three-quarters of

subject   Feeling among citizens that they should obey authority but not participate much in politics.

parochial   Narrow; having little or no interest in politics.

rule of anticipated reactions Politicians form policies based on how they think the public will react.

turnout   Percent of eligible voters who vote in a given election.

the electorate (but is declining there, too). How, then, can the United States boast of its democracy? Theorists reply that a democratic culture does not necessarily require heavy voter turnout. Rather, it requires an attitude that, if aroused, the people will participate—vote, contribute time and money, organize groups, and circulate petitions—and that elected officials know this. Democracy in this view is a psychological connection between leaders and followers that tends to restrain officials from foolishness. It is the potential and not the actual participation that makes a democratic culture.

Another of Almond and Verba's key findings was the response to the question of what citizens of five countries would do to influence local government regarding an unjust ordinance. Far more Americans said that they would "try to enlist the aid of others." Americans seem to be natural "group formers" when faced with a political problem, an important foundation of U.S. democracy. In what Almond and Verba called "subject" cultures, this group-forming attitude was weaker.

Other studies show that Americans are prouder of their system and more satisfied with the way democracy works in their country compared with the citizens of other lands. A 1995 Gallup survey found that 64 percent of the Americans polled expressed some degree of satisfaction. Sixty-two percent of Canadians responded likewise, as did 55 percent of Germans, 43 percent of French, 40 percent of Britons, 35 percent of Japanese, and only 17 percent of Mexicans and Hungarians. Americans may complain about government, but their faith in democracy is still the strongest in the world.

THE DECAY OF POLITICAL CULTURE

The political cultures of most of the advanced democracies have recently grown more cynical, and voter turnout has declined. More citizens saw politicians as corrupt and government institutions as ineffective. The steepest drop was in Japan, where the economy was largely stagnant for two decades. In the 1960s and 1970s— the years of the Vietnam War, Watergate, and inflation—U.S. surveys showed a sharp decline in trust in government (see Figure 7.1). In the 1980s, under the "feel-good" presidency of Ronald Reagan, the trusting responses went up but never recovered the levels of the early 1960s. Trust fell in 2004 over the U.S. war in Iraq

Figure 7.1
Americans' trust in government, 1964–2010.

Sources: 1965–1996, American National Election Studies of the University of Michigan; 1997–2010 Pew Research Center for People and the Press

---

secular   Not connected to religion.

and in 2010 over bank bailouts and growing federal debt. The growth in cynicism made America harder to govern and is reflected in an electorate that seems to be permanently split and unhappy with Washington. American political culture is not as unified and legitimate as it used to be.

A related development is America's "culture wars," a nasty polarization between conservatives and liberals, who dislike and vote against each other. For two centuries one spoke of the "Two Spains" because it was badly split by region and religiosity. Now America seems to be two countries. One is conservative, evangelical, small-town, and living in the middle of the country; it votes Republican (the "red states" on news maps). The other is liberal, **secular**, urban, and living on both coasts; it votes Democrat (the "blue states"). Conservatives dislike gay and women's rights, taxes, and Barack Obama (example: Fox News). Liberals dislike big corporations, the Iraq War, and George Bush (example: Michael Moore).

Richard Nixon first exploited this split to win the 1968 election, and it has grown deeper ever since. The causes of this polarization are several and disputed. The 1960s was a time of upheaval in which younger Americans repudiated authority with "drugs, sex, and rock-and-roll." In reaction, what Nixon called the "silent majority" turned to conservative Christianity and the Republican Party, which espoused "family values." This created a big gap between religious and secular America (see box below). America may have also never recovered psychologically from the Vietnam War, and the anger returned with the Iraq War. The big spending of healthcare reform and bank bailouts inflamed conservatives. Economically and demographically, the coasts of America grew while the center stagnated. If polarization keeps growing, some fear for U.S. political stability. Dialogue between the Two Americas fails, as their views are visceral, not rational.

One factor much discussed was the decline of the American tendency to form associations, anything from volunteer fire departments to labor unions. In the 1830s, Tocqueville noted, "Americans of all ages, all conditions, and all dispositions constantly form associations." He was impressed by this tendency, for it was (and still is) largely absent in France, and he held it was the basis of American democracy, a point supported much later by the *Civic Culture* study. Some observers claim that these grassroots associations are fading. Harvard political scientist Robert Putnam noted, for example, that the number of people bowling has increased, but league bowling has declined. His article, "Bowling Alone," caught much attention and controversy. Putnam argued the membership loss of many associations—unions, PTAs, Boy Scouts, and fraternal orders—meant decline of our "social capital" and decay of civil society.

Others argue that Americans volunteer and join as much as ever. Old associations, such as the Scouts and Elks, may be shrinking, but new ones, such as Habitat for Humanity and Meals on Wheels, may be growing. Forty percent of American college students volunteer to help the homeless, feed the needy, tutor, participate in religious life, clean up the environment, and participate in other altruistic activities. The sudden rise of the Tea Party movement shows Americans are still willing to form associations.

Those who see the decline of America's voluntary associations, however, fear political and economic repercussions. With individuals demanding their "rights" without a corresponding sense of "obligations," demands on government become impossible. Democracy becomes less a matter of concerned

COMPARING ■ AMERICA THE RELIGIOUS

The United States has long been known as a religious nation. A 2009 Gallup survey found that 65 percent of Americans said religion plays an important part in their daily lives, far higher than Britons (27 percent), Canadians (42), Germans (40), Japanese (24), or French (30). Among the advanced, industrialized nations, the United States is an "outlier" (see page 289). In general, poorer countries are the most religious—India (90 percent), Brazil (87), and Mexico (73)—as well as Muslim lands—Indonesia (99) and Egypt (97).

U.S. religiosity is also one of the points of cultural divergence between Americans and Europeans, many of whom think the United States is dominated by Christian fundamentalists. Polls find that nearly half of Americans believe in creationism and two-thirds in the devil. A majority believes the Book of Revelation will come true. Americans' favorite reading: the "Left Behind" books, of which more than 40 million have been sold. Sarah Palin, an outspoken evangelical Christian, enjoys much support from conservative Christians. This would not work in Europe or Japan.

subculture   A minority culture within the *mainstream* culture.

citizens meeting face-to-face to discuss a community problem than disgruntled citizens demanding "Gimme!" Furthermore, argued Francis Fukuyama (who earlier brought us the "end of history" theory), trust or "spontaneous sociability" underpins economic growth and stability. If you can trust others, you can do more and better business with them. Hence "high trust" societies tend to become prosperous, low trust societies not.

Another school of thought sees the growth of distrust in government as a natural thing and not necessarily bad. Politicians worldwide have for decades promised citizens more and more, promises they could not possibly deliver; there is simply not enough money. But citizens meantime have become more educated and aware of this gap and more willing to criticize. What some see as the growth of cynicism others see as the growth of "critical citizens" who are actually improving democracy by telling politicians what voters think of them.

Political culture changes. It is a combination of long-remembered and deeply held values plus reactions to current situations. These changes are responses to government performance, which almost always fall short of promises. Political cultures do not fall from heaven; they are created by government actions and inactions.

POLITICAL SUBCULTURES

Elite and Mass Subcultures

The political culture of a country is not uniform and monolithic. One can usually find within it differences between the mainstream culture and **subcultures** as well as differences between elite and mass attitudes. Elites—used here more broadly than the "governing elites" discussed in Chapter 6 (a tiny fraction of 1 percent)—in political culture studies means those with better education, higher income, and more influence (several percent). Elites are much more interested in politics and more participatory. They are more inclined to vote, to protest injustice, to form groups, and to run for office. One consistent finding of the *Civic Culture* study has been confirmed over and over: The more education people have, the more likely they are to participate in politics.

Delegates to both Democratic and Republican conventions—who are clearly very interested in politics—illustrate the differences between elite and mass culture. Usually half the delegates have some postgraduate education (often law school), far more than average voters. Most convention delegates have annual incomes much higher than those of average voters. Delegates are also more ideological than average voters, the Democrats more liberal and the Republicans more conservative. In other words, the people at conventions are not closely representative of typical voters. People with more education, money, and ideological convictions take the leading roles. There is nothing wrong with this; it is standard worldwide.

Why should this be so? Here we return to the concepts mentioned earlier: *political competence* and *political efficacy*. Better-educated people know how to participate in political activity. They have greater self-confidence in writing to officials and the media, speaking at meetings, and organizing groups. They feel that what they do has at least some political impact. The uneducated and the poor lack the knowledge and confidence to do these kinds of things. Many of them feel powerless. "What I do doesn't matter, so why bother?" they think. Those at the bottom of the social ladder thus become apathetic.

The differences in participation in politics between elites and masses are one of the great ironies of democracy. In theory and in law, a democracy is open to all. In practice, some participate much more than others. Because the better-educated and better-off people (more education usually leads to higher income) participate in politics far more, they are in a much stronger position to look out for their interests. It is not surprising that the 2001 tax cut favored the wealthiest, who speak up and donate money; those lower on the socioeconomic ladder do not. There is no quick fix for this. The right to vote is a mere starting point for political participation; it does not guarantee equal access to decision making. A mass political culture of apathy and indifference toward politics effectively negates the potential of a mass vote. An elite political culture of competence and efficacy amplifies its influence.

HOW TO... ■ USE QUOTATIONS

Do not quote everything. Quote only important statements from key figures. You might quote the secretary of state on a major foreign policy, but you should not normally quote a journalist or an academic. Their precise words are rarely that important. Instead, if you want to borrow their ideas, paraphrase them in your own words, but still cite them. For your paper, a short summary is better than a long quote.

Quote

"I have no problem with any of the substantive criticism of President Obama from the right or left," wrote columnist Thomas Friedman. "But something very dangerous is happening. Criticism from the far right has begun tipping over into delegitimation and creating the same kind of climate here that existed in Israel on the eve of the Rabin assassination" (Friedman, 2009).

Paraphrase

Washington pundits grew alarmed at the partisan rage directed at President Obama.

Occasionally, a scholar says something so clear and provocative that it's worth quoting: "Islam has bloody borders" (Huntington 1993). Use partial quotes instead of long quotes. Pick out the interesting or operative phrase and quote it: Pentagon officials said they had "not anticipated" chaos in Iraq (Sinclair 2003). If you must include a long quote—more than three lines—make it an indented block quote. Use ellipses (...) to indicate you have omitted unnecessary words. Use brackets ([ ]) to indicate you have inserted a clarification of words not in the original.

To slow down the tempo means to lag behind. And those who lag behind are beaten. The history of Old Russia shows ... that because of her backwardness she was constantly defeated.... We [the Russians] are behind the leading countries by fifty to one hundred years. We must make up this distance in ten years. Either we do it or we go under. (Stalin 1931)

mainstream   Sharing the average or standard political culture.

integration   Merging subcultures into the *mainstream* culture.

Minority Subcultures

The 2010 census showed that more than a third of U.S. residents are minorities. They might be black, Latino, Asian, Native American, or Pacific Islander. In California, whites are a minority. Even among white Americans, there are differences among ethnic, religious, and regional groups. When the differentiating qualities are strong enough in a particular group, we say that the group forms a *subculture*. Defining subculture is tricky, as not every group is a subculture. The Norwegian-Americans of "Lake Wobegon," Minnesota, do not form a subculture because their culture and politics are **mainstream**.

But African Americans do form a political subculture. They are on average poorer and less educated than whites, more liberal, and solid Democratic voters. In attitudes toward the criminal justice system, blacks sharply diverge from whites, as the 1995 murder trial of O. J. Simpson illustrated. Most blacks, convinced the police and courts are racist and rig evidence, were glad to see Simpson acquitted. Most whites, convinced the police and courts are just and fair, thought the jury (with its black majority) ignored the evidence. Many whites had naively believed that U.S. society had made great strides since the 1950s in **integrating** African Americans; the Simpson trial and the reactions to it showed how great a gap remained. The 2008 election split over race, with a majority of whites for McCain and most non-whites for Obama.

Groups with a different language who dislike being ruled by the dominant culture constitute subcultures. Many of the French speakers of Quebec would like to withdraw from Canada and become a separate country. The Bengalis of East Pakistan, ethnically and linguistically distinct from the peoples of West Pakistan, did secede in 1971. The Basques of northern Spain and the Roman Catholics of Northern Ireland are sufficiently different to constitute political subcultures. The Scots and Welsh of Britain harbor the resentments of the "Celtic fringe" against the dominant English. They vote heavily Labour, whereas the English vote heavily Conservative. They, too, constitute subcultures.

Where subcultures are very distinct, the country itself may be threatened. The Soviet Union and Yugoslavia fell apart because citizens were more loyal to their ethnic groups than to the nation. Ethnic Albanians in Kosovo, by religion (Muslim) and language very distinct from their Serbian rulers, fought for independence. In India, some Sikhs seek independence for the Punjab, their home province, and resort to arms. Prime Minister Indira Gandhi's Sikh bodyguards assassinated her in 1985. Such countries as Lebanon and India are not yet culturally integrated—a dangerous condition.

Should a nation attempt to integrate its subcultures into the mainstream? Such efforts are bound to be difficult, but if left undone the subculture in later years may seek independence, as did the Tamils of Sri Lanka. The Spaniards in Peru who conquered the Incas let them retain their language and culture. But now the Spanish-speaking Peruvians of the cities know little of the Quechua-speaking Peruvians of the mountains. Thirty percent of Peruvians speak no Spanish. Any nonintegrated subculture poses at least a problem and at worst a threat to the national political system.

Starting in the 1870s, France deliberately pursued national integration through its centralized school system. Many regions were backwaters and spoke strange dialects. The French education ministry sent schoolteachers into the villages almost like missionaries. The teachers followed an absolutely standard curriculum that was heavy on rote learning and on the glory and unity of France. Gradually, in the phrase of Eugen Weber, they turned "peasants into Frenchmen." After some decades, a much more unified and integrated France emerged, an example of *overt political socialization* (see discussion following).

The United States has relied largely on voluntary integration to create a mainstream culture in which most Americans feel at home. Immigrants know they have to learn English to get ahead. The achievement-oriented consumer society standardizes tastes and career patterns. The melting pot worked—and, with nearly one in ten U.S. residents an immigrant, is still working—but not perfectly. Many Americans retain subculture distinctions in religion and cuisine, but these may not be politically important. Asian Americans integrated rapidly into the U.S. mainstream. Now some 5 percent of the total U.S. population, they hold several of the 535 elected seats on Capitol Hill.

Not all American groups have been so fortunate. Blacks and Hispanics are not fully integrated, but this too is changing. Now, with 13 percent of the population, African Americans hold about 10 percent of the seats of the House of Representatives.

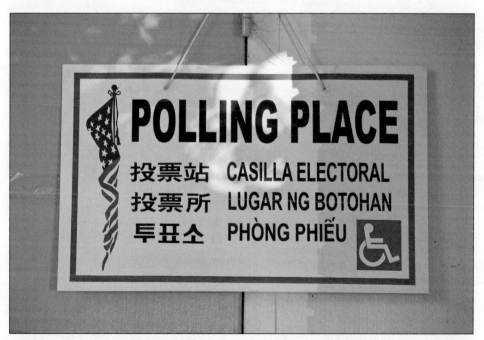

A multilingual sign in California emphasizes the multicultural character of the population of that state. In an effort to promote cultural unity, Californians voted in 1986 to make English the state's only official language. (Ted Soqui/Corbis)

francophone A French speaker.

marginalized Pushed to the edge of society and the economy, often said of the poor and of subcultures.

anglophone An English speaker.

The election of Barack Obama, who had a mother from Kansas and a Kenyan father, helped psychologically integrate African Americans. His election marked a turning point in national integration that Catholics achieved only with John F. Kennedy in 1960.

Should integration be hastened? This has been one of the great questions of post–World War II U.S. politics. With the 1954 *Brown v. Board of Education of Topeka* decision, the Supreme Court began a major federal effort to integrate U.S. schools. It encountered massive resistance. In some instances, federal judges had to take control of local school systems to enforce integration by busing. The integrationist Kennedy and Johnson administrations argued that the United States, in its struggle against communism, could not field a good army or offer an example of freedom and justice to the rest of the world if some Americans were oppressed and poor. Integration was portrayed as a matter of national security.

COMPARING ■ QUEBEC: "MAÎTRES CHEZ NOUS"

The French arrived in North America about the same time the English did, but France was more interested in the lucrative fur trade than in colonization and sent few French settlers; as a result, the population of New France stayed tiny compared with that of the English colonies to the south. The two empires collided in the French and Indian War, which essentially ended when the British conquered Quebec City in 1759. After the historic battle on the Plains of Abraham—which was actually quite small with only a handful killed, including both commanders—the English let the French Canadians keep their language and Roman Catholic religion. It was a magnanimous gesture, but it meant that two centuries later Canada faced a Quebec separatist movement.

Culturally and politically, Quebec province fell asleep for two centuries, an island of tradition in an otherwise dynamic North America. Quebec missed the French Revolution and thus stayed far more conservative than France. Quebec has been called "France without the Revolution." English speakers led the economy, and Montreal became a mostly English-speaking city. Many **francophones** became **marginalized**, living as poor and isolated farmers in their own province. An unstated deal was struck: **Anglophones** would run the economy while francophones, a majority of Quebec's population, would obey local politicians and the Catholic Church.

In the 1960s, Quebec woke up in a "Quiet Revolution." Francophone attitudes shifted dramatically, away from traditional politicians and the priests. It was almost as if a new generation of Québécois said: "You have held us down and backward long enough. We want to be modern, rich, and *maîtres chez nous* (masters in our own house)." Out of this massive shift of values emerged the Parti Québécois (PQ) of René Levesque (pronounced Leveck) with its demand to separate Quebec from Canada. The PQ argued that Quebec really is a different culture and was tired of being under the thumb of English-speaking Canada.

The PQ and related Bloc Québécois became the province's largest parties. A 1980 referendum on separation failed 60–40 percent, but a 1995 referendum failed only by a whisker. Since then, Quebec separatism has subsided, and the PQ's vote has declined. Quebeckers simply got tired of the issue. For Americans, Quebec served as an example of what goes wrong with bilingualism and multiculturalism: They can lead to national fragmentation.

By the same token, should language integration be forced? Should African Americans abandon
black dialect in favor of standard English, and should
Hispanics learn English? If they do not, they will be

socialization The learning of
culture.

severely handicapped their whole lives, especially in employment. But some
blacks, Hispanics, and Native Americans cling to their language as a statement
of ethnic identity and pride. The U.S. Constitution does not specify any national
language, nor does it outlaw languages other than English. In some areas of the
United States, signs and official documents are in both English and Spanish. In
1986, California voters approved a measure making English the state's official
language by a wide margin. People could, of course, continue to speak what they
wished, but official documents and ballots would be in English only. In 1998,
California voted to end bilingual education in order to speed the assimilation of
subcultures. California is often an indicator of nationwide trends, and other states
passed similar laws.

POLITICAL SOCIALIZATION

In the **socialization** process, children acquire what are often lifelong manners and
speech patterns. Although some is formally taught, most is absorbed by imitating
others. In the same way, political socialization teaches political values and specific

---

KEY CONCEPTS ■ CULTURE AND DEVELOPMENT

The recent economic growth of East Asia
brought cultural explanations of why some
countries stay poor while others get rich. Japan,
South Korea, Taiwan, Hong Kong, and Singapore have no natural resources, but they do
have disciplined people who work hard, save
their money, and trust each other. (Most also
turned into democracies.) Some point to their
common Confucian heritage, which promotes
such values. China, the origin of Confucianism, has enjoyed incredible economic growth
recently. The Middle East, on the other hand,
has rigidly Islamic people who do not trust each
other. Its oil wealth has brought only superficial
modernization, no democracy, and the world's
highest unemployment.

A century ago, Max Weber argued that Protestantism laid down the cultural basis of capitalism. A "Protestant work ethic" pushed people
to work hard and amass capital. The Protestant
countries of northwest Europe were the first
capitalist and democratic nations. Even today,
these countries are rich, have high levels of
trust and rule of law, and have little corruption.
Countries lacking this culture, such as Rwanda or Egypt, do not take quickly to economic
growth or democracy.

According to the cultural theory of prosperity, countries will stay poor until they rid themselves of traditionalism, mistrust, and fatalism,
all prominent in the Middle East. Without a
shift of values, outside aid often disappears
into corruption. Critics of the cultural theory
point out that decades ago Confucianism
was blamed for keeping East Asia *backward*
and that values often change *after* economic
growth has taken hold. No one has been able
to predict which countries will grow rapidly
based on their culture or anything else; it's
always a surprise.

overt socialization Deliberate government policy to teach culture.	usages. Learning to pledge allegiance to the flag, to sing the national anthem, and to obey authority figures from presidents to police officers is imparted by families, friends, teachers, and television. Children raised in

cultural ghettoes, such as minorities in America's inner cities, pick up subcultures that are sometimes at odds with mainstream culture. Political socialization is thus crucial to stable government.

The Agents of Socialization

The Family What children encounter earliest—the family—usually outweighs all other factors. Attempts at **overt socialization** by government and schools generally fail if their values are at odds with family orientations. Communist countries, such as Poland, had this problem: The regime tried to inculcate socialist values in a child, but the family taught the child to ignore these messages. Where family and government values are generally congruent, as in the United States, the two modes of socialization reinforce one another.

Parents influence our political behavior for decades. Most people vote as their parents did. More basically, the family forms the psychological makeup of individuals, which in turn determines many of their political attitudes. It imparts norms, values, beliefs, and attitudes such as party attachment and trust or cynicism about government. The early years have the strongest effect, especially from ages 3 to 13. Children accept parental values unconsciously and uncritically and may retain them all their lives. People often give back to the world as adults what they got from it as children. One study found that people with authoritarian personalities had been treated roughly as children. Almond and Verba found that those who remembered having had a voice in family decisions as children had a greater adult sense of political efficacy.

The School More deliberate socialization occurs in school. Most governments use history to inculcate children with pride and patriotism. Many African nations try

CLASSIC WORKS ■ THE AUTHORITARIAN PERSONALITY

One of the boldest attempts to link individual character traits with political attitudes was a 1950 book—*The Authoritarian Personality*, by Theodore Adorno and others, mostly refugees from Nazi Germany. Based heavily on the Freudian theory that personality is laid down in early childhood, Adorno and his colleagues devised a 29-item questionnaire that allegedly showed pre-fascist political views, hence its name, the F-Scale. Persons who scored high on it were conventional in lifestyle to the point of rigidity; were intolerant, prejudiced, and hostile toward outsiders and minorities; submitted to and liked power; and were superstitious and mystical. The Adorno study attracted great interest but was soon criticized over its methodology and its direct connection of personality and politics. Many people have all or some of the F-Scale's characteristics but are good democrats. Although it has faded from view, some still find the study accurate and insightful.

to unify their tribes, usually with different languages and histories, by teaching in French or English about a mythical past when they were a great and united nation. It often does not work, as seen recently in the Congo (formerly Zaire). Communist nations also used schools to inculcate support for the regime. As we saw in 1989, though, this effort failed; family and church overrode the attempts of schools to make East Europeans into believing Communists. U.S. schools did a brilliant job of turning immigrants from many lands into one nation, something critics of bilingual education say must be restored.

The amount of schooling also affects political attitudes. Uniformly, people with many years of education show a stronger sense of responsibility to their community and feel more able to influence public policy than do less-educated citizens. Persons with more schooling are more participatory. College graduates are more tolerant and open-minded, especially on questions of race, than high-school dropouts, who are often parochial in outlook. Education imparts more open-minded attitudes, and educated people generally enjoy higher incomes and status, which by themselves encourage interest and participation.

Peer Groups Friends and playmates also form political values. For example, working-class children in Jamaica who went to school with children of higher social classes tended to take on the political attitudes of those classes, but when they attended school with working-class peers, their attitudes did not change. The relative strength of peer-group influence appears to be growing. With both parents working, children may be socialized more by peers than by families. Upholders of "family values" see this as the underlying cause of youthful drug-taking and violence.

COMPARING ■ CHINA BUILDS UNITY

China, like France, is an example of overt political socialization through education, one that seems to be working. Chinese intellectuals have for centuries stressed that China is one country and must not be broken up. China's many languages, however, work against this. The Cantonese of the south, for example, do not understand the Mandarin of the north. (And there are many dialects within each group.) A century ago, even under the tottering Empire, Beijing began a movement to make *Putonghua* ("common language"), a type of Mandarin, the national language.

It made little headway until the Communists required Putonghua in all schools and use it on television. Now most educated mainland Chinese can speak it, although they may not use it much in daily life. For the first time in history, you can get by with one language in most of China (but not in Hong Kong or Macau, where Cantonese still reigns). The common language helps cement China together.

Adding to this, Chinese are well aware and proud of their record-setting economic growth. The 2008 Beijing Olympics were deliberately calculated to boost Chinese pride. The spiffed-up capital, the extravaganza of the opening and closing ceremonies, and the gold medals won made Chinese (even Hong Kongese and Macanese) proud of their country and see it as a unified whole. The old ideal of one China may at last turn into a reality.

The Mass Media   Gaining in influence are the mass media, especially television. Many fear the influence is negative. Harvard political scientist Robert Putnam argued that heavy TV watching makes people passive and uninterested in community or group activities. As American children watch thousands of hours of television (the "plug-in babysitter") a year, they witness myriad crimes and murders. Some critics charge this tends to make them heartless and violent, but this has not been proven. TV reaches kids early; even 3-year-olds can recognize the president on television and understand that he is a sort of "boss" of the nation. Senators and members of Congress receive much less and less-respectful TV coverage, a view the children may hold the rest of their lives.

As with schools, the mass media may be unsuccessful if their messages are at odds with what family and religion teach. Even Soviet researchers found that families were much bigger influences on individuals' political views than the Soviet mass media. Iran's mass media, all controlled by the shah, tried to inculcate loyalty to him, but believing Muslims took the word of their local *mullahs* in the mosques and hated the shah. Now, ironically, with Iran's media controlled by Islamist conservatives, most Iranians believe the opposite of what the press feeds them. Mass media alone cannot do everything.

The Government   The government itself is an agent of socialization, especially if it delivers rising living standards. Many government activities are intended to explain or display the government to the public, always designed to build support and loyalty. Great spectacles, such as the 2008 Beijing Olympics, have a strengthening effect, as do parades with flags and soldiers, and proclamations of top leaders. The power of government to control political attitudes is limited, however, because messages and experiences reach individuals through conversations with primary groups of kin or peers, who put their own spin on messages. Alienated groups may socialize their children to dislike the government and ignore its messages.

mypoliscikit EXERCISES

Apply what you learned in this chapter on MyPoliSciKit (www.mypoliscikit.com).

Assessment   Review this chapter using learning objectives, chapter summaries, practice tests, and more.

Flashcards   Learn the key terms in this chapter; you can test yourself by term or definition.

Video   Analyze recent world affairs by watching streaming video from major news providers.

Comparative Exercises   Compare political ideas, behaviors, institutions, and policies worldwide.

KEY TERMS

anglophone (p. 130)
cynical (p. 121)
francophone (p. 130)
integration (p. 128)
mainstream (p. 128)
marginalized (p. 130)
overt socialization (p. 132)

parochial (p. 123)
participatory (p. 122)
political competence
(p. 122)
political efficacy (p. 122)
rule of anticipated
reactions (p. 123)

secular (p. 124)
socialization (p. 131)
subculture (p. 126)
subject (p. 123)
turnout (p. 123)
values (p. 120)

FURTHER REFERENCE

Alexander, Jeffrey C. *The Civil Sphere.* New York: Oxford University Press, 2007.

Blondel, Jean, and Takashi Inoguchi. *Political Cultures in Asia and Europe: Citizens, States and Societal Values.* New York: Routledge, 2006.

Brewer, Mark D., and Jeffrey M. Stonecash. *Split: Class and Cultural Divides in American Politics.* Washington, DC: CQ Press, 2007.

Brogan, Hugh. *Alexis de Tocqueville: A Life.* New Haven, CT: Yale University Press, 2007.

Buruma, Ian. *Taming the Gods: Religion and Democracy on Three Continents.* Princeton, NJ: Princeton University Press, 2010.

Carr, Craig L. *Polity: Political Culture and the Nature of Politics.* Lanham, MD: Rowman & Littlefield, 2007.

Damrosch, Leo. *Tocqueville's Discovery of America.* New York: Farrar, Straus & Giroux, 2010.

Diamond, Larry, and Marc F. Plattner, eds. *How People View Democracy.* Baltimore, MD: Johns Hopkins University Press, 2008.

Hunter, James Davison, and Alan Wolfe. *Is There a Culture War?: A Dialogue on Values and American Public Life.* Washington, DC: Brookings, 2006.

Huntington, Samuel P. *Who Are We?: The Challenge to America's National Identity.* New York: Simon & Schuster, 2004.

Lane, Jan-Erik, and Svante Ersson. *Culture and Politics: A Competitive Approach,* 2nd ed. Williston, VT: Ashgate, 2005.

Perlstein, Rick. *Nixonland: The Rise of a President and the Fracturing of America.* New York: Simon & Schuster, 2007.

Putnam, Robert D., and David E. Campbell. *American Grace: How Religion Divides and Unites Us.* New York: Simon & Schuster, 2010.

Riley-Smith, Tristram. *The Cracked Bell: America and the Afflictions of Liberty.* New York: Skyhorse, 2010.

Rimmerman, Craig A. *The New Citizenship: Unconventional Politics, Activism, and Service,* 3rd ed. Boulder, CO: Westview, 2005.

Seabright, Paul. *Company of Strangers: A Natural History of Economic Life.* Princeton, NJ: Princeton University Press, 2004.

Warren, Mark E., ed. *Democracy and Trust.* New York: Cambridge University Press, 1999.

Westen, Drew. *The Political Brain: The Role of Emotion in Deciding the Fate of the Nation.* New York: PublicAffairs, 2008.

Wiseman, Nelson. *In Search of Canadian Political Culture.* Vancouver, BC: University of British Colombia Press, 2007.

Public Opinion

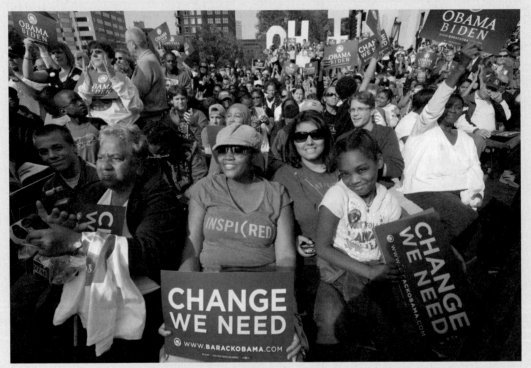

The candidacy of Barack Obama showed a major shift in U.S. public opinion. Here, Obama supporters meet in Columbus, OH. (Peter Turnley/Corbis)

In 2008, as the U.S. financial meltdown threatened to unleash a major recession, economists, bankers, congresspersons, and a Republican president and Fed chief agreed on the need for a federal program to urgently loan billions to giant firms. But this was an *elite* (see Chapter 6) consensus, and at first the public did not know how to react; it was far beyond most Americans' expertise. By 2010, however, a majority opposed the bailouts—even though they had staved off a depression and were being repaid—and threatened electoral punishment against those who had voted for them, including Republicans. Particularly irksome were the massive bonuses financial chiefs gave themselves.

QUESTIONS TO CONSIDER

1. Does government follow or create public opinion?
2. How important is religion in forming U.S. opinion?
3. What is the theory of *political generations*?
4. What are the three classic opinion curves?
5. Why did the *Literary Digest* miscall the 1936 election?
6. Why did polls miscall the 1948 election?
7. What is a random sample?
8. What does presidential "popularity" really measure?
9. What is intensity and volatility?

The episode illustrated a number of points about **public opinion**. There is a big gap between elite and mass opinion. The mass public does not understand much about complicated choices but can react later, in this case lashing out at perceived unfairness. Public opinion can be poorly informed and angry—a poor basis for sound policy. The issue reopened a very old question of who should govern, experts who understand such complex matters or average citizens? Most political scientists are cautious about giving public opinion a leading role in governance.

Public opinion is important in a democracy, as elections provide only a crude expression of the public's will. Elections may indicate what voters generally think of a candidate overall but rarely focus on specific issues. Public opinion surveys fill in the details so officials know what people think about specific problems, such as health care or a war. Public opinion can thus be seen as a backup and detailing device for inputting mass views into politics, a way to fine-tune elections.

Officials often try to create the public opinion they desire by addressing the nation through the media. When Richard Nixon announced in 1971 that he would be the first president to visit China, Americans quickly became more favorable toward China. Spanish Prime Minister Felipe González, head of a party that opposed NATO, changed his mind and supported Spain's affiliation, although polls

public opinion Citizens' reactions to current, specific issues and events.

anecdotal Recounting the views of a few respondents.

showed that most Spaniards were against it. González urged support for NATO in a 1986 referendum, and Spaniards swung around to support him. British socialist Beatrice Webb long ago said: "There is no such thing as spontaneous public opinion. It all has to be manufactured from a center of conviction and energy."

Public opinion is often led or manipulated by interest groups. Bringing grievances to public attention, especially when the media watches, can generate widespread sympathy. The televised brutality of sheriffs' deputies in Selma, Alabama, toward blacks demanding the right to vote turned public opinion in favor of the Voting Rights Act of 1965.

Any government is vulnerable to public opinion. Mahatma Gandhi, by simple dramas of nonviolent protest, used public opinion to win independence for India. A gaunt, bespectacled old man in a loincloth, he led protests, wove his own

KEY CONCEPTS ■ WHAT PUBLIC OPINION IS—AND ISN'T

Political culture and public opinion are linked but are not the same. Political culture focuses on long-standing values, attitudes, and ideas that people learn deeply. Most Americans firmly believe that government power is potentially tyrannical and must be controlled and that democracy is the only just form of government. Public opinion concerns people's reactions to specific and immediate policies and problems, such as sending troops overseas or voting intentions.

Public opinion is not the same as individual opinion. A woman's opinion of her neighbor's religion would not be part of public opinion, but her feeling on prayer in public schools would. Public opinion refers to political and social issues, not private matters. **Anecdotal** evidence is a poor indication of public opinion, as we have no way of knowing if it is representative. Beware of the journalistic "one-person cross-section" of opinion.

Public opinion does not necessarily imply that citizens have strong, clear, or united convictions; such unity is rare. So-called public opinion often involves several small, conflicting groups, plus many who are undecided, plus an even larger number with no interest or opinion on the matter. On most subjects, public opinion is an array of diverse attitudes that can change quickly.

Public opinion sometimes shows widespread ignorance. A 2000 poll found that 71 percent of Americans were unaware there was a federal budget surplus, and 56 percent had no idea who Alan Greenspan was. (The influential chairman of the Federal Reserve Board, now retired. But you knew that, right?) Some respondents manufacture answers in order to sound well-informed. A 1948 poll found that 59 percent of Americans said the (fake) "Metallic Metals Act" would be a good thing but should be left up to the states. Many people are poorly informed. After three years of news reports to the contrary, a 2006 Harris Poll found that half of Americans still thought Iraq had weapons of mass destruction in the 2003 war. And 64 percent said Saddam Hussein had "strong links" with al Qaeda.

So, should survey numbers make policy? Most Americans are opposed to raising taxes on gasoline. Does that mean government should never do it? Should elected leaders always bow to public opinion? President Truman shrugged off public opinion and was vilified for it. Decades later, many celebrated him as a leader who did the right thing without fear of disapproval. Some say current politicians pay too much attention to public opinion. If you are always following, how can you lead?

cloth, and threatened to starve himself to death if the British did not quit India. The movement Gandhi created became so powerful the British had to give India independence in 1947.

Government by sheer violence and coercion cannot last long. Even Stalin's Soviet Union, with all its brutal apparatus for suppressing dissent, depended first on the dream of a classless utopia and on Russian patriotism to repel the Nazi invader, and only secondly on the security police. After Stalin died in 1953, the regime turned to incentives and propaganda to keep up a veneer of legitimacy, which collapsed quickly in 1989 in East Europe and then in the Soviet Union itself in late 1991. Ultimately, lack of public support ended these regimes.

salience   Literally, that which jumps out; the importance of given issues in public opinion or the characteristics of the public holding various opinions.

social class   A broad layer of society, usually based on income and often labeled lower, middle, and upper.

THE SHAPE OF PUBLIC OPINION

Social scientists find roughly who thinks what about politics. No social category, of course, is ever 100 percent for or against something. Indeed, 60 or 70 percent is often quite high. What we look for are differences among social categories, the significance of which can be tested by the rules of statistics. We look for shades of gray, not for black and white. Once we have found significant differences, we may be able to say something about **salience**, the degree to which categories and issues affect the public opinion of a country. In Scandinavia, for example, social class is salient in structuring party preferences: The working class tends to vote Social Democratic, and the middle class votes for more conservative parties. In Latin Europe, social class is weakly salient, with the working class scattering its vote among parties of the left, right, and center. In Latin Europe, religion and region are typically most salient. In the United States, religion and urban–rural differences are salient.

Social Class

Karl Marx saw **social class** as massively salient. Workers, he predicted, would become socialists. Actually, only some of them did, but social class does matter, even in the relatively classless United States. Over the decades, the American manual worker has tended to vote Democratic; the better-off person has tended to vote Republican. But these are only tendencies, and they are often muddied by other factors. Poor people are often very conservative on religious and social issues, and affluent people can be liberal or even radical. During hard times, when bread-and-butter issues, such as jobs, become salient, the American working class tends to rediscover the Democratic Party, as it did in 1992. When these issues lose their salience, however, the working class often focuses on noneconomic issues such as gun control, morality (abortion, gay rights), or leadership in war.

Social class can be hard to measure. There are two general ways: the objective and the subjective. An objective determination involves asking people their

noneconomic issues Questions relating to patriotism, religion, race, sexuality, and personal choice.

economic issues Questions relating to jobs, income, taxes, and welfare benefits.

annual income or judging the quality of the neighborhood. The subjective determination involves simply asking respondents what their social class is, which sometimes diverges from objective criteria. A majority of Americans call themselves middle class, even if they are not. Sometimes even wealthy people, thinking of their modest origins, call themselves middle class.

The way a person earns a living may matter more than the amount he or she makes. Typically, American farmers are conservative, and miners and steelworkers are not. Different political attitudes grow up around different jobs.

Sometimes social class works in precisely the opposite way envisioned by Marx. Highly educated professionals make some affluent U.S. suburbs quite liberal compared with the conservatism of poorer country dwellers. Spanish researchers found an *inverse* relationship between social class and preferring the left; that is, better-off persons were more leftist than poorer Spaniards. In the Spanish study, education was most salient.

Class matters, especially in combination with other factors, such as region or religion. In Britain, class plus region structures much of the vote; in France, it is class plus region plus religiosity (practicing Catholic versus nonpracticing); in Germany, it is class plus region plus denomination (Catholic or Protestant). As Yale's Joseph LaPalombara put it, the question is "Class plus what?"

America in the decades after World War II had a relatively equitable division of income that made most citizens middle class. In the late twentieth century, however, incomes grew more unequal. The income gap between those with a bachelor's degree or higher and those with a high school diploma or less grew from 31 percent in 1979 to close to double in 2006. The share of income of the top 0.1 percent increased greatly while factory workers had their jobs outsourced. Some feared this polarization was turning America into a class society. Social class is taking on renewed salience as the disadvantaged demand curbs on both foreign imports and immigrants.

Education

Educational level is related to social class, and this contributes to the polarization. Some of those with college degrees win big bucks in information technology and finance; those without have to scramble. The better off give their children more and better education, in effect passing on their class position and slowing the social mobility that allowed many Americans to rise during the postwar years.

Education in the United States often has a split political impact, making people more liberal on **noneconomic issues** but more conservative on **economic issues**. Survey data show that college-educated people are more tolerant, favor civil rights, and understand different viewpoints. But on economic issues, many of them are skeptical of efforts to redistribute income by higher taxes on the upper brackets— which happen to be them—and welfare measures. There are, to be sure, some educated people who are consistently liberal on both economic and noneconomic

questions, but in the United States the categories sometimes diverge. The same is often true of the American
working class: Its members want higher wages but
can be intolerant in the areas of race, lifestyle, and
patriotism. Middle-class college youths protesting the

regions   Portions of a country
with a sense of self and sometimes
subcultural differences.

Vietnam War ran into the snarls and fists of unionized construction workers, an
illustration of the split between economic and noneconomic liberalism.

Region

Every country has a south, goes an old saw, and this is true in politics. It is uncertain, however, whether a country's south is more conservative or more leftist than
its north. France south of the Loire River and Spain south of the Tagus have for
generations gone left. The south of Italy, though, is conservative, as is Bavaria in
Germany's south. In Great Britain, England is heavily conservative, whereas Scotland and Wales go for Labour. The U.S. South was famous for decades as the "solid
South," which went automatically Democratic but now is mostly Republican.

A country's outlying **regions** usually harbor resentment against the capital,
creating what are called *center–periphery tensions* (see Chapter 4). Often an outlying region was brought into the nation by force and has never been happy about
it. Regional memories can last for centuries. This is true of Quebec and Scotland
and the southern parts of the United States, France, and Italy. Often the region

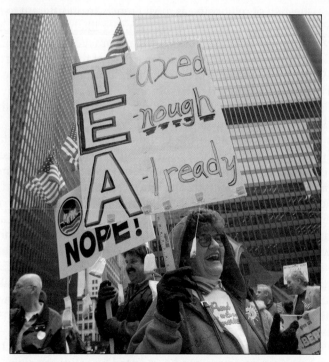

The sudden rise of the Tea Party illustrates volatility in public opinion.
(UPI/Landov)

anticlericalism Movement in Catholic countries to get Church out of politics.

feels economically disadvantaged by the central area. The region may have a different language, as in Spain's Catalonia and the Basque country, Wallonia in Belgium (the French-speaking south), Quebec, Slovenia in ex-Yugoslavia, and several parts of India.

Once a region gets set in its politics, it stays that way for a long time. Region plays a big role in the politics of Britain, France, Germany, and the United States. Most "sunbelt" states in the U.S. South and West (but not California) are conservative on both economic and noneconomic issues and jealous of states' rights. The "frostbelt" of northern and eastern states, where industry has declined, tends to be liberal, especially on questions of government spending programs. In 2001, when President Bush cut taxes, some conservative, southern Democrats supported him, and some liberal, northern Republicans opposed him, illustrating the effects of region on U.S. politics. In the United States, region can trump party.

Religion

Religion is often the most explosive issue in politics and contributes a great deal to the structuring of opinion. Religion can mean either denomination or religiosity. In Germany, Catholics tend to vote Christian Democrat, Protestants Social Democrat. Here it is a question of denomination. In France, where most citizens are baptized Catholic, it is a question of religiosity, as most French are indifferent to religion. The more often a French person goes to Mass, the more likely he or she is to vote for a conservative party. Few Communist voters are practicing Catholics. In Poland, the Roman Catholic Church encouraged Poles to oust the Communist regime and support pro-Church parties. One of the biggest divisions in Catholic countries is between clericalists and **anticlericalists**. France, Italy, and Spain have long been split over this issue, with the conservative parties pro-Church and the parties of the left hostile to church influence.

Religion plays a major role in the United States, where Protestants tend to vote Republican. Religion overlaps with ethnicity. Catholics, especially Polish Catholics, were once among the most loyal Democrats. In the great immigrations of a century ago, big-city Democratic machines welcomed and helped immigrants from Catholic countries, and their descendants stayed mostly Democratic, but this eroded as the Democratic Party endorsed "pro-choice" positions. For a long time it was believed that no Catholic could be elected president; John F. Kennedy in 1960 put that view to rest. In 2004, however, Catholic John F. Kerry lost many Catholic votes when the clergy denounced him for being pro-choice. Many Catholics and fundamentalist Protestants now have a common cause in fighting abortion. The 2000 vice-presidential candidacy of Senator Joseph Lieberman (now a Connecticut independent), an observant Jew, aroused little attention or opposition—a measure of the increased tolerance of Americans.

The rise of the "religious right" in the 1980s was important to U.S. politics. Roughly one American in seven can be counted as religious right, and fundamentalist groups became highly political. Televangelists such as Jerry Falwell mobilized their flocks against pornography, abortion, and gay rights—and for Republicans. The Christian Coalition became a major force inside the Republican Party. Bush 43, himself an evangelical, won with fundamentalist votes, most of whom stayed with McCain in 2008.

life cycle   Theory that opinions change as people age.

political generations   Theory that great events of young adulthood permanently color political views.

gender gap   Tendency of American women to vote more Democratic than do men.

American candidates, especially for the presidency, like to be known as churchgoers, but since the rise of fundamentalism many also wish to be known as "born-again" Christians. Jimmy Carter, Ronald Reagan, and both Bushes claimed to have been born again in Christ. Presidents and spouses attend church most Sundays, often with the president clutching a family Bible. There are few avowed atheists in U.S. politics.

Age

There are two theories on how age affects political opinions, the **life cycle** and generation theories. The first, widely accepted, holds that people change as they age. Thus, young people are naturally radical and older people moderate or even conservative. With few responsibilities, young people can be idealistic and rebellious, but with the burdens of home, job, taxes, and children of their own, people tend to become conservative. In 2008, young voters went strongly to Obama.

This life cycle theory does not always work because sometimes whole generations are marked for life by the great events of their young adulthood. Survivors of wars and depressions remember them for decades, and these experiences color their views on war, economics, and politics. German sociologist Karl Mannheim called this phenomenon **political generations**. Many who lived through the Vietnam War were instinctively critical of the U.S. war in Iraq. Those who personally experienced the Depression of the 1930s were more supportive of federal welfare measures than younger people who had been raised in postwar prosperity. In the 2004 elections, those 75 and older were the strongest age group for Kerry, who vowed to maintain their Social Security and Medicare. Aging does not necessarily make one conservative.

Gender

Even before the women's movement, gender made a difference in politics. Traditionally, and especially in Catholic countries, women were more conservative, more concerned with home, family, and morality. But as a society modernizes, men's and women's views change. Women leave home to work, become more aware of social and economic problems, and express their own political views. In the United States, a **gender gap** appeared in the 1980s as women became several percentage points more liberal and Democratic than men. And this was precisely because women had found the federal government necessary to support home and family. Further, many women disliked the Republican emphasis on war. In 1996, 2000, and 2008, women were more than 10 percentage points more likely to vote Democrat for president

skewed A distribution with its peak well to one side.

unimodal A single, center-peaked distribution; a bell-shaped curve.

bimodal A distribution with two large clusters at the extremes and a small center.

polarize To drive opinion into a *bimodal* distribution.

than were men. It may be that, in the modern political world, women will be the natural liberals.

Ethnic Group

Ethnicity is related to region and religion but sometimes plays a distinct role of its own, especially in the multiethnic United States, where some ethnic groups form political subcultures (see previous chapter). America was long touted as a "melting

KEY CONCEPTS ■ CLASSIC OPINION CURVES

The ways people feel about issues are summarized statistically in curves that show the distribution of opinions on a range from one extreme position to the other. A matter on which there are few doubters shows opinions **skewed** to one side, a "J-curve." Few Americans, for example, did not wish to destroy Islamist terrorists after September 11 (see chart at top of right column).

On many issues, public opinion forms the familiar "bell-shaped curve," or **unimodal** distribution, which shows few people at the extremes and most in the moderate center. All industrialized democracies show ideological distributions with few extreme leftists or rightists and a big bulge in the center (see chart at middle of right column).

A third characteristic pattern is a **bimodal** distribution, or "U-curve," where the extremes are bigger than the center (see chart at bottom of right column). In 2008 most Democrats opposed the war in Iraq, and most Republicans supported it, with few in the center. The war was a **polarizing** issue in U.S. politics (see chart at bottom of right column).

Bell-shaped opinion curves are the basis of democracy. If many citizens take extreme positions and form a U-curve, the political system can break down. This can lead to extremist takeovers as in Germany in 1933, to civil war as in Spain in 1936, or to a military coup as in Chile in 1973. Almost all democratic countries have unimodal distributions of opinion on basic issues; that is, people cluster in the center. Democracy is a centrist thing.

Stable Curve

"Should we go to war against terrorism?"

For   Against

Bell-Shaped Curve

"Where do you place yourself ideologically: left, right, or center?"

Left   Center   Right

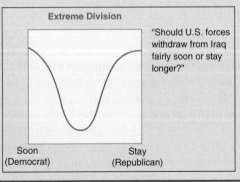

Extreme Division

"Should U.S. forces withdraw from Iraq fairly soon or stay longer?"

Soon   Stay
(Democrat)   (Republican)

pot" of immigrant groups, but ethnic consciousness
lasts many generations. American politics is often
described in ethnic terms, with WASPs (white An-
glo-Saxon Protestants) and other northern Europeans generally conservative
and Republican, and people of southern and eastern European origin, blacks,
Hispanics, and Asians more liberal and Democratic. This oversimplifies the
complexity of individuals and of politics, but many working politicians still
use it as a guide.

survey	A public opinion poll.

Ethnic politics changes over the decades. After the Civil War, most blacks were
Republican, the party of Lincoln. With Franklin D. Roosevelt and the New Deal,
most African Americans became Democrats and stayed that way. In the nineteenth
century, American Jews were mostly Republican, for the Republicans criticized
the anti-Semitic repression of tsarist Russia. The Jewish immigrants of the turn
of the century—introduced to U.S. politics by Democratic machines such as New
York's Tammany Hall—went Democratic. More recently, some Jews, influenced
by neoconservatism (see Chapter 3), swung to the Republicans. Ethnic politics is
not fixed in concrete.

PUBLIC OPINION POLLS

People can be for, against, or undecided about an issue. But the factors of
uncertainty and changeability are so prominent in many areas that we cannot be
totally confident when polls report percent for and against. Do not blindly follow
poll data.

Opinion distribution does not often fall into well-defined patterns, mainly
because most people most of the time pay little attention to politics. They have weak
interest in issues that do not directly touch them and acquire no information about
most issues. Most surveys, for example, find that nearly half of those questioned
cannot name their representative in Congress.

Thus, on most issues, only a small portion of the total public is attentive enough
to news reports and editorials to hold a clear opinion. Reported public opinion
will often be a rather dim reflection of the opinion pattern within this "attentive
public." With all of the uncertainties, personality quirks, and just plain ignorance
involved in public opinion, how are surveys able to reflect an accurate picture of
what people are thinking?

Popularly known as a "public opinion poll," asking a representative sample for
their views is called a **survey**. Published surveys, particularly in election years, are
carefully watched. Almost daily we see statistics and percentages on what Americans
think of war, unemployment, health care, and candidates. This is useful for policymakers and candidates. But debate has developed over some of their political side
effects. For example, do the polls give undue attention and influence to uncertain
opinions? Do journalists create self-fulfilling prophecies by treating the polls as authoritative verdicts? Should public opinion surveys be treated as a fair and democratic
method of deciding public policies? Are polls reliable enough to determine policy?
Who uses surveys, what purpose do they serve, and can we trust them?

quota Drawing a sample to match categories of the population.

sample Those persons to be interviewed in a survey, a small fraction of a population.

Polling Techniques

How can a sample of 1,000 people depict the opinions of 200 million potential voters? The answer is complex, but it revolves around a technique that can be summarized as follows.

Selecting the Sample In deciding whom to sample, the pollster has two major approaches. One, the stratified **quota** sampling, tries to include a proportionally representative cross section of the society. This is very difficult to carry out because interviewers must question precisely x number of blue-collar workers, y number of older women, and z number of Republicans. If they query too many or too few of various groups, they lose proportionality.

The second major approach is a random sample with no picking and choosing among dozens of categories. In a truly random sample, the number of blue collar workers (or any other category) interviewed will be very close to their percentage of

KEY CONCEPTS ■ A SHORT HISTORY OF POLLING

In 1824, the *Harrisburg Pennsylvanian* asked passersby whether they would vote for John Quincy Adams or Andrew Jackson. They called the very unscientific poll "straws in the wind." Other newspapers, using both careful and haphazard methods, conducted "straw polls" in elections thereafter. The popular magazine *Literary Digest* developed a prestigious survey that predicted the 1924, 1928, and 1932 presidential elections. The *Literary Digest*, using a huge sample on the theory that it was more reliable, mailed questionnaires to nearly 10 million of its subscribers, car owners, and people in phone books. In 1936, the magazine predicted Republican Alfred M. Landon would win with 59.1 percent of the vote. Roosevelt's landslide—with more than 60 percent of the vote—signaled the demise of both casual methods of sampling and of *Literary Digest* itself.

But 1936 was also the first year of the newly developed "scientific polling," a branch of another new field, market research. George H. Gallup's survey results, syndicated in newspapers, forecast Roosevelt's victory. Gallup predicted that the *Digest* poll was far off because its sample was drawn heavily from

higher-income people, many of whom were angered by Roosevelt's social and economic policies. The new technique used by Gallup was to select a **sample** as *representative*, rather than as large, as possible.

This scientific sampling method has dominated the field since then, with a generally successful record. But even it failed in the 1948 election, when almost every poll predicted that Thomas E. Dewey would defeat Harry S. Truman by a landslide. Truman won with 49 percent in a four-way contest. The error was in assuming that respondents who said they were undecided would wind up voting in the same ratio as those who had already decided. In fact, the undecideds went much more heavily for Truman—close to 75 percent. The major polls have further refined their methods since that time and today make special efforts to detect late swings. They do not claim to be able to predict divisions within closer than 2 to 3 percentage points. The margin of victory in several presidential elections has been less than 1 percent, so polls cannot confidently predict close elections. Elections such as those of 2000 are called "too close to call."

the population. **Randomization**, done now by computers, produces more dependable results than the quota system.

The most reliable method, "area sampling," has 100 to 200 regular interviewers in different areas around the country who each interview 15 to 20 persons in a designated locality. The sample, which is both random and highly representative, involves selecting which geographic districts to sample, their population characteristics, and random selection of which people to question from various categories. The resulting sample is quite close to that which a completely random selection would obtain and is considerably less expensive.

Reaching the Sample Polling is expensive, and pollsters try to economize. Unfortunately, the least expensive methods tend to be the least accurate. The cheapest is to mail out ballots to a sample, but people who are involved enough to reply will not be representative, the *Literary Digest* error. Telephone polling tries to avoid this problem, but it rarely establishes rapport to obtain candid replies. For telephone surveys, a computer may dial the numbers nationwide at random, even unlisted ones. There are at least two problems with phone surveys: (1) Many people ignore telephone solicitations; and (2) women, the elderly, and unemployed people are the most likely to be home, making the sample nonrandom. Automatic dialing does not call cell phones, so the 2008 polls underpolled young people, who went strongly to Obama. The most dependable method is still the costly face-to-face interview, which requires interviewers to be carefully selected and trained. To cover costs, political questions are often appended to commercial or product questions: "Do you eat Krunchy Flakes?"

Asking the Questions The unbiased wording of questions to avoid slanting responses is also important. In 1999, for example, a *Washington Post*/ABC poll asked half its sample whether President Clinton should resign if impeached or "fight the charges in the Senate." Fifty-nine percent said resign rather than fight. The other half was asked essentially the same question but worded with the alternative of resign or "remain in office and face trial in the Senate." To this, only 43 percent said resign. A slight difference in wording—"fight" sounds nastier than "face trial"—greatly shifted responses. In 1992, answers to a badly worded question (it had a double negative) suggested that one in five Americans doubted the Nazi Holocaust had really happened. When the question was worded clearly in 1994, only 2 percent denied the Holocaust had happened. The pollster must also avoid tones of voice or sympathetic looks that might encourage one response over another and skew the results.

How Reliable Are the Polls?

Public opinion surveys are generally reliable, provided we recognize their limits. Overall, the U.S. opinion-research business takes in several billion dollars a year, and candidates commission thousands of private polls in primary and general elections. Unpredictability of voter turnout is a major limitation of pre-election

volatility Tendency of public opinion to change quickly.

independent variable The factor you think influences or causes something to happen.

dependent variable The factor that changes under the impact of the *independent variable.*

covariance How much two factors change together, indicating how strongly they are related.

polls. Many respondents who say they intend to vote actually do not. These voters and the undecideds are likely not to divide the same way as those who do vote and those already decided. This underlay the mistaken predictions of Truman's defeat in 1948. A heavy turnout may shift election results. Pollsters must adjust raw findings for this factor, but no one can be certain of how high turnout will be or the effects of events such as weather or terrorist strikes.

Public opinion is **volatile**, able to change quickly under the impact of events. In 1965, as Lyndon Johnson escalated the war in Vietnam, an aide told him that "we have overwhelming public opinion on our side." Johnson, a crafty political pro who closely followed the polls, replied, "Yes, but for a very underwhelming period of time." He was right; two-thirds support for the war in 1965 turned into two-thirds opposition in 1968. Roughly the same happened with the war in Iraq: two-thirds for it in 2003 but two-thirds against it by 2006. Americans do not like long, inconclusive wars.

A new problem calls into question all telephone surveys: the high "no response" rate. Americans, harassed by telemarketers, decline or just hang up on callers asking anything. Only a small fraction of those now called respond. With so few answering, the survey is likely not random or representative. Surveys over the Internet have the same problem because respondents are "self-selected" and of above average income

HOW TO ... ■ IDENTIFY AND USE VARIABLES

A variable is a factor that varies; it shows some change. If you can, you quantify these factors. Variables come in two basic types, **independent** and **dependent**. The former is what you think influences or perhaps causes the change, but you cannot always be sure. You might hypothesize, for example, that increases in a country's per capita GDP lead it to democracy. The "per cap" is your independent variable, and democracy is your dependent variable, the one that literally depends on the impact of the other variable.

You might switch the two and make democracy your independent variable to see how it affects wealth. Causality is hard to prove, and the causal flow can go both ways. Some argue that democracy promotes prosperity. In some cases, of course, causality can flow only one way. We can posit "white Protestant male" as the variables leading to a Republican vote, but

we cannot say that voting Republican will turn people into white Protestant males.

If you have two variables with reliable numbers to measure them, you can follow them over time and put two lines on the same graph to show positive **covariance**—as one changes, so does the other—which may go a long way to supporting your thesis. Sometimes you see negative or inverse covariance—as one goes up, the other goes down—but this may still prove your thesis. If there is little or no covariance—if the two lines on a graph wobble around with no relation to each other— you should go back and change your thesis. Sometimes covariance happens with a time lag, giving you a more interesting thesis. For example, the president makes foreign policy decisions, but public opinion reacts to them about six months later.

and education. Any survey that records only those who want to participate is invalid. This may be the main reason the surveys done for the 2000 and 2004 elections did not predict well. (They were better in 2008, overstating Obama's strength only by about 1 percentage point.)

honeymoon High support for presidents early in their terms.

rally event Occurrence that temporarily boosts presidents' support.

AMERICAN OPINION

Presidential Ratings

One of the oldest and most important items in U.S. public opinion polls asks how the president is handling his job, which is not necessarily how much people "like" the president. In practice, however, the respondent who likes the president will approve of the president's job performance, so the term "popularity" is often used for this poll. The correct terms are "support" or "approval."

Typically, presidents start with high support and then decline. During their first year, they enjoy a **honeymoon** with the press and the public. The high point of their support usually comes early in their term. After some years, however, problems accumulate—the economy sours or foreign policies fail. This brings an approval low point. Presidents seldom leave office as popular as they were during their first year.

When a president comes under intense pressure or takes a major action, his support enjoys a temporary upturn or "spike." Americans rally to a president who faces a difficult decision and makes decisive responses. Political scientist John Mueller called these **rally events**. President Carter gained 13 percentage points over the seizure of American hostages in Iran, but he was soon blamed for helplessness and lost reelection the next year. Bush 41 enjoyed an 18-point gain when he began the Gulf War in 1991, but he lost reelection a year and a half later, the casualty of a lingering recession. Bush 43 gained a massive 35 percentage points after 9/11, support that continued through the U.S. conquest of Iraq in 2003 but declined as Iraq dragged on. No rally event has lasted a full year.

Some suspect that presidents, especially later in their terms of office, deliberately try to appear decisive in a dramatic way to boost their sagging popularity. Foreign policy provides for such dramatic moves and (as we will consider in the next chapter) the best television coverage. A meeting with foreign leaders, a bold strike against terrorists, or the rescue of American hostages lifts support for a president. The highest support ratings of Presidents Truman, Kennedy, Nixon, Carter, Reagan, and both Bushes came with a dramatic foreign policy event. Even a failure, the 1961 Bay of Pigs invasion to overthrow Castro, rallied Americans around President Kennedy. When a humiliating situation lasts a long time, however, presidential popularity sinks, as Carter and Reagan both found in dealing with Iran. Similarly, a long war destroys popularity; Truman experienced this in Korea, Johnson in Vietnam, and Bush 43 in Iraq. Economic recession is also bad for popularity; five Republican presidents (Eisenhower, Ford, Reagan, and both Bushes) were rated low during economic downturns, as was Democrat Obama. A good economy is great for presidents; Clinton's approval stayed high in the prosperous late 1990s, even during his impeachment.

attentive public   Those citizens who follow politics, especially national and international affairs.

Presidential approval based on one situation tends to spill over into other areas of presidential activity. As might be expected, President Reagan's support jumped several points in the wake of the successful 1983 U.S. takeover of Communist Grenada and the rescue of American students there. At that same time, approval of Reagan's economic policies also climbed, although little in the economy had actually changed.

Liberals and Conservatives

Republican presidents do not necessarily prove that Americans have become more conservative. For decades, about twice as many Americans have been calling themselves conservative as call themselves liberal, but many still call themselves moderates. Such unimodal distributions—variations on a bell-shaped curve—are standard in all industrialized democracies, a fact that makes democracy possible. Under Reagan and both Bushes, the percentage of Americans identifying themselves as conservatives increased little, and more Americans expressed support for environmental and employment legislation, typically liberal causes. The percentage who think the poverty programs of the 1960s—one of the Republicans' favorite targets—make things better is stable. Americans may like Republican presidents and even call themselves conservative, but they have not repudiated the moderate welfare state. (Many commentators believe the Republicans will not repeal the 2010 healthcare reforms.)

To explain this seeming inconsistency, we return to the difference between *economic* and *noneconomic* liberalism discussed earlier. Americans are not very clear about what they mean by "liberal" or "conservative." Retired people, for example, support Social Security and Medicare—the programs of economic liberals—but many call themselves conservatives because they have traditional values. They use "conservative" in the noneconomic sense. On economic issues, however, such as federal aid for prescription drugs, they (often unwittingly) assume ultra-liberal positions. The problem is self-identification, which often diverges from people's views on specific issues. People who say they are conservative—because where they live it is fashionable to do so—may actually be economic liberals when it comes to getting more federal dollars for themselves.

Who Pays Attention?

Public opinion is fragmented; groups are interested in different questions. Farmers are concerned about crop prices, steel and auto workers about imports, women about wage equality, and minorities about job opportunities. A time when some groups are satisfied may be a time when others are dissatisfied. Blacks and poor people did not much notice the good economic times of the late 1990s; better-off Americans praised the economy.

The **attentive public** (see box on page 151), although fewer in number, has more political impact because they have ideas and articulate them, demonstrating political competence. Sometimes they can rouse the general public. Opposition to the Vietnam and Iraq wars and to South Africa's apartheid started with a few critics who wrote and spoke in churches, newspapers, and colleges. In the early 1990s, while few people were paying attention, some of the attentive public raised concern over atrocities in the Balkans and Africa. The attentive public can act as "spark plugs" for the apathetic and slow-reacting general public.

intensity   The firmness and enthusiasm with which an opinion is held.

This is why all regimes treat intellectuals with caution and sometimes with suspicion. Communist regimes expended great effort to ferret out a handful of dissident intellectuals. In Washington, administration officials devote much time and energy to win over the attentive public to minimize criticism that might influence the general public and the next election. As we will consider in Chapter 9, relations between the White House and the news media are a cat-and-mouse game. Political elites, aware of the ignorance and low interest of the general public, may convince themselves not to pay much attention to public opinion. A 1998 Pew study found that members of Congress, presidential appointees, and senior civil servants believed most Americans do not know enough to form sound opinions on vital issues of the day. Elites, in other words, believe elites must decide questions because they are the only ones following them. Unfortunately for democracy, they may be right.

The general public's indifference and fragmentation mean that their views are often hard to discern and may have little impact on decision making. Elected leaders are apt to pay attention to the group with the most intensely held views. Polls show that most Americans would permit abortion, but few strongly support it. The "pro-life" foes of abortion, although a minority nationwide, feel such great **intensity** about the subject that they often drown out the greater numbers who are not passionately concerned. Jews are only about 2 percent of the U.S. population,

CLASSIC WORKS ■ ALMOND'S THREE PUBLICS

In his 1950 *The American People and Foreign Policy*, political scientist Gabriel Almond proposed that there were three American public opinions, not just one:

1. A *general public* of a majority that does not know or care about much beyond their immediate concerns. For example, they show little interest in foreign policy unless the country is in a war or international crisis.

2. An *attentive public* of a minority who are among the better educated and who follow more abstract political concerns, such as foreign policy. They are the audience the elite plays to; in turn, this attentive public passes on views that mobilize the general public.

3. A *policy and opinion elite* of a few highly influential people who are involved in politics, often professionally. These members of Congress, appointed officials, and top journalists devise foreign and domestic policies and articulate them to the attentive and general publics.

Especially regarding foreign affairs, Almond makes a strong case. The number of Americans who follow the news is decreasing, and surveys show ignorance of world affairs. Attentive and elite opinion—such as business, media, and religious leaders and academics—favored NAFTA, trade expansion, and U.S. missions in the Balkans far more than did the general public.

but among them are such intense supporters of Israel that most elected officials take a pro-Israel stance. Most Americans favor some form of gun control, but they are mostly lukewarm about the issue. The opponents to gun control are red hot and thus quite influential. Intensely held views of a few often override large numbers of indifferent people.

The disproportionate influence of the attentive public and passionate opinion holders underscores one of the problems of public opinion. Often there is little "public" opinion, just the opinions of scattered and small groups who pay attention to issues and care intensely about them. Should their views be excluded as unrepresentative, or should they take on added weight as the only people who really care? Which is the more democratic approach? Most people would say democracy means going with the greatest numbers, even if their views are lukewarm. When it comes to a question that deeply concerns them, however, many people do not want a simple head count, arguing that the majority view is ignorant or mistaken and should not be heeded. We will consider some of these questions when we discuss interest groups in Chapter 10.

IS POLLING FAIR?

Polls do not merely monitor public opinion; they also help make it. Critics charge that published or broadcast poll results can distort an election. For example, the news media may highlight polls showing one candidate leading another by a wide margin. Such publicity, claim underdog candidates, devastates their campaigns by making supporters and contributors lose interest. Poor poll showings, especially early in the campaign, are a self-fulfilling prophecy of defeat for some candidates. Those who lead in the early polls get more contributions, more news coverage, and thus more supporters.

One current controversy is the effect of "exit polls," in which voters are questioned just as they leave the balloting place. With the three-hour time difference between the East and West Coasts, exit polls enable television to predict winners in the East while westerners still have hours in which to cast a ballot. Does the early prediction in the East persuade westerners not to bother to vote? Even if the early prediction of the presidential election is accurate, a falloff in voters could hurt state and local candidates who may have won if more people had voted. Some urge a delay in broadcasting the results of exit polls. No evidence has been found that exit polls influence the presidential vote, but they might influence other contests for the House, Senate, or state legislatures. Polls, especially when broadcast so quickly, are not neutral in their impact, but no constitutionally legal way has been found to control them.

Should the United States Be Governed by Polls?

Considering the preceding discussion, it would seem in most cases that the United States should not be governed by polls. First, public attention varies widely. On many issues, the general public has no knowledge or opinion, which lets the intensity of a minority dominate poll results. Leaders, especially with modern means of communication, influence public opinion in their direction and encourage the kind of feedback they want to hear. Typically, public opinion follows executive decisions.

The wording of the questions and the selection of the sample can seriously skew results. The survey must be done by trained professionals using standardized questions and random samples. Polls designed to sway you—the obnoxious "push polls"—are not worthy of response; hang up on them. The low rate of response to telephone surveys undermines their reliability. Equally serious is the problem of volatility. What the public likes one year it may dislike the next. Decisions made on the basis of a survey may turn sour when the consequences sink in. Bush advisor Karl Rove thought that war with Iraq would play well with voters. It did, for a while. Top officials who "go with the polls" may be trapping themselves. Polls, if done well, are useful snapshots of public opinion at a given moment but are no substitute for careful analyses and prudent anticipation.

mypoliscikit EXERCISES

Apply what you learned in this chapter on MyPoliSciKit (www.mypoliscikit.com).

Assessment   Review this chapter using learning objectives, chapter summaries, practice tests, and more.

Menu

Flashcards   Learn the key terms in this chapter; you can test yourself by term or definition.

Flashcards

Video   Analyze recent world affairs by watching streaming video from major news providers.

Videos

Comparative Exercises   Compare political ideas, behaviors, institutions, and policies worldwide.

Comparative
Exercises

KEY TERMS

anecdotal (p. 138)
anticlericalism (p. 142)
attentive public (p. 150)
bimodal (p. 144)
covariance (p. 148)
dependent variable
   (p. 148)
economic issues (p. 140)
gender gap (p. 143)
honeymoon (p. 149)

independent variable
   (p. 148)
intensity (p. 151)
life cycle (p. 143)
noneconomic issues (p. 140)
polarize (p. 144)
political generations
   (p. 143)
public opinion (p. 138)
quota (p. 146)

rally event (p. 149)
randomization (p. 147)
regions (p. 141)
salience (p. 139)
sample (p. 146)
skewed (p. 144)
social class (p. 139)
survey (p. 145)
unimodal (p. 144)
volatility (p. 148)

FURTHER REFERENCE

Alvarez, R. Michael, and John Brehm. *Hard Choices, Easy Answers: Values, Information, and American Public Opinion.* Princeton, NJ: Princeton University Press, 2002.

Aronowitz, Stanley. *How Class Works: Power and Social Movement.* New Haven, CT: Yale University Press, 2003.

Asher, Herbert. *Polling and the Public: What Every Citizen Should Know,* 8th ed. Washington, DC: CQ Press, 2010.

Berinsky, Adam J. *In Time of War: Understanding American Public Opinion from World War II to Iraq.* Chicago: University of Chicago Press, 2009.

Dalton, Russell J. *Citizen Politics: Public Opinion and Political Parties in Advanced Industrial Democracies,* 5th ed. Washington, DC: CQ Press, 2008.

Elazar, Daniel J. *The American Mosaic: The Impact of Space, Time, and Culture on American Politics.* Boulder, CO: Westview Press, 1994.

Lardner, James, and David A. Smith, eds. *Inequality Matters: The Growing Economic Divide in America and Its Poisonous Consequences.* New York: New Press, 2005.

Mueller, John. *War, Presidents and Public Opinion.* New York: Wiley, 1973.

———. *Overblown: How Politicians and the Terrorism Industry Inflate National Security Threats and Why We Believe Them.* New York: Simon & Schuster, 2006.

Stonecash, Jeffrey M. *Class and Party in American Politics.* Boulder, CO: Westview, 2000.

Traugott, Michael W., and Paul J. Lavrakas. *The Voter's Guide to Election Polls,* 4th ed. Lanham, MD: Rowman & Littlefield, 2008.

Wald, Kenneth D., and Allison Calhoun-Brown. *Religion and Politics in the United States,* 5th ed. Lanham, MD: Rowman & Littlefield, 2006.

Weissberg, Robert. *Polling, Policy, and Public Opinion: The Case Against Heeding the "Voice of the People."* New York: Palgrave, 2002.

PART III

POLITICAL INTERACTIONS

Ch. 9 Political Communication   Modern politics revolves around the media, which the Internet is rapidly changing. Especially important are the elite media. Newspapers are in decline, and television is now the most influential, although the Web is gaining. TV news coverage, however, is spotty and leaves viewers poorly informed. U.S. government and media are frequently at odds, especially after the media finds it has been deceived.

Ch. 10 Interest Groups   Interest groups are a bedrock of pluralism and thus important to democracy. Interest groups, however, can be created by government programs. Big money has led to undue interest-group influence and repeated scandals. Higher socioeconomic status gives interest groups greater access with which to influence legislatures, executives, court decisions, and public appeals. In some systems, strong interest groups work against democracy.

Ch. 11 Parties   Parties are the great organizing device of government, especially in democracies. Parties may be classified in several ways, from degree of centralization and organization through ideology. Most modern democratic parties are now "catch-alls," combinations of many groups and viewpoints. Party systems, logically distinct from parties, discern how the parties interact. They include one-party, dominant-party, two-party, and multiparty systems. The electoral system influences the party system, which under certain circumstances can break down.

Ch. 12 Elections   First we consider who is most likely to vote and find that turnout is uneven among groups. Next we ask who votes how and find that the key variables are party identification, social class, region, religion, age, and urban–rural splits. The theory of electoral realignment, which claims that every few decades many voters switch their party ID to favor one party, has been called into question. The U.S. electorate has shown strong partisan polarization of late. Obviously, personality helps win elections, but some voters take a retrospective overview of incumbent performance. A candidate who modifies positions is merely responding rationally to mass demands.

CHAPTER 9

Political Communication

Sarah Palin, here campaigning in 2008, used the media to turn herself into a major force in the Republican Party.
(Whitney Curtis Stringer/Getty)

The Internet has brought a communications revolution, but one with uncertain political impact. Some compare the rise of the Net with the invention of printing in the fifteenth century—a widening of human horizons with the freedom to learn and think for oneself. Now the Internet is supposed to take this even farther, but some are cautious. Blogs and websites are heavy with opinions and partisanship and may further fragment and polarize politics as liberals read liberal blogs and conservatives read conservative blogs, never meeting in a middle ground. As the Internet eats into the mainstream media—both print and broadcast—so also will their centrist and calming factual reporting, some fear.

The *mass media* (see Chapter 6) strongly influence politics. In the 1780s, the *Federalist Papers* were published in newspapers throughout the 13 U.S. states to win support for the new constitution. Andrew Jackson's victory in 1828 over John Quincy Adams was one of the dirtiest "media campaigns" ever; some papers accused Jackson and his wife of immorality. In 1904, Teddy Roosevelt was a "media candidate" with a rough-and-ready image that won press coverage and the election. And Franklin D. Roosevelt's "fireside chats" on the radio, along with hundreds of press conferences, won support for his policies. Today, the mass media are a recognized component of politics worldwide, and modern campaigns depend on television so much that critics complain that candidates no longer run for office on issues; instead, professional marketing consultants package and sell them like products.

QUESTIONS TO CONSIDER

1. How do mass media and face-to-face communication have different impacts?
2. What is the *elite media*, and which are its leading journals?
3. How has the Web changed political communication?
4. What are the weaknesses of television news coverage?
5. Can money buy television time and hence buy elections?
6. Has television created political apathy?
7. Which country has the freest mass media?
8. Was the media to blame for declining support for the Iraq and Afghan wars?
9. How can you stay well informed?
10. Is it good that media and government are adversaries?

face-to-face Communication by personal contact.

stump Verb, to campaign by personally speaking to audiences.

opinion leaders Locally respected people who influence the views of others.

COMMUNICATION IN POLITICS

Political scientists have long recognized the dependence of politics on communication. Karl W. Deutsch showed how modernization and nationalism can be measured by the increase of mail, telephone calls, and newspapers. The more communication, the more modernization (which does not prove which causes which). The political system and the communication system parallel one another; it is doubtful that one could exist without the other.

All political action is a reaction to communication. There are different levels and types of communication. **Face-to-face** communication is the most basic and effective for altering or reinforcing political opinions because it allows for dialogue where mass media cannot. Until the early 1930s, face-to-face communication was the main method of political campaigning. Candidates **stumped** (in the old days, many spoke from tree stumps) their districts and addressed small groups of voters, appealing for their support with the help of ward bosses, precinct captains, and political organizers. The rise of television has largely bypassed grassroots stumping, except as a means of getting free media coverage.

The mass media reach an infinitely larger audience and therefore yield a greater voter or public opinion return than face-to-face communication. A speech at even the largest rally is heard by only a few thousand, but the mass media are one-way communication. Viewers cannot immediately tell the president they disagree with his TV message. Mass media generally reinforce existing political opinions but rarely convert anyone. Radio and television do have stronger persuasive power than the printed word because they mimic face-to-face communication, but their impact still depends partly on chats with friends afterward.

Television may have eroded the role of *opinion leaders* as television newscasters become opinion leaders on a grand scale. Television not only transmits direct political messages but also indirectly changes society by bringing news and ideas into the homes of all. Most observers agree that the 1960s civil rights movement would not have succeeded without television. Racial discrimination in the South was largely unnoticed in the print media and radio. But television news showing fire hoses and

CLASSIC WORKS ■ THE TWO-STEP FLOW OF MASS COMMUNICATIONS

How do the mass media influence political opinions? Indirectly, said Paul Lazarsfeld and Elihu Katz, whose research in the 1940s and 1950s found a "two-step flow" in this process. The first step is the media messages, but the crucial second step is respected local **opinion leaders**—what Almond called the "attentive public" (see Chapter 8). These people get political ideas from the mass media and pass them on to their less attentive friends in face-to-face contact. Mass media persuasion depends on these opinion leaders.

police dogs attacking peaceful marchers turned most Americans in favor of equal rights for black people. Some believe that television coverage of the Vietnam War—the world's first television war—turned many against the war and against President Johnson. Photos of the mistreatment of Iraqi prisoners had a similar impact in 2004.

introspective   Looking within oneself.

oligopoly   A few big firms dominate a market.

Fewer Americans now are interested in news than they were one and two generations ago. Fewer than a third regularly watch television news or read newspapers. And news is shifting from politics and world affairs to human interest and "news you can use" about health, business, and lifestyles. This shift parallels the decline in Americans' interest in politics in general, confirming the close connection between communications and politics. The causes of this decline are debated. Some see a shift in values, especially among a new and **introspective** generation addicted to entertainment. Only terrorist attacks, involvement in war, or a financial meltdown can jolt them into paying attention to the real world.

The various modern media appeal to different audiences distinguished by education, income, and age. The more educated individuals are, the more media they consume. College graduates and better-off people tend to read newspapers, magazines, and books as well as follow radio and television. Those with less education mostly use television, and largely for entertainment. Better-off people are regular magazine and book readers; few low-income people are.

KEY CONCEPTS ■ THE TENDENCY TO MEDIA MONOPOLY

If many competing media voices are good, America has some concerns, for media ownership has moved toward **oligopoly**. Some 20 corporations control most of what Americans read, hear, and view, as they own newspapers and radio and television stations. The five biggest:

- *Murdoch*, an Australian-born press baron, owns Fox TV, HarperCollins (books), the *Weekly Standard* (influential neocon magazine), the *Wall Street Journal, New York Post, London Times,* and DirecTV.
- *General Electric* owns NBC and Universal-Vivendi, itself a major conglomerate.
- *Time-Warner* was the merger of a big magazine publisher and major studio that now includes CNN and HBO.

- *Disney* owns ABC and ESPN.
- *Comcast*, the biggest cable company, has tried to take over Disney.
- *Clear Channel* owns a large fraction of U.S. radio stations and programs them centrally, eliminating local content.

What happens to free speech and multiple sources of information? Media critics worry that we receive bland uniformity and unquestioning acceptance of White House pronouncements. The president says it, so it must be true. Some feel there is still adequate diversity and criticism, now bolstered by the Internet with its innumerable sources and viewpoints. The Federal Communications Commission is supposed to guard against oligopoly but in recent years has seen no problem with bigness and fewness.

status quo   Keeping the present situation.

elite media   Highly influential newspapers and magazines read by elites and the attentive public.

Age also affects mass media usage. Older people pay far more attention to the editorial and news content of newspapers and magazines than teenagers and young adults, who tend to use newspapers for entertainment. Young readers follow sports, rock stars, and feature articles rather than hard news. The college student who keeps up on the news and editorial opinion is rare.

Modern Mass Media

Newspapers   In 1910, the United States had more than 2,600 daily newspapers, and most American cities had two or more competing papers. Today, half that number remains, and few U.S. cities have two papers. Many major newspapers, long money losers, have drastically cut their staffs and Washington and overseas bureaus. Some have folded. As news on the Internet grows, many citizens use it and do not get a variety of political and editorial opinion. Big corporations, seeking profits and not controversy, own some 75 percent of U.S. newspapers, giving them a **status quo** orientation. Few newspapers present the news in an obviously partisan manner, for both practical and idealistic reasons. Most newspaper revenue comes from advertising, and ad rates depend on the papers' circulation. Thus, high circulation is the main concern, and this usually leads to a middle-of-the-road news policy that does not antagonize but makes newspapers bland.

KEY CONCEPTS ■ THE ELITE MEDIA

The *New York Times*, *Washington Post*, *Wall Street Journal*, and *Financial Times* are read by a small fraction of the U.S. population, but they carry by far the most clout. Decision makers in Washington read them and take both their news stories and editorials seriously. Leading thinkers fight battles on their "op-ed" pages (opposite the editorial page). That is why these papers have influence out of all proportion to their circulation. They are the **elite media** because the people who read them are generally wealthier and better educated and have much more influence than readers of hometown papers. Many are *opinion leaders* (see page 158).

The elite press pursues "investigative reporting," looking for government and partisan wrongdoing, something the average paper shuns for fear of lawsuits. The *New York Times*

jolted the nation when it published the *Pentagon Papers* on the Vietnam War in 1971 (see page 89). The dogged pursuit of the 1972 Watergate burglary by the *Washington Post* brought down the Nixon administration in 1974. The *Wall Street Journal* and *Financial Times* influence economic decisions in Washington. Originating in London, the lively and brainy *Financial Times* is distributed across the United States and has taken some of the readers of the NYT and WSJ.

Some small-circulation magazines of opinion are also influential. The conservative *National Review*, the liberal *American Prospect*, the leftist *Nation*, and the neoconservative *Weekly Standard* have considerable impact on opinion leaders. Students often ignore the elite press, but those who aspire to leadership should follow one or more of these journals.

Journalism has a long tradition of objectivity in news reporting (not so on the editorial page). The profession's own standards influence newspeople to present the news fairly and honestly. Further, much news in U.S. newspapers is from a service, The Associated Press, which takes special pains to be objective and to refrain from editorializing.

wire service   News agency that sells to all media.

How much political impact, then, do U.S. newspapers have? Not as much as they used to. In the 1960s, some 80 percent of Americans read a daily paper; now fewer than 35 percent do. Young people have largely abandoned newspapers in favor of Web sites and blogs. Americans raised on television do not read much. The content of newspapers is mostly advertisements (one important reason people read them) and wire-service copy. The editorials of most newspapers carry little weight. The exceptions are the "elite" media.

Radio   Like newspapers, radio is not what it used to be. Now three companies own half of America's radio stations. Clear Channel Communications alone controls more than 1,200 stations. It is programmed from its headquarters with homogenized news and no local content, not even tornado warnings. Between the two world wars, however, radio was popular, and radio news, comments, and political addresses—such as Franklin D. Roosevelt's famous "fireside chats," which served as models for both Jimmy Carter and Ronald Reagan—were quite influential. With the rise of television in the 1950s, radio became less important, with two exceptions. Popular "talk radio" shows, often hosted by angry right-wingers, reinforce conservative views. Reinforcing liberal views, National Public Radio offers world events, economics, politics, and critical opinions.

The News Services   Most hard news in newspapers and on radio, and even a good deal of television's news, is not produced in-house but comes from a printer hooked up to the New York offices of The Associated Press (AP), hence the old-fashioned name **wire service**. The elite newspapers disdain wire service copy, as it is a matter of pride to have their own reporters cover the story. But many papers in the United States are little more than local outlets for the AP, which provides them with photos, sports coverage, even recipes, as well as news.

The AP is a publishers' cooperative, with members paying thousands of dollars a week in assessments based on their circulation. Member papers also contribute local stories to the AP, which may rewrite them for national and even world transmission. The AP is one of the few news services not owned, subsidized, controlled, or supervised by a government. It is free of government influence and proud of it, but it too is in financial difficulty. Why buy information when you can get it free online? Britain's Reuters, France's AFP, and Germany's DPA have discreet government supervision, and China's Xin Hua is Beijing's spokesman. United Press International (UPI) used to compete with AP, but now Rev. Sun Myung Moon, a conservative and eccentric Korean millionaire, owns UPI, which is a faint shadow of its former self.

No government controls the AP, but it has other problems that limit its quality and influence. First, it moves fast; every minute is a deadline. This means it does no digging; its stories are often superficial. Second, the wire services' definition of

AP photographer Eddie Adams snapped the summary execution of a captured Vietcong assassin in 1968. Adams later said he was sorry he took the history-making photo, which made the Vietcong look heroic. In truth, the Vietcong assassin had just murdered the family of one of the assistants to South Vietnam's police chief, who took speedy revenge. Images can mislead. (AP Photo)

source Who or where a news reporter gets information from.

news is something from an official **source**. Most of its stories are attributed to police, the White House, the State Department or Pentagon, and so on. If it's not official, it's not news, and if it is official, it must be true. This causes the wire services to miss explosive situations in the world because they do not report on the thoughts of opposition people or average citizens who might have a completely different—and sometimes more accurate—perspective than official spokespersons. The news media failed to notice the coming of the Iranian revolution for this reason. Often, the best news stories are not about a key event or statement but about what people are saying and thinking, which is a strong point of the blogs.

THE GIANT: TELEVISION

When most people say "the media," they mean television, for television still has the greatest impact. Americans tend to get their news from television—more from cable channels than from broadcast networks nowadays—and most accord it higher credibility than newspapers. This may be eroding as more people, especially young ones, turn to the digital media, including YouTube.

Post World War II, television touched and changed almost everything in politics. Election campaigns now revolve around the acquisition of television time; winners are usually those who raise the most money to hire the best media consultants. Television has become a suspect in the decline of both U.S. election turnout and political parties. Some observers

blog   Short for "Web log"; online free magazine, often partisan and idiosyncratic.

KEY CONCEPTS ■ THE WEB: THE NEWEST MASS MEDIUM?

The political impact of the Internet is growing. You can look up whatever you want on it—such as a candidate's proposals—but that is often "preaching to the converted," to people who already like the candidate. Fewer Americans follow news on TV and in newspapers, but news on the Web climbs, especially among young people.

News on the Web is free. You can read it any time and focus only on what interests you. Most prefer sports and financial matters to political news. Howard Dean's 2004 bid for the Democratic presidential nomination featured online fund-raising for the first time. It was quite successful and was copied by Barack Obama in 2008.

Some praise the Internet for catching stories the conventional media overlook. Beholden to no one, blogs uncovered dubious political contributions, torture, warrantless surveillance, and the financial crisis earlier and deeper than newspapers or television. *Talking Points Memo* first noticed in 2007 how the Bush administration was firing U.S. attorneys it deemed liberal. The online magazine *Salon* broke the story of Rev. Moon's coronation in the U.S. Capitol as the messiah. Such discoveries jolt the conventional media into covering what they previously neglected. In comparison to the Web, mainstream media can be remarkably incurious.

Defenders of the conventional media point out that only they practice "quality journalism" by professionals who know their areas and check their facts. Only the conventional media cover the basic news of government, the courts, wars, and natural disasters. This is expensive, and the Internet simply puts out the stories as news digests without paying for them, under the slogan "Information wants to be free." Blogs, operating on a shoestring, send no reporters into the field and base their stories on e-mails from unpaid volunteers (the good ones sift them carefully).

Newspapers and television boast of their "balance" (covering two sides of everything), something that does not interest the blogs.

Will the Web overall make well-informed citizens? Many doubt it. The Internet has drastically lowered the cost of entering the media world (just as digitized music has drastically lowered the cost of entering the music world). This has enabled thousands to put out their own magazines, **blogs**, most of them highly partisan. One study found that 85 percent of blog links were to those of the same political viewpoint. Thoughtful synthesis is not the Internet's strong point. You can get all manner of detailed information online, but you have to *want* to do it. You can read Japan's top daily at www.asahi.com/english, but how many will?

Many newspapers and magazines now have parallel online publications as their regular circulation declines. Millions now read the *New York Times* free on their computer; online advertising is supposed to pay for it but does not. One big media question today is whether news organizations should charge a subscription fee for their news online; some already do.

Digital media can undermine undemocratic regimes. Iranians mobilized by computer and cell phones against the rigged elections of 2009. For the sake of economic growth, most countries allow the new media, but with the economic and technical come the political and critical, cracking the regime's information monopoly. With chat rooms comes dissident chat. Iran and China censor their Web systems, just as they muzzle their conventional media. China has tens of thousands of Web-watchers and arrests critical bloggers, who nonetheless work around the "Great Firewall." The Web is not always positive; pornography, racism, and bomb-making instructions are online and impossible to control.

media event News incident
planned to get media coverage.

see television, which focuses on "sound bites" of a
few seconds, as contributing to the trivialization of
politics. Calm analysis is out; the catchy phrase is in.

Television News

Television, by definition, favors the visual. "Talking heads" provide no more
news than radio. (Talking heads do provide a sense of personality and hence
credibility, an imitation face-to-face communication.) News producers pay more
attention to a news story with "good visuals" than without. As with the wire
services, abstract, deeper topics go by with little coverage, but dramatic action—
if there was a camera crew on hand to catch it—gets played up. Television, like
most of the rest of the U.S. news media, ignored the hatred that was brewing
against the shah of Iran for years but caught the dramatic return of the Ayatollah
Khomeini. Television never did explain what the Vietnam War was about, but
a brief film clip of a Saigon general shooting a Vietcong assassin in 1968 helped
sicken Americans and turn them against the war. Just as the wire services are
hooked on official sources, television news is hooked on the eye-catching. The
2004 Abu Ghraib photos underscored this. Television is inherently a more emotional medium than the others; its coverage can go straight to the heart, bypassing
the brain altogether.

Television camera crews are expensive to maintain in the field, especially
overseas, so they usually arrive where the action is only *after* having read it on
the AP wire. Television needs to know in advance what's going to happen; then
it can schedule a camera crew. This makes television news lopsided with press
conferences, speeches, committee hearings, and official statements. Some critics
call these **media events**, things that would not have occurred without television
coverage. A media event is not fake, but it is planned in advance with an eye to
catching TV coverage. Officials understand this, and so do protest groups, who
stage marches, sit-ins, and mass arrests to get television exposure for their cause.
Chanted protesters at the 1968 Democratic convention in Chicago: "The whole
world is watching!" The number of film clips of events that were obviously sched-
uled in advance greatly outnumbers those that were not.

Analysis is also not television's strong point. An average news story runs
one minute; a four-minute story is an in-depth report. Walter Cronkite, long the
dean of television anchors, emphasized that television news was just a "headline
service," meaning that if viewers wanted detail and depth they would have to
go elsewhere. Many Americans, of course, look no deeper and are left with the
tardy, the eye-catching, and the media event as their daily diet of information.
Thus, it is not surprising when polls repeatedly discover that Americans are
poorly informed.

Television and Politics

Television changed politics in several ways. Incumbency, especially in the White
House, has always brought recognition, and television has enhanced this, but not

always in the **incumbent's** favor. Television news is heavily focused on the president. Congress gets much less coverage, the courts even less. This deepens a long-term American tendency to president-worship. The president—especially with the way television socializes small children—is seen as an omnipotent parental figure, a person who can fix all problems. That

incumbent Official who already occupies the office.

bandwagon Tendency of front-runners to gain additional supporters.

should make a president happy. But then things go wrong, the president fails to fix the problems, and ultracritical media imply he is making them worse. The flip side of being treated as all-powerful is catching all the blame. The media, especially television, whip up president-worship and then whip up mass dissatisfaction with the president's performance. Expectations, heightened by the media, are too high, and disappointments are correspondingly bitter. Some critics charge that the media wreck the political system with that kind of coverage, making the country unstable and ungovernable.

Nomination by Television   Television does much to nominate presidential candidates. With all eyes focused on the early presidential primaries, commentators grandly proclaim who is the "real winner" and who has "momentum." The candidate thus designated as front-runner goes into the remaining primaries and the national convention with a **bandwagon** effect, enhanced recognition, and even more television coverage. In the nominating process, television has become a kind of kingmaker. It is no wonder that candidates arrange their schedules and strategies to capture as much television exposure as possible.

Television coverage of candidates focuses on their personalities, not on issues. Television, with its sharp close-ups and seeming spontaneity, gives viewers what they think is a true glimpse of the candidate's character. Actually, this may not be so; some candidates play the medium like professionals (Ronald Reagan), and others tense up and hide their normal personalities (Robert Dole). How candidates perform on television is a poor indicator of how they will perform in office, but it is the one most voters use.

While television is playing this major role in nominating and electing candidates, political parties are bypassed. Party organizations and bosses are important only as fund-raising organizations, as candidates on television go right over their heads to the voters. Because the leading contenders have already picked up their "momentum" going into the convention, they do not need party professionals to broker a nominating deal. Politics has come out of the proverbial smoke-filled back room and into the glare of television lights, not always for the better. The party and its chiefs used to know a thing or two about politics and were often capable of putting forward effective candidates. With television, a candidate can come out of nearly nowhere and win the top national office with little political experience.

We must be careful, though, in blaming television for the weakening of parties. American parties, with the exception of a few urban machines, were never as strongly organized as most European parties (which are also declining). American parties began declining long ago, not just with the advent of television. Other

cross-pressured   Pulled between opposing political forces; said to produce apathy.

factors—special-interest groups, political action committees, and direct-mail and online solicitation—have also undermined party strength. Television is not the sole culprit.

Television and Apathy   Observers have long suspected that television induces passivity and apathy. Harvard political scientist Robert D. Putnam (see his discussion of "bowling alone" on page 125) believes "the culprit is television." Reviewing the decline of "civic engagement" in the United States, Putnam found older people, those born before World War II, are more trusting and more inclined to join groups and participate in politics. The reason: They were raised before the television age began in the 1950s. Younger people, raised on television, lack these qualities. Says Putnam: "Each hour spent viewing television is associated with less social trust and less group membership, while each hour reading a newspaper is associated with more."

A related charge is that television has lowered Election Day turnouts. There is a close coincidence in time; U.S. turnout dropped 13 percentage points from 1960, when television first established itself as the top means of campaigning, to 1988; then, it stayed at the same low level until the uptick of 2004. Television saturates viewers so far in advance that they lose interest. The top two candidates usually sound so similar that many voters see little difference. Negative campaigning disgusts many voters. Charges and countercharges in political spots come so thick and fast that the voter is **cross-pressured** into indecision and apathy. In Western Europe, where paid-for political television spots are generally prohibited and campaigns are much shorter—usually about a month instead of the year or more in the United States—voter turnout is higher. Only the United States does not regulate TV political ads.

U.S. television costs billions. Depending on the time of day and locale, a one-minute spot can go for $100,000 or more. The cost factor has transformed American politics. Some members of Congress need little television advertising, but virtually all senatorial and presidential candidates need it. About half of presidential campaign chests now go for television. Political consulting—the right themes, slogans, and speeches presented in scripted television spots—has become a big business. In most contests, the winner is the one who spent the most money, most of it on television. This heightens the importance of special-interest groups and political action committees, which in turn has weakened the role of the parties and perhaps deepened feelings of powerlessness among average voters.

Voters increasingly ignore party labels. The trend, alarming to some political scientists, is called voter "dealignment," citizens *not* lining up with a party (explored in Chapter 12). Lacking party identification, these voters are open to persuasion via the media, especially television. In 2004 most Americans believed that Bush had sent 3 million jobs overseas and that Kerry voted for higher taxes 350 times. Voters believe absurd TV ads.

Television Ownership and Control

The U.S. government exercises the *least* control of communications of any industrialized country. Since the invention of the telegraph, the American government has stood back and let private industry operate communications for profit. In Europe, in contrast, telegraphy was soon taken over by the postal service, as were telephones. The U.S. government—partly because of First Amendment guarantees of free speech and partly because of the U.S. ethos of free enterprise—simply does not like to butt in. For European nations, with traditions of centralized power and government paternalism, national control of electronic communications is as normal as state ownership of the railroads. Now European TV is partly state-run and partly private, and both types face continual charges of politically partisan coverage.

The U.S. attitude of **nonpaternalism** has led to the freest airwaves in the world, but it has also brought some problems. With the rapid growth of radio in the 1920s, the **electromagnetic spectrum** was soon jammed with stations trying to drown each other out. To bring some order out of the chaos, the Radio Act of 1927 designated the airwaves public property that should serve "the public interest, convenience and necessity." The Federal Communications Commission (FCC), which licenses broadcasters, does not supervise the content of programs.

nonpaternalism Not taking a supervisory or guiding role.

electromagnetic spectrum The airwaves over which signals are broadcast.

HOW TO... ■ DEFINE VARIABLES

You must define the variables you use so clearly that neither you nor the reader can mistake them for anything else. This means deliberate narrowing. For example, it is difficult to use the term "democracy" in all the complexity of the description on pages 98–104. There are just too many things to keep track of. You would find countries have some of the characteristics but not all. A good definition allows you to easily put items into categories. You might define a flat or falling economy in presidential election years as "bad times" and see if incumbents lose.

Even something like "voting" needs to be narrowed. Do we mean voting in primary, local, presidential, or congressional elections? We cannot compare turnout in the 2008 presidential election with turnout in the 2010 congressional elections; presidential elections bring higher turnout. We must compare like elections, such as the presidential elections every four years.

Especially difficult are broad and unclear terms that carry emotional baggage, such as "isolationism." How would you demonstrate that senators of certain regions or parties are more isolationist? If you ask them, all will deny being isolationists, as the term connotes ignorance. You might come up with a narrower term, such as "noninterventionist," and define it as unwillingness to send U.S. troops overseas. Then, by surveying senators' voting records, you might discern patterns of noninterventionism.

ARE WE POORLY SERVED?

The U.S. mass media do not serve Americans very well. First, news coverage is highly selective, overconcentrating on some areas while ignoring others. This is called "structural bias." The presidency, which occupies more than half the news time given to the federal government, is inherently more dramatic and eye-catching than the other branches. Editors and producers are afraid that full coverage of Congress and the courts will bore readers and viewers. The president gets in and out of helicopters, greets foreign leaders, travels overseas, and gets involved in scandals; all provide good television footage. Congress may get some attention when its committees face tense, controversial, or hostile witnesses. Then the committee members hurl accusatory questions, the witness stammers back denials, and sometimes shouting erupts. That's good drama; the rest of Congress is pretty dull. And the courts face the biggest obstacle of all: No cameras are allowed in most courtrooms. Accordingly, Americans grow up with the notion that the White House does most of the work and has most of the power, whereas Congress and the courts matter far less.

Especially undercovered are the civil service and state governments. Myriad departments, agencies, and bureaus govern any country, but bureaucrats give boring interviews, and regulations are unintelligible. Still, many of next year's news stories lurk in the federal bureaucracy. What agency using what criteria allows deep-sea oil drilling? The media pay no attention until a massive oil spill occurs. What department gave millions in contracts to presidential-campaign contributors? Risky and sometimes crooked doings in the financial industry went on for years unnoticed by regulators and the media. What federal agency decides whether power plants have adequate emission standards? The news media rarely cover such things; they wait until something goes wrong and then evince shocked surprise. The very stuff of politics is in the federal agencies, but few pay attention.

Coverage of state governments may be even worse. Much of the problem here is that there are national media—the big networks and elite newspapers—and there are local media—your town's stations and paper. But there are no state media, partly because states are not "market areas" (population centers) that advertisers try to reach. Accordingly, outside of state capitals, there is little news about state politics, even important items.

On the world scene, the news media wait for something to blow up before they cover it. Except for the elite media, there is little background coverage of likely trouble spots. Thus, when terror hits the United States or a distant land erupts in violence, most Americans are surprised. They shouldn't be; even moderate news coverage of these problems over the years would have kept Americans informed about the increasing problems. But the U.S. media send few reporters overseas. Latin America, with all its implications for the United States, is largely uncovered. We live in a tumultuous world, but the U.S. media pay little attention until the shooting starts. Providers of "good visuals" rather than analysis and early warning is the way they define their role, and this sets up Americans to become startled and confused.

The biggest problem with the U.S. media is that they do not give a coherent, comprehensive picture of what is happening in the world. Operating under tight deadlines, flashing the best action footage, and basing reports

---

framing   A news story's basic direction and interpretation.

---

heavily on official sources, the media bombard us with many little stories but seldom weave them together into a big story. They give us only pieces of a jigsaw puzzle. Part of this problem is the nature of any news medium that comes out daily: Newspapers and television take events one day at a time. Such news is usually incomplete and

---

KEY CONCEPTS ■ THE FRAMING OF NEWS

Developed by sociologist Erving Goffman, **framing** is used by many social scientists but has special relevance in communication studies to mean the basic line of a news story. Akin to oversimplifying and stereotyping, framing means setting up a frame of reference, which for a while dominates news stories on a given topic. Newspersons call it the *lead*, sometimes deliberately misspelled "led" or "lede," the crucial first paragraph, which sets the story's direction.

Framing does not necessarily mean conscious slanting; rather, it is a necessary narrowing that allows reporters, editors, and readers to make sense of the news. You cannot lead with, "Gee, this financial reform sure is complicated." Instead, newspeople must pick one frame at any given time—such as, "Failure to pass a finance-reform measure could lead to another collapse"—and pay little attention to other facets of the story, such as wrongdoing or alternative solutions. Later, they may shift to another frame, often in near unison. Notice how mainstream media stories have the same leads; almost all accept the prevailing frame.

Politically, framing gives great power. Whoever frames a problem guides public discourse. The Bush administration framed the Iraq War in terms of weapons of mass destruction and terrorism and won support from the media, at least initially. Later, when the media learned they had been misled, they reframed the Iraq story as one of civil war and chaos. The White House hated that. The Iraq War was a high-stakes framing contest between the White House and the media.

One of the big questions: Who frames news stories? The White House blames the media, but usually the media at first accept the frames provided by the White House or other elites. They must; they have no other sources. When huge U.S. financial firms threatened to collapse, newspeople had to interview financiers, who favored a bailout plan. Later, some newspeople developed different and critical frames from academic and think-tank economists. For weeks in 2008, the media did not question the White House frame that we were on the verge of another Great Crash. News stories uniformly led with "Doom threatens if we don't accept the Paulson plan, and fast!" No lede suggested that the Paulson plan might not work or that there were better alternatives. Skeptical frames did not make page one—or any page. Elites have the upper hand in framing: Media are the sheep; political elites are the border collies.

What can you do to protect yourself from sometimes misleading frames? First, use multiple news sources; blogs may be among the first to question the standard frame. Second, be aware that several sides are trying to frame stories for their own political or financial ends, to win elections or promote the flow of money. Third, note the sources used in news stories: Do they have a stake in the issue? If so, expect a self-serving frame. Finally, treat all news stories with skepticism and patience; be prepared to wait a week or two to gain a balanced perspective. Panic works against sound judgment.

adversarial Inclined to criticize and oppose, to treat with enmity.

often misleading. We see people shooting, but we do not know why. The media world is, in Shakespeare's phrase, "full of sound and fury, signifying nothing."

What Can Be Done?

The mass media—except for the elite media—do not provide *meaning*. Some, such as the wire services, have until recently shunned analysis and interpretation as unobjective or editorializing. Few reporters are equipped to explain historical background or long-term consequences. Reporters are expected to be generalists, to be able to cover anything. All you have to do is write down what the official source says. It is for this reason that editorials and columns of opinion often contain more "news" than the straight news stories, for the former set the news into a meaningful context, while the latter just give scattered bits and pieces. Unfortunately, most Americans make do with the bits and pieces as they make decisions on candidates, economic matters, and sending troops abroad.

Can anything be done? Professional newspeople often agree that the public is ill-informed and that news coverage could be wider and deeper. But the limiting factor, they emphasize, is the public itself. Few people want to be well-informed, especially about things that are distant or complicated. Audience surveys find that people care least about foreign news and most about local news. Only intellectuals follow complicated, in-depth analyses. Do the media have any responsibility in educating the mass public so that citizens can comprehend our complicated world? Some idealists in the media do feel a responsibility, but they are offset by hardheaded business types, who have the last word. We cannot expect major improvements soon. For you, however, the student of political science who is already among the more attentive, the answer is the elite media. Use the mass media for sports coverage.

THE ADVERSARIES: MEDIA AND GOVERNMENT

The role of the press as critic in a democracy has long been recognized. Thomas Jefferson wrote in 1787: "Were it left to me to decide [between government without] newspapers and newspapers without government, I should not hesitate a moment to prefer the latter." In Russia, Ukraine, and Mexico, journalists who investigate corruption and abuse of power are routinely killed, and no suspects are caught. Many news organizations there now practice "self-censorship" to stay open and alive.

Over the centuries, the press has criticized government. In the late 1960s and early 1970s, however, a new **adversarial** relationship between media and government emerged that is still with us. The elite media and television adopted hostile stances toward the executive branch.

The causes are not hard to see: Vietnam and Watergate. In both episodes, the executive branch lied to the media to soothe public opinion. Many media people resented being used and struck back with sharp questioning in press conferences and investigative reporting. Nixon's presidency made things worse; he had long feared and hated the press. On losing the governor's race in California in 1962, he slouched off muttering that the press "won't have Nixon to kick around anymore." Before presidential press conferences, Nixon used to calm his nerves by relaxing in a darkened room. He liked to operate in secrecy and then spring his decisions on the public in direct telecasts without any newspeople getting in the way. In turn, the press resented him all the more.

In Saigon, the U.S. military held afternoon press briefings, dubbed the "five o'clock follies," in which upbeat spokesmen tried to show progress in the war. Journalists soon tired of the repetitive, misleading, and irrelevant briefings and took to looking around for themselves. They found a corrupt, inept Saigon regime that was not winning the hearts and minds of its people, a Vietcong able to roam and strike at will, and tactics and morale inadequate to stop them. One young *New York Times* reporter was so critical of the Diem regime that his stories undermined American confidence in Diem and paved the way for Diem's 1963 ouster and murder by his own generals. Such is the influence of the elite media.

Vietnam is described as the first television war: bloody bodies of young GIs in full color. We should be careful of the widely accepted charge that television coverage turned Americans against the Vietnam War. The Korean War (1950–1953) reached few Americans via television, but U.S. public opinion turned against it

KEY CONCEPTS ■ THE MEDIA AND WATERGATE

In 1972, a news story began that brought the fall of the Nixon administration and, for at least portions of the media, a new self-image as guardians of public morality. Persons connected to the White House were caught burglarizing and planting telephone "bugs" in the Democratic campaign headquarters in the Watergate office and apartment complex. Dogged investigation by two young *Washington Post* reporters, who later wrote the book *All the President's Men*, revealed a massive cover-up led by the Oval Office. The more Nixon promised to come clean, the guiltier he looked. Nixon was never impeached. A House special committee voted to recommend impeachment; then Nixon resigned. The House certainly would have voted impeachment, and the Senate probably would have convicted.

Would the same have happened without media coverage? Ultimately, the legal moves came through the courts and Congress, but the media made sure these branches of government would not ignore or delay their duties. Did the media bring Nixon down? The Nixon people thought so, but they always loathed the press. Others have argued that the same would have happened without the investigative reporting but more slowly and with less drama. The point is that media and government are intertwined and part of the same process.

Since Watergate, some branches of the media, namely the elite press and the national television networks, have adopted generally adversarial stances toward the executive branch. Criticism of later presidencies of both parties was immoderate and sometimes unreasonable. Typically, all presidents now claim the media are out to get them. Presidential policies are almost automatically doubted and criticized. The media see scandal everywhere in Washington and then descend in a "feeding frenzy" that leaves no reputation untarnished.

precisely the same way: As U.S. casualties mounted, support dropped. It was combat deaths, not television coverage, that changed Americans' minds. Vietnam also brought the *Pentagon Papers* in the *New York Times* and *Washington Post* (see page 89). The Nixon administration was outraged—although the *Papers* made the Johnson officials the chief culprits—and ordered their publication halted, the first time the U.S. government ever censored newspapers. The Supreme Court immediately threw out the government's case, and the presses ran again. By this time, there was open warfare between government and the media.

KEY CONCEPTS ■ THE MEDIA AND WAR

The 2003 Iraq War had strong media support going into it and during it. 9/11 was a huge "rally event" (see page 149) that produced emotional and uncritical support for President Bush, including from the press. The media accepted administration claims that Iraq was building weapons of mass destruction (WMD). After the war, however, no WMD were found, and implanting a stable democracy amid deadly chaos was long and difficult. As if in revenge for having been misled before the war, much of the media turned critical, and the administration again fumed that the press was misinforming the public and undermining morale.

Was the media to blame for declining public support for the war? Political scientist John Mueller demonstrated that during Korea (1950–1953), Vietnam (1965–1973), and Iraq (starting in 2003), two-thirds of the public initially supported the wars, but within three years one-third or fewer did. And the Korea war was essentially pre-television, so we cannot blame TV for this decline. Time and mounting casualties seem to cause the decline, not television. Americans simply do not like long wars. Opinion on Iraq declined more quickly, probably because no WMD were found.

The U.S. military still blames the media and keeps it under close control. In 2003 journalists could cover the Iraq War "embedded" into combat units. This generally brought positive coverage, as the newspeople quickly bonded with the soldiers. But it was narrow-angle coverage (the view from one Humvee) that did not explain what was happening overall. And it did not extend into the looting and violence that soon erupted. Public support for the occupation declined, but was it due to news coverage or to reality? A major moral shift—comparable to the impact of the 1968 Mylai massacre in Vietnam—came with photos of U.S. guards sexually humiliating Iraqi prisoners in 2004. These photos were not taken by the media but by U.S. soldiers. In the digital age, images travel worldwide in seconds.

In unusual apologies, the *New York Times* and *Washington Post* in 2004 regretted having believed administration claims that led to the 2003 war. They had not been sufficiently skeptical, editors said, and should have asked more questions. Later, several newspapers reported on secret U.S. antiterrorism programs, and the Bush administration threatened prosecution under the 1917 Espionage Act. The papers claimed a public right to know; the administration claimed it hurt antiterrorism efforts. Again, the media and the White House were in a snarling match.

By 2006, columnists of all sorts—including conservative Republicans—were denouncing the administration for a botched job in Iraq. Neither the White House nor the Pentagon can suppress bad news for long. There is no sure way to "manage" news coverage; reality eventually emerges, often angrily. The media seem to follow a "bounce-back" pattern: Initially the media accept administration frames but then, discovering that they have been misled, turn angry and negative.

Has the press gone too far? Some people are fed up with the high-handedness with which the media impugn all authority. The media seem to think they are always right, the government always wrong. Republicans charge that the media are strongly liberal. Radicals, on the other hand, charge that the media defer to the president and big corporations. There is some truth to both charges, but one should note that eventually most institutions come under media scrutiny. The press washed President Clinton's dirty laundry in prime time. It is as if the media is "out to get" all politicians.

Sullivan   Short for *New York Times v. Sullivan*, 1964 Supreme Court decision protecting media against public officials' libel suits.

Studies show that news reporters and writers indeed tend to be liberals and Democrats, and this sometimes shows up in their coverage. Owners of stations and newspapers, though, tend to be conservative and Republican, and they curb the liberal impulses of their employees. Radio talk shows tend to the angry right, documentary films and blogs to the radically liberal. Charges of media bias are hard to prove, because you can usually show that the media mistreat all politicians, Republican and Democrat. The Bush 43 White House tried to keep a tight rein on information, which the media resented.

What is the proper role of the media in a democracy? How much should they criticize? Should they presume wrongdoing and cover-up everywhere? Should many reporters model themselves after Woodward and Bernstein of Watergate fame and ferret out scandals? The press is largely protected from charges of libel, for under the Supreme Court's **Sullivan** rule, "public" persons are presumed to be open to media scrutiny. This has left some public figures feeling helpless and bitter at the hands of an all-powerful press and has increased cynical attitudes about politics in general. Public opinion has grown critical of the too-critical media. Perhaps the United States can find some happy middle ground.

mypoliscikit EXERCISES

Apply what you learned in this chapter on MyPoliSciKit (www.mypoliscikit.com).

 Assessment   Review this chapter using learning objectives, chapter summaries, practice tests, and more.

Menu

 Flashcards   Learn the key terms in this chapter; you can test yourself by term or definition.

Flashcards

 Video   Analyze recent world affairs by watching streaming video from major news providers.

Videos

 Comparative Exercises   Compare political ideas, behaviors, institutions, and policies worldwide.

Comparative
Exercises

KEY TERMS

adversarial (p. 170)
bandwagon (p. 165)
blog (p. 163)
cross-pressured (p. 166)
electromagnetic spectrum
   (p. 167)
elite media (p. 160)

face-to-face (p. 158)
framing (p. 169)
incumbent (p. 165)
introspective (p. 159)
media event (p. 164)
nonpaternalism (p. 167)
oligopoly (p. 159)

opinion
   leaders (p. 158)
source (p. 162)
status quo (p. 160)
stump (p. 158)
Sullivan (p. 173)
wire service (p. 161)

FURTHER REFERENCE

Alterman, Eric. *What Liberal Media? The Truth About Bias and the News.* New York: Basic Books, 2004.

Bennett, W. Lance, Regina G. Lawrence, and Steven Livingston. *When the Press Fails: Political Power and the News Media from Iraq to Katrina.* Chicago: University of Chicago Press, 2008.

Boehlert, Eric. *Bloggers on the Bus: How the Internet Changes Politics and the Press.* New York: Simon & Schuster, 2010.

Brader, Ted. *Campaigning for Hearts and Minds: How Emotional Appeals in Political Ads Work.* Chicago: University of Chicago Press, 2006.

Buell, Emmett H. Jr., and Lee Sigelman. *Attack Politics: Negativity in Presidential Campaigns since 1960.* Lawrence, KS: University Press of Kansas, 2008.

Campbell, W. Joseph. *Getting It Wrong: Ten of the Greatest Misreported Stories in American Journalism.* Berkeley, CA: University of California Press, 2010.

Cohen, Jeffrey E. *The Presidency in the Era of 24-Hour News.* Princeton, NJ: Princeton University Press, 2008.

Fuller, Jack. *What Is Happening to News: The Information Explosion and the Crisis in Journalism.* Chicago: University of Chicago Press, 2010.

Gant, Scott. *We're All Journalists Now: The Transformation of the Press and Reshaping of the Law in the Internet Age.* New York: Simon & Schuster, 2007.

Geer, John G. *In Defense of Negativity: Attack Ads in Presidential Campaigns.* Chicago: University of Chicago Press, 2006.

Graber, Doris A. *Mass Media and American Politics,* 8th ed. Washington, DC: CQ Press, 2009.

Jones, Alex S. *Losing the News: The Future of the News That Feeds Democracy.* New York: Oxford University Press, 2009.

Kumar, Martha Joynt. *Managing the President's Message: The White House Communications Operation.* Baltimore, MD: Johns Hopkins University Press, 2009.

Luyendijk, Joris. *People Like Us: Misrepresenting the Middle East.* Berkeley, CA: Soft Skull, 2009.

Mark, David. *Going Dirty: The Art of Negative Campaigning.* Lanham, MD: Rowman & Littlefield, 2006.

Mindich, David T. Z. *Tuned Out: Why Americans Under 40 Don't Follow the News.* New York: Oxford University Press, 2004.

Perlmutter, David D. *Blogwars.* New York: Oxford University Press, 2008.

Pfau, Michael, J. Brian Houston, and Shane M. Semmler. *Mediating the Vote: The*

Changing Media Landscape in U.S. Presidential Campaigns. Lanham, MD: Rowman & Littlefield, 2007.

Prior, Markus. *Post-Broadcast Democracy: How Media Choice Increases Inequality in Political Involvement and Polarizes Elections.* New York: Cambridge, 2007.

Seib, Philip. *Beyond the Front Lines: How the News Media Cover a World Shaped by War.* New York: Palgrave, 2004.

Starr, Paul. *The Creation of the Media: Political Origins of Modern Communications.* New York: Basic Books, 2004.

Wasik, Bill. *And Then There's This: How Stories Live and Die in Viral Culture.* New York: Penguin, 2010.

West, Darrell M. *Air Wars: Television Advertising in Election Campaigns, 1952–2008,* 5th ed. Washington, DC: CQ Press, 2009.

CHAPTER 10

Interest Groups

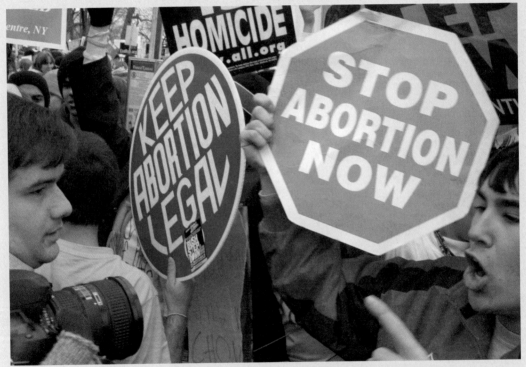

Pro-life and pro-choice groups sometimes engage each other directly and angrily. (Karen Bleir/Getty)

In 2010, Americans were spectators to two fierce back-to-back lobbying wars, the first over healthcare, the second over finance. The healthcare lobby alone had more than 3,300 registered lobbyists—many of them former staffers or Congresspersons—in Washington and dished out millions to elected officials of both parties. Their goal: Make sure nothing in the legislation limited the incomes of private insurers, pharmaceutical companies, doctors, or hospitals. The finance lobby was not far behind. Its goal: Make sure no regulatory reforms hurt the ability of banks and investment houses to make lots of money.

QUESTIONS TO CONSIDER

1. Can democracy exist without interest groups?
2. Are all citizens equal in organizing interest groups?
3. How does government create interest groups?
4. Are interest groups and their money too powerful?
5. What are PACs, 527s, and "soft money"?
6. Why are the French anti-pluralist?
7. Which is more effective: lobbying legislators or lobbying executives?
8. Can interest groups bypass democracy?

Critics denounce the influence of "big money" on politics, but in a democracy, there is nothing to stop it. To curb such influence would require limiting group inputs to the political process. Who would decide which groups should have how much influence?

The theory here argues that on your own, even in the finest democracy, you can do little. The solution: Form a group of like-minded individuals. After hard work organizing, fund-raising, and lobbying, you can start having an impact. In this view—a pluralist view (see Chapter 6)—the crux of politics is groups. It is a somewhat naïve view, as it pays no attention to the very unequal resources of various groups. Federal lobbying now runs at some $3.5 billion a year. Rich industries have major influence, average citizens little or none. Interest-group activity is especially strong in the pluralistic United States but is found everywhere, even in dictatorships, where groups quietly try to win the favor of the dictator.

WHAT IS AN INTEREST GROUP?

The term *interest group* (see page 106) covers just about any collection of people trying to influence government. Some interest groups are transient, others permanent. Some focus on influencing a particular policy, others on broad changes. Some work through the executive or administrative agencies, others through the judicial or legislative sectors, and still others through public opinion. But all are non–publicly accountable organizations that attempt to promote shared private interests by influencing public policy outcomes.

Who Belongs to Interest Groups?

Every advanced society is pluralistic, with many industrial, cultural, economic, educational, ethnic, and religious groups. Divergent interests lead almost automatically to group formation. In a pluralist democracy, a multiplicity of interest groups push their own claims and viewpoints, creating a balance of opposing interests that, in theory, prevents any one group from dominating the political system. In this optimistic view, government policy is the outcome of competition among many groups, which represent the varied interests of the people.

Interest groups, however, overrepresent the better-off and businesses. Because some groups are rich and well-connected, the democratic playing field is not level. Elite theorists argue that if group theory really operated, the poor would organize

---

KEY CONCEPTS ■ HOW INTEREST GROUPS DIFFER FROM POLITICAL PARTIES

Interest groups are a bit like political parties. Both try to influence public policy, but interest groups do it outside the electoral process and are not responsible to the public. A party must win elections. Interest groups may influence the nomination of candidates who are sympathetic to their cause, but the candidates run under the party banner—not the interest group banner.

Goals

Parties seek power though elections. Interest groups usually focus on specific programs and issues and are rarely represented in the formal structure of government. Instead, they try to influence legislators and executives. They often seek the favor of all political parties. Economic groups want the support of both the Republicans and the Democrats. Some interest groups favor one party. The National Rifle Association, for example, strongly supports Republican candidates.

Nature of Memberships

Political parties seek broad support to win elections and draw many interests into their ranks. Even the Republican Party includes people in all income brackets. The Democratic Party, billing itself as the party of the common person, has many wealthy supporters, including those from big finance. Interest groups have a narrower membership. Labor unionists share similar living and working conditions and goals. Idealistic interest groups draw those aiming at religious, environmental, or gender goals. Some groups link disparate groups, as when Roman Catholics and fundamentalist Protestants unite to oppose abortion.

For several reasons, including the length of a ballot, there are rarely more than a dozen or so political parties. But there is no limit on interest groups, and some countries, such as the United States, foster their growth. As Tocqueville observed in the 1830s, "In no country of the world has the principle of association been more successfully used or applied to a greater multitude of objects than in America." Tocqueville is still accurate. Open a Washington, DC, phone book to "National…" and count the hundreds of national associations, federations, and committees. Washington's prosperity is based on its attraction as a headquarters for more than 20,000 interest groups.

groups to get a bigger piece of the economic pie. But the poor, who have less education, are slow in forming groups to promote their interests. Better-off and better-educated people are more likely to participate in politics, and this includes organizing and running interest groups. In this area, too, the poor get shortchanged.

With few organizations to represent their interests, the lower classes may act explosively rather than as groups working within the political system. Their grievances can burst out, as in the 1789 storming of the Bastille at the start of the French Revolution. In the 1960s, U.S. inner-city riots reflected the anger that race-related poverty produced among many African Americans. The ghetto riots, while publicizing grievances, did little to challenge the power of business, labor unions, or other groups that keep things as they are. Not all sectors of society can effectively form and use interest groups.

Interest Groups and Government

Interest groups try to influence government. But what if there is not much government? In Afghanistan, near-anarchy prevails. The government's writ barely extends outside the capital, Kabul. There are plenty of groups: tribes, clans, warlords, opium growers, and Taliban fighters. In Mexico, drug-related crime is a major economic activity and leads to armed interest groups. The weak states of which we spoke in Chapter 4 are characterized by the interpenetration of crime and politics. Not all "interest group" activity is good or peaceful; it depends on the groups' willingness to operate within the law, which in turn requires strong states.

Interest groups presuppose an existing government that is worth trying to influence. Government, in fact, virtually calls many interest groups into life, for

KEY CONCEPTS ■ HOW GOVERNMENT CREATES INTEREST GROUPS

In 1938, as part of FDR's program to get out of the Depression, Congress created the Federal National Mortgage Association—soon known as "Fannie Mae"—to underwrite home loans and thus encourage home purchases and construction. In 1968, Congress made Fannie Mae private, turning it into a regular corporation that makes money by buying banks' mortgages, repackaging them, and selling them like bonds. To ensure competition in this important "secondary mortgage market," Congress in 1970 created the Federal Home Loan Mortgage Corporation ("Freddie Mac"), which is also private and does the same things as Fannie Mae.

Platoons of Fannie and Freddie lobbyists made sure Congress kept supporting the two mortgage giants. Wits described Fannie and Freddie as basically lobbying operations with mortgage side businesses. When the U.S. housing market turned sour in 2008, Congress quickly authorized unlimited taxpayer dollars to back up Fannie and Freddie, which were deemed "too big to fail." Many criticized the bailout that let Fannie and Freddie keep profits private but passed risks on to taxpayers.

This circular flow is common: Congress creates a program, the program creates an interest group, and then the interest group works on Congress to keep supporting it. U.S. farm subsidies, originally to help struggling farmers during the Depression, now cost billions a year, much of it to corporate "agribusiness," and few try to curb it. Programs, once set up, are hard to terminate due to interest group influence.

corporatism The direct participation of interest groups in
government.

they are intimately associated with government programs. There are farm lobbies because there are farm
programs, education lobbies because there are education programs, and veterans' lobbies because the government goes to war.

Once government is funding something, the groups that benefit develop
constituencies with a strong pecuniary interest in continuing the programs. As
government has become bigger and sponsored more programs, interest groups
have proliferated. By now, virtually every branch and subdivision of the U.S.
government has one or more interest groups watching over its shoulder and
demanding more grants, a change in regulations, or their own agency. The
Departments of Education and Energy were created under these circumstances,
and Ronald Reagan vowed to abolish them. He was unable to do so: The interests
associated with them—in part created by them—were too powerful.

Sometimes interest groups participate in government legislation and implementation. In Britain, "interested members" of Parliament are those who openly
represent industries or labor unions. This is not frowned on and is considered
quite normal. (Quietly selling government influence to British interest groups,
however, is considered "sleaze" and has produced scandals.) In Sweden, interest
groups are especially large and powerful. Swedish "royal commissions," which
initiate most new legislation, are composed of legislators, government officials, and
interest-group representatives. After a proposal has been drafted, it is circulated
for comments to all relevant interest groups. Some Swedish benefits for farmers
and workers are administered by their respective farm organizations and labor
unions. Some call this **corporatism**, meaning interest groups taking on government
functions. Top representatives of business, labor, and the cabinet meet regularly
in Sweden to decide a great deal of public policy. Critics charge that this too-cozy
relationship bypasses parliamentary democracy altogether.

KEY CONCEPTS ■ COUNTERVAILING POWER

One of the theories of pluralists is that no
interest group can monopolize power because
there are always one or more groups working
against it. The theory of countervailing power
argues that business associations are offset by
labor unions, the Jewish lobby by the Muslim
lobby, industries fearful of imports by industries
eager to export, and drug companies by retiree
associations. Such balances keep us free and
democratic, argue pluralists.

But do things always balance? As in most
of the world, U.S. unions have been declining in membership and are now much weaker
than business associations. Producers of electric
power and gasoline form powerful lobbies that
face no countervailing lobby of 300 million consumers. The battle over healthcare reform was
fought by giant insurers, hospital and physician
organizations, employers, and drug companies, spending $1.4 million a *day* in lobbying.
The 2010 bill contained no provision for public
insurance options—only private—because the
insurance industry blocked them. Consumers of
health care, on the other hand, are essentially
unrepresented. The theory of countervailing
power does not mean that it actually exists.

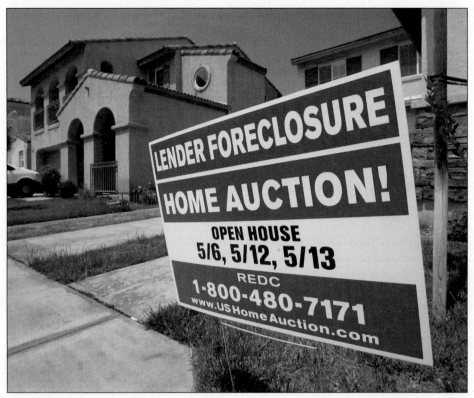

As a wave of foreclosures shattered the U.S. housing market, Americans pressed Congress to find out what had gone wrong. The influence of the mortgage, banking, and finance industries came under fire. (Mark Avery/Corbis)

Bureaucrats as an Interest Group

Government and interest groups are related in another important but sometimes overlooked way: Bureaucracies have become big and powerful interest groups. Civil servants are not merely passive implementers of laws; they also have input in the making and application of those laws. Much legislation originates in specialized agencies. Many of the data and witnesses before legislative committees are from the executive departments and agencies. In Japan, the powerful bureaucrats of the finance and trade **(METI)** ministries routinely tell the **Diet** what to legislate.

METI   Japan's Ministry of Economy, Trade, and Industry; formerly MITI, Ministry of International Trade and Industry.

Diet   Japan's national legislature.

Bureaucracies develop interests of their own. They see their tasks as terribly important and demand bigger budgets and more employees every year. When was the last time a civil servant recommended abolishing his or her agency or bureau? It was earlier proposed that interest groups are offshoots of society and the economy. That is only partly true, for they are also offshoots of government. Government and interest groups, to paraphrase Thomas Hobbes, were born twins. The more government, the more interest groups.

To say that every political system has interest groups says little, for interest groups in different systems operate quite differently. One key determinant in the way interest groups operate is the government. Here we can refine our definition of pluralism discussed in Chapter 6. Pluralism is determined not by the mere existence of groups, each trying to influence government, but by the degree to which government permits or encourages the open interplay of groups. Pluralism has a normative component, an "ought" or a "should."

EFFECTIVE INTEREST GROUPS

Political Culture

Interest groups flourish in pluralistic societies that have traditions of local self-governance and of forming associations. Where this is weak (see box on France below), interest groups have tough going. Americans, Britons, and Swedes are more likely to participate in voluntary associations than French, Italians, and Mexicans. The more educated are more likely to belong to an interest group. Not all groups are political, but even nonpolitical groups, by discussion among members, have some political influence. Members of a bicycle club become involved in politics when they support rails-to-trails bicycle paths. In societies where many join groups, people have a greater sense of political competence and efficacy. Some worry that the U.S. tendency to form groups has declined (see Chapter 7).

The Rise of Big Money

Money is probably the single most important factor in interest group success. With enough money, interests hardly need a group. Money is especially important for

COMPARING ■ FRENCH ANTIPLURALISM

The United States and Britain are highly pluralistic, for interest group activity is acceptable and desirable, and lobbying is normal for a healthy democracy. In France, on the other hand, interest group activity, although it does exist, is frowned on and considered dirty. France is heir to centuries of centralized and paternalistic government. The French are used to Paris ministries setting national goals and supervising much of the economy.

Further, the philosopher Jean-Jacques Rousseau still has a hold on the French mind.

Rousseau argued that there must be no "particular wills" to muddy and distort the "general will," that which the whole community wants. Rousseau presumed there was such a thing as a general will, something pluralists deny. Accordingly, interest groups are seen as trying to pervert the good of the whole community. French bureaucratic elites pay little attention to interest groups, considering them "unobjective." French interest groups operate in a more constrained atmosphere than their American or British counterparts.

elections, and groups help candidates who favor their causes. Most democracies have recognized the danger in too close a connection between interests and candidates, the danger that we will have the "best Congress money can buy," but in 2009 the U.S. Supreme Court lifted limits on direct corporate giving. It is but a very short step from influence-buying to **corruption**. U.S. peanut, sugar, corn, and cotton growers give generously to candidates and get federal subsidies. The healthcare and financial industries are the biggest campaign contributors—to both parties—and receive ample consideration. Said California political boss Jesse Unruh: "Money is the mother's milk of politics."

Many countries have tried reforms. Japanese reformers tried to break "money politics," the extreme dependence of politicians on interest groups—business conglomerates, banks, farmers, even gangsters—but have not yet succeeded. Germany and Sweden provide for almost complete **public financing** of the major parties in national elections. Spain, which rejoined the democracies only in 1977, subsidizes parties after the election according to how many votes they received and parliamentary seats they won. Some countries—Britain, France, and Germany, among others—try to limit campaign spending.

The United States has been reluctant to go to public financing of campaigns for several reasons. First, there is the strong emphasis on freedom. The U.S. Supreme Court has interpreted the First Amendment to include dollars as a form of free speech. When a person gives money to a candidate or cause, those are political statements. Second, U.S. campaigns are much longer and more expensive than in other democracies, the result of our weak, decentralized parties and nominating system. In Western Europe, elections can be short and cheap because the parties are already in place with their candidates and platforms. And third, given these two previous conditions, American legislators have not been able to find a formula for public financing that really works in the manner intended. Some efforts turn out to have negative **unforeseen consequences**.

Some individuals and **political action committees** contribute to parties and interest groups not directly working for a candidate's election campaign. This **soft money** funds groups that produce "issue ads" aimed *against* the other side without mentioning their own candidate's name, a big loophole in federal campaign laws. Soft money thus contributes to the trend toward negative advertising in political campaigns. In 2004, for example, a special "Swift-boat committee" that was clearly Republican ran TV ads accusing John Kerry of exaggerating his war heroism. In 2008, MoveOn.org (a "527," see next page), clearly Democratic, spent without limit on anti-Republican ads.

In 2002, after a hard struggle, the McCain-Feingold Campaign Reform Act passed. In 2003, the Supreme Court ruled it constitutional. Many cheered, but by 2004 it was irrelevant, skirted in three ways. First, limits are not very limiting; individuals may give

corruption Use of public office for private gain.

public financing Using tax dollars to fund something, such as election-campaign expenses.

unforeseen consequence Bad or counterproductive result when laws or policies do not work as expected.

political action committee (PAC) U.S. interest group set up specifically to contribute money to election campaigns.

soft money Campaign contributions to parties and issue groups so as to skirt federal limits on contributions to candidates.

single-issue group   Interest association devoted to one cause only.

AFL-CIO   American Federation of Labor-Congress of Industrial Organizations, the largest U.S. union federation.

NAM   National Association of Manufacturers, a major federation of U.S. industrial executives.

up to $2,000 directly to a presidential candidate, $25,000 to a national party, and much more to state and local parties and candidates. Second, many presidential hopefuls simply walked away from public campaign financing, which imposed spending ceilings, in favor of funds they raised on their own (now often gathered online), which have no limit. Barack Obama did this. Third, well-funded groups with no formal ties to candidates—called "527 committees" after a section of the tax code—spent prodigiously on "issues" that clearly favored one side; 527s operate under looser rules than PACs.

It is now apparent that parties and candidates will work around whatever reforms or laws attempt to curb big money in politics. In 1907, Teddy Roosevelt, reacting to the big money politics of his predecessor McKinley, supported the first reform, the Tillman Act, prohibiting corporations from giving funds. It looked good but was ineffective and has now been ruled unconstitutional. The Supreme Court's decision seems to rule that any statutory limits on campaign contributions are restrictions on free speech.

Critics fear that money politics is out of control. Defenders say this is just the workings of pluralist democracy, and the amounts are peanuts compared with the overall U.S. economy. Can or should anything be done about interest groups and money? Some suggest we go to a European-type system in which parties are better organized and campaigns are short and relatively cheap. But that is simply not the U.S. nominating and electoral system, which is complex and long. And Europe's interest groups still give plenty (sometimes under the table) to their favored candidates.

Public financing of all candidates—presidential nominees who gain at least 5 percent of the national vote are already entitled to federal financing—would be terribly expensive. Many U.S. taxpayers do not check off the option on their tax returns to contribute a few dollars to presidential campaigns, even though it costs them nothing. For the foreseeable future, it will not be possible to break the tie between big money and candidates in the United States.

The Rise of Single-Issue Groups

Perhaps the second-greatest factor in the influence of interest groups (after money) is the intensity of the issue involved. The right issue can mobilize millions, give the group cohesion and commitment, and boost donations. There have always been American interest groups pursuing one or another idealistic objective, but since the 1970s the rise of **single-issue groups** has changed U.S. politics. Typically, interest groups have several things to say about issues, for their interests encompass several programs and departments. Organized labor tries to persuade government on questions of Social Security, medical insurance, education, imports and tariffs, and the way unemployment statistics are calculated. The **AFL-CIO** has a long-term, across-the-board interest in Washington. The same can be said for many business groups, such as the **NAM**.

But to the single-issue groups, only one issue matters, and it matters intensely. Typically, their issues are moral—and therefore hard to compromise—rather than material. The most prominent of them is the right to life, or antiabortion, movement. In 1973, the Supreme Court ruled that states could not arbitrarily restrict a woman's right to an abortion. Many Roman Catholics and Protestant fundamentalists were shocked, for they believe that human life begins at the moment of conception and that aborting a fetus is therefore murder. "Pro-life" people would like to amend the Constitution to outlaw abortion. Opposing them are "pro-choice" forces, many linked to the women's movement. Feminists argue that abortion is a matter for the individual woman to decide and no one else; the right to choose gives women control over their lives and is part of their liberation from second-class status.

> **socioeconomic status** Combination of income and prestige criteria in the ranking of groups.

The antiabortionists make life miserable for many legislators. They care about nothing else—where officials stand on taxes, jobs, defense, and so on. They want to know where they stand on abortion, and a compromise middle ground—the refuge of many politicians faced with controversial issues—is not good enough. How can you be a "moderate" on abortion? Some elections turn on the abortion issue. Meanwhile, the pro-choice forces organize and grow militant to offset the pro-life forces. The 2005 Terri Schiavo case—whether to pull the plug on a comatose woman—also rallied pro-lifers.

Other single-issue causes appear, such as prayer in public school and same-sex marriage. Taken together, these two and the abortion question are sometimes referred to as the "morality issue." Gun control grew into a major issue, fanned by the assassinations of John and Robert Kennedy and Martin Luther King Jr. The powerful National Rifle Association (NRA) opposes such groups as Handgun Control. None of these issues makes elected representatives any happier. They like to be judged on a wide range of positions they have taken, not on one narrow issue on which it is hard to compromise.

Size and Membership

Their size and the intensity of their members give groups clout. The biggest and fastest-growing U.S. interest group is AARP (formerly the American Association of Retired Persons), with more than 40 million members (one American in eight), many of them educated, forceful, and strongly committed to preserving and enhancing Social Security and Medicare. Both parties proclaim that they want to preserve the two vast programs. When AARP speaks, Congress trembles.

Size alone, however, is not necessarily the most important element in interest group strength. Money and intensity often offset size. The well-funded American-Israel Public Affairs Committee (AIPAC), supported by many evangelical Christians, keeps Congress pro-Israel. The NRA fights gun control laws, mostly successfully. These three—AARP, AIPAC, and the NRA—are reckoned as Washington's most influential lobbies. All things being equal, a large group has more clout than a small one—but things are never equal.

The **socioeconomic status** of members gives groups clout. Better-off, well-educated people with influence in their professions and communities can form

structured access   Long-term friendly connection of interest group to officials.

groups that get more respect. The socioeconomic status of doctors, organized as the American Medical Association (AMA), helps them prevail in Washington. As Japanese Americans climbed educationally and professionally, their Japanese American Citizens' League (JACL) started having an impact and won apologies for the unconstitutional internment in World War II; JACL then worked on getting compensation. The National Association for the Advancement of Colored People (NAACP), on the other hand, speaks for millions but has relatively little influence. Disadvantaged groups with the biggest grievances are among the least likely to be listened to.

Access

Money, issue, and size may not count for much unless people in government are willing to listen. The careful cultivation of members of Congress and civil servants over the years makes sure doors are open. When a group has established a stable and receptive relationship with a branch of government, it is said to enjoy, in the words of Joseph LaPalombara, **structured access**. Greek-American members of Congress are, quite naturally, receptive to Greek arguments on questions concerning Turkey, Macedonia, and Cyprus. Michigan legislators likewise heed the complaints of the automobile industry. Arab Americans complain bitterly that Jews enjoy too much access on Capitol Hill and organize their own groups to gain access. There is nothing wrong with access as such; it is part and parcel of a working democracy.

But what happens when groups are shut out and have no access? Pluralists think this cannot happen in a democracy, but it does. Black and Native American militants argued that no one was listening to them or taking their demands seriously. Only violence in urban ghettos and on Indian reservations got Washington to listen. When the wealthy and powerful have a great deal of access, the poor and unorganized may have none. The consequences sometimes lead to violence.

COMPARING ■ HOW POWERFUL ARE U.S. UNIONS?

Labor unions in the United States are not very powerful, especially in comparative perspective. Since the 1950s, the percentage of American workers in labor unions has dropped by more than two-thirds. The percentages of the workforce that were unionized around 2006 are shown in the right column.

U.S. unions seem powerful because they attract much attention when they strike at major firms, but their biggest numbers are actually among government employees, including schoolteachers, who are often prohibited from striking. Business in the United States has far more clout than unions. U.S. unions are now striving for new members to get back some of their former strength.

Sweden	78%
Britain	28
Germany	20
Japan	19
United States	12
France	8

Strategies of Interest Groups

lobbying   Interest-group contact with legislators.

Approaching Lawmakers   **Lobbying** receives the most attention. The campaign contributions and favors to legislators given by corporations convince many that lobbyists buy Congress. Indeed, any major interest threatened by new laws spares no expense to make sure the laws are not passed, and they are usually successful. Senator John McCain (R-Ariz.), a critic of big money, said sadly, "Money buys access." He referred to a 2003 energy bill as "no lobbyist left behind." Big tobacco, which is especially generous to incumbent Republican candidates, routinely blocks or dilutes antismoking legislation. One favor big companies provide cooperative congresspersons: trips in the corporate jet. The average lobbying group, however, has little money to give, so most see themselves as providers of information.

Approaching the Administration   Depending on the issue, the executive branch may be a better interest-group target. The interest group may not need or want a new law, merely favorable interpretation of existing rules and regulations. For this, they turn to administrators. Antipollution groups, for instance, seek tighter definitions of clean air; industry groups seek looser definitions. Interest groups concentrate on the department that specializes in their area. Farm groups deal with the Department of Agriculture, public service companies with the Federal Power Commission, and so forth. As a rule, each department pays heed to the demands and arguments of groups in its area. In fact, many government bureaucracies are "captured" or "colonized" by the groups they deal with. The flow goes the other way, too. Some 200 former senators and Congress members along with many former top administration officials stay in Washington—with offices on famous K Street—as lobbyists, billing clients $500 an hour.

Interest groups employ many of the same tactics on executive departments that they use on legislators, including personal contacts, research, and public relations. Some provide money; in most of the world, corruption of public officials is the norm. The U.S. federal bureaucracy is one of the least corrupt in the world—state and local is something else. Federal officials caught on the take are usually political appointees and not career civil servants. Interest groups really make their influence felt in nominations to top-level government posts, including cabinet secretaries, to get officials who serve their interests.

Approaching the Judiciary   Interest groups may also use the courts, especially in the United States, for the U.S. judicial system has far more power than most judiciaries, which are merely part of the executive branch. In countries where rule of law is strong, the courts become an arena of interest group contention, as in Germany, where groups have taken cases on abortion and worker rights before the Federal Constitutional Court.

Every year, U.S. state and federal courts hear cases filed or supported by such interest groups as the American Civil Liberties Union and Sierra Club. In recent years, the U.S. Supreme Court has dealt with several social issues brought to it by interest groups, including women's rights, the death penalty, guns, and school

class action   Lawsuit on behalf of a group.

amicus curiae   Statement to a court by persons not party to a case.

prayer. Interest groups use two judicial methods to pursue their goals. First, they may initiate suits directly on behalf of a group or class of people whose interests they represent (such suits are commonly referred to as **class actions**). The second is for the interest group to file a "friend of the court" brief (**amicus curiae**) in support of a person whose cause they share.

Aware of the importance of the U.S. judicial system, especially of the Supreme Court, the National Association for the Advancement of Colored People (NAACP) focused much of its fight against racial segregation on the courts. It paid off. The legal staff of the NAACP, whose chief attorney was Thurgood Marshall (later a U.S. Supreme Court justice), successfully challenged the constitutionality of all state laws requiring racial segregation in public schools in the famous *Brown* decision of 1954. Then, the NAACP went on to challenge the legality of state laws on segregation in public transportation, restaurants, lodging, and other areas. The vast changes in U.S. civil rights happened first in the courts, not through legislation, because Congress would not tackle the issue—Southerners blocked it—until the mid-1960s. The Supreme Court led; Congress followed.

Appeals to the Public   Organized interests often take their case to the public with peaceful—or not so peaceful—appeals. Even powerful interest groups realize the importance of their public image, and many invest in public relations campaigns to explain how they contribute to the general welfare and why their interests are good for the country. For example, railroads used television to explain their case for "fair" government policies so they could stay alive and compete with trucking. The gasoline lobby explained why environmental restrictions work against building new refineries.

Some interest groups maintain a low profile by promoting their objectives without advertising themselves. Such groups may plant news stories that promote their cause and quietly work against the publication of stories detrimental to them. The Tobacco Institute, for example, discreetly funds research that casts doubt on findings that smoking is bad for your health. The American Petroleum Institute seeks no news coverage but has its officers quoted as unbiased experts above the political fray.

Demonstrations   Certain organizations, such as the American Cancer Society and the Heart Fund, may get free advertising space and time, but most interest groups do not, and many cannot afford to purchase such publicity. Such a disadvantaged group may hold demonstrations to publicize its cause. Mahatma Gandhi used this tactic to get the British to leave India. Gandhi learned about nonviolent protest from an influential essay on "civil disobedience" by American Henry David Thoreau, who protested the war with Mexico in 1846–1848. Thoreau's idea was also adopted by the Rev. Martin Luther King Jr. to push for African American civil rights in the 1950s and 1960s.

Some protesters against nuclear plants, facing the financial and political resources of power companies, felt that marching, picketing, and blocking plant entrances were their only options. News media coverage of their protests brought them adherents, contributors, and sometimes access in Washington. Their powerful opponents, of course, often prevailed, leading some protesters to become frustrated and bitter.

Violent Protest A group that loses faith in conventional political channels may see violent protest as its only alternative. The United States is no stranger to violent protests, which require a psychological buildup nurtured by poverty, discrimination, frustration, and a sense of personal or social injustice. An incident may spark pent-up anger, and mob behavior can escalate. Shootings and arrests of African Americans have sparked riots in U.S. cities. Defenders of the rioters claim they are simply *opposing* the violence they suffer daily at the hands of police, all levels of government, and an economy that keeps them underpaid or unemployed.

Does violent protest work? Perhaps it was no coincidence that the Great Society was passed during a period of U.S. urban riots. The British got out of India and Palestine when violence made the areas impossible to govern. The white government of South Africa started offering reforms only when blacks turned to violence.

HOW TO... ■ CREATE TABLES

A table is a list of the things you are studying—counties, countries, years, voters, legislators, interest groups—with numerical measures attached to each. Later, you may use some of these as "variables" (see page 148). Measures are whatever is relevant to the case you wish to make—dollars, population, or how many listings in a phone book. You list these things in some order—the biggest, most, or latest. Alphabetical order is often useless. In this chapter, we might list which PACs gave the most money, with the biggest givers first.

To take another example, the relative wealth of countries can be measured in several ways. The most basic is gross domestic product (GDP, see page 33), the first column of numbers, now usually corrected for cost of living (purchasing-power parity, PPP). Dividing that by population (the second column) gives per capita GDP (GDPpc) at PPP, the third column, the best comparison of relative wealth. Note how the table goes from richest to poorest.

Country	GDP ($ Billion)	Population (Million)	Per Capita GDP at PPP
United States	$14,300	307	$47,000
France	2,000	64	32,700
Russia	2,200	140	15,800
Mexico	1,600	111	14,200
Colombia	399	46	8,900
China	7,800	1,338	6,000
Syria	94	20	4,800
India	3,300	1,166	2,800

Source: *CIA World Factbook*

---

subprime   Risky mortgage made to unqualified borrower.

In certain circumstances, violence works. As black radical H. "Rap" Brown put it, "Violence is as American as cherry pie." (He is now in prison for murder.)

INTEREST GROUPS: AN EVALUATION

Interest groups are part of every democracy, but how well do they serve the needs of citizens? Interest groups help represent a wider range of interests in the legislative process—a good thing. Many smaller organizations, however, have neither the members nor the money to have any input. Unless they are able to form coalitions, they cannot defend their interests from larger, more powerful groups. The mere fact that interest groups articulate demands does not mean the demands will be heeded. Resources are highly unequal among interest groups. Some are rich and powerful and have a lot of influence. Others are ignored.

There is a further problem: What about individuals who are not organized into groups? Who speaks for them? Many citizens are not members or beneficiaries of interest groups. They vote for elected leaders, but the leaders pay more attention to group demands than to ordinary voters. If legislators and executives are attuned to interest groups, who is considering the interests of the whole country? At times, it seems as if no one is. Then we may begin to appreciate Rousseau's emphasis on the "general will" over and above the "particular wills" that make up society (see page 182).

For this reason, the "citizens' lobby" Common Cause was formed in 1970. Supported by donations, it won public funding of presidential campaigns, an end to the congressional seniority system, and disclosure of lobbying activities. In a similar vein, Ralph Nader set up several public interest lobbies on law, nuclear energy, tax reform, and medical care. Although groups such as these have done much good work, they raise an interesting question: Can a society as big and complex as America's possibly be represented as a whole, or is it inherently a mosaic of groups with no common voice?

Another problem is whether interest groups really speak for all their members or represent the views of a small but vocal minority. Most interest group leaders, like leaders of political parties, have stronger views than followers. Leaders are often red-hot, ordinary members lukewarm.

Skewing Policy

Interest group input may skew policy. The finance industry, for example, is a major interest group that contributes heavily to both parties and lobbies intensively. (Barack Obama got nearly $15 million from Wall Street and $19.4 million from health-related groups during his 2008 campaign. McCain got lesser amounts.) Since Reagan, Congress has generally delivered whatever the finance industry specified, and regulations and safeguards were rolled back so much of U.S. finance was little supervised. It was supposed to be "self-policing." One result was the 2006 "**subprime** crisis" that turned into a world-shaking

financial crisis in 2008. Lenders had pushed unqualified borrowers to take out home mortgages they
could not afford. The dubious loans were packaged

scandal   Corruption made public.

and sold off in pieces, like bonds. They were sold as safe investments, but then
home foreclosures shot up, and billions of dollars were lost. Frantically, Washington pumped taxpayer money into banks and into Fannie Mae and Freddie
Mac (see page 179), as their collapse threatened a new Depression.

The subsequent bailout of major financial institutions created a **scandal**, but it
was nothing new; indeed, there is about one every decade. In the 1980s, savings and
loans got Congress to roll back restrictions so they could make foolish and sometimes crooked loans. Then the whole thing collapsed, and the federal government
had to step in. In 2001, the mighty Enron, which manipulated electricity prices,
collapsed amid massive, hidden debts. Enron executives walked away with more
than $1 billion while employees and investors lost everything. Enron had also given
$5.9 million in political contributions, mostly to Republicans, to Bush 43, to 71 sena-
tors, and to 19 of the 23 members of the House energy committee. Several Enron
executives were convicted, and the blue-chip accounting firm of Arthur Andersen
(also a major Bush contributor) was found to have rigged audits and was forced to
close. Congress, by deregulating reasonable safeguards, bears much responsibility.

CLASSIC WORKS ■ OLSON'S THEORY OF INTEREST GROUPS

American economist Mancur Olson's 1965
Logic of Collective Action is widely accepted
and cited. He noted that small and well-organized groups, especially with money, often
override the broader public interest. The reason: The former have much to gain from favorable but narrow laws and rulings, so they lobby
intensely. The latter see nothing to gain, are
not organized or intense, and lobby little. The
public does not care if the price of shoelaces
jumps up, but shoelace manufacturers do. The
few trump the many.

Related to this is Olson's "free-rider syn-
drome": Why buy a ticket when you can ride
for free? People will not invest their time and
money in a cause when they get the same
results anyway. Why pay union dues when you
are already under a union contract? Why should
Europeans contribute much to NATO when the
Americans provide them with free security?

Olson warned in his 1982 *The Rise and
Decline of Nations* against what happens when
interest groups become too strong: They choke

off change and growth, leading to national
stagnation. Politicians, responding to one or
more powerful interests, do not consider the
wider public good. A prime example is Britain,
which, with highly organized interests and
politicians listening closely to those interests,
went into economic decline until Margaret
Thatcher blasted policy loose from both unions
and owners.

Germany and Japan, with their organized
interests destroyed in World War II, were free
for spectacular growth in the decades after
the war. By the late twentieth century, however, both were so gunked up with labor, industry, and farming associations that their growth
slowed to a trickle. Japan has an "iron trian-
gle" of economic interest groups, politicians,
and bureaucrats that defies reform. Some
followers of Olson fear that such "sclerosis"
is the fate of all countries. Has the United
States fallen victim to overstrong interests, or
has it been able to periodically shake loose
from them?

Such scandals are found worldwide; most trace back to laws that interest groups set up to favor themselves.

Stalemating Political Power

Interest groups compete with one another and in so doing limit the influence that any group can have on the legislature or a government agency. Interest groups may stalemate government action. Certain issues are "hot potatoes" because government action either way angers one group or another. Typically, such issues are ardently supported and vehemently opposed by competing groups with enough voting power and influence to drive politicians to equivocation. Government may get stuck, trapped between powerful interests and unable to move on important problems. Italy has been called a "stalemate society" for this reason.

In two-party systems, especially, issues tend to be muted by political candidates who try to appeal to as broad a segment of the voting public as possible. The result is a gap between the narrow interest of the individual voter and the general promises of an electoral campaign—a gap that interest groups attempt to fill by pressing for firm political actions on certain issues. But how well do interest groups serve the needs of the average citizen? The small businessperson, the uninformed citizen, and minority groups with little money tend to get lost in the push and pull of larger interests and government. The successful interest groups, too, tend to be dominated by a vocal minority of well-educated, middle- and upper-class political activists. In some cases, interest groups have become so effective that they overshadow parties and paralyze policymaking with their conflicting demands. The precise balance between the good of all and the good of particular groups has not yet been found.

mypoliscikit™ EXERCISES

Apply what you learned in this chapter on MyPoliSciKit (www.mypoliscikit.com).

 Assessment   Review this chapter using learning objectives, chapter summaries, practice tests, and more.

 Flashcards   Learn the key terms in this chapter; you can test yourself by term or definition.

 Video   Analyze recent world affairs by watching streaming video from major news providers.

 Comparative Exercises   Compare political ideas, behaviors, institutions, and policies worldwide.

KEY TERMS

AFL-CIO (p. 184)
amicus curiae (p. 188)
class action (p. 188)
corporatism (p. 180)
corruption (p. 183)
Diet (p. 181)
lobbying (p. 187)
METI (p. 181)

NAM (p. 184)
political action committee
(p. 183)
public financing (p. 183)
scandal (p. 191)
single-issue group (p. 184)
socioeconomic status
(p. 185)

soft money (p. 183)
structured access
(p. 186)
subprime (p. 190)
unforeseen
consequence (p. 183)

FURTHER REFERENCE

Berry, Jeffrey M. *The New Liberalism: The Rising Power of Citizen Groups.* Washington, DC: Brookings, 2000.

Biersack, Robert, Paul S. Herrnson, and Clyde Wilcox, eds. *After the Revolution: PACs, Lobbies, and the Republican Congress.* Needham Heights, MA: Allyn & Bacon, 1999.

Browne, William P. *Groups, Interests, and U.S. Public Policy.* Washington, DC: Georgetown University Press, 1998.

Cigler, Allan J., and Burdett A. Loomis, eds. *Interest Group Politics,* 7th ed. Washington, DC: CQ Press, 2006.

Graziano, Luigi. *Lobbying, Pluralism and Democracy.* New York: Palgrave, 2001.

Grossman, Gene M., and Elhanan Helpman. *Special Interest Politics.* Cambridge, MA: MIT Press, 2002.

Johnson, Haynes, and David S. Broder. *The System: The American Way of Politics at the Breaking Point.* Boston: Little, Brown, 1996.

Kaiser, Robert G. *So Damn Much Money: The Triumph of Lobbying and the Corrosion of American Government.* New York: Knopf, 2009.

Lindsay, D. Michael. *Faith in the Halls of Power: How Evangelicals Joined the American Elite.* New York: Oxford University Press, 2007.

Rauch, Jonathan. *Government's End: Why Washington Stopped Working.* New York: PublicAffairs, 1999.

Sabato, Larry J., and Glenn R. Simpson. *Dirty Little Secrets: The Persistence of Corruption in American Politics.* New York: Times Books/Random House, 1996.

Smith, Bradley A. *Unfree Speech: The Folly of Campaign Finance Reform.* Princeton, NJ: Princeton University Press, 2001.

Thomas, Clive S., ed. *Political Parties and Interest Groups: Shaping Democratic Governance.* Boulder, CO: Lynne Rienner, 2001.

Tilly, Charles, and Sidney Tarrow. *Contentious Politics.* Boulder, CO: Paradigm, 2006.

Wilcox, Clyde, and Carin Larson. *Onward Christian Soldiers? The Religious Right in American Politics.* Boulder, CO: Westview, 2006.

CHAPTER 11

Parties

Prime Minister Vladimir Putin, Russia's powerful chief, created the United Russia Party, a personalistic vehicle to ensure his reelection. (AFP/Getty)

To many Americans, a **political party** means little. The two major U.S. parties claim they are very different, but their basic values and proposals often overlap. In elections, candidate personality and fund raising is usually more important than party. This weakness of American parties is curious, for the United States was the first country to develop mass political parties, which appeared with the presidential election of 1800, decades before parties developed in Europe. Europeans, however, may have developed political parties more fully. Americans have tended to forget that parties are the great tools of democracy. As E. E. Schattschneider put it, "The rise of political parties is indubitably one of the principal distinguishing marks of modern government. Political parties created democracy; modern democracy is unthinkable save in terms of parties."

QUESTIONS TO CONSIDER

1. Can you have a democracy without competing parties?
2. What is "interest aggregation," and how do parties do it?
3. What good is party centralization, as in Britain?
4. How can a party seemingly commit electoral suicide?
5. How did Communist parties differ from democratic parties?
6. How do you classify parties on an ideological spectrum?
7. What is a "catchall" party?
8. What are the several types of *party systems*?
9. How do competitive party systems handle corruption?

Almost all present-day societies, whether they are democratic or not, have parties that link citizens to government. Military dictators—such as Franco in Spain, Pinochet in Chile, or generals in Pakistan—tried to dispense with parties, blaming them for the country's political problems. But even these dictators set up obedient parties to bolster their rule, and after the dictators departed, free parties appeared almost immediately. Whether they love political parties or hate them, countries seem to be unable to do without them.

FUNCTIONS OF PARTIES

In both democracies and authoritarian systems, parties perform several important functions that help hold the political system together and keep it working.

political party Group seeking to elect officeholders under a given label.

interest aggregation Melding separate interests into general platforms put forward by a political party.

A Bridge Between People and Government

To use a systems phrase, political parties are major "inputting" devices, allowing citizens to get their needs and wishes heard by government. Without parties, individuals would stand alone and be ignored by government. By working in or voting for a party, citizens can have some impact on political decisions. At a minimum, parties give people the feeling that they are not utterly powerless, and this belief helps maintain government legitimacy, one reason even dictatorships have a party.

Aggregation of Interests

If interest groups were the highest form of political organization, government would be chaotic and unstable. One interest group would slug it out with another, trying to sway government officials. There would be few overarching values, goals, or ideologies that could command nationwide support. (Some worry that the United States already resembles this situation.) Parties help tame and calm interest group conflicts by **interest aggregation**—pulling together their separate interests into a larger organization. The interest groups then find that they must moderate their demands, cooperate, and work for the good of the party. In return, they achieve at least some of their goals. Parties, especially large parties, can be analyzed as coalitions of interest groups.

A classic example of a party as interest aggregator was the Democratic Party that Franklin D. Roosevelt built in the 1930s, a coalition that got Democrats elected five times in a row. It consisted of workers, farmers, Catholics, Jews, and blacks. Labor unions, for example, working with the Democrats, got labor legislation they could never have won on their own. As long as this coalition held together, the Democrats were unbeatable; since then the coalition has fallen apart. In the 1980s, Ronald Reagan aggregated economic and noneconomic conservative groups into the Republican Party, a coalition revived by Bush in 2000.

Integration into the Political System

Parties also pull into the political system groups that had previously been left out. Parties usually welcome new groups into their ranks, giving them a say or input into the formation of party platforms. This gives the groups both a pragmatic and a psychological stake in supporting the overall political system. Members of the group feel represented and develop a sense of efficacy and loyalty to the system. The British Labour Party and the U.S. Democratic Party, for example, enrolled workers by demanding union rights, fair labor practices, welfare benefits, and educational opportunities. Gradually, a potentially radical labor movement learned to play by democratic rules and support the system. Now, ironically, British and American workers are so successfully integrated into the political systems that many vote Conservative or Republican. In countries where parties were unable to integrate workers into the political system, labor movements turned radical and sometimes revolutionary. In the United States, parties also integrate successive waves of immigrants and minorities into American political life.

Political Socialization

Parties also teach their members how to play the political game. Parties introduce citizens to candidates or elected officials and show members how to speak in public, to conduct meetings, and to compromise, thus deepening their *political competence* (see page 122) and building among them legitimacy for the system as a whole. Parties are also the training grounds for leaders. Historically, some

---

HOW TO... ■ CREATE A CROSS-TABULATION

A cross-tabulation ("cross-tab") is a table that shows two variables, arrayed so the reader can see a relationship between the two. When one is high, for example, so mostly is the other. Let's take two variables, per capita GDP (see page 33) and Freedom House's ranking of countries' freedom on a scale from 1 to 7 (see page 98).

Readers quickly see that rich countries (the United States and France) and a middle-income country (Mexico) are democracies (what Freedom House calls "free") but poorer countries generally are not. A cross-tab is not your whole paper; it is just a starting point and may raise questions.

Here, for example, two countries, India and Russia, do not fit. Why is poor India a democracy and middle-income Russia not? We might study the long development of India's Congress Party and how it set India on the course (sometimes unsteady) to democracy. Russia, whose experience with parties was approximately the opposite, sank down in the FH ratings even as its oil income climbed. Kenya for a long time was not free but recently held reasonably free and fair elections. This cross-tab shows that economic level is only part of the story; you must get into each country's history, institutions, and culture as well.

Country	2009 Per Capita GDP at PPP	Freedom House 2010 Rating	
United States	$46,000	1	(free)
France	32,600	1	(free)
Russia	15,100	5.5	(not free)
Mexico	13,200	2.5	(free)
Colombia	9,200	3.5	(partly free)
China	6,600	6.5	(not free)
Syria	4,600	6.5	(not free)
India	3,100	2.5	(free)
Kenya	1,600	4	(partly free)

Sources: *CIA World Factbook* and Freedom House

mobilization Rousing people to participate in politics.

centralization Degree of control exercised by national headquarters.

European parties attempted to set up distinct subcultures—with party youth groups, soccer leagues, newspapers, women's sections, and so on. The effort was self-defeating, however, for as these parties socialized their members to participate in politics, they emerged from their subcultures. The fading remnants of this effort can still be found in Italy both in the renamed Christian Democrats, now the Popular Party, and the renamed Communists, now the Democratic Party of the Left. Some American parties provided social services. New York's Tammany Hall welcomed European immigrants, found them jobs and housing, and enrolled them as Democrats.

Mobilization of Voters

Parties get out the vote. In campaigning for their candidates, parties are **mobilizing** voters—whipping up interest and boosting turnout. The 2008 U.S. election is an example. Without party advertising, many citizens would ignore elections. Most political scientists believe there is a causal connection between weak U.S. political parties and low voter turnout. In Sweden, strong and well-organized parties have produced voter turnouts of 90 percent (recently lower). Some critics object that party electoral propaganda trivializes politics. This is true, but simplifying and clarifying issues is a worthwhile function that enables voters to choose among complex alternatives.

Organization of Government

The winning party gets government jobs and power and shifts policy its way. The party with the most seats in the U.S. House of Representatives or Senate appoints the chamber's leaders and committee chairpersons. A new president can appoint some 3,000 people to executive departments and agencies, allowing the party to steer policy for at least four years. Party control of government in Britain is tighter than in the United States because Britain's parliamentary system gives simultaneous control of both the legislative and executive branches to the winning party. What a prime minister wants, he or she usually gets—and with minimal delay because party discipline is much stronger. In no system, however, does a party completely control government, for bureaucrats are also quite powerful (see Chapter 14). Parties *attempt* to control government; they do not always succeed.

PARTIES IN DEMOCRACIES

In democracies, three points of party organization are important: the degree of **centralization**, the extent to which a party participates in policy, and how parties finance themselves.

Centralization

The amount of control party leadership exerts on its elected people varies widely. Israel has highly centralized candidate selection; each party draws up a *party list* (see page 71) of 120 nominees to the Knesset (parliament), and voters pick one list. Under proportional representation (see page 70), only those listed at the top can expect to win seats. Party chiefs place tried and trusted people higher on the list and newcomers lower. This ensures centralized party discipline.

coherence   Sticking together to make a rational whole.

Britain is a little less centralized. British parties select candidates by bargaining between national headquarters and local constituency organizations. The national headquarters may suggest a candidate who is not from that district—often the case in Britain—and the local party will look the person over to approve or disapprove the candidate. The local party may also run its own candidate after clearing the nomination with national headquarters.

Germany, like Israel, uses party lists but is divided into 16 states, thus partly decentralizing national party control. The varying degrees of centralization of these systems gives their parties **coherence**, discipline, and ideological consistency. When you vote for a party in Israel, Britain, or Germany, you know what it stands for and what it will implement if elected. Once elected, members of these parliaments do not go their separate ways but vote according to party decisions.

Party discipline in the United States, where parties have historically been decentralized, is weaker. In most cases, candidates rely on themselves to raise funds and campaign. Candidates for the House and the Senate, in effect, create a new local or state party organization every time they run. Between elections, U.S. parties lie dormant. The Republican and Democratic National Committees may not have many resources to distribute to candidates. Candidates appeal directly to voters through television and other media. Increasingly, TV spots do not even mention the candidate's party affiliation. Candidates are thus in a position to tell their national parties, "I owe you little. I didn't get much party help to win, and I won't necessarily obey you now that I'm in office." This makes U.S. parties decentralized and often incoherent. Elected officials answer to their conscience, to their constituents, and to their PACs, not to their political parties. (President Reagan made the Republican Party more coherent.)

Setting Government Policy

To what extent can the winning party enact its legislative program? Here, the U.S. party system faces its severest criticism. In parliamentary systems, the majority party must resign when it can no longer muster the votes in parliament to carry on its program. The U.S. problem is often identifying where the majority lies. "Blue Dog Democrats"—typically, those elected from conservative districts—vote with Republicans on some issues. Some change parties, as did Senators Jim Jeffords of Vermont and Arlen Specter of Pennsylvania. The platform the president won on is not binding on congressional members of the party. Often, the president's party is not the majority party in one or both houses. And who determines a party's

neoinstitutional theory Institutions take on lives of their own, sometimes disconnected from electorates.

legislative program? The president? The speaker of the House? The Senate majority leader?

The U.S. president may present a legislative program, but it must be acted on by 535 individual senators and representatives, all ultimately responsible for their own vote, as they are for their own reelection. Is the president, then, to be blamed for failing to fulfill campaign promises, or does the fault lie with too-loose party discipline? Schattschneider argued that, because U.S. national parties are so decentralized, they cannot agree on a strong national platform, making Washington "a punching bag for every special and local interest

KEY CONCEPTS ■ PARTIES THAT IGNORE VOTERS

Can a political party in a democracy ignore voters? According to democratic theory, no, for they will soon lose elections and have to change their tune. But according to **neoinstitutional theory** (page 36), they can be so self-absorbed that they rumble on with little regard to what voters want. An old, established party with strong traditions and leadership patterns may be so focused on struggles *inside* the party that they neglect voter opinion *outside* the party. The party as institution can take on a life of its own apart from trying to win elections. The British Labour Party, talking mostly to itself and assuming positions too far left for most voters, lost four elections in a row. Finally getting sensible and centrist, they won in 1997, 2001, and 2005. Again losing direction and coherence, they lost in 2010.

The Canadian Progressive Conservatives (PC) in 1983, under Brian Mulroney, won a majority of the House of Commons's 295 seats. Mulroney and the PC adopted Thatcherite free-market policies and stayed with them even though unemployment climbed and their popularity declined. The PC and Mulroney campaigned on the new free trade agreement (NAFTA) and won again in 1988 but with a reduced majority. A worsening economy, the Quebec question, and favoritism to certain firms brought the PC into public disrepute. Why didn't the PC change? Why didn't Mulroney resign? Eventually he did but not until late in his second five-year term; he passed power to Kim

Campbell, Canada's first woman prime minister, a short-lived sacrificial lamb. In the 1993 elections, the PC almost disappeared, winning only two (2!) seats. The Liberals took over Ottawa, and the PC disappeared, replaced by a new Conservative Party, which won Canada's 2006 elections.

Japan's Liberal Democratic Party (LDP), which governed Japan for decades, also ignored voters. In 1990 Japan entered a long economic slump. Inept LDP leaders talked about financial reforms but delivered little. Factions inside the LDP blocked each other. LDP chiefs figured they would always be reelected because Japanese voters dislike change, but the voters grew fed up with the LDP and in a series of elections brought it down to less than half of the Diet seats. Many LDP politicians left the party to start new parties. Voters finally booted out the LDP in favor of the DPJ in 2009.

The result in Canada and Japan of corrupt old parties was new parties. How could ruling parties shoot themselves in the foot? Don't they read the polls? They do, but politics inside the parties and payoffs from interest groups mattered more to them than voters. They forgot their original purpose, to win elections. Actually, every time a major party loses big, it is a sign that the party is too self-absorbed: the U.S. Republicans under Goldwater in 1964, the British Conservatives under Major in 1997, and the German Christian Democrats under Kohl in 1998.

in the nation." Most Americans, however, prefer our senators and representatives to vote their consciences rather than the dictates of party leadership as is the case in Europe.

Great Society President Johnson's ambitious program of social reforms.

political appointment Government job given to non–civil servant, often as reward for support.

transparency Political money and transactions open to public scrutiny.

Party Participation in Government

A European type of parliamentary system is more conducive to what Schattschneider regarded as responsible party government. The U.S. system, with its checks and balances, makes it difficult for parties to bridge the separation of powers to enact platforms. Occasionally, when a powerful president controls both the White House and Congress, party platforms turn into law, as when Lyndon Johnson got his **Great Society** program through the Democratic Congress of 1965–1966. No European parliamentary system had ever passed so many sweeping reforms so quickly.

In European parliamentary systems, the winning party is the government, or, more precisely, the party's leadership team becomes the cabinet. This system allows for more clear-cut accountability and voter choice than in the decentralized American party system. In both systems, parties participate in government by providing jobs for party activists in departments and agencies. In Britain, about 100 members of the winning party's parliamentary faction take on cabinet and subcabinet positions, compared with the 3,000 Americans who can receive **political appointments** when a new president takes office.

Financing the Party

Parties must finance their activities, and these are increasingly expensive, deepening the parties' dependence on rich interest groups. There is little **transparency** in these relationships. As one political scientist put it, "Whole books could remain unwritten if we just knew how parties funded themselves." Japan's Liberal Democrats were notorious for the sums they received from businesses, banks, farmer federations, and even *yakuza* gangsters. The traditional European style of small membership dues does not provide nearly enough, and parties have become desperate to raise money. Some do it crookedly. Almost every democratic country suffers scandals related to party fund-raising: the United States, Britain, France, Germany, and Japan. The problem may be incurable, related to the political competition that is the crux of democracy. In 1976, an estimated $500 million was spent on U.S. political campaigns. In 2008, more than $5 billion was spent for presidential and congressional campaigns. In contrast, total spending in the 2010 British general elections was only $150 million, but it too is growing rapidly.

As we discussed in the previous chapter, many democracies have laws to restrict or regulate political contributions. Germany, Spain, Sweden, and Finland use government funds to subsidize political parties in proportion to each party's electoral strength. This obviously discriminates against new parties. The U.S. Congress in 1974 passed a similar plan (the Presidential Campaign Fund), which allowed taxpayers to

nationalization Putting major industries under government ownership.

authorize the Internal Revenue Service to designate $3 of their income tax payment for the fund, which subsidized presidential nominees in proportion to the votes they received, provided they got a minimum of 5 percent nationwide. But only one taxpayer in four pays into the Presidential Campaign Fund, far too few to cover campaign expenses. PACs and 527s (discussed in Chapter 10) have filled the vacuum with a vengeance.

CLASSIFYING POLITICAL PARTIES

One basic way to classify parties is on a left-to-right spectrum, according to party ideology (see Chapter 3). Left-wing parties, such as Communists, propose leveling of class differences by **nationalizing** major industries. Center-left parties, such as the Socialist parties of Western Europe, favor welfare states but not nationalized industries. Centrist parties, such as the German and Italian Liberals, are generally liberal on social questions but conservative (that is, free market) on economics. Center-right parties, such as the German Christian Democrats, want to rein in (but not dismantle) the welfare state in favor of free enterprise. Right-wing parties, such as the British Conservatives under Thatcher, want to dismantle the welfare state, break the power of unions, and promote vigorous capitalist growth. Sweden has a rather complete political spectrum (see Figure 11.1).

Figure 11.1 ▶

The eight parties in Sweden's 349-member Riksdag (parliament) illustrate the left-right spectrum. Sweden uses proportional representation (see Chapter 4). The ruling "Alliance" of Moderate, Christian Democrat, Liberal, and Center parties, still just short of a majority, depends on occasional votes from other parties.

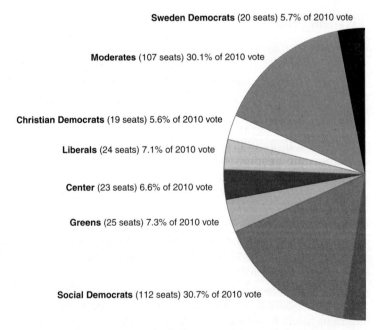

Sweden Democrats (20 seats) 5.7% of 2010 vote

Moderates (107 seats) 30.1% of 2010 vote

Christian Democrats (19 seats) 5.6% of 2010 vote

Liberals (24 seats) 7.1% of 2010 vote

Center (23 seats) 6.6% of 2010 vote

Greens (25 seats) 7.3% of 2010 vote

Social Democrats (112 seats) 30.7% of 2010 vote

Party of the Left (19 seats) 5.6% of 2010 vote

Communist systems—that is, countries ruled by Communist parties—have become rare. In Eastern Europe and the Soviet Union, Communist parties were voted out of power. China, Vietnam, North Korea, and Cuba try to preserve the party-controlled state, but they too appear ripe for change.

The "classic" Communist system founded by Lenin and developed by Stalin in the Soviet Union featured the interlocking of a single party with government and the economy. The Communist Party did not rule directly; instead, it supervised, monitored, and controlled the personnel of the state and economic structures. Members—about 10 percent of the adult population—were hand-picked from among the most intelligent, energetic, and enthusiastic. Most Soviet officials wore two hats: one as government functionary and another as Communist Party member. Every level of government, from local to national, had a corresponding party body that nominated its candidates and set its general lines of policy. At the top of the state structure, for example, was the legislature, the Supreme Soviet. Corresponding to it in the party system, the Central Committee oversaw the nomination of candidates to the Supreme Soviet, set its agenda, and guided its legislative outcomes. Supervising the Central Committee, the **Politburo** of a dozen or so top party leaders was the real heart of Soviet governance. Guiding the Politburo was the party's general secretary, who could appoint loyal followers to high positions and thus amass great power.

Why did Soviet President Mikhail Gorbachev (1985–1991) deliberately undermine this structure? A single party that attempts to control everything important develops severe problems over the years. Because it gives members the best jobs, housing, and consumer goods, the party fills up with **opportunists**, many

Politburo   Russian for "political bureau"; the ruling committee of a Communist party.

opportunists   Persons out for themselves.

mass party   One that attempts to gain committed adherents; usually has formal membership.

cadre party   One run by a few political professionals and only intermittently active.

devotee party   One based on a single personality.

personalistic   Based on personality of strong ruler.

CLASSIC WORKS ■ DUVERGER'S THREE TYPES OF PARTIES

One of the first typologies of political parties was devised by French political scientist Maurice Duverger (1917–), who developed three categories: mass, cadre, and devotee. The **mass parties** are well organized and strive for a large and ideologically committed membership, such as West European Socialist parties. They fund themselves with members' dues. In contrast, **cadre parties**, such as the U.S. Democratic and Republican Parties, are weakly organized and based on a politically active elite. **Devotee parties** are those such as the Nazis under Hitler, where the party is built around one person. Akin to that are the **personalistic** parties of Latin American strongmen, such as Perón of Argentina and Vargas of Brazil. One example was Saddam Hussein's Ba'ath (Arab Renaissance) Party in Iraq. Personalistic parties, however, have trouble outliving their founders.

apparatchik Russian for "person of the apparatus"; full-time Communist party functionary.

Weltanschauung German for "worldview"; parties that attempt to sell a particular ideology.

catchall Large, ideologically loose parties that welcome all.

of them corrupt. The party **apparatchiks** also become highly conservative. The system favors them, and they have no desire to reform it. With such people supervising it, the Soviet economy ran down and fell further behind the American, West European, and Japanese economies. A Communist Party that was to lead the Soviet Union into a radiant future came to be seen as leading the country backwards. Gorbachev concluded that to save his country he had to break the party's monopoly on power. Gorbachev failed to understand (as did many Western political scientists) how brittle the system was. Unable to reform, it collapsed.

The Soviet experience suggests that single parties that monopolize power are not workable over the long-term. Without the invigorating elements of debate, competition, and accountability, Communist-type parties become corrupt, inflexible, and unable to handle the new, complex tasks of a modern world. Study Communist systems while you can; soon there may be none left.

CLASSIC WORKS ■ KIRCHHEIMER'S "CATCHALL" PARTY

Accompanying the tendency of most democracies to *two-plus* party systems (see page 207) has been the growth of big, sprawling parties that attempt to appeal to all manner of voters. Before World War II, many European parties were ideologically narrow and tried to win over only certain sectors of the population. Socialist parties were still partly Marxist and aimed their messages largely at the working class. Centrist and conservative parties aimed at the middle class, agrarian parties at farmers, Catholic parties at Catholics, and so on. These were called **Weltanschauung** parties because they tried not merely to win votes but also to promote their view of the world.

After World War II, Europe changed a lot. With prosperity, people began to reject the old ideological narrowness. In most of Western Europe, big, ideologically loose parties that welcomed all voters either absorbed or drove out the *Weltanschauung* parties. German political scientist Otto Kirchheimer coined the term **catchall** to describe this new type of party. His model was the German Christian Democratic

Party, a party that sought to speak for all Germans: businesspersons, workers, farmers, Catholics, Protestants, women, you name it.

The term now describes virtually all ruling parties in democratic lands; almost axiomatically, they must be catchall parties to win. The British Conservatives, Spanish and French Socialists, and Japanese Democrats are catchall parties. And, of course, the biggest and oldest catchall parties of all are the U.S. Republicans and Democrats.

Most political scientists welcome this move away from narrowness and rigidity, but with it comes another problem. Because catchall parties contain many viewpoints, they are plagued by factional quarrels. Struggles within parties replace struggles between parties. Scholars counted many factions in the Italian Christian Democrats and Japanese Liberal Democrats, parties that resembled each other in their near-feudal division of power among the parties' leading personalities. A good deal of American politics also takes place within rather than between the major parties.

PARTY SYSTEMS

"Party systems" are not the same as "parties." Parties are organizations aimed at winning elections. **Party systems** are the interactions of parties with each other. With parties, we look at the trees; with party systems, we look at the forest. Much of the health of a political system depends on the party system, whether it is

party system How parties interact with each other.

electoral system Laws for running elections; two general types: single-member district and proportional.

inchoate Not yet formed.

stable or unstable, whether it has too many parties, and whether the parties compete in a *center-seeking* or *center-fleeing* manner (see page 209). An unstable party system can wreck an otherwise good constitution. Stable, moderate party systems made democracy possible in West Germany after Hitler and in Spain after Franco. In turn, much of the country's party system depends on its **electoral system**—whether it is based on single-member districts or on proportional representation.

Britain's party system led to a "hung parliament" and shaky government following the 2010 elections. As usual, Britain's perennial third party, the Liberal Democrats, won about 20 percent of the vote but fewer than 10 percent of the seats. But the Tories lacked a majority of seats, so the Lib Dems became indispensible coalition partners. The Lib Dems' price: reform of Britain's FPTP electoral system (see page 69) to give them a fairer slice of seats. Party system, in part related to electoral system, really matters in politics.

Classifying Party Systems

The simplest way to classify party systems is to count the number of parties in them: one, two, and multiparty. In between one and two we put "dominant-party system." In between two and multiparty we put "two-plus party system." Theoretically, there can be a no-party system, but, as we discussed, even dictators like obedient parties to support them. And some systems may be so messy we call them fluid or **inchoate** party systems.

One-Party Systems Associated with totalitarian regimes, this is a twentieth-century phenomenon that lingers into the twenty-first. The Soviet Union, China, and many of the emerging nations of Africa and Asia are or were one-party states. These have a single party that controls every level of government and is the only legal party. The leaders of such parties rationalize that they are still democratic because they represent what the people really want and need. No fair election or public opinion poll can substantiate this claim. When allowed, as in East European countries, citizens repudiate one-party systems. Some developing lands, especially in Africa, argue that having several parties spells chaos and violence, for they form along tribal lines.

Dominant-Party Systems In contrast to one-party systems, opposition parties in dominant-party systems contest elections, but they rarely win. Some democratic nations had dominant-party systems, but they tend not to last because voters get fed up with the dominant party's corruption and ineptitude. India was long governed by the Congress Party, Japan by the Liberal Democrats, and Mexico by the Party of Institutional Revolution (PRI). In 2000, Mexico's conservative National Action Party (PAN) overcame PRI's lock on the presidency with the election of Vicente Fox, thus moving Mexico from a dominant-party to a multiparty system (flanked on the left by the Revolutionary Democratic Party). The Democratic Party of Japan finally ousted the Liberal Democrats in 2009. Russia now has a dominant-party system under Putin's United Russia Party.

Two-Party Systems   Most familiar to us is the two-party system of the United States and Britain. Here two major parties have about an equal chance of winning. Although third parties such as the U.S. Libertarians and Britain's United Kingdom Independence Party (UKIP) seldom win, they serve to remind the two big parties of voter discontent. Often one or both of the two main parties then offer policies calculated to win over the discontented. In this way, even small third parties can have an impact. Some observers argue that new political ideas come mostly from third parties, as the big parties are too stuck in their ways.

Multiparty Systems   These have several competing parties. The Swedish party system (see page 202) has parties arrayed on a left-to-right spectrum. Each receives seats in parliament in proportion to their share of the vote. This system is often criticized as being unstable. Israel and Italy are examples of having too many parties; both had trouble keeping a government in power for a long time. A fragmented party system makes it harder for any one party to win a governing majority, but this is not always

KEY CONCEPTS ■ WHAT IS A "RELEVANT" PARTY?

Columbia University political scientist Giovanni Sartori asks just what counts as a party. Is there some minimum size—such as winning a certain percentage of votes or a seat in parliament— that makes a small group a party? We should count as relevant, Sartori argues, parties that the main parties have to take into account either in campaigning for votes or in forming coalitions. If a party is so small that no major party needs to worry about trying to win over its adherents, it is irrelevant. Likewise, if it is unnecessary in forming a governing coalition, it is irrelevant. Thus, British Trotskyists and Irish Communists are ignored by all and do not count as parties, but Sweden's Liberals and Israel's small religious parties, each with only a few percent of the vote, may be necessary coalition partners and thus count as relevant parties.

Using Sartori's definition of relevant parties, would we include various American third-party efforts? Although the Democrats in 1948

denied the importance of the States' Rights Party (Dixiecrats) and in 1968 the importance of Wallace's forces, in both elections they took them into account. In 1968, Democratic nominee Hubert Humphrey visited the South and emphasized that the Democratic Party was a "very big house" that could accommodate many viewpoints, a lame attempt to make white Southern voters forget the civil rights reforms of the Johnson administration. In 1980, the independent candidacy of John Anderson probably forced President Carter to emphasize foreign and ecological policies he might otherwise have minimized. In 1992, Ross Perot forced Bush 41 and Clinton to pay more attention to the federal budget deficit. In 2004, John Kerry paid attention to Ralph Nader's effort, for it had cost the Democrats the 2000 election. In 2010 the Republicans had to pay attention to Tea Party complaints. In these cases, we could say the United States had relevant third parties.

the case. The Netherlands, Sweden, and Norway generally construct stable multiparty coalitions that govern effectively. The number of parties is not the only reason for cabinet **instability**. Much depends on the political culture, the degree of agreement on basic issues, and the rules for forming and dissolving a cabinet. Scholars have long debated which is better: two-party or multiparty systems. It's hard to say, for both have fallen prey to indecision and **immobilism**. In the meantime, there has been a drift in both systems toward a middle ground, "two-plus" party systems.

> **instability**   Frequent changes of cabinet.
>
> **immobilism**   Getting stuck over a major political issue.

Two-Plus Party Systems   Many democratic countries now have two large parties with one or more relevant smaller parties. Germany has large Christian Democratic and Social Democratic parties, but the Free Democratic, Green, and Left parties win enough votes to make them politically important. Austria was long dominated by two big parties but now has a third party, the highly nationalistic and anti-immigrant Freedom Party. Britain is usually referred to as a two-party system, but it has long had third parties of some importance. In 2010, Britain's Liberal Democrats were courted because neither Conservatives nor Labour had a majority of seats. If the Lib

---

COMPARING ■ MULTIPARTY SYSTEMS ARE MORE FUN

In a multiparty system, you get to choose from a bigger menu. With several relevant parties, as in Sweden (see page 202), you can find a party that matches your preferences much better than just the two big U.S. parties. In most of Europe, people concerned about the environment can vote for a Green Party. Serious Christians can vote for a Christian Democratic Party. Leftists can vote for a Socialist Party and conservatives for a Conservative Party.

True, U.S. ballots (depending on the state) may list more than a dozen parties, ranging from Green to Libertarian to Socialist Workers, but if you vote for them you feel you are throwing your vote away. Such is the impact of our winner-take-all electoral system, so a vote for a third party in the United States is simply a protest vote. Voters in much of Europe and in Israel know they are not throwing their votes away; if their party gets some minimum threshold (5 percent in Germany, 2 percent in Israel), the party wins some seats in parliament. The interesting choices on European ballots help explain Europe's higher voter turnout.

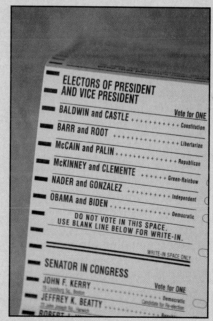

The United States has a two-party system, but many small parties appear on the ballot. They stand no chance but hope to catch a protest vote. (David Brabyn/Corbis)

two-plus party system Country having two big and one or more small parties.

Dems get electoral reform, they will make Britain a clear two-plus party system. Scottish Nationalists and Plaid Cymru (the Welsh nationalists) are nontrivial British regional parties. Spain, which has a history of multiparty fragmentation, now has a **two-plus party system**: a large Socialist Party, a large center-right Popular Party, and a scattering of smaller parties. Looked at more closely, the U.S. system is also really two-plus, for it too has long had third parties. The Tea Party movement could potentially turn into a third party, something Republicans strive to prevent.

Fluid Party Systems New and unstable democracies often have party systems so fluid and inchoate they change before your eyes and fit none of the previous categories. "Mess" is the only way to describe them. In such countries, parties rise and fall quickly—sometimes existing just for one election—and are often personalistic vehicles to get leaders elected but otherwise stand for no program or ideology. Poorly organized, many of them soon fall apart. Charismatic Latin American politicians often invent new parties, but they rarely last. In Poland, Czechoslovakia, and Hungary, broad catchalls ousted the Communists in 1989, won free elections, but soon fragmented. The Russian party system was fluid; President Putin founded his own Unity Party just before the 1999 election and by 2004 turned it into Russia's largest, but it is personalistic, just a tool for Putin to govern with. The Japanese system broke down from a dominant-party system to an inchoate one in the 1990s but has consolidated into a multiparty system.

As long as there are at least two parties, we call the system a "competitive party system," the essence of which is to impede corruption. A single party that locks itself in power, whatever its ideological rationale, tends to become corrupt. One way to keep corruption in check is by an "out" party hammering away at corruption in the administration of the "in" party. The utility of a competitive party system was underscored in 1989 in East Germany, where Communist leaders skimmed millions from foreign-trade deals and stashed them in Swiss banks for personal use. When such antics are uncovered in competitive-party systems, the "ins" are soon out.

The Party System and the Electoral System

How a nation gets its party system is complex. Much is rooted in historical developments. When and under what circumstances was the electoral franchise expanded? Some very different countries have similar party systems: Culturally segmented India produced a dominant party system (under the Congress party), as did culturally homogeneous Japan (under the Liberal Democrats). Single-factor explanations do not suffice, but political scientists generally agree on the importance of the electoral system.

As we discussed in Chapter 4, single-member election districts, such as U.S. congressional districts, where a simple plurality wins, tend to produce two-party or two-plus systems. The reason is clear: Small third parties are underrepresented in such systems and often give up trying. Such is the case in the United States and Britain, based on the original English model. The British call this "first past the post"

(FPTP), as it resembles a horse race; even a nose better wins. There is a big premium in single-member districts on combining political forces to form the party with a majority or at least a plurality. If one party splits, it often throws the election to the party that hangs together. The factions within a party may not love each other, but they know they must stay together to have any political future. This factor goes a long way toward explaining why the two big American parties remain intact despite considerable internal differences.

polarized pluralism   System in which parties become more extremist.

center-seeking   Parties become moderate, aiming for large block of votes in center of political spectrum.

center-fleeing   Parties become extremist, ignoring voters in center.

Proportional representation (PR) allows and perhaps even encourages parties to split. PR systems use multimember districts and assign parliamentary seats in proportion to the percentage of votes in that district. Accordingly, there is not such a big premium on holding parties together; a splinter group may decide that it can get one or two people elected without having to compromise with other viewpoints. Israel's PR system elects a dozen parties to the Knesset. Modification of electoral laws can change a country's party system, pushing a country from a multiparty to a two-plus system, as in Germany; from a multiparty system to a "two-bloc" system, as in France; or from an exceedingly fragmented multiparty system to a moderate one, as in Poland.

Are Parties Fading?

Parties are not what they used to be. In most democracies, party membership is down, and voters are less loyal. The big ideological clashes of the twentieth century are over; most major parties are centrist and similar. The mass media and interest

---

CLASSIC WORKS ■ SARTORI'S TYPES OF PARTY COMPETITION

Giovanni Sartori (see box on page 206), among others, is not satisfied with simply counting the number of parties to classify party systems. Also important is the degree and manner in which the parties *compete*. The term *multiparty system* does not differentiate between those systems that are stable and those that are unstable. Sartori does; he delineates party systems of "moderate pluralism" from those of **polarized pluralism**.

In the former, there are usually five parties or fewer, and they compete in a **center-seeking** or centripetal manner; that is, their platforms and promises appeal to middle-of-the-road voters. Left-wing parties curb their radicalism and right-wing parties dampen their conservatism, for both know that the bulk of the voting public

is in the center. Thus, political life in moderate pluralism tends to be calm and stable, with ideological considerations toned down.

When the number of parties is greater than five or six, Sartori finds, there is the danger of polarized pluralism. Here, the parties compete in a **center-fleeing** or centrifugal manner, becoming ideologically extreme and engaging in a "politics of outbidding" with their rivals. Some parties offer more and more radical solutions, either radical left or radical right. Some are "antisystem" or revolutionary. Parties that stick to the center find themselves attacked from both sides. Such a situation causes political instability, sometimes leading to civil war, as in Spain in the 1930s, or to military takeover, as in Chile in 1973.

groups have taken over some of the functions of parties. New policy ideas often come from specialists in think tanks. But what will take the place of parties? 527s? Television? Neither prospect is appealing.

U.S. parties may foreshadow the future of parties elsewhere. Dependent on big money, parties fall under special-interest influence. Because U.S. parties are weakly organized and decentralized—in effect, every congressional district and state has its own parties, little related to each other—the parties do not cohere well at the national level. Said one nineteenth-century politician: "I belong to no organized party, sir. I'm a Democrat." (The same could be said today.) Because there are only two main parties, each aiming for the political center, they do not offer voters much to choose from. These characteristics are no longer just American but also found in Europe and Japan.

Can anything be done? Parties and party systems are rooted in their countries' history, society, and institutions. The U.S. Constitution never recognized parties, and the Founding Fathers warned against them. Americans, who share most basic values, may not need more than two parties to express their general divisions. Single-member districts with only a simple plurality needed to win tend to produce two-party systems. Realistically, we can expect no major change in America's two-party system, although some would like to see a viable third party.

There has been some movement toward U.S. party centralization. Ronald Reagan made the Republicans a more coherent conservative party with a reasonably clear program, pushing the Democrats to get their act together. Information technology is helping to centralize the parties. Computerized mailing lists induce state and local party organizations to cooperate with national headquarters. The national party committees can also channel PAC money to loyal candidates. In the long run, this may make the two parties more cohesive and ideologically consistent.

And there may be an advantage in *not* having strong parties, which may fall into the hands of oligarchic leaders who control too much and stay too long, getting the party stuck in rigid and outmoded viewpoints. The U.S. system, by virtue of its very fluidity, may be better able to process demands from a wider range of citizens. The lack of programmatic coherence confers the benefit of flexibility.

 EXERCISES

Apply what you learned in this chapter on MyPoliSciKit (www.mypoliscikit.com).

Assessment   Review this chapter using learning objectives, chapter summaries, practice tests, and more.

Flashcards   Learn the key terms in this chapter; you can test yourself by term or definition.

Video   Analyze recent world affairs by watching streaming video from major news providers.

Comparative Exercises   Compare political ideas, behaviors, institutions, and policies worldwide.

KEY TERMS

apparatchik (p. 204)
cadre party (p. 203)
catchall (p. 204)
center-fleeing (p. 209)
center-seeking (p. 209)
centralization (p. 198)
coherence (p. 199)
devotee party (p. 203)
electoral system (p. 205)
Great Society (p. 201)
immobilism (p. 207)

inchoate (p. 205)
instability (p. 207)
interest aggregation (p. 196)
mass party (p. 203)
mobilization (p. 198)
nationalization (p. 202)
neoinstitutional theory
(p. 200)
opportunists (p. 203)
party system (p. 205)
personalistic (p. 203)

polarized pluralism
(p. 209)
Politburo (p. 203)
political appointment
(p. 201)
political party (p. 196)
transparency (p. 201)
two-plus party
system (p. 208)
Weltanschauung
(p. 204)

FURTHER REFERENCE

Bibby, John F., and L. Sandy Maisel. *Two Parties—Or More? The American Party System.* Boulder, CO: Westview, 1998.

Carty, R. Kenneth, William Cross, and Lisa Young. *Rebuilding Canadian Party Politics.* Vancouver, BC: University of British Columbia Press, 2000.

Cohen, Jeffrey E., Richard Fleisher, and Paul Kantor, eds. *American Political Parties: Decline or Resurgence?* Washington, DC: CQ Press, 2001.

Dalton, Russell J., and Martin P. Wattenberg, eds. *Parties without Partisans: Political Change in Advanced Industrial Democracies.* New York: Oxford University Press, 2001.

Duverger, Maurice. *Political Parties: Their Organization and Activities in the Modern State,* 3rd ed. London: Methuen, 1964.

Eldersveld, Samuel J., and Hanes Walton Jr. *Political Parties in American Society,* 2nd ed. New York: Palgrave, 2000.

Hershey, Marjorie Randon. *Party Politics in America,* 14th ed. New York: Longman, 2010.

Hetherington, Marc J., and William J. Keefe. *Parties, Politics, and Public Policy in America,* 11th ed. Washington, DC: CQ Press, 2009.

Karvonen, Lauri, and Stein Kuhnle, eds. *Party Systems and Voter Alignments Revisited.* New York: Routledge, 2001.

Lawson, Kay, and Peter H. Merkl, eds. *When Parties Prosper: The Uses of Electoral Success.* Boulder, CO: Lynne Rienner, 2007.

Luther, Kurt, and Ferdinand Müller-Rommel, eds. *Political Parties in the New Europe: Political and Analytical Challenges.* New York: Oxford University Press, 2005.

Mair, Peter. *Party System Change: Approaches and Interpretations.* New York: Oxford University Press, 1997.

Morris, Ian. *Why the West Rules—For Now: The Patterns of History, and What They Reveal About the Future.* New York: Farrar, Straus & Giroux, 2010.

Rosenblum, Nancy. *On the Side of the Angels: An Appreciation of Parties and Partisanship.* Princeton, NJ: Princeton University Press, 2008.

Rosenstone, Steven J., and John Mark Hansen. *Mobilization, Participation, and Democracy in America.* White Plains, NY: Longman, 2002.

Ware, Alan. *Political Parties and Party Systems.* New York: Oxford University Press, 1996.

CHAPTER 12

Elections

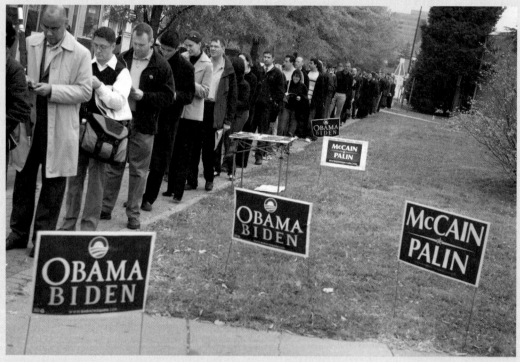

Voters in Arlington, VA, had to wait in long lines for the 2008 election, which saw a major uptick in turnout. (Ken Cedeno/Corbis)

In this chapter, we ask three general questions about elections, each followed by a more specific question about U.S. elections. First, we ask why people vote. This leads us to the puzzle of why voting *turnout* (see Chapter 7) in the United States is low. Second, we ask how people vote. This brings us to the question of whether party loyalties in the United States are shifting. Finally, we ask what wins elections. This takes us to some of the strategies used in U.S. elections.

QUESTIONS TO CONSIDER

1. Why has U.S. voting turnout risen recently?
2. What went wrong with the U.S. electoral system in 2000?
3. Should we view U.S. nonvoting with alarm?
4. How does party ID help decide elections?
5. Why is there a "gender gap" in U.S. voting?
6. Does income predict how a person votes?
7. Are we seeing electoral realignment, dealignment, or neither?
8. How does the economy influence elections?

WHY DO PEOPLE VOTE?

Although committed to democracy and participation, Americans vote less than citizens of other democracies. In the 2008 U.S. election, 61.7 percent of those eligible voted, a major improvement from previous years. One reason: Both parties worked hard to turn out their potential supporters. Historically, voter turnout in the United States was never high; its previous peak in 1960 was 63 percent. Turnout in Sweden, Germany, and Italy has reached 90 percent. Black South Africans in 1994, allowed to vote for the first time, produced a turnout of 86 percent, a measure of how much they appreciated the right to cast a ballot.

In nonpresidential elections, U.S. turnout seldom exceeds 40 percent. Why do Americans vote so little? Typically, more than half of U.S. nonvoters say they are uninterested in or dissatisfied with candidates. Many feel their vote makes no difference or that none of the candidates is really good. Another reason is the U.S. party system, in which the two large parties may not offer an interesting or clear-cut choice; both tend to centrist positions. In 2008, both candidates sounded similar in their emphasis on "change." Television saturates voters so long in advance—often with primitive, dirty political spots that disgust many with both parties by Election Day. Fewer than one in 20 American adults is involved enough in politics to attend a political meeting, contribute money, or canvass a neighborhood.

U.S. nonvoting has brought major debate among political scientists. One school fears that low electoral participation means that many Americans are turning away from the political system, which loses legitimacy. Another school is unworried, arguing that low turnout means that many Americans are basically satisfied with

213

the system or not sufficiently dissatisfied to register and vote. Countries with very high voter turnouts may have a sort of political fever in which partisan politics has become too intense. The United States experienced some of this intensity in 2008, when interesting personalities and a divided electorate brought out more voters. Some thinkers propose mandatory U.S. voting (several countries do), but Americans resent impositions on their freedom.

Why the difference between European and American turnout? One obvious reason is that in Europe registration is automatic; upon reaching 18, local authorities register you. Americans must register personally, months before the election and before campaign excitement mounts. U.S. elections are held on Tuesdays; in much of Europe, they're held on Sundays. (In 2008, many states allowed early voting, which likely boosted turnout.) The United States' long ballot with many local, state, and national candidates plus referendums baffles voters. European ballots are simple, usually just a choice of party, and most countries control and limit television political advertising; some allow none.

WHO VOTES?

Voters in most democracies tend to be middle aged and better educated with white-collar jobs, more urban and suburban than rural. They are also more likely to identify with a political party. Nonvoters show the reverse of these characteristics: young, lacking education, and with blue-collar or no jobs. Income and education, race, age, gender, and area of residence are key factors in who votes.

Income and Education

High-income people vote more than the less affluent, the well-educated more than high-school dropouts. These two characteristics often come together (good education leads to good incomes) and reinforce each other. High income gives people a stake in election outcomes, and education raises levels of interest and sophistication.

Factory workers in small towns may see little difference between candidates. They pay taxes, follow rules, make a living, and notice little change from one administration to another. In contrast, executives and professionals feel involved and see a direct relationship between who wins and their personal fortune. Blue-collar workers are also affected by a change in administration, but they are less likely to know it.

The difference between voters and nonvoters is a feeling of *efficacy*, the feeling that one has at least a little power. It tends to be low for workers and high for professionals. Better-off and better-educated people have seen interest groups succeed in changing policy. Ordinary workers often see political life as a "silent majority." Friends, neighbors, and family rarely had much wealth and rarely organized to pressure the government.

Well-educated people have broader interests in elections beyond personal economic stakes. The college-educated person—wealthy or not—is more interested, better informed, and more likely to participate in elections. As we discussed in

Chapter 7, education lifts the sense of participation and abstract intellectual curiosity, which makes people more likely to follow political news and feel involved. Much research shows that education is the strongest

postmaterialism Theory that modern culture has moved beyond getting and spending.

determinant of who votes, but this leads to a puzzle, as declining U.S. turnout happened precisely as U.S. educational levels *climbed.* Americans, with the highest percentage of young people in college and college-educated citizens, should be very participatory and eager to vote.

Several explanations, none definitive, have been advanced. Education may not mean what it used to. The sheer numbers of U.S. college graduates have diluted its former elite status. A college degree, in terms of getting a job nowadays, is more like a high-school diploma before World War II. Many majors are vocational or career-related and do not awaken curiosity or knowledge of the nation and world. And voting may not mean what it used to. Even well-educated citizens may not see a great choice between parties and candidates. Potential voters may be turned off by negative campaigning and conclude that all politicians are dirty. As we considered in Chapter 9, some blame television for a decline in political participation.

Postmaterialism offers another explanation. According to this cultural theory, in all industrialized nations the economy has moved away from manufacturing and into knowledge and information industries. With this has come a shift of values, away from society and toward self. Only personal things matter in the New Age: relationships, correct diet, outdoor activities, and music. Social and political questions no longer interest many. If the postmaterialism theory is accurate, education will not necessarily make citizens more participatory.

Race

Despite federal laws and black organizations, African American voting rates are lower than white voting rates, a gap that is slowly closing as black income and education levels rise. The 1965 Voting Rights Act overcame some of the barriers placed in the way of black registration, chiefly in the South. Many blacks have gone through political consciousness-raising and learned the value of participation and voting, a trend accelerated by Obama's candidacy. Some previously racist white politicians

CLASSIC WORKS ■ DOWNS'S THEORY OF VOTING

Contributing to rational-choice theory, Anthony Downs's landmark 1957 work, *An Economic Theory of Democracy*, theorized that people vote if the returns outweigh the costs. That is, if the stakes seem important, citizens will go to the trouble of voting. Property owners fearing tax hikes are more likely to vote than renters not immediately hurt by the tax. The cost of political information, both financial and personal, also determines whether a person will vote. Not all have the energy or interest to follow political news or attend political meetings. Accordingly, the poor and uneducated in most societies are the least likely to vote. (India may be an exception.)

Black voter registration in recent decades has enfranchised a group of citizens who previously had little political clout but who are now courted by candidates of both parties. (Scott Olsen/Getty)

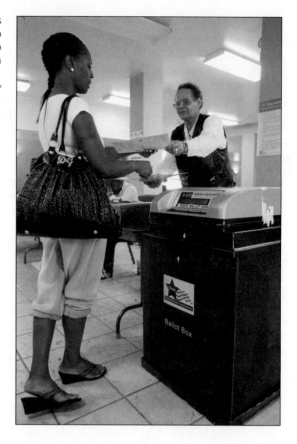

got the message and became respectful toward their black constituents. Latinos faced similar problems. Race, accordingly, is still a factor in U.S. election turnout.

Age

Young people—those under 25—feel less politically involved, and they vote less. About half of U.S. citizens aged 18 to 25 are not registered to vote. Young people, with little income and property, also feel economically uninvolved with election outcomes. When they start paying taxes, their interest grows. Focused on the concerns of youth, few have time for or interest in political questions, which seem abstract and distant.

franchise The right to vote.

In 1971, the Twenty-Sixth Amendment lowered the U.S. voting age from 21 to 18 at almost the same time that most other democracies did. The results were similar: With their new **franchise**, young people did not vote as much as their elders did. Middle-aged and older people are more likely to vote than the young, probably because the middle-aged person is at peak earning power, and the old person is concerned about Social Security and Medicare. In recent U.S. elections, those over 70 showed the highest turnout.

Gender

Traditionally, men were more likely to vote than women in almost every society. Women only comparatively recently won the right to vote. (Switzerland enfranchised women only in 1971.) Since 1920, when female **suffrage** was granted in the United States, the gap between men's and women's voter turnout narrowed and then reversed; in recent U.S. elections women have voted more than men, a reflection of women's higher education levels.

suffrage   The right to vote.

multicausal   Several factors making something happen.

if-then statement   Says that two variables are linked: Where X happens, so does Y.

tendency   Finding that two variables are linked but not perfectly.

Place of Residence

In most of the world, cities have higher turnouts than rural areas, partly because urbanites on average have higher education levels. Polling stations are nearer in cities. People who have long lived in the same place are more likely to vote than are transients or newcomers, for longtime residents feel more involved in local affairs and are more likely to participate in groups and activities in the community.

Voter turnout in the U.S. South is somewhat lighter than in the North and West, a reflection of lower living standards and a lack of party competition. But the South and its politics have changed, and now turnout in the South is approaching that of other areas. Other nations are also characterized by regional differences in voter participation. In France, the areas south of the Loire River have a lower voter turnout than the northern areas of the country.

HOW TO . . . ■ HANDLE TENDENCIES

It is hard to show that one thing causes another, especially in the social sciences. Often the best we can do is show how one thing correlates to or covaries with another. For example, we have noted how rich countries are democracies and poor not, but this is only approximately true. There are many exceptions, so instead of saying "is," we say "tends to." Further, which causes which? Does being rich make countries democratic? Or does being democratic make countries rich?

Most social scientists are cautious about making causal statements—X causes Y—and say that causality is indirect and complex. X might give rise to Q, which in turn might influence Z to move in the direction of Y. In our example, wealth creates a large middle class, which places a high value on education and articulates its interests, which in turn undermines authoritarian rule. Simple it ain't.

Much of what we study is **multicausal**: P, Q, and R working together lead to Z. Which matters most—per capita GDP, education, or interest-group formation—to the founding of democracy? They all matter and are hard to disentangle. They tend to come as a package. Instead of making causal statements, we learn to make **if-then statements**: If we find X, then we also find Y. We also learn that this connection is rarely one-to-one: Where we find X, two-thirds of the time we find Y. This is called a **tendency** statement, the standard fare of the social sciences. For example: "Poor countries tend not to be democracies, but several are." And, remember, individuals often defy the tendency of their group: "African Americans tend strongly to vote Democratic, but some vote Republican."

party identification   Long-term voter attachment to a given party.

swing   Percentage of voters switching parties from one election to the next.

class voting   Tendency of a given social class to vote for a party that promotes its economic interests.

WHO VOTES HOW?

The reasons that people vote as they do are many and complex. Factors can be divided into *long-term* and *short-term* variables. Loyalty to a political party is a long-term influence that can affect a person's votes for a lifetime. Short-term variables may cause a person to vote one way for one election but another way four years later. Margaret Thatcher shrewdly called British elections in 1983 to catch the glow of military victory in the Falklands and again in 1987 during an economic upswing and disarray in Labour's ranks. Her Conservatives won both times. Similarly, in 1976 in the United States, Jimmy Carter benefited from a "morality factor" brought by the Watergate scandal. Economic conditions matter; the 2008 downturn hurt the Republicans. Such short-term variables, however, rarely mean a permanent shift in party loyalty.

Party Identification

Party identification—party ID, for short—is an attachment many feel toward one party for a long time, sometimes all their lives. Strong party identifiers habitually vote for that party; weak identifiers can be swayed to vote for another party. People with no party ID are up for grabs and may shift their votes every election. Remember, party ID is something that people carry in their heads; it is not something that parties have.

Party ID is heavily influenced by parents early in life. Some children proclaim they are Democrats or Republicans and may never change what they learned from their parents, like the early learning of a religion. It is also easier to vote along party lines, especially important with complicated U.S. ballots. Party ID is a "standing decision" on how to vote. Strong identifiers feel good about their party's candidates and view other candidates with suspicion.

Party ID is important to electoral stability. People who stick largely to one party allow politicians to anticipate what people want and to try to deliver it. Weak party ID produces great volatility in voting, as citizens shift their votes too easily, often in response to clever TV ads. Political scientists worry that declining party ID in the United States bodes ill for democracy.

Party identification in much of Europe (but not in France) and Japan used to be stronger than in the United States, but the differences may be fading. Britain, Germany, Sweden, Japan, and other countries were long characterized by consistent splits between their two biggest parties. Typically, the **swing** from one major party to another ranged from only about 1 percent to 5 percent, as most voters stuck with the same party. Strong party ID anchored voters to parties. With the decline in **class voting** and rise of *postmaterialism* (see page 215), party ID has been fading and volatility increasing, sometimes to U.S. levels. French voters are less likely than Americans to have a party ID, partly the result of the splitting, merging, and renaming that French parties engage in. Such changes do not give party IDs time to take root. The result: French voting is and always has been volatile.

Using the social categories discussed in Chapter 8 (on public opinion) and earlier in this chapter (on voting turnout), political scientists can describe what kinds of people tend to identify with the various parties. No social cat-

> **voting bloc**   Group with a marked tendency.

egory votes 100 percent for a given party; some people disregard group norms. If more than half of a given social category votes for one party, there is probably a significant relationship between the category and the party. If three-quarters votes for a party, there is a strong relationship. We are making statements here that indicate a tendency, not an absolute relationship. (See the box on tendency statements in this chapter.)

Practicing politicians and political scientists call a group with a tendency to identify with a certain party a **voting bloc**. The candidates' strategy is then to secure enough blocs to deliver a plurality of the electorate, and they tailor their campaign to win over the blocs most likely to vote for them. The concept of voting blocs is an oversimplification; there is no such thing as a solid bloc.

Class Voting

Social class is one determinant of party identification and voting behavior. Even in the United States, where class distinctions are blurred, wage workers tend to register and vote Democratic, especially in families in which breadwinners are union members. In 2008, a big majority from families earning under $50,000 a year voted for Obama; however, many well-off professional people went for Obama as well, suggesting he enjoyed bimodal support. In most European countries, class voting is stronger, for unions are often connected to social-democratic or labor parties. The big Swedish and German unions, respectively the LO and DGB, persuade most of their members to vote Social Democrat. Better-off Britons, French, Germans, and Swedes are likely to support their respective conservative parties.

Two things muddy class voting. Some working-class people—because they consider themselves middle class, have a family tradition, or have individual convictions—vote for conservative parties. Sometimes a majority of the U.S. and British working class vote, respectively, Republican and Conservative. Conversely, some middle- and even upper-class people—because they are of working-class origins, have a family tradition, or picked up liberal views in college—vote for parties on the left. Such people are especially important in providing working-class parties with educated leadership. This two-way crossover—working class going conservative and middle class going left—dilutes class voting. Class voting has receded everywhere; it just happened first in the United States.

Regional Voting

Some regions identify strongly with certain parties. Often these are areas that were conquered and subjugated centuries ago, something inhabitants still resent. In the Middle Ages, Paris kings extended their reach, often by the sword, south of the Loire River, where people still tend to vote Socialist. Scotland and Wales, England's "celtic fringe," go Labour. Scots still remember losing the Battle of

Electoral College   U.S. system of weighting popular presidential vote to favor smaller states.

anachronism   Something out of the past.

Culloden in 1746. The Civil War made the southern United States solidly Democratic—because the damn Yankees were Republicans—but since the 1980s the South has been the strongest Republican region. The Northeast—which following the Civil War had been a Republican bastion—is now the strongest for the Democrats.

COMPARING ■ IS THE U.S. ELECTORAL SYSTEM DEFECTIVE?

No electoral system can guarantee translating the public's will into governance in a way that is both fair and simple. All have problems. If the system is fair (say, proportional representation), it is likely not simple. If the system is simple (say, single-member districts with plurality win), it is likely not fair. In the United States and Britain, the latter systems have recently run into difficulties. The 2000 U.S. presidential election was a double disaster, both issues foreseeable: (1) An anachronistic **Electoral College** denied victory to the popular vote winner, and (2) a defective balloting mechanism really mattered. Gore, with a nontrivial half-a-million more votes (0.51 percent more), lost in electoral votes to Bush, 271–266. Similar situations happened three times in the nineteenth century.

States and counties use whatever balloting system they wish, including defective ones. Some still use paper ballots, some hand-lever voting machines designed in 1892, and some light-scanned ballots. Counties are slow to upgrade to electronic and touch-screen systems because of cost. The worst system was in Palm Beach County, Florida, which used a common and cheap 40-year-old technology: Voters put an IBM-type card into a frame and punched out a rectangle by their choice. Some of the little "chads"—as high as 6 percent—were not completely punched out, so counting machines read them as "no vote." The system was long known to be defective and had spawned court cases in several states; Massachusetts had outlawed it.

Making things worse in Palm Beach was a two-page "butterfly ballot" that confused voters, many of whom accidentally voted for right-wing populist Pat Buchanan instead of the intended Al Gore. Those who tried to fix the error by making another punch invalidated their ballot. This strongly Democratic county lost some 20,000 votes for Gore, several times more than were needed to win Florida and thus win the electoral vote.

The Electoral College was designed to overrepresent states with fewer voters, especially the Southern states, where slave-owners rejected notions of "one person, one vote." Each state gets as many electors as its senators and representatives, so even very small states get three electors. A vote for president in a thinly populated state has several times the power of a vote for president in a populous state. A vote in Wyoming is worth almost four times that of a vote in California. And small states, a huge swath of the middle of America, tend to go Republican. States with big cities, clustered in the Northeast and on the Great Lakes and West Coast, tend to go Democrat.

The Electoral College is widely thought to be an **anachronism** but cannot be seriously reformed because 17 small states with five or fewer representatives like being overrepresented. These states can block constitutional change, which requires two-thirds of each house plus three-fourths of the state legislatures.

The United States is not alone in its problems with electoral system. The 2010 British elections produced a "hung Parliament," one where

Outlying regions may harbor economic and cultural resentments at rule by a distant capital, *center-periphery tensions* (see page 63). Scotland and Alberta do not like sharing their oil revenues, respectively, with London and Ottawa. The south of Italy resents the north, and vice-versa; they vote differently. Germany's *Ossis* (easterners) resent rule by *Wessis* (westerners) and vote that way. India's many languages are reflected in voting patterns: Hooray for our local language!

no party held a majority of seats. The last time this happened was 1974. The United States, with its separation of powers, could shrug off such a situation; the president still governs. But Britain, where a majority of Commons selects the prime minister, the Conservatives had to form a coalition with the Liberal Democrats and promise them to consider reforming Britian's FPTP (see page 69) electoral system to make it fairer to the Lib Dems.

FORM 3
(Subsections 116(1) and 138(1))

FORM OF BALLOT PAPER

Front

FORMULAIRE 3
(paragraphes 116(1) et 138(1))

FORMULAIRE DU BULLETIN DE VOTE

Recto

············DOE, John············
········Independent / Indépendant·········

··········DOE, Sandra··········
·Political Affiliation / Appartenance politique·

······UNETELLE, Anne······

·········UNTEL, Pierre·········
·Political Affiliation / Appartenance politique·

The Canadian ballot—paper marked with pencil—is clear, simple, standard, bilingual, and hand-counted in four hours nationwide. Any hints for the United States?

Religious Blocs

Religious versus secular is the single strongest predictor in U.S. voting. In 2008, McCain won three-fourths of white Protestant evangelicals; Obama won two-thirds of the "seculars" (nonreligious). A majority of Catholics swung to Obama in 2008, as did more than three-fourths of Jews. In France, devout Catholics vote mostly conservative; secular people vote mostly left. In Italy, the Popular Party was founded by and is still linked to the Roman Catholic Church. Catholic areas of Germany vote more Christian Democrat than do Protestant areas.

Age Groups

Younger people are not necessarily more radical than their elders. Rather, they tend to catch the tide that is flowing in their youth and stay with it. Young people socialized to politics during the Depression tended to vote Democratic all their lives. The enthusiasm for Reagan among young voters in the 1980s gave some of them a permanent sense of identification with the Republican Party. Age groups react in part to the economic situation. In 2008, two-thirds of 18-to-29-year-old voters went for Obama, partly because they are more open on race and worried about their jobs during the economic downturn. Older voters were less open on the race question and feared economic experiments.

Gender Gap

It also used to be assumed that women were more traditional and conservative than men, but that has reversed in the United States and several other countries. Women now vote Democrat by several percentage points more than men. Women tend to like the Democrats' support for welfare measures and abortion rights and to dislike the Republicans' opposition to such views and support for a militarized foreign policy.

Marriage Gap

Starting in 2000, observers noticed a "marriage gap." (It had probably existed earlier but had not been included among survey questions.) Unmarried people are several percentage points more Democrat than are married. The responsibilities of raising a family make voters conservative, and Republicans stress "family values."

Race

Blacks are the most loyal Democrats by far; more than 80 percent of blacks who vote generally vote for Democrats, 95 percent in 2008. Hispanic voters shifted temporarily from Democrat to a nearly even split in 2004 but went back to two-thirds Democrat in 2008. The affinity of racial minorities for the Democrats, however, costs the party white votes. A majority of whites voted for McCain in 2008. Although rarely stated openly, racial fear and resentment of minorities pulls whites to the Republicans.

Arizona's tough 2010 law against illegal immigrants, passed by a Republican state legislature and signed by a Republican governor, drew strong white support but mostly Hispanic opposition. America's two parties are polarizing along racial lines.

critical election One showing a realignment.

realignment Major, long-term shift in party ID.

Urban Voting

Big cities worldwide tend strongly to vote liberal or left. The working-class vote is concentrated in cities. Cities are also centers of education and sophistication, places where intellectuals are often liberal and leftist. Country and suburban dwellers tend to embrace conservative values and vote for conservative parties. England votes overwhelmingly Tory, but the city of London does not. Germany's Bavaria is a conservative stronghold, but not Munich. Italy was long dominated by the Christian Democrats, but not Italy's cities, most of which had leftist mayors.

A map of U.S. elections shows a major urban–rural split. Cities went strongly for Obama in 2008, suburbs not so strong. McCain and especially Sarah Palin represented rural values—religion, plain speech, anti-abortion, anti–gun control, anti-tax, and pro-military—that won most rural areas.

ELECTORAL REALIGNMENT

Political scientists have long debated a theory of **critical** or **realigning elections**. Typically, people retain their party identification for decades, but, according to this theory, in several watershed presidential elections the party loyalties of many voters dissolved, and they established new, durable party IDs. These "critical elections" do not determine how every election will go, but they set the terms of debate and the main topics. They give one party dominance but not absolute control. The critical or realigning elections in U.S. history are usually seen as the following:

1800, the emergence of Jeffersonian Democratic Republicans
1828, the emergence of Jacksonian populist Democrats
1860, the emergence of Lincoln Republicans
1896, the emergence of business Republicanism
1932, the emergence of Roosevelt's New Deal Democrats

Between these critical elections, party IDs are stable and most people vote according to them. This is called the "normal vote" or "maintaining elections." Occasionally, enough voters disregard their party identification to elect the weaker party: Democrat Grover Cleveland in 1884 and 1892, Democrat Woodrow Wilson in 1912 and 1916, and Republican Dwight Eisenhower in 1952 and 1956. These are called "deviating elections" because the party shift was only temporary; afterward, voters went back to their long-term party ID.

A New Realignment?

Republicans argued that the Reagan sweeps of 1980 and 1984 marked a realignment in their favor. Party registration rose for Republicans and declined for Democrats until the parties were about equal. Young people in particular registered and voted Republican, and Reaganite thinkers restructured the ideological debate in a conservative direction (see Chapter 3). Using government to fix social ills and provide welfare were less fashionable than cutting taxes, government spending, regulation, and the federal deficit. Before Reagan, even Republicans went along with the welfare state, and some of the biggest expansions of welfare programs occurred under Nixon. After Reagan, even the Democrats demanded fiscal responsibility. Said President Clinton: "The era of big government is over."

---

dealignment   Major, long-term decline in party ID.

In 2008, it was the Democrats' turn to argue that the U.S. electorate had realigned in their favor. The economic downturn and racial breakthrough indicated the emergence of a new, liberal electorate, they said, with Obama as the new FDR who would use the powers of Washington to reform the country, a dubious claim. Many political scientists argue that there was neither a Republican nor a Democratic realignment, just voters reacting to current economic conditions. It will take several elections to tell if there has been a realignment, that is, a durable shift in voting patterns. Most are betting against it.

And if there has been a realignment, it may be difficult to spot the precise election in which it occurred. After Nixon's 1968 election, Kevin Phillips concluded that a Republican majority was emerging. But which was the critical election, Nixon's in 1968 or Reagan's in 1980? Or neither? If it was 1968, it would mark Carter's election in 1976 as a "deviating election," and, indeed, Carter's victory was largely the result of the Watergate scandal. The Nixon administration, however, lacked the ideological conservatism that came with Reagan. Perhaps the ingredients for a Republican realignment came with the 1968 election but did not coalesce until 1980 and was confirmed and deepened in 2004. Instead of a single "critical" election, it occurred over many years. Instead of national realignment, some researchers see *regional* realignment: the South and Plains states more purely Republican, the Northeast and West more purely Democrat. The 2008 election bears this out.

There are problems with realignment theory. Some political scientists would throw the whole package out. Many argue that it applies only to voting for president, which is often out of sync with voting for Congress. Americans sometimes vote for "divided government"—legislative and executive under different parties—to deadlock them and limit the damage they can do. (French voters do the same.) The Clinton victories in 1992 and 1996 and the Obama victory of 2008, all based on the economy, undermine the theory of electoral realignment. If voters react mostly to current situations and candidates' personalities, the basic supposition of party identification will have to be reconsidered. Perhaps party ID is not as important as it once was.

Instead of realignment, some suggest we are going through **dealignment**. Since the mid-1960s, the number of voters committed to neither major U.S. party increased. In 1948, fewer than 20 percent of U.S. voters called themselves independents, but in some elections since then this has grown to a third. Independents tend to be young and college-educated. Many came of age in turbulent times. In 1964, they heard Lyndon Johnson promise not to send Americans to fight in Vietnam. In 1974, they saw Nixon resign in shame. After the 2003 war, they learned that Iraq had no weapons of mass destruction. Their faith in conventional party politics was shaken; both major parties appeared to be dishonest—and numerous scandals did not improve their image.

polarization Opinion fleeing the center to form two hostile camps.

religiosity Depth of religious conviction (not same as choice of denomination).

Some political scientists noted that this process—which proceeded during both bad and good economic times—coincided with three trends: (1) declining voter turnout, (2) declining party ID, and (3) declining trust in Washington. Do the three items

KEY CONCEPTS ■ PARTISAN POLARIZATION

Political scientists note growing **polarization** in the U.S. electorate. Party identifiers have become more militant, as have dislikes and slurs against the other party. Although the trend was under way for some time, by the 1990s Republicans despised Clinton even when the economy boomed. In the 2008 election, Republicans and Democrats were hostile to each other. Reason and consistency were not in command. Several factors contributed to the polarization tendency:

1. Under Reagan (1981–1989) the Republicans became more consistently conservative, until there were few moderate Republicans in Congress. To a lesser extent, the Democrats tended to become more consistently liberal.

2. Elites articulated more strongly ideological agendas than previously. New think tanks, periodicals, and Web sites, especially on the conservative side, took positions that the big parties, always seeking the centrist vote, had usually avoided.

3. The Supreme Court's 1972 "one person, one vote" rule (see page 290) required states to make their congressional districts equal in population. Now most states redistrict after every census. Computers gerrymander with great accuracy, so that congressional districts now contain like-minded

voters who consistently return incumbents to office. These incumbents, knowing they cannot lose, turn more ideologically partisan and less concerned about votes in the center.

4. Mobile Americans move to areas that culturally suit them, making whole regions of the country purer ideologically, the South conservative and the Northeast liberal. What the media designated as "red" (Republican states) and "blue" (Democratic states) did not speak nicely to each other. Researchers—some political, some marketing—can tell you the tastes of each ZIP Code.

5. The trend reflects America's "culture wars" (see page 124), based heavily on **religiosity**. Religious Americans rallied to the "moral values" espoused by Republicans. Less-religious Americans focused on the economy, Iraq, and health care and rallied to the Democrats. The two cultures, interested in totally different issues, disdain and vote against each other.

Some historians and political scientists say U.S. politics has always been like this; regional and cultural politics have always loomed large in U.S. elections. Polarization is not all bad. In 2008, it markedly boosted voter turnout.

charismatic   Having strong personal drawing power.

hang together? Which causes which? Declining trust is probably the underlying cause. The higher turnout of 2008 suggested that American voters were giving Washington another chance.

Some researchers doubt there is much dealignment and independent voting. Many voters who call themselves "independent" actually lean to one party or the other, so that only 15 percent are genuine neutrals, and this amounts to only 11 percent who actually cast ballots (because true independents tend to vote less). By the time you count the weak identifiers, these researchers say, party ID in the United States is largely unchanged.

WHAT WINS ELECTIONS?

In theory, elections enable citizens to choose and guide their government. In modern elections, however, the element of rational choice is heavily manipulated by the twin factors of personality and the mass media. People vote without clearly realizing what they are voting for or why, and this could become a threat to democracy.

Modern parties showcase their leaders' personalities. Especially in the advanced industrialized world, ideology is seldom emphasized. Ads and TV spots feature the leaders' images, sometimes without even mentioning their parties. The leader is presented as **charismatic** and decisive but calm and caring. Ronald Reagan and Barack Obama are excellent examples of winning political personalities, and leaders in other countries have adopted similar approaches. British Prime Minister Tony Blair won in part by copying the style of Bill Clinton. French presidential candidates (but not Sarkozy) often project an image of a caring, parental figure above the political fray, almost nonpartisan. German candidates for chancellor project a tried-and-true, reliable, and upbeat image but also say little about what policies they will pursue. The pattern worldwide: Keep it general, keep it happy, don't mention parties, and smile a lot.

U.S. presidential candidates who present the most upbeat image of America almost always win. Pessimistic candidates, who worry about things going wrong, tend to lose. In 2008, Obama was more optimistic than McCain. The leaders' personalities are sold through the mass media, especially through television, where the candidate's image is controlled; even physical appearance can be altered. "Photo opportunities" instead of question-and-answer sessions avoid embarrassing probes by journalists. The photo op shows seemingly spontaneous candidate activity; words explaining the activity can be added later. The photo op is wordless; the candidates' professional "handlers" worry that their candidate could say something foolish and ruin a carefully built-up image. Journalists must be kept distant.

And this is happening worldwide. One British observer argued that "television very largely *is* the campaign." In 2010, for the first time the chiefs of the top three British parties debated each other live on TV. (The United States has held TV debates since 1960.) The three debates riveted Britons' attention and may have boosted turnout. In France, journalists complain about the *hypermédiatisation* of French politics. On television, everything is professionally controlled: set, lighting, music, makeup, narration—a mini-drama more perfect (and often more expensive) than many regular programs. The television spot, developed in America, now blankets Europe. The French call it *le clip politique.* French political scientist Jean-Paul Gourevitch saw three types: (1) the "jingle clip," a simple attention-getting device; (2) the "ideological clip," which sets an idea in images; and (3) the "allegorical clip," which portrays the hero-candidate in an epic. Increasingly, elections are won by the candidate with the sunniest personality and best ads. This generally means the candidate with the most money wins, for television is terribly expensive. Candidates, desperate for money, sell themselves to interest groups. Parties become little more than fund-raising organizations. This is not just an American problem; it started in the United States but has since spread to Europe.

retrospective voting Voters choosing based on overall incumbent performance.

Retrospective Voting

Few voters carefully evaluate issues in a presidential election, but they do form an overall evaluation of the performance of an incumbent president. They feel the president has done a good job or a poor one, especially on the economy. Morris P. Fiorina called the accumulated or package views of voters toward incumbent presidents **retrospective voting** because it views in retrospect a whole four years of performance in office. When voters think the government in general is doing a good job, they reward the incumbent's party: Johnson in 1964, Nixon in 1972, Reagan in 1984, Clinton in 1996, and Bush in 2004. When they think the government in general is doing a poor job, they punish the incumbent's party: Humphrey in 1968, Ford in 1976, Carter in 1980, Bush 41 in 1992, and McCain in 2008. The Index of Consumer Confidence—a measure of how economically secure Americans feel—predicts most presidential elections. When people feel good about the economy, they generally vote for the incumbent's party. The financial meltdown of 2008 turned the election decisively to Obama.

Retrospective voting is colored, naturally, by party identification, issues, and the candidate's personality. For weak party identifiers plus independents, the perception of overall performance determines much of their vote. A strong positive retrospective view could even turn into party identification. Voting behavior is complex. When people say they "like" candidates, it could mean that they like the candidates' party, their stands on issues, their personal images, or the performance of the economy. Unraveling such puzzles is the crux of campaign strategy.

Candidate Strategies and Voter Groups

Campaign strategies have two goals: keeping "one foot on home base" by not alienating the normal party supporters and trying to win over votes from the undecided and from the opposition. Presidential candidates focus on states with more electoral votes and close to 50–50 voting, concentrating on such "battleground" states as Florida, Ohio, and Pennsylvania. States lopsided for one party—such as California (Democrat) and Texas (Republican)—are considered "not in play" and get less time and money. Campaign strategy is highly rational.

constituency The people or district that elects an official.	Most campaigns are designed to fit the opinions and needs of the candidate's **constituency**, often determined by public opinion polls. Candidates must be aware of pockets of party strength and resistance,

what various groups are thinking about, what districts have the lowest turnouts (and therefore merit less candidate time), and which issues anger constituents. Aware of the direction and intensity of voter opinion, candidates then typically try to assemble enough "voting blocs" to win.

Voting blocs parallel the public opinion blocs discussed in Chapter 8. Religion, geography, and class—probably in that order—are the most important influences in opinion formation, and these partially predict voting. Coalitions of several smaller blocs of voters often win. On a national scale, the Democrats used to represent a coalition of labor, blacks, Catholics, Jews, and urban voters; the Republicans received their support from a coalition of rural and farm voters, the remaining Protestants, and nonunion workers. By the 1960s, though, these traditional blocs had begun to break up, and neither party has managed to reconstruct them in a durable way. The breakup of the blocs, it should be noted, coincides with the declining voter turnout and party loyalty discussed earlier.

KEY CONCEPTS ■ CHANGING POSITIONS

Candidates are endlessly opportunistic and modify their positions on issues to win the most votes. Many call this "slippery" or "unprincipled," but it is really just democracy in action. Elected officials who support discredited or unpopular policies get voted out. Those who urge politicians to stand by their principles and "do the right thing" meet the hard-nosed reply: "But if I'm not reelected, all the good and just things I'm trying to accomplish will be thrown away. So I've got to bend on this issue." Soon pure expediency reigns.

The 1994 Republican "Contract with America" included a ten-year phaseout of farm subsidies, something the GOP had long championed. By 2002, Republicans were shoveling more money into farm subsidies than ever. To do otherwise, said President Bush, would be "political suicide" for his 2004 reelection. Democrats, seeking those same farm-state votes, also supported the subsidies.

The 2008 election cycle began with the candidates far apart on Iraq. McCain mentioned he would be willing to keep U.S. forces

in Iraq "a hundred years." Obama said he would bring them home "immediately." During the campaign, both modified their positions toward the middle. McCain (and indeed President Bush) now said "as soon as possible," when Iraq stabilized, possibly in a couple of years. Obama now said withdrawal should not be precipitate, possibly in 16 months. By the fall of 2008, they were not far apart, as both played for the big vote in the center. This dynamic means that issues seldom dominate U.S. political campaigns: By Election Day, both candidates have adjusted their positions toward the center.

Can it be otherwise in a democracy? Should politicians go against the mass will for the sake of "consistency" or "principle"? Their changes are frequently held up to ridicule by the media and their opponents, but they are really adjusting to new realities on a continuous basis. Asked what drove his policies, British Prime Minister Harold Macmillan (1957–1963) replied, "Events, dear boy, events." Much of political life is the opportunistic reaction to events.

The "blocs" are not what they used to be, and many Americans do not fit demographic, ethnic, or religious pigeonholes. Instead, attitudes on religion, free enterprise, welfare, patriotism, civil rights, and other issues cut across the old voting blocs. "Liberal" and "conservative" are tricky categories because people are often liberal on some things and conservative on others. Neither does party ID matter much in an era of dealignment and rapid shifts between parties. Clusters of *values* may now count for more than social categories. Thus, candidates strive to align themselves with their constituents' values.

mypoliscikit EXERCISES

Apply what you learned in this chapter on MyPoliSciKit (www.mypoliscikit.com).

 Assessment Review this chapter using learning objectives, chapter summaries, practice tests, and more.

Menu

 Flashcards Learn the key terms in this chapter; you can test yourself by term or definition.

Flashcards

 Video Analyze recent world affairs by watching streaming video from major news providers.

Videos

 Comparative Exercises Compare political ideas, behaviors, institutions, and policies worldwide.

Comparative
Exercises

KEY TERMS

anachronism (p. 220)
charismatic (p. 226)
class voting (p. 218)
constituency (p. 228)
critical election (p. 223)
dealignment (p. 224)
Electoral College (p. 220)

franchise (p. 216)
if-then statement (p. 217)
multicausal (p. 217)
party identification (p. 218)
polarization (p. 225)
postmaterialism (p. 215)
realignment (p. 223)

religiosity (p. 225)
retrospective voting
 (p. 227)
suffrage (p. 217)
swing (p. 218)
tendency (p. 217)
voting bloc (p. 219)

FURTHER REFERENCE

Birnir, Johanna Kristin. *Ethnicity and Electoral Politics.* New York: Cambridge University Press, 2007.
Bishop, Bill, and Robert G. Cushing. *The Big Sort: Why the Clustering of Like-Minded*

America Is Tearing Us Apart. Boston: Houghton Mifflin, 2008.
Campbell, David E., ed. *A Matter of Faith: Religion in the 2004 Presidential Election.* Washington, DC: Brookings, 2007.

Caplan, Bryan. *The Myth of the Rational Voter.* Princeton, NJ: Princeton University Press, 2007.

Ceaser, James W., and Andrew E. Busch. *Red Over Blue: The 2004 Elections and American Politics.* Lanham, MD: Rowman & Littlefield, 2005.

Claggett, William J. M., and Byron E. Shafer. *The American Public Mind: The Issues Structure of Mass Politics in the Postwar United States.* New York: Cambridge University Press, 2010.

Douthat, Ross, and Reihan Salam. *Grand New Party: How Republicans Can Win the Working Class and Save the American Dream.* New York: Doubleday, 2008.

Flanigan, William H., and Nancy H. Zingale. *Political Behavior of the American Electorate,* 12th ed. Washington, DC: CQ Press, 2009.

Gelman, Andrew. *Red State, Blue State, Rich State, Poor State: Why Americans Vote the Way They Do.* Princeton, NJ: Princeton University Press, 2008.

Gerken, Heather K. *The Democracy Index: Why Our Election System Is Failing and How to Fix It.* Princeton, NJ: Princeton University Press, 2009.

Heilmann, John, and Mark Halperin. *Game Change: Obama and the Clintons, McCain and Palin, and the Race of a Lifetime.* New York: HarperCollins, 2010.

Hill, Steven. *Fixing Elections: The Failure of America's Winner Take All Politics.* New York: Routledge, 2003.

Ifill, Gwen. *The Breakthrough: Politics and Race in the Age of Obama.* New York: Doubleday, 2009.

Johnson, Dennis W. *No Place for Amateurs: How Political Consultants Are Reshaping America.* New York: Routledge, 2007.

Kenski, Kate, Bruce W. Hardy, and Kathleen Hall Jamieson. *The Obama Victory: How Media, Money, and Message Shaped the 2008 Election.* New York: Oxford University Press, 2010.

Lewis, Charles. *The Buying of the President 2004.* New York: HarperCollins, 2004.

Mayer, William G. *The Making of Presidential Candidates, 2008.* Lanham, MD: Rowman & Littlefield, 2008.

McCarty, Nolan, Keith Poole, and Howard Rosenthal. *Polarized America: The Dance of Ideology and Unequal Riches.* Cambridge, MA: MIT Press, 2006.

McDonald, Michael D., and Ian Budge. *Elections, Parties, Democracy: Conferring the Median Mandate.* New York: Oxford University Press, 2005.

Minow, Newton N., and Craig L. LaMay. *Inside the Presidential Debates: Their Improbable Past and Promising Future.* Chicago: University of Chicago Press, 2008.

Nelson, Michael, ed. *The Elections of 2008.* Washington DC: CQ Press, 2009.

Nivola, Pietro S., and David W. Brady, eds. *Red and Blue Nation?: Characteristics and Causes of America's Polarized Politics.* Washington, DC: Brookings, 2007.

Patterson, Thomas E. *The Vanishing Voter: Public Involvement in an Age of Uncertainty.* New York: Knopf, 2003.

Polsby, Nelson W., and Aaron Wildavsky. *Presidential Elections: Strategies and Structures of American Politics,* 12th ed. Lanham, MD: Rowman & Littlefield, 2007.

Schaller, Thomas F. *Whistling Past Dixie: How Democrats Can Win Without the South.* New York: Simon & Schuster, 2008.

Schier, Steven E. *You Call This an Election?: America's Peculiar Democracy.* Washington, DC: Georgetown University Press, 2003.

Todd, Chuck, and Sheldon Gawiser. *How Barack Obama Won: A State-by-State Guide to the Historic 2008 Presidential Election.* New York: Vintage, 2009.

White, John Kenneth. *Barack Obama's America: How New Conceptions of Race, Family, and Religion Ended the Reagan Era.* Ann Arbor, MI: University of Michigan Press, 2009.

PART IV

POLITICAL INSTITUTIONS

Ch. 13 Legislatures   Presidential systems, like the one in the United States, have a powerful chief executive who is elected separately from the legislature and cannot be easily ousted, a *separation of powers*. Parliamentary systems, like the one in Britain, on the other hand, have the national legislature elect a prime minister from its own ranks, a *fusion of powers*. Parliaments can recall prime ministers with a *vote of no confidence*, which usually happens when the governing coalition has fallen apart. Federal systems need an upper house, like the U.S. Senate, but unitary systems can be unicameral, although many are still bicameral. In theory, legislatures formulate laws, but in practice they take their cues from the executive and deliver "pork" to their constituencies. Supervision and criticism of the executive is now perhaps their most useful function. Legislatures have, perhaps unfortunately, declined in importance as executives have grown.

Ch. 14 Executives and Bureaucracies   The U.S. presidential system frequently suffers from *deadlock* whereas parliamentary systems suffer from *immobilism*. These issues are normal for democracies; only authoritarian systems eliminate executive-legislative difficulties, as Putin has done in Russia. Prime ministers have tended to "presidentialize" themselves by gathering more power. Some American scholars fear an overstrong president, one who prevails by projecting a friendly personality. Within the executive branch, power has been flowing to bureaucrats because they are the only ones who understand complex situations and policies. Japan's bureaucrats virtually rule the country. No political system has succeeded in controlling its bureaucracy.

Ch. 15 Judiciaries   Law plays an especially strong role in the U.S. system, which makes the judiciary an equal branch; this is not the case in most countries. Common law systems, like the one in the United States, feature "judge-made law" that changes over time. Code law systems, like those of Europe, feature relatively fixed formulas, some of them tracing back to ancient Rome. Likewise, the Anglo-American accusatory and adversarial system is quite different from European inquisitorial systems. Few other countries have a Supreme Court as important or interesting as the American one, which decides issues related to the constitution, a power it gave itself with *Marbury v. Madison*. The political impact of the Warren Court was especially strong and controversial; it changed civil rights, criminal procedure, and legislative districts.

CHAPTER 13

Legislatures

On the banks of the Thames in London, Westminster, mother of Parliaments, represents the slow, gradual march to democracy over many centuries. (Douglas Pearson/Corbis)

Political institutions, it is theorized, become more specialized, complex, and differentiated as they become more modern. Primitive extended families had nothing more than a single leader who decided most things. Tribes added councils to debate major problems and adjudicate disputes. City-states such as Athens had assemblies that combined legislative, executive, and judicial functions. The Roman senate combined several roles, and its powers declined as Rome went from republic to empire. In the Middle Ages, the prevailing feudal system was a balance among a monarch, nobles, and leading churchmen, and it is in **feudalism** that we first glimpse the "balance of power."

QUESTIONS TO CONSIDER

1. How did parliaments first come to be?
2. What is the difference between presidential and parliamentary systems?
3. Why does the U.S. Congress overspend?
4. What is executive-legislative "deadlock"?
5. What good is a bicameral legislature in a unitary system?
6. Do legislatures originate the laws they pass?
7. Is the "pork barrel" necessary for the system to work?
8. Have legislatures declined in importance? Why?

Countries with limits on government have usually had feudal pasts, which teach that dispersion of power is good and concentration of power is bad. Countries with mostly absolutist traditions, such as China, have trouble founding democracies. An example of this balancing of power is the oath the nobles of medieval Aragon (in northeast Spain) pledged to a new king, "We, who are as good as you, swear to you, who are no better than we, to accept you as our king and sovereign lord provided you observe all our statutes and laws; and if not, no."

Ambitious monarchs, who were often at war, desperately needed revenues. Some of them started calling assemblies of notables to levy taxes. In return for their "power of the purse," these assemblies got a modest input into royal policies. Such were the beginnings of the British **Parliament**, which had two houses (Lords for peers and church leaders and Commons for knights and burghers), and the Swedish **Riksdag**, which originally had four chambers (for nobles, clerics, burghers, and farmers). The French **Estates General**, with three houses (for nobles, clerics, and commoners), got off to a weak start and was soon forgotten as French monarchs gathered more and more personal power in what became known as **absolutism**.

In Britain, Sweden, and some other European countries, though, legislatures slowly grew in power and were able to resist monarchs' absolutist demands. In

feudalism System of political power dispersed among layers.

parliament National legislature; when capitalized, British Parliament, specifically House of Commons.

Riksdag Sweden's parliament.

Estates General Old, unused French parliament.

absolutism Post-feudal concentration of power in monarch.

presidential systems Those with separate election of executive (as opposed to symbolic) president.

president In U.S.-type systems, the chief political official; in many other systems, a symbolic official.

parliamentary systems Those with election of parliament only, which in turn elects the prime minister.

prime minister Chief political official in parliamentary systems.

coalition Multiparty alliance to form a government.

fall In parliamentary system, a cabinet is voted out or resigns.

Britain in the sixteenth century, Henry VIII, who broke with Rome over a divorce, developed a partnership with Parliament because he needed its support in passing laws to break England away from the Roman Catholic Church. By the seventeenth century, Parliament considered itself coequal with the monarch and even supreme in the area of taxes. The English Civil War was a quarrel between royalists and parliamentarians over who had top power. In 1649, Parliament decided the issue by trying and beheading Charles I.

John Locke, the English philosopher who lived through this momentous period, extolled the power of the "legislative" as the most basic and important. During the Age of Enlightenment in the eighteenth century, Montesquieu (see page 237) declared that liberty could be secured only if government were divided into two distinct branches, the legislative and the executive, with the ability to check and balance the other. Modern governments still have these two branches, but only in the United States do they check and balance each other. Theoretically at least, the legislature enacts laws that allocate values for society, and the executive branch enforces the statutes passed by the legislature. (A coequal judicial branch is rare; it is a U.S. invention found in few other systems.) But these responsibilities often overlap, and the separation of powers is rarely clear-cut.

PRESIDENTIAL AND PARLIAMENTARY SYSTEMS

Presidential systems most clearly show the separation of power between the executive and legislative branches. These systems, a minority of the world's governments, have a **president** who combines the offices of head of state with chief of government. He or she is elected more or less directly by the people (in the United States, the quaint Electoral College mediates between the people and the actual election), is invested with considerable powers, and cannot be easily ousted by the legislature. In **parliamentary systems**, the head of state (figurehead monarch or weak president) is an office distinct from the chief of government (**prime minister**, premier, or chancellor). In this system, the prime minister is the important figure.

Notice that in parliamentary systems voters elect only a legislature (see Figure 13.1); they cannot split their tickets between the legislature and executive. The legislature then elects an executive from its own ranks. If the electoral system is based on proportional representation (see Chapter 4), there will likely be several parties in parliament. If no one party has a majority of seats, two or more parties must form a **coalition**. Whether one party or several, a majority of parliament must support the cabinet; if not, it "**falls**." Usually a monarch (as in Britain and Spain)

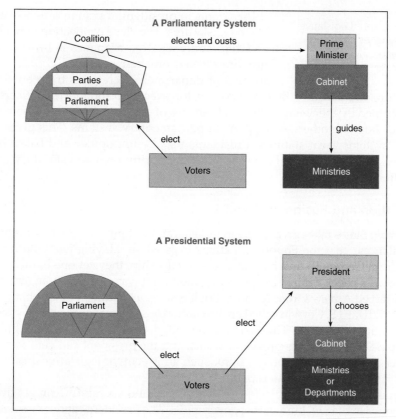

Figure 13.1
Parliamentary versus presidential systems.

or weak president (as in Germany or Israel) "asks"—there's no real choice in the matter—the head of the largest party to become prime minister and "form a government."

Cabinet and **government**, used interchangeably, are what Americans call an **administration**. One used to say the Cameron government but the Obama administration. Recently, however, some other countries have begun using the term "administration." The prime minister, after consulting with the parties likely to support him or her, names a team of ministers for the cabinet who are themselves members of the parliament. These ministers then guide the various ministries or departments of government that form the executive branch. The prime minister and cabinet are "responsible" (in the original sense of the word, "answerable") to the parliament. (Prior to democratization in the nineteenth century, ministers were responsible only to the monarch.)

cabinet Top executives who head major ministries or departments.

government In Europe, a given cabinet, equivalent to U.S. "administration."

administration Executives appointed by U.S. president, equivalent to European "government."

separation of powers   Legislative
and executive branches checking
and balancing each other.

Presidents in presidential systems are not responsible to legislatures. The close connection between the
legislative and executive branches is broken. Presidents are elected on their own and choose cabinet
ministers or department secretaries from outside the
legislature. In the United States, of course, top executive and judicial officers must
be confirmed by the Senate. The two branches of government cannot control, dissolve, or oust the other, as happens in parliamentary systems. This gives presidential systems great stability. Presidents may be unpopular and face a hostile
Congress, but they can still govern with the constitutional and statutory powers
they already have.

Separation and Fusion of Powers

The United States takes great pride in its **separation of powers**, the famous "checks
and balances" that the Founding Fathers insisted on. Having just won independence from George III and his executive dictatorship, they set one branch of government as a check against the power of another. It was a clever arrangement and
has preserved America from tyranny. But it is slow and cumbersome, what political
scientist Edward S. Corwin called an "invitation to struggle" between the executive
and legislative branches. The two branches often stymie each other. Congress can
fail to pass something the president wants, and the president can veto something
Congress wants. Some scholars think such an executive-legislative *deadlock* (see
page 254) is common for the U.S. presidential system.

Important questions, such as economic policy and tax reform, can get stuck for
years between the two branches of government. The president cannot dissolve Congress and hold new elections, which are set by the calendar. Congress cannot oust
a president except by the impeachment procedure. Only two presidents, Andrew
Johnson and Bill Clinton, have ever been impeached, and the Senate did not convict
either of them. Richard Nixon resigned before the House of Representatives could

KEY CONCEPTS ■ HEAD OF STATE VERSUS CHIEF OF GOVERNMENT

Two terms that sound almost alike often confuse students. A *head of state* is theoretically
the top leader but often has only symbolic
duties, such as the queen of England or king
of Sweden. These monarchs represent their
nations by receiving foreign ambassadors and
giving restrained speeches on patriotic occa-
sions. In republics, their analogues are presidents, some of whom are also little more than
figureheads. The republics of Germany, Hungary, and Israel, for example, have presidents

as heads of state, but they do little in the way
of practical politics. (They are also not well
known. Can you name them?)

The *chief of government* is the real working
executive, called prime minister, premier, or chancellor. They typically also head their parties, run
election campaigns, and guide government. In
Britain this is Prime Minister David Cameron, in
Germany Chancellor Angela Merkel. The United
States combines the two offices, for our president
is both head of state and head of government.

vote to impeach him. The disputes between the Obama administration and a Republican-dominated House of Representatives are standard in U.S. history. Some prefer this sort of "divided government" because it holds down spending and foolish policies.

West Europeans consider the American system inefficient and unintelligible, and they actually have more modern systems that evolved after the U.S. Constitution was devised. Their parliamentary systems have a **fusion of power** that does not set the branches against each other. In fact, it's hard to distinguish between legislative and executive branches, for the top executives are themselves usually members of parliament. In the British, German, Japanese, and Dutch systems, prime ministers must be elected to parliament, just like ordinary legislators, before they can become chief of government. As leaders of the biggest parties, they are formally called on (by the monarch or figurehead president) to form a government. The individuals forming this government or cabinet have both their seats in parliament and offices in the executive departments. They report back often to parliament. At any time, about a hundred British **MPs** (members of Parliament) also serve in the executive ministries and departments. Legislators are also executives. The cabinet, in effect, is a committee of parliament sent over to supervise the administration of the executive ministries.

When Britain's parliament is in session, the cabinet members show up to answer questions from their fellow MPs. Britain's House of Commons holds a Question Hour most afternoons. The members of the two main parties sit facing each other across an aisle on, respectively, the "government benches" and "**opposition** benches." The front bench of the former is reserved for cabinet ministers, the front bench of the latter for the opposition's "shadow cabinet," the MPs who would become ministers if their party were to win the next election. MPs with no executive responsibilities sit behind the cabinets and are called

fusion of power   Executive as an offshoot of the legislature.

MP   British member of Parliament, namely, the House of Commons.

opposition   Those parties in parliament not supporting the government.

backbencher   Ordinary member of parliament with no leadership or executive responsibilities.

CLASSIC WORKS ■ WHERE DID THE U.S. SYSTEM ORIGINATE?

The U.S. system of checks and balances originated with a French nobleman, the Baron de Montesquieu (1689–1755), who traveled all over Europe to gather material for one of the classics of political science, *The Spirit of the Laws*. In trouble with the king of France, Montesquieu spent some years in England and admired its liberties, which he thought came from the balancing of the king (the executive) and Parliament (the legislative). The French parliament, the Estates General, was unused for

generations; French kings ran everything on an absolutist basis.

Actually, by the time Montesquieu wrote about English checks and balances, they had been overturned, and Parliament was supreme over king. Montesquieu was describing an idealized version of the English mixed monarchy that had slid into the past. The U.S. Founding Fathers, however, read Montesquieu literally and attempted to construct his theory of checks and balances. Few other countries have done this.

National Assembly Lower, more important chamber of French parliament.

Bundestag Lower, more important chamber of German parliament.

bicameral Parliament having two chambers, upper and lower.

unicameral Parliament with one chamber.

Bundesrat Upper, weaker chamber of German parliament.

Lords Upper, weaker chamber of British parliament.

life peer Distinguished Briton named to House of Lords for his or her life, not hereditary.

backbenchers. Most questions to the prime minister and his or her cabinet come from the opposition benches—first written questions and then oral follow-ups. The answers are criticized, and the opposition tries to embarrass the government with an eye to winning the next election. Most parliamentary systems operate in a similar fashion.

In the U.S. system, with its separation of powers, committees of the Senate or House can summon cabinet members and other officials of the executive branch to committee hearings. But appearing before a committee is not the same as a grilling before the entire legislative body. The president, of course, as equal to and separate from Congress, cannot be called to testify.

KEY CONCEPTS ■ BICAMERAL OR UNICAMERAL?

Some two-thirds of parliaments in the world have two chambers, an upper house (the U.S. Senate, British House of Lords, French Sénat, German Bundesrat) plus a lower house (the U.S. House of Representatives, British House of Commons, French **National Assembly**, German **Bundestag**). These are called **bicameral** (two chambers) legislatures. Despite its name, the upper house usually has much less power than the lower house. Typically, if the upper house objects to something passed by the lower house, the lower house can override the upper house's objections, often by a simple majority. Only the two houses of the U.S. Congress are coequal and must pass identically worded versions of a bill.

A smaller number of parliaments are **unicameral** (one chamber), such as China's National Peoples Congress, Sweden's Riksdag, and Israel's Knesset. Yugoslavia once experimented with a five-chambered parliament. South Africa had a curious and short-lived three-chambered parliament with one house each for whites, mixed-race peoples, and East Indians. The majority black population was unrepresented. (Since 1994, South Africa has had a bicameral parliament with a black majority.)

The reason for two chambers is clear in federal systems (see Chapter 4). The upper house represents the component parts, and the lower house represents districts based on population. This was the great compromise incorporated in the U.S. Constitution: The Senate represented the states and the House the people. A federal system requires an upper chamber. Germany's **Bundesrat**, for example, represents the 16 *Länder* and is coequal to the lower house on constitutional questions. On other issues, however, it can be overridden by the Bundestag.

The utility of an upper house in unitary systems is unclear. Britain's House of **Lords**—reformed in 1999 by keeping **life peers** and excluding most hereditary peers—is still mostly an elderly debating society that sometimes catches errors in laws passed too quickly and obediently by Commons. Otherwise, the Commons overrides any objection from the House of Lords with a simple majority vote. This is also true of the French Sénat, an indirectly elected body that largely expresses farming interests. New Zealanders, Danes, and Swedes—all with unitary systems—concluded that their upper houses served no purpose and abolished them in recent decades.

The Finnish parliament is unicameral—with no upper chamber—and consists of 200 seats arrayed in a semicircle, the standard layout for parliaments. Also standard are the buttons on each member's desk to register his or her vote, which is then electronically tabulated and displayed instantly. (Mikko Stig/Getty Images)

Advantages of Parliamentary Systems

There are several advantages to a parliamentary system. The executive-legislative deadlock, which happens frequently in the American system, cannot occur because both the executive and legislative branches are governed by the same party. If the British Conservative Party wins a majority of the seats in the House of Commons, the leaders of the party are automatically the country's executives. When the Conservative cabinet drafts a new law, it is sent to the House of Commons to be passed, which is rarely difficult or delayed because the Conservative MPs obey the party's leaders.

vote of confidence Vote in parliament to support or oust government.

If members of the governing party disagree with their own leaders in the cabinet, they can withdraw their support and vote "no confidence" in the government. This is rare. The government then falls and must be replaced by a new leadership team that commands the support of a majority of the House of Commons. If a new election gives the opposition party the numerical edge in parliament, the cabinet resigns and is replaced by the leaders of the newly victorious party. Either way, there cannot be a long disagreement between executive and legislative branches; they are fused into one.

The prime minister and cabinet can be speedily ousted in parliamentary systems. Any important vote in parliament can be designated a **vote of confidence**. If the prime minister loses—a "vote of no confidence"—the cabinet falls. There is no

---

whip Legislator who instructs other party members when and how to vote.

Capitol Hill Home of U.S. Congress. (Note spelling: -ol.)

minority government Cabinet lacking firm majority in parliament.

portfolio Minister's assigned ministry.

---

agony of impending impeachment of the sort that paralyzed Washington under Presidents Nixon and Clinton. A new prime minister and cabinet are voted in immediately. If the government makes a major policy blunder, parliament can get rid of the cabinet without waiting for its term to expire. When Americans become unhappy with presidents' policies, there is little the system can do to remove them from the White House early. Parliamentary systems do not get stuck with unpopular prime ministers.

Parliamentary systems have other difficulties, however. First, because members of parliament—supervised by their parties' **whips**—generally obey their party leaders, votes in parliament can be closely predicted. The parties supporting the government vote for any bill the cabinet has drafted. Parties opposing the government vote against it. Floor speeches and corridor persuasion have no impact; the legislators vote the way their party instructs. MPs in such systems have lost their independence, and their parliaments have become little more than rubber stamps for the cabinet. The passage of legislation is more rational, speedy, and efficient, but parliament cannot "talk back" to the executive or make independent inputs. This makes European parliaments rather dull and less important than **Capitol Hill** in Washington, where legislators often oppose the president, even of their own party. Many European legislators are jealous of the independence and separate resources that American representatives and senators enjoy.

Second, depending on the party system and electoral system, parliamentary democracies often have many parties, with no single party controlling a majority of seats in parliament. This means the largest party must form a coalition with smaller parties to command more than half the seats. In Britain's 2010 elections, Conservatives emerged as the largest party (with 306 out of 650 seats) but lacked a majority, so they had to form a coalition with the smaller Liberal Democratic Party, which got five positions in the cabinet and a promise to reconsider the electoral system.

The only other alternative would have been to form a **minority government** that depended on the passive support of smaller parties. Then, if the Tories failed to get support on an important bill—say, the budget—they would have lost a vote of no confidence and would probably have to hold new elections. This happened before, in the 1970s, when a minority Labour government depended on the support of small parties. In 1979, however, they stopped supporting the cabinet, which was ousted on a vote of no confidence. Notice how Britain's legendary governing stability weakens when no party commands a majority of parliamentary seats. As we discussed in previous chapters, party system determines much of governing stability.

In coalitions, the head of the largest party becomes prime minister, and the head of the second largest party usually becomes foreign minister. Other cabinet positions, or **portfolios**, are assigned by bargaining. Italy and Israel are examples of coalition governments, and they illustrate what can go wrong: The coalition partners quarrel over policy, and one or more parties withdraws from the coalition, bringing it below the required majority in parliament. The government then falls for lack of parliamentary support, with or without a formal vote of no confidence. This leads to instability, frequent cabinet changes, and loss of executive authority. Italy, for example, has had some sixty governments since World War II.

This is not as bad as it sounds—remember, the "government" simply means "cabinet"—and the cabinets are often put back together again after bargaining among the same coalition partners. The trouble is that prime ministers must concentrate on not letting the coalition fall apart, and thus they hesitate to launch new policies that might alienate one of the member parties. The problem here is not one of too much change but of too little: the same parties in the same coalitions getting stuck over the same issues. *Immobilism* (see Chapter 11), the inability to decide major questions, is the danger of multiparty parliamentary systems. Notice how this parallels the problem of *deadlock* in presidential systems.

Not all parliamentary systems, to be sure, suffer from immobilism. In Britain, the largest party usually has a majority of seats and can govern alone. Some coalition cabinets, as in Sweden, are cohesive and effective because their parties are in general agreement. German and British governments have fallen on votes of no confidence only once each since World War II. In general, the more parties in a coalition, the less stable it is. Israel's multiparty cabinet is often immobilized.

WHAT LEGISLATURES DO

Consider the old high-school civics question: How does a bill become law? They may have told you that individual members introduce proposals, but these usually cover small matters, such as getting a tax break for a constituent. Most important bills originate in the government or administration. Typically, an executive agency develops an idea, the cabinet drafts a proposal, and the largest party introduces it to the legislature, which then debates and modifies it.

The Committee System

Much power in modern legislatures resides in their committees, which can make or break proposals. Democratic parliaments often hold public hearings to get expert testimony and input from interest groups. If the bill is reported favorably out of committee, it goes to "the floor," the full chamber, where it needs a majority vote to pass.

Virtually every legislature has a number of standing or permanent committees and may from time to time create special ad hoc committees to study urgent matters. The British House of Commons has five standing committees plus several specialized committees. These committees are less important than their U.S. counterparts, for the fusion of powers of the British system means that Parliament is not supposed to criticize or reject bills the cabinet has submitted. It may, however, modify them. With separation of powers, the committees of the U.S. Congress are most fully developed. The House of Representatives has 27 standing committees—the Senate, 21—and they often make the news. Assignment to the more prestigious of these committees, such as the House Ways and Means Committee or Armed Services Committee, can help careers, for they give members media exposure.

U.S. congressional committees screen the thousands of bills that are introduced at every session and pick out the few that merit serious consideration. A government bill in a parliamentary system is automatically important; "private members' bills" may be quickly weeded out in committee. Second, legislatures are so large that bills cannot be drafted by the entire membership; to work out an agreement on the precise wording and scope of legislation, proposals must be referred to committees. The bulk of legislative work is not performed on the floor but in committee rooms.

In the United States, each committee has several specialized subcommittees; the two houses have a total of about 250 subcommittees. Changes in the 1970s weakened the sometimes tyrannical powers of committee chairpersons by making it easier to establish subcommittees. Chairpersons are weaker than they used to be, but now subcommittees and their chairpersons have decentralized and fragmented power too much, weakening Congress as an institution. A cure for one problem produced new problems, the story of many political reforms.

These same reforms of the 1970s broke the power of appointment of the senior House and Senate leaders of both parties. Committee chairs and membership were generally assigned on the basis of seniority. Now, when the parties caucus at the beginning of a session in each house, members vote for committee chairpersons by secret ballot, effectively breaking the seniority system. Party committees in each house make committee assignments and usually try to take members' interests and expertise into account. On the Hill, specialization is the name of the game. The larger committees, such as the Senate Foreign Relations Committee, may have a dozen subcommittees. Capitol Hill is now more open and democratic than it used to be, but this has not enhanced its power vis-à-vis the executive branch.

Standing committees in the U.S. Congress are balanced to represent both political parties and the states or geographic regions with the greatest interest in the committee's work. A Nebraskan is often on the Agricultural Committee and a New Yorker on the Education and Labor Committee. Each standing committee is bipartisan, made up of Democrats and Republicans in proportion to each party's seats.

A Closer Look at Legislatures

The main purpose of legislative bodies, in theory, is to formulate laws. This, however, varies among political systems and is generally in decline. Ideally, legislatures initiate laws, propose constitutional amendments, ratify treaties, control tax revenues, and scrutinize government activities. In authoritarian systems, however, legislatures are for show.

Lawmaking   Although legislatures *pass* laws, few of them *originate* laws—which is why we must take their "rule-initiation function" with a grain of salt. As we noted, much legislation originates in government departments and agencies. In parliamentary systems, especially where one party has a majority of seats, the cabinet gets what it wants. Party discipline makes sure that members of the ruling parties will automatically vote the way party leaders instruct. Votes in such legislatures are highly predictable along party lines; some observers say such parliaments have become rubber stamps for the executive.

In the U.S. Congress, where party discipline is more lax, members sometimes buck their own party. But even here much of the legislative agenda is set by the White House: economic initiatives, wars, and expanding or cutting programs. Even the budget, the original "power of the purse" that gave legislatures their importance, is now an annual congressional reaction to the budget produced by the White House budget office. Typically, Congress takes the president's budget, adds its own pork spending, and passes it. Accordingly, "lawmaking" is not the only, or perhaps even the most important, thing that legislatures do.

constituency casework   Attention legislators pay to complaints of people who elect them.

ombudsman   Swedish for "agent"; lawyer employed by parliament to help citizens wronged by government.

pork barrel   Government projects aimed at legislators' constituencies, also called earmarks.

log rolling   Legislators mutually supporting each other to get pork-barrel bills passed.

Constituency Work   Legislators spend much time helping constituents. Most have staffs to answer letters, make sure people get their government checks, and generally show that the elected representatives really care. Often "lawmakers" are so busy with **constituency casework** that they pay little attention to making laws. In effect, elected representatives have partly transformed themselves into **ombudsmen**, specialists who intervene with government on behalf of people with complaints. (Standard

KEY CONCEPTS ■ PORK-BARREL POLITICS

Legislators everywhere ensure their reelection by looking after their districts. Projects that bring improvements to or spend money in their district are called **pork barrel**, after the gifts of plantation owners to their slaves of a barrel of pickled pork parts. Under the politer label "earmarks," these programs include highways, bridges, flood control, military contracts, and farm subsidies. The U.S. pork barrel takes second place to the Japanese, whose legislators are famous for delivering massive (and often unneeded) public works projects to their districts and shielding farmers from competition.

Individual legislators support others' earmarks so their projects will get support, a process called **log rolling**: "You help roll my log, and I'll help roll yours." Republicans long denounced Democratic pork but do not resist it when they have control of Congress. Legislators do whatever gets them reelected, and that usually means earmarks. If the United States and

Japan wish to reduce their pork intake, they will have to break the close connection between elected representatives and home districts. But this connection is precisely what these democracies prize. Would you want a system in which congresspersons are distant and uncaring about their districts?

Besides, much good and important legislation would not pass if leaders could not use pork as inducements to vote for it. Every U.S. federal budget includes thousands of earmarks, little bribes to every state and congressional district to get legislators to support the White House budget. Even Republicans use pork to get things done. Earmarks are only about 0.5 percent of the U.S. federal budget, so not much could be saved by eliminating them. Returning to a theme of Chapter 1, do not get angry at a fact like earmarks; instead, analyze it. Why does it exist? What functions does it serve? You may find that it is built into the system and cannot be fixed.

Question Hour Time reserved
in Commons for opposition to
challenge cabinet.

longitudinal Studying how something changes over time.

complaint: "Where's my check?") Is there anything
wrong with this? Is it not a perfectly valid and necessary role for legislators to play? It is, but something gets
lost: the wider view that a representative should have in
looking out for the good of the whole country. A legislator immersed in constituency casework has no time for
or interest in bigger questions, so the initiative goes more
and more to the executive branch, and democracy grows a little weaker.

Constituency service is mainly how representatives keep getting reelected.
They are in a position to do favors. They frequently visit their home districts to listen to local problems and arrange for government help, something an out-of-office
challenger cannot do. Thus, legislators in systems as different as the United States
and Japan can lock themselves into power.

Supervision and Criticism of Government   Potentially, the most important role
of modern legislatures is keeping a sharp and critical eye on the executive branch.
Even if they originate little legislation, parliaments can powerfully affect the work
of government by monitoring government activity to make sure it is in the nation's
interest, incorrupt, and effective.

In Britain, the **Question Hour** allows members of Parliament to grill ministers, sometimes with devastating results. Even if the British cabinet knows that it
is almost immune to a vote of no confidence—because it controls the majority of

HOW TO... ■ CONDUCT A LONGITUDINAL STUDY

One good way to study something is to see how it changes over time, a **longitudinal** study. For example, suppose you want to see if interest groups headquartered in Washington have grown in number. You could find a reliable secondary source (perhaps Common Cause) that keeps track of these things. You might also count the numbers of "National" and "Associa-tions" in D.C. phone books over several years. Then you would list the numbers, probably with most recent first, looking something like this:

2009	1,827
2008	1,779
2007	1,654
2006	1,628
2005	1,607
2004	1,592

For a longer-range study, you might take every fifth or tenth year over many decades or a century. Other longitudinal studies might take a closer look at the behavior of one or sev-eral interest groups, campaign spending, laws initiated by Congress, or presidential votes by states. You may be able to display such num-bers graphically, which helps readability. (See pages 262–263.)

Not all longitudinal studies need to be quan-tified. Some do not lend themselves to num-bers. A longitudinal study of Senator J. William Fulbright, for example, might use quotes and paraphrases from his speeches and writings to show how he changed over time, from sup-porting the administration on foreign affairs to opposing it over the Vietnam War.

Commons—its members must answer questions carefully. A bad, unconvincing answer or lie can hurt the ruling party in the next election.

apartheid   System of strict racial segregation formerly practiced in South Africa.

Virtually every U.S. administration must modify its policies because Congress raises difficult and sometimes embarrassing questions, even though it may pass little legislation on these matters. Members of both parties on Capitol Hill criticized the Obama administration for spending too much, for bailing out financial institutions, and for a complex healthcare reform. The Obama administration had to change many of its policies because of congressional criticism. Keeping the government on its toes is one of the best things a legislature can do, even if it passes few laws.

Education   Legislatures also inform and instruct the citizenry on the affairs of government; they create mass demands by calling public attention to problems. In the mid-1960s, Senator J. William Fulbright (D-Ark.), chair of the Senate Foreign Relations Committee, educated Americans about the Vietnam War by televising his committee's hearings. Democratic control of Congress later allowed Congress to hold critical hearings on the Iraq War. All democratic countries carry extensive press reports on parliamentary debate, and many now televise them.

Representation   The most elemental function of a legislature is to represent people, or at least make them feel they are represented. Although legislators are elites, most legislators in democracies consider the interests of their constituents; it gets them reelected. Even in the U.S. South, now that African Americans are voting in considerable numbers, members of Congress take care not to offend them. A large part of representation is psychological; people need to feel they are represented. When they do not, they resent government power, and the government loses legitimacy. "No taxation without representation," chanted American colonials. Tea Party supporters, feeling estranged from Washington, vow to "take back" the government. The **apartheid** laws of South Africa, passed by a whites-only legislature, evoked no support and much disobedience from the black majority. Because of this, the apartheid system cracked.

The foregoing are some of the roles performed by legislatures. Notice that only one of them is lawmaking, and that is usually just a follow-up on ideas initiated by bureaucrats and executives. Still, if legislatures carry out the other functions mentioned, they are doing a lot.

THE DECLINE OF LEGISLATURES

By the late nineteenth century, observers were noticing that parliaments were not working the way they were supposed to. Contrary to Locke's expectations, legislatures were losing power to the executive. Most political scientists would agree that the trend has continued and grown. Some, however, hold that the original Lockean expectations were too high and that parliaments provide useful checks on the executive even though they do not originate much legislation. For better or worse, a high-tech age has shifted power away from legislatures.

Structural Disadvantages

In parliamentary systems, party discipline is strong, and legislators obey party whips. In European parliaments we can usually predict within a vote or two how the issue will be decided: in favor of the government, because the government (that is, the cabinet) commands a majority of seats. In such systems, individual members do little and there is no special excitement in the press and public about parliamentary affairs. Only when coalitions break up or when members of one party defect to another do things get unpredictable and therefore interesting. The European parliaments really are more rational and efficient than the U.S. Congress, but they are also less powerful and less interesting. Efficiency has led to atrophy.

The U.S. Capitol Hill has no such problem with efficiency. Its near-feudal dispersion of power with weaker party discipline and its tendency to deadlock with the executive has made it most inefficient. But this is why Congress is lively and important. In few other countries can the national legislature as a whole disagree with the executive and even override a presidential veto. On occasion, members change parties to show their displeasure. Nevertheless, even in the United States power has drifted to the executive. The president speaks with one voice, Congress with many. Congress is fragmented into committees and subcommittees—with chairpersons vying for media attention—and this delays and often prevents agreement. Congress expects and even demands presidential leadership and usually gives presidents most of what they want after some controversy and debate.

Lack of Expertise

Few legislators are experts on technical, military, economic, or social problems. Of the 535 senators and representatives in both houses of Congress, typically over half are lawyers. (Tocqueville first noted the tendency of U.S. politicians to be lawyers in the 1830s.) European parliaments have fewer lawyers and more schoolteachers, journalists, and full-time party people. But hardly anywhere are technical experts elected to legislatures, and few legislators are professionally equipped to deal with such matters as intelligence estimates, medical care, reckless lending, and environmental pollution. Accordingly, legislators must rely chiefly on experts from the executive departments. Much legislation originates with these specialists, and they are often called as witnesses to committee hearings. The ensuing legislation usually grants these executive specialists considerable discretion in applying the law.

Most parliaments have little or nothing in the way of independent research support; their data come either from the government or from private interest groups. Only the U.S. Congress—again, based on the idea of separation of powers—can generate its own data. The Government Accountability Office (GAO, formerly the

General Accounting Office), Congressional Research Service (CRS), and Congressional Budget Office (CBO) are all part of the legislative branch. They provide independent evaluations and data to lessen Congress's dependence on the executive. No other legislature in the world has a fraction of this research capability, which still cannot counterbalance the massive information advantage of the executive branch.

aggregate Thing or population considered as a whole.

Psychological Disadvantages

Citizens everywhere are more impressed with presidents or prime ministers than with parliaments. There may be a deep human need to respond to a single chief. A president can have charisma, but a legislature cannot. American children are socialized to revere the president but to disdain members of Congress. As was mentioned in Chapter 12, even in parliamentary systems voters now respond to the personalities of the candidates for prime minister. Television, by giving much more air time to chief executives than to other political figures, heightens this tendency. People come to see their president or prime minister as a parental figure, calmly

---

KEY CONCEPTS ■ CONGRESSIONAL OVERSPENDING

The tendency of most legislatures to overspend is built into their situation. In the abstract, they are all for a balanced budget. When it comes to their pet interests—usually linked to getting reelected—they like spending increases. New bridges and highways, military hardware, and farm subsidies often directly benefit their constituents (see box on "Pork-Barrel Politics" on page 243). Paying for prescription drugs under Medicare shows they hear the cries of senior citizens. Rationally, individual self-interests drive the system as a whole to overspend, allegedly something nobody wants. What's good for the individual is not necessarily good for the **aggregate**.

At various times, the U.S. Congress tries to restrain itself. In 1985, Congress attempted to hand the power to limit spending to an appointed congressional official. The Supreme Court threw it out as unconstitutional. Congress then attempted to hand the power to the White House with the 1996 "line-item" veto, a major shift in power from the legislative

to the executive. The Supreme Court threw it out; the Constitution does not permit the veto of part of a bill. It was almost as if Congress said, "We give up; we're too divided. So here, Mr. President, you take over our constitutional duties." The astonishing thing about the U.S. Congress, the last Mohican of independent parliaments, is that it *wants* to surrender power to the executive.

The Republicans who took over both houses in 1994 were determined to end deficits (see page 300) by setting "spending caps." The caps were evaded almost immediately, but an economic boom provided unforeseen tax revenues and budget surpluses by the turn of the millennium. Quickly, the limits were forgotten as both Republicans and Democrats put forward their pet spending projects. With the end of the boom, the 2001 tax cut, and the mammoth financial bailouts of 2008 and 2009, revenues shrank and deficits soared. As the baby boom generation retires, spending will only go up. Is Congress inherently unable to balance the budget?

guiding the country toward safety while the silly parliamentarians squabble among themselves. This leads to what some political scientists fear is "president worship."

The Absentee Problem

If you visit a legislature in session, you might be disappointed, for usually the chamber is nearly empty. Most of the time, most members need not be present, and they aren't. They have many other things to do: helping and visiting constituents, talking with interest groups, and sitting on committees. Why bother listening to speeches? They will not change anyone's vote, and everyone knows their content in advance. The speeches are for the mass media.

Absent most of the time, the member is really needed only to vote and sometimes not even then. British party whips can get a high turnout for an important vote. In Sweden, an electronic system summons members from all over the Riksdag after the speeches are over. They press their *ja* or *nej* button according to their parties' wishes, glance up at the electronic tabulation (which was never in doubt), and then leave. The Riksdag chamber has been full for fewer than 10 minutes.

Most systems have ways of recording members' votes without their presence. When the French National Assembly votes, a few members of each party move down the rows of absent fellow party members' desks and flick their voting switches to a *pour* or *contre* position, as the party has commanded. The press then reports that the measure passed by a vote of around 300 to 200, but that is deceptive, as often only three dozen members were present. Theoretically, the French system could function with just one member present from each party.

The U.S. House and Senate require members to be present to vote, but even if absent they can arrange to have their votes "paired against" that of another absent legislator with the opposite viewpoint. The yes vote cancels out the no vote, so the passage of the measure is unaffected, and the member can still claim to have voted for or against something.

What is the impact of legislative absenteeism? It may indicate that the legislator is busy doing other important things. It may also indicate just plain laziness. But it surely means that legislators no longer regard legislating as their chief function. By their absence they admit that they are not important, at least not in the way originally intended. Is there any way to fix the problem? Only by weakening party discipline and party-line voting so that no one could predict how a vote would go. If bills were up for grabs, some excitement and tension would return to floor debate, and members would have an interest and incentive to show up and participate. The trade-off would be that the passage of legislation would be more chaotic and unpredictable.

Lack of Turnover

In democratic parliaments, members tend to become career, lifetime legislators. Once elected, they usually get reelected as long as they wish to serve. This means little fresh, young blood enters parliament with new ideas, and on average parliamentarians are rather old, in their fifties. In U.S. House contests, typically some 90 percent of incumbents win. Incumbency brings terrific advantages: gerrymandered districts, name recognition, favors done for constituents, media coverage, and plentiful campaign funds from corporations and interest groups. Unless representatives are tarred by scandal, they almost cannot lose. Challengers are so discouraged that several dozen House incumbents run unopposed. In many other contests, opposition is only token. Why waste time and money in a hopeless race?

What happens to democracy when elected representatives stay until death or retirement? It loses some of its ability to innovate and respond to new currents in public opinion. It gets stodgy. The Founding Fathers made the House term deliberately short, just two years, to let fresh views wash into the chamber. Alexander Hamilton praised the frequent elections to the House: "Here, sir, the people govern. Here they act by their immediate representatives." He could not imagine that turnover is higher in the Senate, a chamber that was designed to be insulated from mass passions. All this raised the question of limits on congressional terms, which some promised but few practiced. Once in power, they discover they are the only ones who can serve their constituents.

Parliamentary systems have similar problems. Few legislators are replaced by elections, and most consider their membership in parliament a career. In proportional representation systems, the more senior party people are higher up on the party list, ensuring their election. Young newcomers may be entered at the bottom of their party lists with scant chance of winning. However, PR systems do have the advantage of letting new, small parties into parliament with fresh faces and new ideas. In the 1980s, the Greens (ecology parties) entered several West European parliaments, forcing the big, established parties to pay attention to environmental problems.

The Dilemma of Parliaments

What Russia has gone through recently illustrates the dilemma of parliaments. In the 1990s Russia experienced a deadlock between President Boris Yeltsin and the Russian legislature, the Duma. To get things done, power must be concentrated in the hands of a powerful executive. To keep things democratic, however, power must be dispersed, that is, divided between an executive and a legislature. Russia urgently needed vast reforms—the economy teetered on the brink of collapse—but the Duma, dominated by Communists and nationalists who opposed Yeltsin, disputed and blocked reforms. Putin solved the problem by founding his own party, which now controls two-thirds of the Duma's seats. Putin owns parliament, but Russia is no longer a democracy.

Even in the United States, Congress works as intended only when dominated by the party opposed to the president, what is called "divided government," something many voters prefer. Locke was right: Parliaments are the foundation of democracy. But worldwide their functions have atrophied, and power is flowing to executives and bureaucrats.

mypoliscikit EXERCISES

Apply what you learned in this chapter on MyPoliSciKit (www.mypoliscikit.com).

 Assessment   Review this chapter using learning objectives, chapter summaries, practice tests, and more.

 Flashcards   Learn the key terms in this chapter; you can test yourself by term or definition.

 Video   Analyze recent world affairs by watching streaming video from major news providers.

 Comparative Exercises   Compare political ideas, behaviors, institutions, and policies worldwide.

KEY TERMS

absolutism (p. 234)
administration (p. 235)
aggregate (p. 247)
apartheid (p. 245)
backbencher (p. 237)
bicameral (p. 238)
Bundesrat (p. 238)
Bundestag (p. 238)
cabinet (p. 235)
Capitol Hill (p. 240)
coalition (p. 234)
constituency casework (p. 243)
Estates General (p. 234)
fall (p. 234)
feudalism (p. 234)

fusion of power (p. 237)
government (p. 235)
life peer (p. 238)
log rolling (p. 243)
longitudinal (p. 244)
Lords (p. 238)
minority government (p. 240)
MP (p. 237)
National Assembly (p. 238)
ombudsman (p. 243)
opposition (p. 237)
parliament (p. 234)
parliamentary systems (p. 234)
pork barrel (p. 243)

portfolio (p. 240)
president (p. 234)
presidential systems (p. 234)
prime minister (p. 234)
Question Hour (p. 244)
Riksdag (p. 234)
separation of powers (p. 236)
unicameral (p. 238)
vote of confidence (p. 239)
whip (p. 240)

FURTHER REFERENCE

Brady, W. David, and Craig Volden. *Revolving Gridlock: Politics and Policy from Jimmy Carter to George W. Bush,* 2nd ed. Boulder, CO: Westview, 2005.

Copeland, Gary W., and Samuel C. Patterson, eds. *Parliaments in the Modern World: Changing Institutions.* Ann Arbor, MI: University of Michigan Press, 1994.

Deering, Christopher J., and Steven S. Smith. *Committees in Congress,* 3rd ed. Washington, DC: CQ Press, 1997.

Dodd, Lawrence C., and Bruce I. Oppenheimer, eds. *Congress Reconsidered,* 9th ed. Washington, DC: CQ Press, 2008.

Hayes, Michael T., and Lou Frey Jr., eds. *Inside the House: Former Members Reveal*

How Congress Really Works. Lanham, MD: University Press of America, 2001.

King, Anthony. *Running Scared: Why America's Politicians Campaign Too Much and Govern Too Little.* New York: Free Press, 1997.

Laver, Michael, and Norman Schofield. *Multiparty Government: The Politics of Coalition in Europe.* New York: Oxford University Press, 1990.

Lijphart, Arend, ed. *Parliamentary versus Presidential Government.* New York: Oxford University Press, 1992.

Mann, Thomas E., and Norman J. Orenstein. *The Broken Branch: How Congress Is Failing America and How to Get It Back on Track.* New York: Oxford University Press, 2006.

Mayhew, David R. *Congress: The Electoral Connection,* 2nd ed. New Haven, CT: Yale University Press, 2004.

Polsby, Nelson W. *How Congress Evolves: Social Bases of Institutional Change.* New York: Oxford University Press, 2003.

Rawls, W. Lee. *In Praise of Deadlock: How Partisan Struggle Makes Better Laws.* Baltimore, MD: Johns Hopkins University Press, 2009.

Suleiman, Ezra N., ed. *Parliaments and Parliamentarians in Democratic Politics.* New York: Holmes & Meier, 1986.

Wolfensberger, Donald R. *Congress and the People: Deliberative Democracy on Trial.* Baltimore, MD: Johns Hopkins University Press, 2000.

Executives and Bureaucracies

British Prime Minister David Cameron, elected in 2010, speaks in the cabinet room of 10 Downing Street, London. (Pool/Corbis)

A political movement has recently rippled across the United States, the Tea Party, demanding a rollback in the size and cost of government. Its number-one target: bureaucrats. Tea Partiers portrayed civil servants as robbing Americans of their freedom and property. Actually, the Tea Party was merely the latest upsurge of an old American tradition, one that mistrusts the national government.

Tea Partiers are right to worry about an expensive, overlarge government, but a major rollback is unlikely. Economic and technological change in a continent-sized republic mean we can no longer get by with the minimal governance the U.S. Founding Fathers had in mind for the 13 largely rural original states. The Founders had an ingenious solution for the time: a legislative branch that would check and balance a potentially abusive executive. But, as we considered in the last chapter, executives have become more powerful than legislatures. Furthermore, some political scientists fear another trend: Within the executive branch, power is shifting from elected officials to bureaucrats. There is no simple cure for these two trends.

There have been executives a lot longer than there have been legislatures. Tribal chiefs, kings, and emperors appeared with the dawn of civilization; only recently have they had legislatures to worry about. Indeed, the word *government* in most of the world means the executive branch. In Europe, *government* equals *cabinet*. The "Cameron government" is just another way of saying British Prime Minister David Cameron's cabinet plus some additional subcabinet assistants. In the United States (and increasingly in some other countries), this configuration is called the *administration*. What Americans call "the government," meaning all of the bureaus and bureaucrats, is known in the rest of the world as the **state**.

QUESTIONS TO CONSIDER

1. Is power shifting first to executives and then to bureaucrats?
2. Why have prime ministers become more like presidents?
3. Is the U.S. presidency too powerful?
4. What are the various styles of presidential leadership? What is the current president's style?
5. Explain Lasswell's psychology of political power.
6. Are cabinets as important as they used to be?
7. Must every large organization be bureaucratic?
8. How did Max Weber characterize bureaucracy?
9. Why is it hard for a government to control bureaucrats?

PRESIDENTS AND PRIME MINISTERS

As discussed in Chapter 13, in parliamentary systems a national legislature indirectly elects a chief executive from its own ranks, a prime (originally meaning "first") minister. Such parliaments serve as electoral colleges that stay in session to consider legislation. They can also oust a prime minister and cabinet by a vote of no confidence, although this is now rare. Still, prime ministers are responsible to parliament. If they represent a party with a majority of seats, they are secure in office and can get legislative programs passed quickly and with little backtalk. A British prime minister with a sizable and disciplined majority in the Commons wields powers that might make a U.S. president jealous.

state   In Europe, all branches of the national political system; what Americans call "the government."

deadlock   In presidential systems, executive and legislative branches blocking each other.

minister   Head of ministry, equivalent to U.S. departmental secretary.

If no party has a majority, however, a government is formed by a *coalition* of parties, each of which gets one or more ministries to run. Sometimes the coalition partners quarrel over policy and threaten to split up. This weakens the hand of the prime minister, as he or she knows that any major policy shift could lead to new quarrels. It is not quite right to say that prime ministers are "weaker" than presidents in presidential systems; it depends on whether prime ministers have a stable majority in parliament.

A presidential system bypasses this problem by having a strong president who is not dependent on or responsible to a parliament but is elected on his or her own for a fixed term. The U.S. Congress may not like the president's policies and may vote them down, but it may not vote out the president. The U.S. president and Capitol Hill stand side by side, sometimes glaring at each other, knowing that there is nothing they can do to get rid of each other. It is sometimes said that presidents are "stronger" than prime ministers, and in terms of being able to run the executive branch for a fixed term, they are. But they may not be able to get vital new legislation or budgeting out of their legislatures. This "**deadlock** of democracy," the curse of the U.S. political system, parallels parliamentary *immobilism* (see page 207). Neither system can guarantee cooperation between legislative and executive. Any system that could would be a dictatorship.

"Forming a Government" in Britain

Great Britain is the classic of parliamentary systems, one in which we still see its historical roots. The monarch, currently Queen Elizabeth II, formally invites the leader of the largest party in the House of Commons to become prime minister and "form a government," meaning take office with a cabinet. The prime minister appoints two dozen **ministers** and a greater number of subcabinet officials. All are members of Parliament (MPs) and mostly from the prime minister's party, usually chosen to represent significant groups within the party. Theoretically, the prime minister is *primus inter pares* (first among equals) and guides the cabinet to consensus. But the prime minister is the chief and can dismiss ministers. Ministers who oppose government policy are expected not to go public but to resign and return to their seats in Commons. Recently, the British cabinet mostly concurs on decisions the prime minister has reached earlier with a few advisors, on the American pattern.

> **chancellor** Germany's prime minister.
>
> **premier** France's and Italy's prime ministers.
>
> **Knesset** Israel's 120-member unicameral parliament.

"Constructive No Confidence" in Germany

The **chancellor** of Germany is as strong as a British prime minister. The chancellor, too, is head of the largest party in the lower house (Bundestag). Once in the office the chancellor can be ousted only if the Bundestag votes in a replacement cabinet. This is called *constructive no confidence,* and it has contributed to the stability of Germany's governments. It is much harder to replace a cabinet than just oust one; as a result, constructive no confidence has succeeded only once, in 1982, when the small Free Democratic Party defected from the Social Democrat–led coalition to the opposition Christian Democrats. A prime minister with constructive no confidence is more powerful than one without it, as one might see in a comparison of the average tenures of Italian and German cabinets (several months as compared with several years).

"Cohabitation" in France

President Charles de Gaulle of France (1958–1969) designed a semipresidential system that has both a working president and a prime minister. The president was elected directly for seven years (now reduced to five) and a parliament elected for five years. If both are of the same party, there is no problem. The president names a like-minded **premier**, who is the link between president and parliament. In 1986 and again in 1993, though, a Socialist president, François Mitterrand, with two years left in his term, faced a newly elected parliament dominated by conservatives. The constitution gave no guidance in such a case. Mitterrand solved the

---

COMPARING ■ ISRAEL'S DIRECTLY ELECTED PRIME MINISTERS

Under a new law, in 1996 Israelis elected a parliament and a prime minister *separately and directly,* something never before done in the world. Each Israeli voter had two votes, one for a party in the legislature and one for prime minister. By definition, parliamentary systems elect prime ministers indirectly, usually the head of the largest party in parliament, whereas presidential systems directly elect their chief executives. So Israel turned from purely parliamentary to presidentialism, but not all the way. The **Knesset** could still vote out the prime minister on a motion of confidence, and coalition cabinets were as hard to form as ever.

Even worse, Israeli voters, figuring that selection of prime minister was taken care of by one ballot, used the other to scatter their votes among a dozen small parties, making the Knesset even more fractionated. After two unhappy tries of the unique hybrid system, the Knesset repealed it in 2001. The experiment showed that halfway borrowings from one system (presidentialism) into another (parliamentary) do not work. If you want stability, go all the way to presidentialism.

Although German Chancellor Angela Merkel and French President Nicolas Sarkozy seem cordial here, they were often at odds. (Reuters/Philippe Wojazer/Landov)

problem by naming opposition Gaullists as premiers and letting them dismantle many Socialist measures. Mitterrand reserved for himself the high ground of foreign policy. The French called the arrangement "cohabitation," like an unmarried couple living together. In 1997, the reverse happened: Gaullist President Jacques Chirac called parliamentary elections early, lost them, and had to face a Socialist-dominated National Assembly. The solution was cohabitation again; Chirac named Socialist chief Lionel Jospin as premier. Cohabitation works, and the French accept it. France thus handled the problem of deadlock that is common in the United States. The 1993 Russian constitution incorporated a French-style system with both president and premier, and it produced executive-legislative deadlock, no longer the case under Putin, who controls both the executive and the Duma.

The "Presidentialization" of Prime Ministers

Parliamentary systems tend to "presidentialize" themselves. Prime ministers with stable majorities supporting them in parliament start acting like presidents, powerful chiefs only dimly accountable to legislators. They know they will not be ousted in a vote of no confidence, so the only thing they have to worry about is the next election, just like a president. This tendency is strong in Britain and Germany.

Increasingly, elections in parliamentary systems resemble presidential elections. Technically, there is no "candidate for prime minister" in parliamentary elections.

Citizens vote for a party or a member of parliament, not for a prime minister. But everybody knows that the next prime minister will be the head of the largest party, so indirectly they are electing a prime minister. For these reasons, virtually all European elections feature posters and televised spots of party chiefs as if they were running for president. As in U.S. elections, personality increasingly matters more than policy, party, or ideology.

dissolve   Send a parliament home for new elections.

Executive Terms

Presidents have fixed terms, ranging from four years for U.S., Brazilian, and Colombian presidents (they can be reelected once) to a single six-year term for Mexican presidents. French and many other presidents can be reelected without limit. When presidents are in office a long time, even if "elected," they become corrupt and dictatorial, as President Robert Mugabe did in three decades at Zimbabwe's helm, even as the country's economy collapsed.

In parliamentary systems, prime ministers have no limits on their tenure in office, provided their party wins elections. As noted, increasingly their winning depends on the personality of their leader, almost as if they were presidential candidates. Britain's Margaret Thatcher was elected for a third time in 1987, but by 1990 her mounting political problems persuaded her to resign after 11 years in office. German Chancellor Helmut Kohl won four elections in a row and served 16 years (1982–1998). Most prime ministers can **dissolve** parliament when they wish, namely, when they believe they'll do best in elections. A good economy, sunny weather, and high ratings persuade prime ministers to call elections a year or two early. Powers such as these might make an American president jealous.

CLASSIC WORKS ■ LASSWELL'S PSYCHOLOGY OF POWER

Harold Lasswell of Yale introduced concepts from Freudian psychology into political science. In his 1936 classic *Politics: Who Gets What* and other works, Lasswell held that politicians start out mentally unbalanced and that they have unusual needs for power and dominance, which is why they go into politics. Normal people find politics uninteresting. If Lasswell is right, many executives should be removed from office, and only people who don't want the job should be elected. This is the kind of analysis that cannot be applied in practice; it is fascinating but useless.

It was Plato who first wrote that even sane people who become too powerful in high office go crazy. They've got to, for they can trust no one. They imagine, probably accurately, that they have many enemies, and they amass more and more power to crush these real and imaginary foes, thus creating even more enemies. It's an insightful description of Hitler and Stalin. According to Plato, tyrants must go insane in office; there's no such thing as a sane tyrant. The problem is not personal psychology but the nature of a political office that has grown too powerful. The solution, if Plato is right (and we think he is), is to limit power and have mechanisms to remove officeholders who abuse it. In the U.S. system, the threats of electoral defeat and impeachment tend to keep the presidency and its occupants healthy.

Tory Nickname for British Conservative.

impeachment Indictment by the House for the Senate to try the president.

KGB Soviet Committee on State Security, powerful intelligence and security agency.

On the other hand, British prime ministers can get ousted quickly if they lose the support of a majority of parliament. When Labour Prime Minister James Callaghan, head of a *minority government* (see page 240), lost the support of just 11 Scottish Nationalist MPs in 1979, he slipped below a majority in Commons and was replaced overnight by **Tory** chief Thatcher. Some Italian premiers have held office only briefly as their coalitions disintegrated. Japanese prime ministers, the playthings of powerful faction chiefs within the ruling party, average less than two and a half years in office, some just a few months. Theoretically, prime ministers can serve a long time; in practice, their tenure depends on political conditions such as elections, coalition breakups, and scandals. Parliamentary systems practice a kind of easy-come, easy-go with their prime ministers, something an American president would dislike. Presidents in presidential systems are partially insulated from the ups and downs of politics. The Iraq War, for example, made President Bush 43 unpopular, but there was no way to oust him until his term expired.

A U.S. president can face **impeachment**, but this is a lengthy and uncertain procedure that has been attempted only three times. Andrew Johnson was impeached by the House in 1868 but acquitted in the Senate by one vote. Richard

COMPARING ■ AUTHORITARIANISM RETURNS TO RUSSIA

Vladimir Putin (president 2000–2008, prime minister currently) consolidated authoritarian power. The 1993 Russian constitution, which set up a de Gaulle–type semipresidential system (see pages 255–256), tilted power to the presidency. Putin made the Russian presidency even stronger. Putin had been a **KGB** colonel and headed the post-Soviet equivalent, the Federal Security Service (FSB in Russian). Unstable President Yeltsin plucked Putin from obscurity and named him his fifth prime minister in 17 months.

Some thought Putin would be another temporary, but Putin pulled what amounted to a KGB coup. He used his police sources—who knew who had robbed what—to keep and expand his power. With Russia in steep decline, the unpopular Yeltsin in late 1999 handed over the presidency to Putin, who was easily elected to it in 2000 and reelected in 2004. He set up his own United Russia Party, which won most of the Duma seats.

Putin pulled Russia out of a climate of despair and immediately became popular. Russians like a strong hand at the top, and Putin continually strengthened his. He brought the energy industry and television back under state control, waged war against Chechens, and cracked down on uncooperative regional governors and the "oligarchs"—people who had gotten rich fast through insider privatization deals. Putin called it "managed democracy," staffed it with KGB comrades—the *siloviki*, the "strong men." He paid little attention to the Duma, where few opposed him. Some who criticized Putin were arrested or assassinated, but few Russians cared when the economy was good, thanks to oil and natural gas revenues. In 2008, Putin pulled a bold switch: He named an obedient protégé, Dmitri Medvedev, to be elected president and accepted, by prearrangement, the prime ministership. Putin "demoted" himself but stayed in charge and set things up so he could return to the presidency a few years later.

Nixon was about to be impeached by the House but resigned just before the vote. Bill Clinton was impeached but not convicted. If a problem character becomes chief executive, parliamentary systems have

appropriation   Government funds voted by legislature.

KEY CONCEPTS ■ AN IMPERIAL PRESIDENCY?

"The accumulation of all powers, legislative, executive, and judiciary, in the same hands," James Madison wrote in *The Federalist* no. 47, "may justly be pronounced the very definition of tyranny." Checks and balances, John Adams declared, are like "setting a thief to catch a thief." In recent years, however, many fear that the modern presidency has amassed power and overturned the checks and balances of the constitution.

Congress and the presidency no longer balance—maybe they never did. Samuel Huntington noted that from 1882 to 1909, Congress initiated 55 percent of significant legislation; between 1910 and 1932, the figure dropped to 46 percent; and from 1933 to 1940, Congress initiated only 8 percent of all major laws. The legislative function, said Huntington, "has clearly shifted to the executive branch."

As the Vietnam War wound down and Watergate boiled up, historian Arthur Schlesinger Jr. captured the worried feeling of the time in his book *The Imperial Presidency*. Lyndon Johnson had taken the country to war without a declaration of war. Richard Nixon had expanded that war into Laos and Cambodia, again with no declaration. Nixon also "impounded" **appropriations** made by Congress; he simply refused to spend funds in certain areas, in effect exercising an illegal item veto. Was the president overstepping constitutional bounds? Was America becoming an imperial presidency, going the way of ancient Rome, from republic to rule by Caesars?

Congress attempted to reassert some of its authority, passing the War Powers Act in 1973 and moving toward impeachment of Nixon the following year. It looked like the beginning of a new era, with Congress and the president once again in balance. But this failed to happen, for

the U.S. system *needs* a strong president to function properly.

When Jimmy Carter took office in 1977, he attempted to deimperialize the presidency, but this led to an ineffective White House. As an outsider, Carter was ignorant of the ways of Washington and quickly alienated a Congress dominated by his own party. His legislation stalled on Capitol Hill and was diluted by amendments, especially his energy proposals. By the 1980 election, much of the American electorate and Congress wished for a more forceful and experienced chief executive.

Congress's reassertion of independent authority in the 1970s proved brief, for with the arrival of Ronald Reagan in the White House in 1981, the president once again commanded Capitol Hill. In 1986 it was revealed that officials of the president's National Security Council bypassed Congress in selling arms to Iran and using the money to fund the overthrow of the Nicaraguan government. Even Reagan's supporters in Congress turned angry and grilled his appointees in committee hearings. Once again, a Congress disappointed with executive misuse of power tried to check the executive branch it had repeatedly invested with enormous powers.

With the terrorist attacks of 2001, Congress gave even more powers to the executive branch. Bush 43 advisors argued a "unitary executive theory" that gives the president essentially unlimited power to safeguard the country, including warrantless wiretaps, imprisonment and trial outside of normal courts, and "aggressive interrogation techniques." As he signed new laws, Bush issued more than 800 "signing statements," telling Congress that he would enforce this law as he saw fit. Critics feared the unitary executive theory was a step toward one-man rule.

a big advantage over the U.S. system—a simple vote of no confidence and the rascal is out. This helps explain why, even though there are many scandals in parliamentary systems, few have the opportunity to become as big and paralyzing as Watergate.

EXECUTIVE LEADERSHIP

Back to back, America saw two distinct leadership styles. President Carter (1977–1981) was a hands-on, detail person; he tried to supervise much of his administration. With intelligence and energy, he put in long hours and memorized much data. Critics, including management experts, say this is the wrong approach, that chief executives only scatter and exhaust themselves if they try to run everything.

President Reagan (1981–1989) was a hands-off president; he supervised little and left most administration to trusted subordinates. He took afternoon naps and frequent vacations. Critics say Reagan paid no attention to crucial matters, letting things slide until they turned into serious problems. The Iran-contra fiasco showed what happens when subordinates get only general directions and go off on their own. The National Security Council staff thought it was doing what the president wanted when it illegally sold arms to Iran and illegally transferred the profits to the Nicaraguan contras.

Can there be a happy middle ground between hands on and hands off? Some say President Eisenhower (1953–1961) achieved it by appearing to be a hands-off president with a relaxed style. Princeton political scientist Fred Greenstein, however, analyzed Eisenhower's schedule and calendar and concluded that he was a very active president who made important and complex decisions but did not show it, preferring to let others take the credit (and sometimes the blame). Greenstein called it the "hidden-hand presidency." In 1954, for example, faced with the sending of U.S. forces to help the French in Indochina, Eisenhower called top senators to the White House. He knew they would be cautious, for we had just ended the unpopular Korean War. The senators opposed sending U.S. forces, and Eisenhower went along with their view. Actually, he never wanted to send troops, but he made it look as if the senators had decided the issue.

President Franklin D. Roosevelt (1933–1945) used a style that some call deliberate chaos. Setting up numerous agencies and advisers, some of them working at cross-purposes, Roosevelt would let them clash. The really difficult and important decisions would reach his desk; the others would be settled without him. This, too, was a kind of middle ground between hands on and hands off. The Clinton White House borrowed this spontaneous and creative approach, but Clinton participated personally in many policy deliberations in a more hands-on manner. Bush 43 seemed to revert to a Reagan style of setting the direction but leaving implementation to subordinates. Obama seemed to partially follow the Carter style; critics complained he was too thoughtful and took too long to make decisions.

CABINETS

Chief executives are assisted by cabinets. A cabinet member heads one of the major executive divisions of government called a *department* in the United States and a **ministry** in most of the world. The former is headed by a *secretary* and the latter by a *minister*. Cabinets range in size from a compact 15 in the United States to 20 or more in Europe.

ministry   Major division of executive branch; equivalent to U.S. *department*.

The United States enlarges its cabinet only slowly and with much discussion, for it takes an act of Congress and the provision for its own budget. For most of its history, the United States had fewer than ten departments. Health and Human Services, Housing and Urban Development, Transportation, Energy, Education, Veterans Affairs, and Homeland Security were added only since the 1960s. In Europe, chief executives add, delete, combine, and rename ministries at will; their parliaments routinely support it. In the 1980s, for example, most West European governments added environmental ministries. The U.S. Environmental Protection Agency stayed at the sub-cabinet level, and environmental responsibilities were divided between it and several other departments.

What is the right size for a cabinet? That depends on how the system is set up and what citizens expect of it. The United States has been dedicated to keeping government small and letting the marketplace make decisions. When this led to imbalances—for example, bankrupt farmers, unemployed workers, and collapsed businesses—the U.S. system added the Departments of Agriculture, Labor, and Commerce. The Department of Energy was added after the "energy shocks" of the 1970s. Slowly, U.S. cabinets have been creeping up to European size.

Who Serves in a Cabinet?

In parliamentary systems like those of Britain and Germany, ministers are drawn from parliament and keep their parliamentary seats. They are both legislators and

CLASSIC WORKS ■ AMERICAN PARANOIA

In 1964, historian Richard Hofstadter wrote his celebrated essay "The Paranoid Style in American Politics" to explain the right-wing takeover of the Republicans and their nomination of hawkish Barry Goldwater. More generally, the work pointed to a persistent tendency in U.S. politics, the "sense of heated exaggeration, suspiciousness, and conspiratorial fantasy." With this comes a belief in evil empires out to get us, "a conflict between absolute good and absolute evil."

The paranoid then aims at "total triumph," whatever it may cost. This, wrote Hofstadter, leads to impossible goals, but failure to reach them "heightens the paranoid's sense of frustration," and he redoubles his efforts. Only traitors and weaklings criticize; they must be denounced and ignored. The media are branded cowardly and defeatist. Some critics claimed the paranoid tendency appeared in the Bush 43 administration. Actually, paranoia is an ever-present danger in all regimes, especially those with no checks on power such as Stalin's, Hitler's, and Saddam Hussein's.

Y axis   The vertical leg of a graph.

X axis   The horizontal leg of a graph.

executives. Usually they have had years of political experience in winning elections and serving on parliamentary committees. The chair of Germany's Bundestag defense committee, for example, is a good choice

HOW TO... ■ CREATE GRAPHS

Thanks to computers, graphs are easy and colorful but sometimes misused. A bunch of numbers does not necessarily make a good graph. The numbers should display some pattern. If upward, you would show the growth of something; if up and down, they might indicate cycles. We could do a longitudinal study of the growth of Washington-based interest groups of the sort we discussed on page 244, taking them over 30 years, from 1980 to 2010. Our hypothesis is that they grow over time.

We can either have the computer set up a graph or do it with paper and a ruler. First, draw a big "L." The upright leg is the **Y axis**, on which you draw a scale, usually from zero to a little more than the highest number we find, say 2,827, plus a little more to make it 3,000. Divide that scale into increments of whatever interval fits the study. It might be every 5 percent or every $5,000 per capita GDP or every hundred interest groups. A metric ruler can make drawing scales easier.

Now take the horizontal leg, the **X axis**, and mark off steps from 1980 to 2010. Measuring rightward from the Y axis, mark with a dot the number of interest groups above the year on the X axis. For easier readability, you may connect the dots (or have the computer do it), thus making a **line graph**.

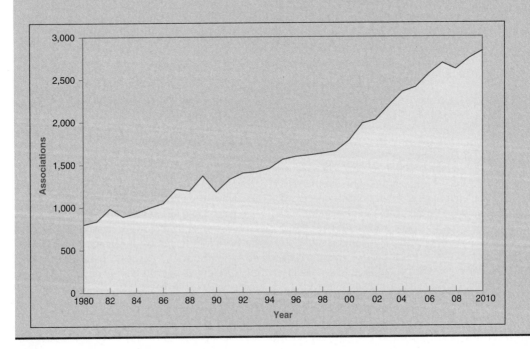

to become defense minister. In a presidential system like those of the United States or Brazil, secretaries or ministers are generally not working politicians but businesspersons, lawyers, and academics. They may

line graph Connection of data points showing change over time.

bar graph Stand-alone data points comparing categories.

If the line generally rises (and it will always have some ups and downs), you have demonstrated your thesis, that interest groups keep growing in Washington. If the line trends downward, alter your thesis, now stating a decline of D.C.-based interest groups (unlikely). And if the line is generally flat, neither trending up nor down, change your thesis to match your findings.

If you want to compare how two or more things change over time (covariance), you could use different colored lines, say blue for the percent Democratic vote in Altoona, PA, and red for size of the railroad workforce in Altoona, to show how both decline at about the same rate. (Unionized workers tend to vote

Democrat.) Pie charts are not very useful; use them to show popular preferences in pies.

Not every graph should be a line graph. The zig-zags of line graphs show change over time but are meaningless for comparing categories at the same time. For that, use a **bar graph**. A line graph indicates that one data point sets the stage for the next; a bar graph does not. If you want to show change over time, say, percent voting Republican over several elections, use a line graph. If you want to show differences between items at the same time, say, voting differences among income levels in the 2008 election, use a bar graph. Our GDP data from page 189 would go on a bar graph, not a line graph.

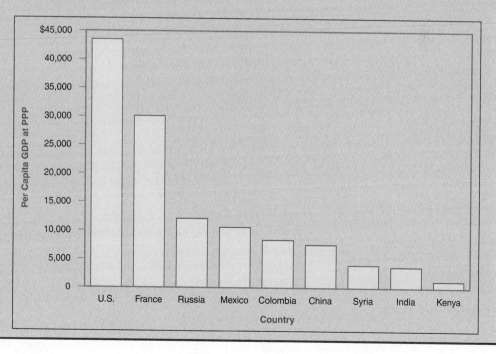

have some background in their department's subject area, but few have won elective office. President Bush 41 named four members of Congress to his cabinet; Presidents Clinton and Obama named three each. This made U.S. cabinets look a bit European, but the secretaries had to first resign their seats in Congress.

Which is better, a cabinet member who is a working politician or one from outside government? The elected members of European parliaments who become ministers have a great deal of both political and subject-area knowledge. They know the relevant members of parliament personally and have worked closely with them. Ministers and parliament do not view each other with suspicion, as enemies. The ministers are criticized in parliament but from the opposition benches; their own party generally supports them.

Outsiders appointed to the cabinet, the traditional U.S. style, may bring with them fresh perspectives, but they may also be politically naive, given to brash statements and unrealistic programs that get them in trouble with Congress, where members of their own party do not necessarily support them. Their lack of political experience in the nation's capital leads to another problem.

In the United States especially, the cabinet counts for less and less. A cabinet meeting serves little purpose and takes place rarely. Few Americans can name three or more cabinet members. Why has the cabinet fallen into such neglect? Part of the problem is that few cabinet secretaries are well-known political figures. And their jobs are rather routine: Get more money from Congress to spend on their department's programs. Cabinet secretaries are in charge of administering established programs with established budgets, "vice presidents in charge of spending," as Coolidge's Vice President Charles G. Dawes called them. As such, they are not consulted on much. They are largely administrators, not generators of ideas.

THE DANGER OF EXPECTING TOO MUCH

In both presidential and parliamentary systems, attention focuses on the chief executive. Presidents or prime ministers are expected to deliver economic growth with low unemployment and low inflation. Americans criticized President Obama for not solving the massive recession in a few months. Government chiefs are expected to keep taxes low but government benefits high. They are held responsible for anything that goes wrong but told to adopt a hands-off management approach and delegate matters to subordinates. The more problems and pressure, the more they have to delegate.

How can they do it all? How can they run the government, economy, subordinates, and policies? They cannot, and increasingly they do not. Instead, the clever ones project a mood of calm, progress, and good feeling to try to make most citizens happy. President Reagan was a master of this tactic. The precise details of governance matter little; they are in the hands of advisers and career civil servants, and few citizens care about them. What matters is getting reelected, and for this personality counts for more than policy, symbols more than performance.

Worldwide, power has been flowing to the executive, and legislatures have been in decline. The U.S. Congress has put up some good rear-guard actions, but it too has been in slow retreat. Some observers have argued that this cannot be helped, that several factors make this shift of power inevitable. If true, what can we do to safeguard democracy? Democracies still have a trump card, and some say it is enough: electoral punishment. As long as the chief executive, whether president or prime minister, has to face the

bureaucracy The *career* civil service that staffs government executive agencies.

career Professional civil servant, not political appointee.

electorate at periodic intervals, democracy will be preserved. The "rule of anticipated reactions," of which we spoke in Chapter 7, will keep them on their toes. Perhaps the concept of checks and balances was a great idea of the eighteenth century that does not fit the twenty-first. Maybe we will just have to learn to live with executive dominance.

BUREAUCRACIES

The term **bureaucracy** has negative connotations: the inefficiency and delays citizens face in dealing with government. The great German sociologist Max Weber, who studied bureaucracy, disliked it but saw no way to avoid it. A bureaucracy is any large organization of appointed officials who implement laws and policies. Ideally, it operates under rules and procedures with a chain of command or *hierarchy* of authority (see Chapter 6). It lets government operate with some rationality, uniformity, predictability, and supervision. No bureaucracy, no government.

Another definition of bureaucracy—or "civil service"—is that it is the *permanent* government. Much of what we have studied might be called the "temporary government" of elected officials who come and go. The **career** civil servants often

CLASSIC WORKS ■ WEBER'S DEFINITION OF BUREAUCRACIES

Max Weber (1864–1920) was the first scholar to analyze bureaucracy. His criteria for defining bureaucracy included the following:

1. Administrative offices are organized hierarchically.
2. Each office has its own area of competence.
3. Civil servants are appointed, not elected, on the basis of technical qualifications as determined by diplomas or examinations.
4. Civil servants receive fixed salaries according to rank.
5. The job is a career and the sole employment of the civil servant.

6. The official does not own his or her office.
7. The official is subject to control and discipline.
8. Promotion is based on superiors' judgment.

Weber felt he was studying a relatively new phenomenon. Some of the above characteristics could be found in imperial China, but not all. Like the nation-state, bureaucracies started in Western Europe around the sixteenth century but were reaching their full powers, which Weber distrusted, only in the twentieth century.

stay with one agency. They take orders from elected officials, but they also follow the law and do things "by the book." They usually know a lot more about their specialized areas than their new politically appointed boss, who wants to redo the system with bold, new ideas. The bureaucrats, who have seen bold, new ideas come and go, move with caution. A bureaucracy, once set up, is inherently conservative; trying to move it is one of the hardest tasks of politicians.

Almost any large organization has a bureaucracy. In the Middle Ages, when Europe was loose confederations of feudal powers, the Roman Catholic Church had a complex and effective administrative system. Through a hierarchy of trained people who spent their life in the Church, authority flowed from the pope down to the parish priest. Until they developed their own administrators in the Renaissance, kings depended on clerics, who were among the few who could read and write. Armies also have bureaucratic structures, based on the military chain of command and myriad regulations. Bureaucracy comes automatically with any large organization, public or private.

BUREAUCRACIES IN COMPARISON

The United States

Fewer than 15 percent of American civil servants are federal. Of our 21.5 million civil servants, some 15 million are employed by local governments, 4 million by state governments, and fewer than 3 million (not counting military personnel) by the federal government. Remember, most government services—schools, police, and fire protection—are provided by local governments.

The 15 current U.S. cabinet departments (George Washington started with four) employ between 85 and 90 percent of all federal civil servants. They share a common anatomy. Each is funded by congressional appropriations and headed by a secretary appointed by the president (with the consent of the Senate). The undersecretaries and assistant secretaries are also political appointees and, thus, in Weber's definition (see box on page 265) are not bureaucrats. This differs from most other systems, where officials up through the equivalent of our undersecretaries are permanent civil service.

The departments carry out legislative and executive policies whose intent is often unclear. Most laws are general and let the department establish specific working policy, so experts can tune policy. Bureaucrats have a lot of knowledge, and knowledge is power. The Reagan administration said it would abolish the Department of Energy (DOE). One of the authors of this book asked a friend, an official of the department, why he wasn't worried. "They won't abolish us," he asserted knowingly. "They can't. DOE manufactures nuclear bombs, and the administration needs the DOE budget to disguise how big the nuclear bomb budget is." Reagan did not abolish DOE. The U.S. bureaucracy is relatively small and light compared with many other countries. Europe and Latin America, with their strong statist traditions (see page 73), have much more bureaucracy and regulation than the United States.

Communist Countries

The Soviet Union was one of the world's most bureaucratic nations, and that was one of the causes of
its collapse. Tied to the Communist Party, the Soviet
civil service was corrupt, inefficient, and unreform-
able. According to Marxist theory, a dictatorship of
the proletariat had no need for Western-style bu-
reaucracy, but immediately after the 1917 revolution the Soviets instituted strict
bureaucratic management, and Stalin increased it with his **Five-Year Plans** in
the 1930s.

Five-Year Plans Stalin's plans for rapid, centrally administered Soviet industrial growth.

nomenklatura Lists of top Soviet positions and those eligible to fill them, the Soviet elite.

Top Soviet bureaucrats, the **nomenklatura**, were a privileged elite, often
the most energetic and effective. They got nice apartments, special shops, and
country houses. At the top of each ministry was a minister, who was a member
of the Council of Ministers (roughly equivalent to a Western cabinet), the highest
executive authority that was made up of high-ranking party members, some of
whom were also members of the party's Politburo. Trusted party members were
placed in subordinate positions to carry out party policy. This made the Soviet
bureaucracy conservative, an obstacle no Soviet president could overcome.

In China too officials are party members. The party is supposed to fight corruption, but China's administration is dangerously decentralized to the provincial and local levels, leaving officials free to collect bribes and fake "taxes" and to
transfer land from peasants to developers. In 2008, provincial and local officials

KEY CONCEPTS ■ BUREAUCRATIC RULE-MAKING

One vivid example of bureaucratic rule-making was the fight to place health warnings on cigarette packages and in advertisements. Congress would never have moved by itself because the tobacco industry is generous to candidates. Change came via a branch of the bureaucracy—public health specialists and statisticians equipped with computers. In 1965, the Advisory Committee on Smoking and Health and the surgeon general (the nation's chief public health officer) presented solid data that cigarette smoking increased lung cancer and shortened lives.

The report disturbed the public, and public pressure on Congress increased. Since 1966, cigarette manufacturers have to print warnings on all packs. In 1969, the FCC banned cigarette advertising on radio and television. Since 1971, cigarette ads must show health warnings. Political scientist A. Lee Fritschler, in his *Smoking and Politics*, concluded:

The initiation and continuation of the cigarette controversy were possible because of both the political power and delegated authority possessed by bureaucratic agencies. Had the decision on cigarettes and health been left to Congress alone, it is safe to assume that the manufacturers would have triumphed, and no health warnings of any kind would have been required. The cigarette-labeling controversy is a clear example of agencies' power to influence and even formulate public policy.

vice minister   Top bureaucrat in a
Japanese ministry.

MITI   Japan's Ministry of International Trade and Industry.

managed to not notice that milk was being poisoned. Major riots break out in China every year over such corruption, which is the system's Achilles' heel. The Communist Party's Central Commission for Discipline Inspection has broad powers to demote or expel party members or send cases to criminal courts, where some are sentenced to death. The regime touts its Central Commission as the cure for corruption, but it continues, probably because the local officials are precisely who the regime depends on to maximize economic growth.

France

In the seventeenth and eighteenth centuries, France set the pattern for most of Europe with the highly bureaucratized state. After the French Revolution destroyed the monarchy, Napoleon restored central control by the bureaucracy and made it more rational and effective. Napoleon, with the *intendants* of Richelieu as his model, created the *prefects* to carry out government policy. Top French civil servants are now graduates of one of the "Great Schools," such as the Ecole Polytechnique, an engineering college, or, since World War II, the Ecole Nationale d'Administration, created to train government officials. The instability of the Third (1871–1940) and Fourth (1947–1958) Republics increased the bureaucracy's power

COMPARING ■ JAPAN: BUREAUCRATS IN COMMAND

Japan is an extreme example of rule by bureaucrats. Modeled on the French civil service by the Meiji modernizers in the 1870s, Tokyo's ministries were always powerful. Before, during, and after World War II, the same bureaucrats were in charge, boosting economic growth by guided capitalism rather than the free market. Japan's bureaucrats view elected officials as clowns who should be ignored.

The key Tokyo ministries are finance, international trade and industry, agriculture, and construction. They guide their respective economic sectors by arranging loans, subsidies, and government contracts. Top Japanese bureaucrats are often graduates of Tokyo University (nicknamed "Todai"), Japan's most selective school. Many civil servants retire young to go into lush jobs in the industries they supervised.

Tokyo's ministries are self-contained and do not cooperate with each other or seek the good of the whole, provoking some to say that in Japan "no one is in charge." The ministry supervises its economic sector, which mostly obeys the ministry. The minister is a political appointee, usually a member of the Diet, but the **vice minister**, who really runs things, is a career civil servant, much like a British "permanent secretary" (see page 269).

The most famous ministry was **MITI**, the brains of Japan's export mania that set economic growth records after World War II and suggested Japanese guided capitalism as a model for others. Since the 1990s, however, the Japanese economy has been flat, and bureaucratic supervision was blamed for industrial overexpansion, money-losing investments, bankrupt banks, and the world's highest consumer prices. A new generation of Japanese politicians is now trying to reform their bureaucracies and bring them under democratic control.

because it had to run France with little legislative or executive guidance. France is still heavily bureaucratic, and centralization is often extreme.

Junker   (Pronounced: YOON-care) Prussian state nobility.

merit civil service   One based on competitive exams rather than patronage.

apolitical   Not interested or participating in politics.

Germany

Prussia and its ruling class, the **Junkers**, put their stamp on German administration. Obedient, efficient, and hard-working, the aristocratic Junkers were a state nobility, dependent on Berlin and controlling all its higher civil service positions. Frederick the Great of Prussia, who ruled from 1740 to 1786, had a passion for effective administration and established universities to train administrators. Germany unified in 1871 under Prussia's leadership, which brought Prussian culture, namely loyalty to nation and emperor, to much of Germany. One of the reasons the short-lived Weimar Republic (1919–1933) failed was because the civil-servant class had only contempt for democracy. With the coming of the Third Reich, they flocked to Hitler.

The current German government has a strongly federal structure that puts most administration at the *Land* level. Today's German civil servants are committed to democracy. A section of Berlin's interior ministry, for example, in cooperation with *Land* agencies, does educational programs to fight political extremism. Generally trained in law—throughout Europe law is at the undergraduate level—German bureaucrats tend to bring with them the mentality of Roman law, that is, law neatly organized into fixed codes rather than the more flexible U.S. and British common law (see next chapter).

Britain

Britain, unlike France, has strong traditions of local self-government and dispersion of authority. This pattern of administration is an outgrowth of the Anglo-American emphasis on representative government, which encourages legislative control of administrative authorities. During the nineteenth century, the growth of British government at the local level also encouraged the dispersion of administrative authority; it was not until the twentieth century that the central government began to run in local affairs. Until the 1854 Northcote-Trevelyan reforms, the bureaucracy was rife with corruption and nepotism. Positions in the bureaucracy (for instance, military commissions) were openly bought and sold. By 1870, however, a **merit civil service** based on competitive examinations had been established.

British ministers are accountable to Parliament, but real bureaucratic power is in the hands of the career "permanent secretary" and the career deputy secretaries, undersecretaries, and assistant secretaries who serve at lower ranks. Thus, even though the British and American bureaucracies share the same tradition of decentralized authority, control over the bureaucracy is tighter in Britain than in America. British bureaucrats pride themselves on being **apolitical**, so they faithfully carry out the ministry's policies, whichever government is in power.

THE TROUBLE WITH BUREAUCRACY

The world does not love bureaucracy. The very word is pejorative. In France and Italy, hatred of the official on the other side of the counter is part of the political culture. Americans like to hear candidates denounce "the bureaucrats," but none ever solve the problem because at least some regulation is necessary. Incoming U.S. administrations, particularly Republican, often vow to bring business-type efficiency to public administration by drastic deregulation of private industry. As a result, no one said no to Wall Street's reckless loans and investments. Efficiency, profitability, and **productivity** are hard to apply in government programs. Cutting a program like Social Security or Medicare is impossible.

productivity   The efficiency with which goods or services are produced.

bureaucratic politics   Infighting among and within agencies to set policy.

KEY CONCEPTS ■ BUREAUCRATIC POLITICS

Some political scientists argue that struggles— often behind the scenes—among and within bureaucracies contribute to or even control policy decisions. Bureaucrats provide the information on which top officials depend. He who controls information controls policy, goes the theory. America's many bureaucracies gather, analyze, and disseminate information in different ways, often quarreling among themselves.

Harvard's Graham Allison found that the 1962 Cuban Missile Crisis turned on when the photographic evidence arrived at the White House. It had been delayed because the Air Force and Central Intelligence Agency quarreled over who should pilot the U2 spy plane. Competition among agencies and "standard procedures" created the informational world in which Kennedy and his advisors operated. With a widely read 1969 article, Allison founded the **bureaucratic politics** model, which political science briefly embraced.

Control of information became a hot issue with 9/11 and the 2003 U.S. invasion of Iraq. Before 9/11, the FBI and CIA did not share information, partly due to legal restrictions. The new Department of Homeland Security did not solve the problem, as the FBI and CIA are not part of it. Department of Defense (DoD) analysts claimed to have solid evidence that Iraq had weapons of mass destruction (WMD) and was sponsoring terrorism. State and CIA analysts were cautious, saying evidence was unclear. DoD prevailed, making war a certainty. No WMD were found after the war. Furthermore, State, claiming that it had the expertise, drew up plans for the occupation of Iraq after the war. DoD ignored State and its plans. The result was a chaotic occupation and great anger in the State Department.

The bureaucratic politics model is still not persuasive because the president really is in charge. He often has strong personal preferences in advance and decides which agency to listen to. In 2003 President Bush had long hated Iraq, and DoD told him that Iraq was guilty. DoD even had a special staff to make the case for attacking Iraq; it excluded evidence to the contrary. By structuring bureaucracies, the White House created the informational world it preferred. Washington bureaucracies played a blame game for 9/11 and Iraq's WMD—several of the CIA's top people resigned—but it was more a question of how these agencies were used. Bureaucrats mostly obey.

At its worst, bureaucracy can show signs of "Eichmannism," named after the Nazi official who organized the death trains for Europe's Jews and later told his Israeli judges that he was just doing his job. Nazi bureaucracy treated people like things, a problem not limited to Germany. On the humorous side, bureaucracy can resemble Parkinson's Law: Work expands to fill the staff time available. Parkinson never called himself a humorist, and many who have worked in featherbedded, purposeless, paper-shuffling agencies confirm Parkinson's Law.

Bureaucracy and corruption are intertwined. Wherever officials carry out rules, some are bent for friends and benefactors. The more regulations, the more bureaucrats, the more corruption. A few countries with a strong ethos of public service—Finland and Singapore, for example—have been able to maintain incorrupt public administration. Most countries are corrupt, some a little and some egregiously (see box on page 289). Chile became the least corrupt Latin American country by cutting the amount of administration and number of bureaucrats. Under the argument that only specialists from private industry can monitor that industry, businesses sometimes "capture" or "colonize" administrative agencies. Top financiers were placed atop the U.S. Securities and Exchange Commission. They gutted its regulatory role and let it march straight to the 2008 financial meltdown. It should be noted, however, that political appointees, not career civil servants, made these dangerous decisions.

Early theorists of bureaucracy assumed that professional bureaucrats would never make public policy but merely carry out laws. Indeed, nonpartisan administration was the original motivation behind merit civil services, but most nations have administrators who make policy but are not publicly accountable. Japan (see box on page 268) shows this to an extreme. Making bureaucracies flexible, creative, and accountable is one of the great tasks of this century.

mypoliscikit EXERCISES

Apply what you learned in this chapter on MyPoliSciKit (www.mypoliscikit.com).

Assessment Review this chapter using learning objectives, chapter summaries, practice tests, and more.

Menu

Flashcards Learn the key terms in this chapter; you can test yourself by term or definition.

Flashcards

Video Analyze recent world affairs by watching streaming video from major news providers.

Videos

Comparative Exercises Compare political ideas, behaviors, institutions, and policies worldwide.

Comparative
Exercises

KEY TERMS

apolitical (p. 269)
appropriation (p. 259)
bar graph (p. 263)
bureaucracy (p. 265)
bureaucratic politics
(p. 270)
career (p. 265)
chancellor (p. 255)
deadlock (p. 254)
dissolve (p. 257)

Five-Year Plans (p. 267)
impeachment (p. 258)
Junker (p. 269)
KGB (p. 258)
Knesset (p. 255)
line graph (p. 263)
merit civil service (p. 269)
minister (p. 254)
ministry (p. 261)
MITI (p. 268)

nomenklatura (p. 267)
premier (p. 255)
productivity (p. 270)
state (p. 254)
Tory (p. 258)
vice minister
(p. 268)
X axis (p. 262)
Y axis (p. 262)

FURTHER REFERENCE

Ackerman, Bruce. *The Failure of the Founding Fathers: Jefferson, Marshall, and the Rise of Presidential Democracy.* Cambridge, MA: Harvard University Press, 2005.

Burke, John P. *The Institutional Presidency: Organizing and Managing the White House from FDR to Clinton,* 2nd ed. Baltimore, MD: Johns Hopkins University Press, 2000.

Cheibub, José Antonio. *Presidentialism, Parliamentarianism, and Democracy.* New York: Cambridge University Press, 2007.

Greenstein, Fred. *Inventing the Job of President: Leadership Style from George Washington to Andrew Jackson.* Princeton, NJ: Princeton University Press, 2009.

Hamilton, Nigel. *American Caesars: Lives of the Presidents from Franklin D. Roosevelt to George W. Bush.* New Haven, CT: Yale University Press, 2010.

Helms, Ludger. *Presidents, Prime Ministers and Chancellors: Executive Leadership in Western Democracies.* New York: Palgrave, 2005.

Jones, Charles O. *The American Presidency.* New York: Sterling, 2009.

Jreisat, Jamil E. *Comparative Public Administration and Policy.* Boulder, CO: Westview, 2002.

Kerwin, Cornelius M., and Scott R. Furlong. *Rulemaking: How Government Agencies Write Law and Make Policy,* 4th ed. Washington, DC: CQ Press, 2010.

Lindblom, Charles E. *The Policy-Making Process,* 3rd ed. Englewood Cliffs, NJ: Prentice Hall, 1992.

Maranto, Robert, Tom Lansford, and Jeremy Johnson, eds. *Judging Bush.* Stanford, CA: Stanford University Press, 2009.

Miklis, Sidney M., and Michael Nelson. *The American Presidency: Origins and Development,* 5th ed. Washington, DC: CQ Press, 2007.

Morris, Irwin L. *The American Presidency.* New York: Cambridge University Press, 2010.

Neustadt, Richard E. *Presidential Power and the Modern Presidents: The Politics of Leadership from Roosevelt to Reagan.* New York: Free Press, 1991.

Peters, Guy. *Politics of Bureaucracy: An Introduction to Comparative Public Administration,* 6th ed. New York: Routledge, 2009.

Pika, Joseph A., and John Anthony Maltese. *The Politics of the Presidency.* 7th ed. Washington, DC: CQ Press, 2009.

Poguntke, Thomas, and Paul Webb, eds. *The Presidentialization of Politics: A Comparative Study of Modern Democracies.* New York: Oxford University Press, 2005.

Rudalevige, Andrew. *The New Imperial Presidency*. Ann Arbor, MI: University of Michigan Press, 2005.

Savage, Charlie. *Takeover: The Return of the Imperial Presidency and the Subversion of American Democracy*. New York: Little, Brown, 2007.

Savoie, Donald J. *Power: Where Is It?* Montreal: McGill-Queen's University Press, 2010.

Wills, Gary. *Bomb Power: The Modern Presidency and the National Security State*. New York: Penguin, 2010.

Wilson, James Q. *Bureaucracy: What Government Agencies Do and Why They Do It*. New York: Basic Books, 1990.

Zelizer, Julian E., ed. *The Presidency of George W. Bush: A First Historical Assessment*. Princeton, NJ: Princeton University Press, 2010.

Judiciaries

Members of the U.S. Supreme Court huddle in their judicial robes at the inauguration of President Obama. The oath was administered by Chief Justice Roberts, lower left. (Jeff Christensen/AP Photo)

The United States prides itself on "rule of law." One indication of this is the number of American lawyers—281 for every 100,000 people, as compared with 94 in England, 33 in France, and only 7 in Japan. Law plays very different roles in these systems. America's legions of lawyers express the country's ethos of freedom and competitive individualism. In few other countries does the "little person" have our ability to sue the powerful. Many Americans complain that we have too many lawsuits, but few would accept a Japanese system where citizens are expected simply to obey government and corporations. Law without lawyers means law administered by bureaucrats. If you want freedom under **law**, you must have lots of lawyers.

QUESTIONS TO CONSIDER

1. Why is the U.S. political system so dependent on the courts?
2. What are the differences between natural and positive law?
3. What are the differences between common and code law?
4. Can you describe the U.S. court system?
5. How are European trials quite different from ours?
6. What does Germany have that resembles the U.S. Supreme Court?
7. How did an 1803 case give the Supreme Court vast powers?
8. In what major cases did the Warren Court make new law?
9. Have subsequent courts reversed Warren Court decisions?

TYPES OF LAW

We focus on **positive law**, that which is written and compiled by humans over the centuries. Unlike natural law (see box on page 276), positive law uses law books to discover right and wrong. Our complex society requires many types of law, of which there are five major branches.

Criminal Law

With 1.6 million people (more than 1 percent of all adults) in U.S. jails, the criminal law system is the one we hear most about. Modern criminal law is largely statutory and covers a specific category of wrongs that are considered social evils and threats to the community. Consequently, the state, rather than the victim, is the prosecutor, or **plaintiff**. Offenses are usually divided into three categories. *Petty offenses*, such as traffic violations, are normally punished by a fine. Serious but not major offenses such as gambling and prostitution are *misdemeanors*, punishable by larger fines or short jail sentences. Major crimes, *felonies*, such as rape, murder, robbery, and ex-

law That which must be obeyed under penalties.

positive law That which is written by humans and accepted over time—the opposite of natural law.

plaintiff The person who complains in a law case.

common law "Judge-made law," old decisions built up over the centuries.

civil law Noncriminal disputes among individuals.

higher law That which comes from God.

natural law That which comes from nature, understood by reasoning.

tortion, are punished by imprisonment. In the United States, some criminal offenses, such as kidnapping and interstate car theft, are federal; others, such as murder and robbery, are mainly state concerns; and a few, such as bank robbery and drug trafficking, are both.

Civil Law

Many statutes govern civil rather than criminal matters. In most English-speaking countries, **common law** supplements statutory law in civil cases. Marriage and divorce, inheritance, contracts, and bankruptcy are civil concerns. **Civil law** provides redress for private plaintiffs who can show they have been injured. The decisions are in dollars, not in jail time. Private individuals, not the state, conduct most civil litigation. Some cases can be pursued as both criminal and civil cases, as when the federal government accuses investment houses of wrongdoing and investors who lost money sue them.

Constitutional Law

Written constitutions are usually general documents. Subsequent legislation and court interpretation must fill in the details. An important role of U.S. courts, under our system of *judicial review* (see Chapter 5), is to make sure that statutory laws and administrative usages do not violate the Constitution. Judicial review is America's great contribution to governance; since World War II, most democracies added some sort of judicial review.

In the United States the ultimate responsibility of interpreting the Constitution rests with the U.S. Supreme Court, and this means that laws change over time: The Constitution is what the Supreme Court says it is. In 1896, for example, the Court

CLASSIC WORKS ■ THE ROOTS OF LAW

Higher law is an old concept that grew out of the Christian melding of Greek philosophy with Judeo-Christian thought. Attributed to God or the Creator, it was thus higher than laws made by humans. It is behind the idea that people are "endowed by their Creator" with the rights to life, liberty, and the pursuit of happiness and the right to own property and enjoy the fruits of their labor—rights that no just government can take away. Many argue that higher law takes precedence over laws enacted by humans, and some justify their defiance of ordinary laws by citing it. Mahatma Gandhi in

India and Martin Luther King Jr. in the United States claimed that their actions, which violated human-made laws, were moral because they conformed to higher law.

Natural law, developed by medieval Catholic theologians, argues that some law is basic to human nature and can be understood just by thinking about it. You need no law books to tell you that murder is wrong, for example. Israel's attorney general, in prosecuting Nazi official Adolph Eichmann in 1961, argued from natural law that Eichmann had to know that mass murder is wrong.

ruled in *Plessy v. Ferguson* that state laws requiring racial segregation in public transportation did not necessarily violate the Fourteenth Amendment, which provides for equal protection under the laws, as long as the transportation facilities for whites and blacks were physically equal. In *Brown v. Board of Education of Topeka* (1954), the court reversed itself and ruled that separate public schools for whites and blacks are *inherently* unequal, even if physically alike. The Constitution had not changed, but society's conception of individual rights did. **Constitutional law** (indeed, law itself) is not static but a living, growing institution.

constitutional law   That which grows out of a country's basic documents.

reciprocity   Mutual application of legal standards.

consistency   Applying the same standards to all.

Administrative Law

A relatively recent development, administrative law covers regulatory orders by government agencies. It develops when agencies interpret statutes, as they must. For example, federal statute prohibits "unfair or deceptive acts" in commerce. But what business practices are "unfair"? The Federal Trade Commission must decide. As the agencies interpret the meaning of Congress's laws, they begin to build up a body of regulations and case law that guides the commission in its future decisions. These rulings may be appealed to the federal courts. The federal government now codifies administrative regulations, and they fill many volumes.

International Law

International law (IL) consists of treaties and established customs recognized by most nations. It is different because it cannot be enforced in the same way as national law: It has some judges and courts, but compliance is largely voluntary. IL is generally observed because it is in the interests of most countries not to break it. IL's key mechanisms are **reciprocity** and **consistency**. Countries like being treated nicely, so they must extend the courtesy to others. They also do not like being accused of applying different standards to various countries, so they try to keep their dealings consistent. Some IL is enforced by national courts. The U.S. Supreme Court has ruled that U.S. states have to observe international treaties that the United States has ratified. A U.S. business harmed abroad can seek redress in U.S. courts against the assets of the foreign firm that did the damage. We mostly study international public law, but international private law is a rapidly growing field as more businesses operate globally.

Primitive legal systems are oral and consist of customs and beliefs. Modern legal systems are written and largely codified, that is, systematically arranged. Putting laws in writing makes them more precise and uniform. Codification began in ancient times and has been a major feature in the development of civilization. The Ten Commandments and the Code of Hammurabi were early law codes, but the great ancient code was Roman law. Its details, covering all aspects of social life and based on "right reason," were so universal, flexible, and logical that they are still in use in much of the world today. Roman law was incorporated by the Catholic Church in its canon law and in the East by the Byzantine Emperor

precedent Legal decisions based on earlier decisions.

canon law Laws of the Roman Catholic Church, based on Roman law.

Justinian, whose celebrated Code of Justinian (*Corpus Juris Civilis*) of 533 A.D., is the foundation of most of Europe's modern legal systems. Modern European law is based on an amalgamation of Roman, feudal, and church law.

THE COURTS, THE BENCH, AND THE BAR

As legal systems developed, so did judicial systems, for they handle day-to-day administration of the law. Judicial systems are always hierarchical with different courts having specific jurisdictions; that is, they hear different kinds of cases or have authority in specific geographical areas.

The U.S. Court System

Our court system is unique, consisting of 51 judicial structures: the national system, comprising the federal courts, and 50 state systems. The federal system

KEY CONCEPTS ■ COMMON LAW VERSUS CODE LAW

The English common law started with the customary usages of Germanic tribal law of the Angles and Saxons who took over England in the third to the fifth centuries. This law stressed the rights of free and equal men and developed on the basis of **precedent** set by earlier judges; it is thus called "judge-made law." The Normans who conquered England in 1066 decided the local, decentralized nature of this law hindered governance of the country as a whole, and they set up central courts to systematize the local laws and produce a "common" law for all parts of England. They also added new features, such as trial by jury.

In administering justice, English judges and courts were forced to improvise. Most had a church education and were familiar with **canon law**. Accordingly, when royal law was inadequate, the judges applied canon law. If these were not applicable, they used common sense and the common practices of the English people. Over the centuries, a substantial body of common law developed—an amalgam of Roman law, Church law, and local English customs.

Common law has three distinctive features. First, it is *case* law; that is, it is based on individual legal decisions rather than on a comprehensive code of statutes. Second, common law was made by *judicial decision* and thus has great flexibility. Judges can reinterpret or modify previous rulings and principles to fit new cases. Third, common law relies heavily on *stare decisis* ("let the decision stand"), or precedent. Because no two cases are exactly alike, a judge can point to difference to break precedent. In this way, common law retains a marvelous flexibility. With the rise of Parliament as a dominant institution in seventeenth-century England, *statute* (see page 80) law supplemented and then supplanted much of the common law. Today, when the two conflict, statute law always takes precedence.

Common law has declined in importance but still has influence in England (but not Scotland), the United States (but not Louisiana), Canada, Australia, New Zealand, and a number of former British colonies. Much of statute law is the formal enactment of old common-law provisions. Common law shaped the development of English society and politics and imparted distinctive political habits to America.

overlaps that of the states. The federal courts hear many cases in which the issue is one of state laws but the parties are residents of different states, the so-called "diversity jurisdiction." Also, of course, they hear cases concerning federal laws. Conversely, issues of federal law (constitutional or statutory) may first arise in state courts. The Supreme Court of the United States can review the state court's judgment on a federal question.

Roman law System based on codes of ancient Rome.

code law Laws arranged in books, originally updated Roman law.

The National Court Structure The 94 federal district courts form the base of the U.S. national court system. They employ more than 500 judges and serve as trial courts in civil suits arising under federal law, criminal cases involving federal infractions, and the diversity jurisdiction. Most criminal cases, however, even those involving federal law, are tried in state courts.

Federal district court decisions can be appealed to a U.S. court of appeals. The 13 courts of appeals, presided over by 132 judges, may also review the rulings of administrative tribunals and commissions, such as the Federal Trade Commission,

The legal systems of continental Europe (France, in particular) developed very differently. As French kings were overturning feudalism in favor of absolutism (see Chapter 4), legal scholars revived **Roman law** to bolster central government and encourage commerce. French jurists saw the value of Roman law; it was universal, written, worked well for the ancient world, and was already known through canon law.

Codifying the law was Napoleon's lasting contribution to French justice and, eventually, to much of the world. His *Code Napoléon* of 1804, the first modern codification of European law, discarded feudal laws and broke civil law away from religious influence. It preserved many of the gains of the French Revolution, such as elimination of torture and arbitrary arrest and imprisonment, civil liberty, and civil equality. Napoleon conquered most of Europe and brought the code with him; Europe's legal systems are still based on it. It is also in use in Louisiana and Asia, Africa, and Latin America. The centralization of French life even to this day is a reflection of its basic philosophy.

Today, much of the world lives under some form of the Code Napoléon. Most **code law** is detailed, precise, comprehensive, and understandable by laypersons. Judges are not expected to "make" law, merely to apply it. Precedent carries less weight. The judiciary is not independent of the executive as in the American system. Therefore, its powers of judicial review are limited—either shared with the legislative branch or assigned to a special constitutional court, which most European countries now have, a relatively new feature.

The differences between the common law and code law are marked. The former is general and largely judge-made, and it relies on precedent and custom. The latter is specific and is largely the product of legislation. Both systems developed to serve the needs of modernizing and centralizing monarchs—Henry I and II in England and Louis XIII and Napoleon in France. The two systems, however, are becoming more and more alike. As the volume of statute law increases in the English-speaking nations, the importance and relevance of common law decreases. In both systems, administrative agencies increasingly fill in the details of legislative enactments, producing regulations that are now part of legal systems.

appeal   Taking a case to a higher court.

brief   Written summary submitted by one side giving relevant facts, laws, and precedents.

bench   The office of judgeship.

the Federal Aviation Administration, and the Food and Drug Administration. Each court of appeals consists of three or more judges, depending on need. Panels of three judges hear arguments but rarely question the facts of the case; they consider only whether the law has been misinterpreted or misapplied. The court of appeals bases its majority-vote verdict on the **appeal** primarily on the **briefs** submitted by the attorneys for both parties; oral arguments are limited.

The pinnacle of the federal court system is the U.S. Supreme Court, consisting of one chief justice and eight associate justices. Its jurisdiction is almost entirely appellate, from lower federal or state supreme courts. For example, if a state supreme court declares a federal statute unconstitutional, it is almost certain that the U.S. Supreme Court will hear the case. Unlike a court of appeals, however, it is not obliged to hear every case and accepts only a small fraction of the petitions that it receives. The Court will generally not hear a case unless it involves a substantial constitutional question, a treaty, or some significant point of federal law. Because the U.S. system is based on precedent, the Court's ruling *is* national law.

The State Court System   Each of the 50 states has its own court systems, and those court systems handle perhaps 90 percent of the nation's legal business. Most of their cases are civil, not criminal. Generally, state trial courts operate at the county level and have original jurisdiction in all civil and criminal cases. In rural areas, justices of the peace try minor matters. In urban areas, magistrate's or police courts do the same. These local courts operate without juries (serious cases go to state courts), and most of their penalties are fines or short jail sentences.

Judges

Federal Judges   Federal judges are nominated by the president and must be approved by the Senate. To free them from executive and political pressure, they may serve for life unless impeached. Some federal judges owe their appointments to party affiliation, but most are well qualified. The attorney general lists eligible candidates; as vacancies occur, the president selects a few names from that list. The president considers the reputation-based ratings of prospective judges by the American Bar Association (ABA). Bush 43 discontinued the practice, believing the ABA was too liberal, but Obama resumed it. The FBI checks out each candidate. Senate approval used to be routine but is now highly political. The opposition party accuses the president of trying to fill the **bench** with incompetent partisans and often tries to block confirmation. Under Clinton, many federal judgeships went unfilled because Senate Republicans rejected nominees as too liberal. Later, Senate Democrats tried to block Bush's choices as too conservative.

Some presidents wanted a federal judiciary that was nonpartisan, or at least bipartisan. Eisenhower, for example, appointed some Democrats to the federal bench (including Supreme Court Justice William J. Brennan) and sought a kind of balance.

Presidents now, however, appoint judges of their own political party who share their judicial philosophy. President Johnson, for example, appointed Thurgood Marshall—a liberal who believed that the Court should take an active role in promoting social justice—to the Supreme Court. President Nixon, in contrast, appointed four conservative justices who believed that the Warren

> **adversarial**   System based on two opposing parties to a dispute.
>
> **accusatorial**   Like adversarial but with a prosecutor accusing a defendant of crimes.

Court of the 1950s and 1960s went too far in protecting the rights of suspects and hampered law enforcement. President Reagan followed the Nixon example with the appointment of conservative Sandra Day O'Connor, the first female on the Court. The five conservative justices really mattered when the Supreme Court refused five to four to prolong Florida vote recounts and thus gave the 2000 presidential election to George W. Bush. Bush 43 appointed conservatives as several vacancies occurred on the Supreme Court. In this way, his conservative legacy lived long after his presidency. President Obama appointed two liberal women justices in an attempt to counterbalance the conservative tilt.

State Judges   State judges are either popularly elected or appointed, for terms ranging up to 14 years. Both parties often nominate the same slate of judges so that the judicial elections have become largely nonpartisan. In a 1986 referendum, Californians ousted their state chief justice, Rose Bird, who had opposed the death penalty. California justices are appointed but later have to be confirmed by voters. Some argue that elected state judges turn into crowd-pleasing politicians with shaky judicial skills. Others counter that appointed state judges can be the governor's political pals.

COMPARING COURTS

What role should judges play? Should they act as umpires, passively watching the legal drama, just ruling on disputed points of procedure? Or should they actively direct the trial, question witnesses, elicit evidence, and comment on the proceedings? The second pattern strikes Americans as strange and dangerous, because we have been raised in the common-law tradition of passive judges. Yet in code-law countries, judges play just such an active role.

The Anglo-American Adversarial and Accusatorial Process

English and American courts are passive institutions that do *not* look for injustices to correct or lawbreakers to apprehend. Instead, they wait until a law is challenged or a defendant is brought before them. The system operates on an **adversarial** and **accusatorial** basis. In the adversary process, two sides (plaintiff and defendant) compete for a favorable decision from an impartial court. Courts do not accept a case that does not involve a real conflict of interest; the plaintiff must demonstrate how and in what ways the defendant has caused damage. During the trial, the judge acts as an umpire. Both parties present their evidence, call and cross-examine witnesses, and try to refute each other's arguments. The judge rules on the validity of evidence and testimony, on legal procedures, and on disputed points. After both sides have presented their cases, the judge rules on the basis of the facts and the relevant law. If a jury is hearing the case, the judge instructs its members on the weight of the evidence and relevant laws and then almost always accepts the jury's verdict.

In criminal cases, the police investigate and report to a public prosecutor, often a county's district attorney, who must decide whether to prosecute. The actual trial proceeds like a civil one, but the government is the plaintiff and the accused the defendant. Unless a jury has been waived, the jury determines guilt under instructions from the judge on laws and facts. One weakness of the adversarial system—especially when applied in poor, developing countries—is that the decision often goes to the side that can hire the best attorney. Thus, money may tilt the scales of justice.

The British Court System

Britain's court system was established by the Judicature Act of 1873 and largely continues common law traditions. It is divided into civil and criminal branches.

Selection and Tenure of Judges   British judges are nominally appointed by the monarch, but the choice is really the prime minister's, based on recommendations of the lord chancellor, who presides over the House of Lords and is usually a cabinet member. British judges have lifetime tenure and are above politics. Britain used to have no judicial review but by adopting the European Convention on Human Rights in 2000 finally got a bit of judicial review. Now British judges can review statutes and police conduct using the European Convention as the equivalent of the U.S. Bill of Rights, a major step. The British judiciary—like most countries' judiciaries, a part of the executive—is not supposed to be a coequal branch of government.

The Lawyer's Role   The United States and Britain share a common legal heritage, but there are important differences. One is that in Britain the Crown—meaning the government—hires lawyers to prosecute crimes. There are no professional prosecutors like U.S. district attorneys. American lawyers may take on any type of legal work, in or out of the courtroom, but British *solicitors* handle all legal matters except representing clients in court. That is reserved for a few specialized lawyers called *barristers*.

The European Court System

Based heavily on the French system—the pattern for much of the world because of the influence of the *Code Napoléon*—European courts, unlike British courts, do not have separate criminal and civil divisions. Instead, most European countries maintain separate systems of regular and administrative courts. European judges sit as a panel to rule on points of law and procedure, but at the conclusion of the trial they retire *with* a jury to consider the verdict and the sentence. Obviously, the lay jurors often go along with the superior—or at least professional—knowledge and wisdom of the judges. In some systems, such as the German, a judge either sits alone or with two "lay judges."

The European Inquisitorial Process In code law countries—most of the world—judges play a more active role than in common law countries. The prosecutor (French *procureur*, German *Staatsanwalt*) is an official who forwards evidence to an **investigating judge** (*juge d'instruction, Ermittlungsrichter*), a representative of the

investigating judge In European legal systems, judicial officer who both gathers evidence and issues indictments.

COMPARING ■ LAW IN RUSSIA

Russia's post-Communist legal system has continued much of the Soviet legal structure because most personnel were trained under the Communists. Now, Russia is struggling to build "rule of law," including "bourgeois" concepts, such as property law and civil rights. In 1991, a Constitutional Court with 15 justices was established, the first independent tribunal in Russian history. It can theoretically rule on the constitutionality of the moves made by the president and the State Duma.

In practice, Russian presidents have so much power—including power over selection of justices—that the court is no counterweight to the executive. Crime is rampant in Russia. Newly rich *biznesmeny* and *siloviki* hire *keelers* to remove anyone in their way, including members of parliament, journalists, and the competition. "The only lawyer around here is a Kalashnikov," despaired one Russian, referring to the assault rifle.

The basic concepts of Soviet law and the workings of the Soviet judicial process were quite different from those of the Western democracies, even though they were similar in strictly criminal—as opposed to political—matters. Soviet law started with Marx's idea that law serves the ruling class. Capitalists naturally have bourgeois laws designed to protect private property. Proletarians, theoretically in power in the Soviet Union, had socialist law to protect state property, which belonged to all society. Especially after the relaxation of Stalin's climate of fear, theft of state property became the norm for Soviet economic life and helped bring down the system. Almost nothing was said of private property, which scarcely existed. Another part of Soviet law dealt with sedition and subversion, areas of minor

importance in the West. Soviet citizens could receive harsh sentences to Siberia for "antistate activities" or "slandering the Soviet state."

Apolitical cases were generally handled fairly under Soviet law. Prosecutors gathered evidence and brought cases to court but sometimes took into account mitigating social factors and asked for lighter sentences. Defense attorneys were permitted, but they merely advised their clients on legal points and did not challenge the prosecutor's evidence. There were no jury trials. Soviet judges had to be Communist Party members.

Some political cases never came to trial. Obedient Soviet psychiatrists diagnosed dissidents as "sluggish schizophrenic" and put them in prisonlike hospitals with no trial. Nobel Prize–winning writer Alexander Solzhenitsyn was simply bundled onto a plane for Germany in 1974 with no trial. Likewise, dissident physicist Andrei Sakharov was banished to a remote city in 1980 to get him away from Western reporters.

The Committee on State Security (KGB) was powerful and often acted independently of courts. The KGB was succeeded by the Federal Security Service (FSB in Russian) and, staffed by old KGB officials, continues the KGB's primary aim: to make sure those in power stay in power. Regime opponents are shot or poisoned, and no assassin is ever convicted. President Putin graduated in law, served as a KGB officer and head of the FSB, and appointed ex-KGB agents to top positions. Putin used legal-looking procedures to get rid of opponents, who were charged with embezzlement or tax evasion and sent to prison for decades. Rule of law was never established in Russia, and democracy died. The two are closely connected.

indict   Pronounced *in-dite*; to formally charge someone with a crime.

justice ministry who conducts a thorough inquiry (*en-quête*), gathering evidence and statements. Without parallel in the Anglo-American system, these European magistrates first make a preliminary determination of guilt *before* sending the case to trial, something mind-boggling to Americans. French and Italian investigating judges have become heroes by going after corrupt officials. In European criminal procedure the decision to **indict** is made not by a district attorney but by a judge, and the weight of evidence is not controlled by the adversaries (plaintiff and defendant) but by the court, which can take the initiative in acquiring needed evidence.

In the U.S. system, the accused is presumed innocent until proven guilty; in Europe the assumptions are nearly reversed. In an American or British court, the burden of proof is on the prosecution, and the defendant need not say one word in his or her defense; the prosecutor must prove guilt "beyond a reasonable doubt." In code-law countries, the accused bears the burden of having to prove that the investigating judge is wrong.

The Lawyer's Role   Unlike a British or American trial lawyer, the French *avocat* or German *Rechtsanwalt* does not question witnesses; the court does that. Instead, he or she tries to show logical or factual mistakes in the opposition's argument or case and sway the lay jury in the summation argument. For the most part, the role of the European lawyer is not as vital or creative as that of the American lawyer, for the court takes the initiative in discovering the facts of the case.

THE ROLE OF THE COURTS

Judicial review is more highly developed in the United States than in any other country, and Americans expect more of their courts than do other peoples. In few other countries is the courtroom drama a television staple.

Court structures in other Western democracies parallel the U.S. system, but they do not do as much. In Switzerland, for example, cases from the cantonal (state) courts come before the Federal Tribunal, which determines whether a cantonal law violates the Swiss constitution. However, the tribunal does not review the constitutionality of laws passed by the Swiss parliament. The German Constitutional Court reviews statutes to make sure they conform to the Basic Law (the German constitution). The court, located in Karlsruhe, was included in the Basic Law partly on American insistence after World War II; it was a new concept for Europe. It consists of 16 judges, 8 elected by each house of parliament, who serve for nonrenewable 12-year terms. The court decides cases between states, protects civil liberties, and outlaws dangerous political parties. Its decisions have been important. In the 1950s it found that both neo-Nazi and Communist parties wanted to overthrow the constitutional order and declared them illegal. It found the 1974 abortion bill was in conflict with the strong right-to-life provisions of the Basic Law. Because Germany's Constitutional Court operates within the more rigid code law, its decisions do not have the impact of U.S. Supreme Court decisions, which under the common law are literally the law of the land.

The U.S. Supreme Court

The U.S. Supreme Court's power to review the constitutionality of federal legislative enactments is not mentioned specifically in the Constitution and has been vehemently challenged. Judicial review was first considered and debated at the Constitutional Convention of 1787. Delegates suggested that, when in doubt, legislators might call on the judges for an opinion on a proposed law's constitutionality. James Madison stated that a "law violating a constitution established by the people themselves would be considered by the judges as null and void." However, those who feared that such a power would give the Court a double check and compromise its neutrality challenged this position. Others felt it would violate the separation of powers. Elbridge Gerry stated that it would make "statesmen of judges," a prophetic remark. At the close of the convention, judicial review had not been explicitly provided for.

Alexander Hamilton, however, argued in *The Federalist* No. 78 that only the courts could limit legislative authority. John Marshall, chief justice of the Supreme Court from 1801 to 1835, agreed with this position; in fact, he went on record in favor of it nearly 15 years before *Marbury v. Madison* (1803), the landmark decision establishing judicial review. The doctrine has never been universally popular, however. Strong-willed presidents have resisted the authority of the Court. Thomas Jefferson, Andrew Jackson, Abraham Lincoln, and Franklin D. Roosevelt differed sharply with equally strong-willed judges.

From 1803 to 1857, the Supreme Court did not invalidate any act of Congress. In 1857, it threw out the Missouri Compromise of 1820, which had barred slavery in the old Northwest Territory. This touched off a political storm that made Abraham

CLASSIC WORKS ■ MARBURY V. MADISON

President John Adams, a Federalist, appointed William Marbury to the post of a Washington justice of the peace shortly before leaving office. For some unknown reason, however, Secretary of State John Marshall did not deliver the commission to Marbury. Marshall's successor, the Republican James Madison, refused to deliver the commission. Marbury brought suit in original jurisdiction before the Supreme Court, asking the Court to issue a writ of *mandamus* commanding Madison to deliver the commission.

This presented the Court with a dilemma. If Chief Justice Marshall and the Supreme Court issued the writ, and Madison refused to deliver the commission, the prestige and authority of the Court would be dealt a severe blow. If, however, Marshall refused to issue the writ, he would in effect call into question the legitimacy of the hasty judicial appointments given to Federalists in the final days of the Adams administration.

Marshall's solution was brilliant, for it not only criticized Madison and Jefferson but also established the principle of judicial review. On the one hand, Marshall ruled that Marbury was entitled to his commission and that Madison should have given it to him. On the other hand, he stated that the Supreme Court had no authority to issue a writ of *mandamus* in a case brought to it in original jurisdiction and that Section 13 of the Judiciary Act of 1789, "an act of the legislature repugnant to the Constitution[,] is void." The decision infuriated President Jefferson, for he understood how cleverly Marshall had escaped the trap and asserted the authority of the Court. He realized that the precedent for judicial review had been laid and called it "both elitist and undemocratic."

WASP   White, Anglo-Saxon, Protestant.

Lincoln president. In the twentieth century, many laws were overturned. The court itself, however, has always been divided on this. Judicial "activists," led by Hugo Black, William O. Douglas, and Earl Warren, have argued that the Supreme Court must be vigilant in protecting the Bill of Rights. Advocates of judicial "restraint," such as Oliver Wendell Holmes, Felix Frankfurter, and Warren Burger, have argued that only Congress should make public policy and that unless a legislative act clearly violates the Constitution, the law should stand. The Warren Court (1953–1969), named after its chief justice, was markedly activist, issuing decisions in the areas of racial segregation, reapportionment, and rights of the accused that had great impact on U.S. society. The courts that followed have been more cautious, reflecting the fact that most of their members were appointed by conservative Republicans.

The Supreme Court's Political Role

In this country, the Supreme Court's rulings often become political issues, rarely the case in other countries. When the Supreme Court of Franklin Roosevelt's day ruled that many New Deal laws were unconstitutional, FDR referred to the justices as "nine tired old men." Richard Nixon in the 1968 campaign charged that the Warren Court's liberal decisions had worsened crime and endangered society. The U.S. Supreme Court plays an important political role, and the appointment of just one new justice changes split decisions from five to four against to the same number for. It is important to know to what extent judges let their personal beliefs influence their decisions. Are their ideological views incompatible with the idea of the Court as an impartial dispenser of justice?

The Views of Judges

Clearly, justices' personal beliefs influence their decisions. Historically, Supreme Court justices used to be **WASP** upper- or upper-middle-class males, and radical critics claimed that such judges could not appreciate the situation of the poor or oppressed. The situation has greatly changed. The first woman justice was appointed only in 1981; now there are three. The current court has six Catholics and three Jews. (Some wags suggested making a place for a token white Protestant male.) The relatively recent arrival of blacks and women to the high bench has not necessarily overturned conservative tendencies, for such justices can be conservative in their own right. Justice Clarence Thomas, the second black ever on the Court, said he reached conservative conclusions by thinking for himself.

Other factors affect the justices' rulings. They are older, averaging 70. Southern jurists have usually been more conservative on racial matters, though one of the strongest champions of civil rights was Alabama's Hugo L. Black, who had been a member of the Ku Klux Klan in his youth. Former corporation lawyers may be more sympathetic to business problems. Some justices, like Louis D. Brandeis (one of six Jewish justices) and Thurgood Marshall (the first black justice), were active in reform and civil rights causes and brought their liberalism to the bench. Others who have served on state courts believe that states' rights should be strengthened.

The two most important influences on voting, however, seem to be party affiliation and the justice's conception of the judicial role. Democratic justices are more likely to support liberal stands than are Republican justices and to see the Supreme Court as a defender of minorities and the poor. They are more likely to distrust states and to favor federal authority while also seeking to protect individual rights under the Fourteenth Amendment. Republicans are more likely to uphold state authority within the federal system and are less likely to accept the Bill of Rights as a blanket guarantee. There are many exceptions. When President Eisenhower appointed California Governor Earl Warren in 1953, he thought he was picking a good Republican moderate as chief justice. Later, Eisenhower called the choice "the biggest damned-fool mistake I ever made."

Warren Court   The liberal, activist U.S. Supreme Court under Chief Justice Earl Warren, 1953–1969.

Many justices see the Court's role as standing firm on certain constitutional principles, despite public opinion. Justice Jackson put it this way: "One's right to life, liberty and property, to free speech, a free press, freedom of worship and assembly, and other fundamental rights may not be submitted to vote; they depend upon the outcome of no election." But changing public attitudes also influence Supreme Court justices. In the 1936 election, after the Court had struck down several important laws designed to alleviate the Depression, President Roosevelt was given the greatest mandate in the nation's history. In 1937, he submitted legislation to expand the Supreme Court to 15 members and encourage justices 70 or over to retire. The plan failed because many felt that FDR was attacking the constitutional principle of an independent judiciary, but it did force the Court to look beyond its narrow world and accept change. The election of 1936 and the controversy over "court packing" led to the Court's becoming more restrained in dealing with New Deal legislation. As one jokester put it, "A switch in time saves nine."

Another influence is colleagues' opinions. Chief Justices John Marshall, Earl Warren, and currently John Roberts were able to convert some of their colleagues to their judicial philosophies by force of personality and their judicial reasoning. Many factors—not all of them knowable—influence decisions. The fact that Supreme Court justices are appointed for life may be the most important of all. They are independent and immune to congressional, White House, and private-interest pressures. This factor changes them—and in unpredictable ways. Liberals turn into conservatives, activists into restrainers, and vice versa. The seriousness of their position and the knowledge that their votes alter American life make justices think deeply and sometimes change views. The office in part makes its occupant.

The Political Impact of the Court

Our legal system poses a basic conflict. Justices are expected to be impartial, but the importance of the Court gives them political power. In the twentieth century this power increased. The **Warren Court** was active and controversial in three key areas—civil rights, criminal procedure, and legislative reapportionment—where it rewrote constitutional law. In the opinion of some, as 96 Southern members of Congress put it, the Court overturned "the established law of the land" and implemented its "personal political and social philosophy."

sit-in Tactic of overturning local laws by deliberately breaking them, as at segregated lunch counters.

indigent Having no money.

Civil Rights The Supreme Court's decision in *Brown* (1954) triggered a revolution in American race relations, an area Congress had been unwilling to touch. In a unanimous ruling, the Court accepted the sociological argument of Thurgood Marshall (then attorney for the NAACP) that segregated public school facilities were "inherently unequal" because they stigmatized black children and deprived them of the Fourteenth Amendment's guarantee of equal protection. A year later, in *Brown II* (1955), desegregation of public schools was ordered "with all deliberate speed." Southern whites vowed massive resistance.

America's blacks, encouraged by this legal support, sought equal treatment in other areas and by 1963 engaged in confrontation with the white establishment. In *Lombard v. Louisiana* (1963), the Warren Court supported the **sit-in**, ruling that blacks who had refused to leave a segregated lunch counter could not be prosecuted where it appeared that the state was involved in unequal treatment of the races. The Court relied on the Fourteenth Amendment that no state may deny any person the equal protection of the laws. The sit-in became a major weapon in the civil rights struggle. In 1964, Congress followed the Court's lead and passed the Civil Rights Act, which barred segregation in public accommodations such as hotels, motels, restaurants, and theaters. The Court led Congress.

Criminal Procedure The Warren Court's rulings in criminal procedure were even more disturbing to many Americans. In *Mapp v. Ohio* (1961), the Court ruled

Integration came hard to Little Rock, Arkansas, in 1957. Black students needed a National Guard escort to get past jeering white students at Central High School. The problem was not confined to the South or to the 1950s, however. (AP Photo)

that evidence police seized without a warrant was inadmissible in a state court. In 1963, in *Gideon v. Wainwright*, the Court held that **indigent** defendants must be provided with legal counsel. In *Escobedo v. Illinois* (1964), in a five-to-four decision, the Court ruled that a suspect could not be denied the right to have a lawyer during police questioning and that any confessions so obtained could not be used in court. One of the Court's most controversial rulings came in 1966 in *Miranda v. Arizona*. The majority (five to four) ruled that arrested persons must immediately be told of their right to remain silent and to have a lawyer present during police questioning.

Legislative Reapportionment Equally important was the Warren Court's mandating of equal-population voting districts. Until 1962, many states had congressional

scattergram Graph showing position of items on two axes.

outlier Item that deviates from its expected position.

HOW TO... ■ CONSTRUCT A SCATTERGRAM

To make clear that your numbers form a pattern, you can move beyond a cross-tab (Chapter 11) and build a **scattergram**, or scatterplot, which turns items into dots on a graph and can make your argument clear. If you have found something worthwhile, these dots will form a pattern—never perfect—showing more clearly than a cross-tab a relationship between two variables. If, on the other hand, the dots scatter randomly over the graph, they demonstrate that there is no pattern or relationship.

The Corruption Perception Index (CPI) from Transparency International, a Berlin research group, is a compilation of surveys of international businesspeople, asking how much corruption they encounter. It is subjective and imperfect, but objective measures are impossible, as few officials admit to taking bribes. TI ranks countries from 10 (squeaky clean) to 1 (totally corrupt). The scattergram in the figure

below displays per capita GDP on the x (horizontal) axis and the CPI on the y (vertical) axis.

Your computer can draw a "line of best fit" (sometimes curved). In this case, it runs about from Haiti to Canada. Most dots are not too far from the line, demonstrating that, very generally, the wealthier a country, the less corrupt it tends to be. However, there are some **outliers**, countries far from the line. Chile, with a third of the per cap of rich countries, is unusually clean. Italy, Japan, and France—where scandals are standard—are more corrupt than their wealth suggests they ought to be. And the biggest outlier might be the United States. To explain the outliers, study their histories, institutions, and political cultures. For example, how does the extreme localness of U.S. government—as in the powers of counties and school boards—contribute to corruption in America? The outliers frequently tell the most interesting stories.

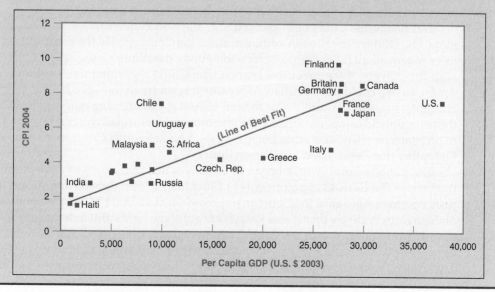

Jim Crow System of segregationist laws in the U.S. South.

districts that overrepresented rural areas and underrepresented cities. In a series of decisions in 1962 and 1964, the Court found that unequal representation denied citizens their Fourteenth Amendment (equal protection) rights. The Court ordered that state legislatures apply the principle of "one person, one vote" in redrawing electoral lines, which most now must do after every census.

These decisions angered people who felt they had been hurt: segregationists who refused to share schools or accommodations with blacks, police who felt hampered in dealing with suspects, and rural people who wanted a more-than-equal vote. Billboards shouted "Impeach Earl Warren," and in 1968 Nixon ran as much against the Supreme Court as against Hubert Humphrey. The Warren Court overthrew **Jim Crow** laws, rewrote the rules for criminal procedure, and redrew legislative maps. With the possible exception of the Marshall Court, it was the most active, groundbreaking Court in U.S. history.

The Post-Warren Courts   The Burger Court (1969–1986) and the Rehnquist Court (1986–2005) were sometimes characterized as conservative, an effort to roll back the Warren Court. Actually, their decisions were not so clear-cut. Overall, there was a conservative drift but an unpredictable one. The most controversial ruling of the century declared abortion was protected by the right to privacy in *Roe v. Wade* (1973), which came from the "conservative" Burger Court (with the chief justice concurring). The Burger Court in the 1978 *Bakke* case found that reserving quotas for black applicants to medical school violated equal protection for whites. The next year, however, in *Weber*, it found that quotas to help black workers attain skilled positions were constitutional. In criminal law, the Burger Court issued some hard-line decisions. In 1984, it added a "good faith exception" to the *Mapp* rule, which excluded wrongfully seized evidence. If the police with a warrant to look for a particular piece of evidence stumble on another, it may be used as evidence. This modified but did not overturn *Mapp*. In 1976, the Burger Court found that capital punishment was not necessarily "cruel and unusual" if the rules for applying it were fair.

The Rehnquist Court both pleased and alarmed conservatives. In 1988, in a move that stunned the Reagan administration, the Court upheld the constitutionality of independent federal prosecutors, something the White House said interfered with the powers of the executive branch. The Court also ruled that burning the American flag could not be outlawed because it is a form of free speech. This ruling brought a mass outcry and a new federal statute outlawing flag burning. In 2003, the court upheld campaign-finance reform, university affirmative-action programs to promote diversity, and other liberal causes. The Rehnquist Court mostly modified rather than repudiated the Warren Court.

The Roberts Court, which began in 2005, was markedly conservative but not uniformly. The Bush 43 appointments of Chief Justice John Roberts and Associate Justice Samuel Alito gave the Court an unprecedented majority of five Catholics, all of them conservatives. *Brown* and *Roe v. Wade* got some limits. But federal authority to curb greenhouse gases was affirmed, and liberals celebrated. In 2008, the Roberts Court decided five to four that a gun in the home is an individual right (see page 88). The Court, however, required the Pentagon to accord terrorist suspects certain rights, including habeas corpus, what many called a "liberal" decision. In 2010, the Court ruled that direct corporate or union funding for political advertisements are constitutional, a form of free speech. President Obama called the decision "devastating," saying that it "will open the floodgates for special interests." Perhaps the most conservative shift of the Roberts Court was that it took notably fewer cases than before, a reversal of the liberal tendency to use the Court as a back-up legislature.

One of the problems with evaluating the thrust of Court decisions is the definition of *conservative*. The term may be applied to the substance of decisions, such as giving minorities special treatment, or it may be applied to the maintenance of existing institutions. Often the two coincide, as when the Court says states can pass laws limiting abortion. That would be both conservative concerning substance and conservative concerning the powers of states. But sometimes the two diverge, as when the Roberts Court upheld the right of habeas corpus for terrorist suspects. Although called a "liberal" ruling, it also upheld Article I, Section 9, of the Constitution, which says habeas will not be suspended, so it was actually "conservative." What the mass media and public opinion call "conservative" is irrelevant to the Court, which is intent only on constitutionality. Although a staunch conservative, Justice Antonin Scalia at times sides with liberals. "Liberal" and "conservative" are simplified labels used by the mass media and politicians; they are not mentioned in Supreme Court decisions.

The U.S. federal courts are an integral part of the policymaking apparatus—not just mechanical interpreters of law. Judicial decisions influence and are influenced by politics. Groups whose welfare depends on the court's decisions will try to influence the court to adopt their point of view; groups that do not succeed with the president or Congress hope that they will have better luck with the courts. Some have called the U.S. judicial system a back-up legislature or parliament of last resort, for it can take on issues the other branches fear. Without Supreme Court decisions leading the way, Congress would not have passed civil rights bills and presidents would not have enforced them. An autonomous and coequal judicial branch is one of America's great contributions to governance. Very slowly, this approach to judicial power is growing worldwide, contributing to rule of law and stable democracy.

mypoliscikit EXERCISES

Apply what you learned in this chapter on MyPoliSciKit (www.mypoliscikit.com).

Assessment   Review this chapter using learning objectives, chapter summaries, practice tests, and more.

Menu

Flashcards   Learn the key terms in this chapter; you can test yourself by term or definition.

Flashcards

Video   Analyze recent world affairs by watching streaming video from major news providers.

Videos

Comparative Exercises   Compare political ideas, behaviors, institutions, and policies worldwide.

Comparative Exercises

KEY TERMS

accusatorial (p. 281)
adversarial (p. 281)
appeal (p. 280)
bench (p. 280)
brief (p. 280)
canon law (p. 278)
civil law (p. 276)
code law (p. 279)
common law (p. 276)
consistency (p. 277)

constitutional
law (p. 277)
higher law (p. 276)
indict (p. 284)
indigent (p. 288)
investigating
judge (p. 283)
Jim Crow (p. 290)
law (p. 276)
natural law (p. 276)

outlier (p. 289)
plaintiff (p. 276)
positive law (p. 276)
precedent (p. 278)
reciprocity (p. 277)
Roman law (p. 279)
scattergram (p. 289)
sit-in (p. 288)
Warren Court (p. 287)
WASP (p. 286)

FURTHER REFERENCE

Bach, Amy. *Ordinary Justice: How America Holds Court.* New York: Holt, 2010.

Barber, Sotirios A., and James E. Fleming. *Constitutional Interpretation: The Basic Questions.* New York: Oxford University Press, 2007.

Baum, Lawrence. *Judges and Their Audiences.* Princeton, NJ: Princeton University Press, 2008.

Belsky, Martin H., ed. *The Rehnquist Court: A Retrospective.* New York: Oxford University Press, 2002.

Bingham, Tom. *The Rule of Law.* London: Allen Lane, 2010.

Breyer, Stephen. *Making Our Democracy Work: A Judge's View.* New York: Knopf, 2010.

Brisbin, Richard, and John Kilwein. *Real Law Stories: Inside the American Judicial Process.* New York: Oxford University Press, 2010.

Burns, James MacGregor. *Packing the Court: The Rise of Judicial Power and the Coming Crisis of the Supreme Court.* New York: Penguin, 2009.

Calvi, James V., and Susan Coleman. *American Law and Legal Systems,* 6th ed. Upper Saddle River, NJ: Prentice Hall, 2007.

Carp, Robert A., Ronald Stidham, and Kenneth Manning. *Judicial Process in America,* 7th ed. Washington, DC: CQ Press, 2007.

Carter, Lief H., and Thomas F. Burke. *Reason in Law,* 8th ed. New York: Longman, 2009.

Cushman, Clare, and Melvin I. Urofsky, eds. *Black, White and Brown: The Landmark School Desegregation Case in Retrospect.* Washington, DC: CQ Press, 2004.

Dworkin, Ronald. *The Supreme Court Phalanx: The Court's New Right-Wing Bloc.* New York: New York Review of Books, 2008.

Greenhouse, Linda. *Becoming Justice Blackmun: Harry Blackmun's Supreme Court Journey.* New York: Times Books, 2005.

Howard, Philip K. *Life Without Lawyers: Liberating Americans from Too Much Law.* New York: Norton, 2009.

Rosen, Jeffrey. *The Supreme Court: The Personalities and Rivalries That Defined America.* New York: Times Books, 2007.

Sunstein, Cass R. *A Constitution of Many Minds: Why the Founding Document Doesn't Mean What It Meant Before.* Princeton, NJ: Princeton University Press, 2009.

Tate, C. Neal. *Comparative Judicial Systems.* Washington, DC: CQ Press, 2005.

Toobin, Jeffrey. *The Nine: Inside the Secret World of the Supreme Court.* New York: Doubleday, 2007.

Urofsky, Melvin I. *Louis D. Brandeis: A Life.* New York: Pantheon, 2009.

PART V

WHAT POLITICAL SYSTEMS DO

Ch. 16 Political Economy   Political economy is a broad term covering the interactions of the economy and government. Even conservatives demand a government role to stabilize the economy. Some would do this through Keynesian counter-cyclical spending while others advocate raising or lowering the money supply through interest rates. The United States has suffered through recurring problems of inflation, tax hikes or cuts, budget and trade deficits, oil shocks, and burst bubbles. Because there is never enough money for everything, the United States must continually reconsider its massive entitlement programs (Social Security and Medicare) that all receive as opposed to welfare aimed at the poor (food stamps and Medicaid).

Ch. 17 Political Violence   Political violence is a symptom of system breakdown, something almost every country has experienced. We can distinguish several types of violence: primordial, separatist, revolutionary, and coup. Terrorism uses violence to weaken a hated political authority. Change and rising expectations may fuel violence. Vietnam was less guerrilla warfare than "revolutionary political warfare." Revolutions sweep out old elites and tend to follow a cycle Crane Brinton discerned long ago— regime decay, a takeover by moderates, another takeover by an extremist reign of terror, and finally a Thermidor or calming. Iran fits this pattern. Revolutions tend to end badly—the worst example is Cambodia—but preventing them is difficult because the ruling class refuses to give up any of its wealth or power.

Ch. 18 International Relations   International relations, because it is anarchic, is different and wilder than domestic politics, where a sovereign attempts to preserve order. Instead, power and national interest determine much of IR. National interest is often hard to tell until years later. The causes of war can be divided into micro and macro theories, misperception, and balances (or imbalances) of power. Various plans to curb war have been urged, ranging from world government to collective security to expanding democracy. Functionalism proposes getting countries to cooperate first on small, practical problems. Diplomacy, sometimes by third-party mediation, followed by peacekeeping operations may calm conflicts. Some suggest the concept of sovereignty may be slipping, allowing supranational bodies, such as the UN or NATO, to intervene. Economic factors now loom large, with protectionism reversing "globalization." U.S. foreign policy tends to alternate between interventionism and isolationism. Americans must get used to living in a chaotic, dangerous world.

CHAPTER 16

Political Economy

In 2008 gasoline prices topped $4 a gallon, something that could happen again. (Mike Blake/Corbis)

The attempts to recover from the financial meltdown of 2008–2009 revived an old debate: Should government stimulate the limp economy by massive spending or practice **austerity** to restore confidence? It was an intensely ideological debate. Liberals and Keynesians (see page 297) favored the first and criticized the Obama administration for not doing enough of it. Conservatives and Hayekians criticized Obama for doing far too much of it. As Britain in 2010 moved sharply to reduce spending, Princeton economist (and Nobel Prize winner) Paul Krugman predicted that "premature fiscal austerity will lead to a renewed economic slump." A frightened world waited to see if he was right.

QUESTIONS TO CONSIDER

1. What policy choices do we now face that are not economic?
2. What was Keynes's solution to the Depression?
3. What started the U.S. inflationary spiral in the 1960s?
4. Are U.S. taxes too high? Compared to what?
5. What went wrong with the U.S. economy after 2000?
6. Why has income inequality grown in the United States?
7. How do entitlements differ from welfare?
8. How does ideology influence our views on poverty?
9. Which U.S. programs can realistically be cut?
10. Why do medical costs tend to escalate?

The heated debate illustrates the close connection between politics and the economy. Most economists said the **bailouts** were necessary; without them, the world might have plunged into a new depression. Governments the world over—even in China—took similar steps. The worst was avoided, but concern quickly grew that government deficits were so huge they might lead to inflation and even currency collapse. Hesitation over bailing out Greece raised questions over the future of the new euro currency and even of the European Union. As some economists say, the content of politics is economics. Most really big quarrels are over economics.

Political economy is an old and flexible term. The classical economists of the late eighteenth and nineteenth centuries—Adam Smith, David Ricardo, John Stuart Mill, and Karl Marx—all wrote on what they called the **political economy**. In doing this, they were taking a leaf from Aristotle, who viewed government, society, and the economy as one thing. The old political economists also had normative orientations, prescribing what government should do to promote a just prosperity. In the late nineteenth century, as economists became more scientific and numbers based, they dropped "political" from the name of their discipline and shifted from "should" or "ought" prescription to empirical description and prediction.

295

austerity Drastically cutting government spending.

bailout Emergency government loan to save firm from collapse.

political economy Influence of politics and economy on each other; what government should do in the economy.

public policy What a government tries to do; the choices it makes among alternatives.

Recently the term has revived, with partisan overtones. Radicals use the term "political economy" instead of Marxism (which is a hard sell these days) to describe their criticisms of capitalism and the unfair distribution of wealth among and within nations. Conservatives use the term to try to get back to the pure market system advocated by Adam Smith. We will avoid taking ideological sides and use the term to mean the interface between politics and the economy. And it is a very big interface.

Economics undergirds almost everything in politics. Politicians get elected by promising prosperity and reelected by delivering it. Virtually all **public policy** choices have economic ramifications, and these can make or break the policy. A policy designed to protect the environment—but that slows industry and costs jobs—is unlikely to last long. An energy policy based on ethanol (alcohol from grain) continues only because Congress subsidizes it by 51 cents a gallon. Ethanol from corn yields only 1.5 times the energy it takes to produce, but it makes farmers happy.

With a growing economy, a country can afford to introduce new welfare measures, as the United States did in the booming 1960s. With a slow economy, an administration has to run massive deficits while devising policies it hopes will spur the economy into growth. Whatever the issue—health care, environment, energy, or welfare—it will be connected to the economy. Some of the worst policy choices are made when decision makers forget this elementary point. Candidates often promise new programs without the faintest idea how to pay for them. Economic policy should take priority over all other policies. Every political scientist should be to some degree an economist. As candidate Bill Clinton constantly reminded himself during the 1992 campaign, "It's the economy, stupid!" And he was right; the economy matters most. Good times buoyed his popularity even as he was impeached. Low inflation and low unemployment made most Americans reasonably content with the Clinton presidency.

GOVERNMENT AND THE ECONOMY

Nowadays, no one, not even conservatives, expects the government to keep its hands off the economy. Everyone wants the government to induce economic prosperity, and if it does not, voters may punish the administration at the next election, as happened in 2008. McCain lost in part because voters (perhaps unfairly) blamed the Republican administration of Bush 43 for the financial meltdown. Obama's support slumped as the economy failed to bounce back. Earlier in the twentieth century, this was not the case. Many European governments as well as Washington followed the "classic liberal" doctrines discussed in Chapter 3 and generally kept their hands off the economy. With the outbreak of the Great Depression in 1929, however, the hands-off policies tended to make things worse, and people demanded government intervention.

A 1936 book by the British economist John Maynard Keynes proposed to cure depressions by dampening the swings of the **business cycle**. During bad times, government would increase "aggregate demand" by "countercyclical spending" on public works and welfare to make **recessions** shorter and milder. An economy growing too fast—with risks of speculative bubbles and inflation—should be cooled by raising taxes. Believers in the classic Adam Smith version of the free market were horrified at "deficit spending," but Keynes argued that we just owe the money to ourselves, and, "In the long run, we'll all be dead." Some say the "Keynesian revolution" brought us out of the Depression. Others say FDR's New Deal never seriously applied Keynesianism; only the massive defense spending of World War II did that. Still others doubt that the New Deal achieved anything lasting except debt and **inflation**.

> **business cycle**   Tendency of economy to alternate between growth and *recession* over several years.
>
> **recession**   Period of economic decline; a shrinking GDP.
>
> **inflation**   A general, overall rise in prices.
>
> **Federal Reserve Board**   "The Fed"—U.S. central bank that controls interest rates and money supply.

After World War II, conservative economists such as Friedrich Hayek and Milton Friedman sidelined Keynesianism with a "neoclassical" theory based on the original supply and demand of Adam Smith. Government regulation of the economy was out, the free market was in. Then the 2008–2009 financial meltdown hit—something only a handful of economists had predicted—and economists quickly rediscovered Keynes. Even Republicans—such as President Bush in 2008—favored pumping billions of federal dollars into shaky firms, a Keynesian effort. Because Congress is so slow, much of the fight to smooth the business cycle shifted to the **Federal Reserve Board**, which, by controlling interest rates, can raise or lower economic activity much faster than Congress can by raising or lowering taxes or delivering emergency funding. Fed chairman Ben Bernanke was closely watched as he struggled to prevent the U.S. economy from falling into another depression.

What are some of our leading economic problems and government responses to them? Consider the approximate sequence of events the United States has gone through since the 1960s, and notice how the problems reoccur. Many are with us today.

Inflation

Until 1965, the U.S. inflation rate was low, but as President Johnson escalated the Vietnam War in 1965, it kicked up. War spending pumped some $140 billion (now worth more than six times that, after adjusting for inflation) into the U.S. economy but not a corresponding amount of goods and services to buy with it. Too many dollars chased too few goods, the classic definition of demand-pull inflation. The Vietnam War brought an inflation that took on a life of its own and lasted into the 1980s. Johnson thought he could win in Vietnam quickly and cheaply, before the war made much economic impact, but the policy failed. Many economists say that we could have avoided the worst of the inflation if LBJ had been willing to raise taxes at the start of the war.

Tax Hike

President Johnson was reluctant to ask for a tax increase to pay for Vietnam for two reasons. First, he had just gotten a tax cut through Congress in 1964; it would have been embarrassing to reverse course the following year. Second, he did not want to admit that he had gotten the country into a long and costly war. By the time Johnson and Congress had changed their minds and introduced a 10 percent tax surcharge in 1968, it was too late; inflation had taken hold. The lesson was that in war you must increase taxes to mop up the increased government spending. Bush 43 ignored the lesson and, like LBJ, both cut taxes and took us to war.

balance of payments   The value of what a country exports compared with what it imports.

fixed exchange rate   Dollar buys set amounts of foreign currencies.

floating exchange rate   Dollar buys varying amounts of foreign currencies, depending on market for them.

Balance of Payments

Starting in the late 1950s, the United States spent more abroad than it sold. With the war-induced prosperity of the 1960s, America sucked in imports without exporting enough to cover them. American industries outsourced, and Americans enjoyed bargain prices on imported goods. Large **balance-of-payments** deficits grew. The too-high value of the dollar in relation to foreign currencies meant it was cheaper to buy foreign goods but harder to sell U.S. goods in foreign markets. Japanese and later Chinese products took a large share of the U.S. market. American dollars flooded the world; they were too plentiful.

Gold Standard

In an effort to correct this imbalance, in 1971 President Nixon cut the link between the dollar and gold, a **fixed exchange rate** that had been in place since 1944. The Bretton Woods agreement—which priced an ounce of gold at $35 and fixed other currencies in relation to the dollar—had been the basis of postwar recovery. But the inflation of U.S. dollars worldwide made our stock of gold way too cheap, so Nixon said no more gold and let the dollar "float" to a lower level in relation to other currencies. This **floating exchange rate** devalued the dollar by about one-fifth. Over time, however, U.S. trade and payment deficits soared even higher.

Wage-Price Freeze

At the same time, Nixon froze wages and prices to knock out inflation. The 1971 wage-price freeze was popular at first, but soon many complained that there was no corresponding freeze on profits so that businesses benefited unduly. A bigger problem with wage-price freezes, however, is that when they are removed, pent-up demand pushes inflation higher than ever. Many economists think Nixon's 18-month freeze just set the stage for greater inflation. Some (mostly liberal) economists supported the idea of wage and price controls—called "incomes policy"—but now few economists of any stripe want to try them again.

Oil Shocks

International oil deals, like most international trade arrangements, were made with U.S. dollars. The dollar's loss in value meant that the oil exporters were getting less and less for their black gold. The price of oil in the 1960s was ridiculously low. As a result of the 1973 Mideast war, the members of the Organization of Petroleum Exporting Countries (OPEC) were able to implement what they had been itching to do: quadruple oil prices. In 1979, in response to the revolutionary turmoil in Iran, they increased prices again. Altogether during the 1970s, world oil prices soared from $2.50 to $34 a barrel, which now looks cheap. In 2008, oil briefly hit $147 a barrel and is recently around $100. With world demand growing—especially in rapidly industrializing economies like China and India—oil prices are certain to rise.

> **stagflation** Combination of slow growth plus inflation in the U.S. economy in the 1970s.

Stagflation

The manifold increase in petroleum prices produced inflation everywhere while simultaneously depressing the economy. During the 1970s, a new word appeared— **stagflation**—to describe inflation with stagnant economic growth. Previously, economists had seen a connection between economic growth and inflation; as one went up, so did the other. In the 1970s, this connection was broken. Inflation hit

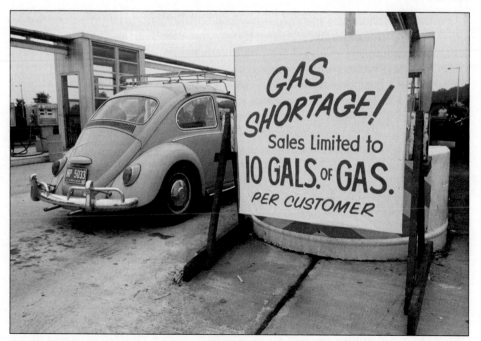

The oil shortages of the 1970s made the United States aware of its dependence on imported oil. (Owen Franken/Corbis)

deficit Spending more in a given year than you take in.

double-digit levels (10 percent or higher), but the economy shrank and joblessness increased. Since 1973, average Americans have had stagnant incomes. The biggest single culprit is believed to be the massive increase in oil prices that affect every corner of the economy, from agriculture and transportation to manufacturing and construction. The United States was especially hard hit, for Americans had gotten used to cheap energy and had based their industry and lifestyle on it.

Interest Rates

President Jimmy Carter attempted to stimulate the economy, but this made inflation worse; in 1980, it was 13.5 percent and probably cost him reelection. The Fed, whose members are appointed by the president for four years and cannot be fired, finally stemmed inflation by boosting interest rates to record levels, at one point higher than 20 percent. This brought slower economic growth and curbed inflation. But it was also painful medicine that brought the greatest rate of unemployment (more than 10 percent) since the Depression. No one wants interest rates like that again. Americans became aware of how important the Fed is in our economic life.

Tax Cut

Again trying to stimulate the economy, President Reagan turned to an approach called "supply-side economics," which focuses on investment and production rather than on consumer demand, as Keynesian policy does. The inspiration of supply-siders was the Kennedy idea that lowering tax rates stimulates economic growth and ultimately generates more tax revenue. Too high taxes discourage effort and investment. Congress bought Reagan's proposal and cut income taxes 25 percent over three years. Actually, this scarcely offset the "bracket creep" that American taxpayers had suffered as a result of inflation; their purchasing power had stayed the same, but they found themselves in ever-higher tax brackets. The Reagan tax cut did stimulate the economy, but it also helped produce another problem.

Budget Deficits

Presidents Reagan and Bush 43 presented Congress with budgets that featured tax cuts and major increases in defense spending. Reagan figured this would force Congress to cut domestic and welfare spending drastically. But Congress cut little, and the U.S. federal budget reached record **deficits**. By issuing Treasury bills, the federal government borrowed the money, and this "crowded out" commercial borrowing and raised interest rates. Because interest rates were high, foreigners found the United States a good place to invest, so in effect much of the U.S. budget deficit was covered by foreign investment. The deficits acted like a gigantic vacuum cleaner that swept in both goods and capital from around the world. This could go on only as long as foreigners trusted the dollar. When Obama ran a $1.3 trillion budget deficit (about 9 percent of GDP; some other countries were worse) in 2010, many feared the dollar would plunge in value. The euro rose against the dollar, reaching $1.40 in 2010.

euro Since 2002, common EU currency used in most of West Europe; value fluctuates but in 2010 worth $1.40.

debt The sum total of deficits over many years.

Trade Deficits

The United States for several decades has consumed more than it produced and imported much more than it exported. U.S. imports now top exports by some half a trillion dollars a year, about 3.5 percent of the GDP. The foreign-trade deficit makes the United States the world's greatest debtor nation. This in turn leads to the buying up of American assets by foreigners. Americans often dislike this, but it is really no problem. If foreigners want to invest in America, it simply makes us more prosperous. Off and on, our trading partners bid down the value of the dollar, and the value of the **euro** climbs, briefly touching $1.60 in 2008. This in effect devalued the dollar and made U.S. products cheaper, something Europeans do not want. Some economists argue that the U.S. trade deficit is irrelevant because the U.S. economy is so strong that foreign creditors know they will be repaid. With increasing urgency, however, others caution that too much hangs on confidence in the dollar; if it collapses, the world would have no standard "reserve" currency to do business with, leading to global recession.

Debt

The 1994 Republican takeover of Capitol Hill brought a determined effort to trim government spending and end the chronic budget deficits, which every year are added to the national **debt**—the sum total owed by the federal government. President Clinton went along with the effort, and the federal budget moved into surplus

---

COMPARING ■ HOW HIGH ARE U.S. TAXES?

Compared with other advanced industrialized countries, U.S. taxes are low. In 2007, countries paid the following percentages of their GDPs in total taxes, including state and local (see right column).

Americans complain their taxes are too high—they would complain if taxes were zero—but we tax relatively little because the United States is not much of a welfare state. Most Europeans, figuring they get a lot from the system (including medical plans), complain less about taxes. The question is how much and what programs are Americans willing to cut to bring taxes even lower? Defense? Social

Denmark	49
France	45
Britain	38
Germany	40
Canada	35
Japan	28
United States	28
China	16

Security? Medicare? Besides, some of the "cuts" in federal programs are just tax burdens shifted to the state and local levels.

HOW TO... ■ CREATE MAPS

Maps are often underutilized, but they are essential for studies with territorial components. They are also easy for readers to understand. Like cross-tabs and scattergrams, maps can relate two variables, sometimes suggesting patterns you overlooked. A study of the 1996 Perot vote in Pennsylvania showed it was most pronounced in the rural counties along the state's northern border, a depressed region where voters have much resentment and low turnout. A map suggested that the Perot vote came from alienated people who typically do not vote.

The basic technique is to shade in territorial components (states, provinces, counties, or electoral districts) to show variation in voting for a certain party. You might take the overall vote for the German Social Democratic party (SPD). In those German *Länder* (states) where the SPD got more than 5 percent below the national average, color them light blue. In those states where the SPD won from 5 percent under to 5 percent over the national average, color them medium blue. In those states where the SPD got more than 5 percent over the national average, color them dark blue. At a glance, you'll have a

German Social Democratic Vote by State

picture of German voting by region. Most countries show regional voting patterns.

For your second variable, you might take religion, coloring in on the same basis in which states Protestants are either at, below, or above Germany's overall percentage of Protestants. You will likely notice that the two maps are similar, as German Catholics tend to vote Christian Democrat and Protestants SPD. Such maps show a rough fit between religion and voting.

U.S. Congressional and state legislative districts have an advantage in drawing up maps that show urban–rural voting differences. By law, U.S. districts for lower houses must have the same number of residents, adjusted after every census. Because territorially large districts are rural and small districts urban, viewers can tell relative population density among districts. Districts of medium size suggest they are suburban. Coloring in Democratic districts in blue and Republican in red will likely show that rural districts went Republican, cities Democrat, particularly true of the 2000, 2004, and 2008 elections. States and counties, of course, were never designed to have equal numbers of residents.

Percent Protestant by State

consumption   Buying things.

outsourcing   U.S. firms producing overseas.

bubble   Market that has gone too high.

manias   Periods of market boom in which greed trumps fear.

panics   Periods of market collapse in which fear trumps greed.

by the late 1990s. The surpluses were less the result of cuts—some of which simply shifted burdens to later years—than of the high-tech and investment boom, which boosted the wealth of the few (the richest 1 percent earn as much as the bottom half of Americans) and thus got more taxes from them. Then recession ended the surplus—both from lower tax revenues and from increased federal spending—and federal budget deficits climbed. The Bush 43 administration had projected a decade of surpluses, so the Republican administration and Congress spent more than ever. Then the Obama administration, fearing a depression, spent more than that, and government debt hit $13 trillion, some 90 percent of GDP. Some other countries, including Japan, are worse. Such levels of debt do not make collapse certain, but they increase fears of it.

Consumer debt was an even bigger problem. The U.S. economy is some 70 percent based on **consumption**, high on a world scale (China: about 35 percent). But Americans as a whole do not earn enough to buy all that is produced to keep prosperity going. To compensate, they were encouraged to take on massive debts, both credit card and home mortgage. Private debt relative to GDP nearly tripled in 30 years. Neither government nor banks attempted to restrain it, and few Americans worried about it. When the debt burden crashed in 2008, home foreclosures and unemployment shot up. The 2008–2009 recession was the longest (18 months) and one of the deepest (minus 4 percent from peak to trough) since the Great Depression. Recovery was slow and jobless. Many people who thought they were middle class discovered they were not.

Inequality

Since the 1970s Americans' incomes have grown less equal and the middle class smaller. The rich get a bigger slice of the nation's economic pie; the poor and much of the middle class get smaller pieces. Those with the right education and skills may do well, but those with a high school education or less do poorly. **Outsourcing**, much of it to newly industrializing Asia, cuts the number and pay of American blue-collar manufacturing jobs. Unions declined to 12.5 percent of the workforce (during the early 1950s, some 40 percent of the U.S. workforce was unionized). Top executives and money managers are compensated extravagantly, and Republican tax cuts favored the rich. In 1977, the richest 1 percent of Americans got 9 percent of the nation's income; in 2007, they got 23.5 percent. Americans who lived off wages, on the other hand, saw their incomes stagnate, offset only by debt and by wives working.

Bubbles

Financial markets tend to produce "**bubbles**," fast growth in investments that let people ignore risk—until the bubbles pop. Some economists blame alternating **manias** and **panics**, both heavily psychological, what Keynes called the "animal spirits" of investor irrationality. He urged government intervention to dampen both. One stock-market bubble ended with the 1929 Crash. The savings and loan bubble of the 1980s, the dot.com bubble of the 1990s, and the housing bubble of the 2000s likewise burst. Asia

entitlement U.S. federal expenditure mandated by law, such as Social Security and Medicare.

has experienced similar bubbles in finance and housing. The big underlying problem with all: Banks and investors lent recklessly, believing there was little risk, and this encouraged high levels of debt. Federal oversight was weak or nonexistent.

The recent home-mortgage crisis is an example: Lenders collected fat fees as they shoveled out risky mortgages to homebuyers who could not repay them. The theory was that home prices only go up, so everyone will be safe. Complex financial "derivatives"—investments that no one could understand—masked the losses so that no one could accurately evaluate assets. When the wave of home foreclosures began, giant institutions literally did not know their own worth, so their shares tumbled and several went bankrupt or were taken over. Economist Robert Shiller called it "the bursting of the largest bubble in history."

WHO IS ENTITLED TO WHAT?

The federal budget is divided into two general categories, discretionary and mandatory. The former can be raised or lowered from year to year. Congress, for example, may decide to increase defense spending and cut highway spending. Mandatory spending—which runs twice as much as discretionary—cannot be so easily changed; it is what the federal budget is stuck with from previous statutory commitments. Mandatory spending in turn is divided into interest payments on the national debt and **entitlements**; together they are half of the federal budget. Interest payments are totally untouchable; if they were cut, future offerings of bonds and treasury notes would have no credibility or customers. The biggest item in the 2011 budget is defense (23 percent), which is also hard to cut. There is not much wiggle room in the U.S. federal budget.

Entitlements are extremely difficult to cut because people are used to them and expect them as a right. They are payments to which one is automatically entitled by law: When you turn 65 and a few months you are entitled to Social Security and Medicare; grow corn or cotton and you get farm-price subsidies. There is no annual cap on entitlement spending; it grows as more people are entitled, what is called "uncontrollable" spending. The 2011 budget devotes 19 percent of all federal spending to Social Security and 13 percent to Medicare. Social Security is in fairly good shape; at current rates it will be solvent until 2041. Medicare, however, will stay solvent only until 2020. These two programs go to seniors, who get seven times what children get from the federal budget. Children don't vote, and oldsters do.

Only a small fraction of federal payments is traditional "welfare" spending; more than 85 percent goes to the middle and upper classes in the form of Social Security, Medicare, government retirement plans, and farm price supports. What goes to poor families includes Medicaid, food stamps, and Supplemental Security

welfare dependency Stuck on welfare with no incentive to get off.

Income. With political realities in mind, what can be cut of the first category—middle-class entitlements? Some people argue that if we eliminated "welfare" spending we could cut taxes, but "welfare" is not the problem; entitlements are. Cuts in welfare spending save little and inflict hardship on society's most vulnerable members, especially children.

How did the U.S. welfare system come about? In the mid-1960s, LBJ launched his War on Poverty, aimed at creating a Great Society. Johnson, who had been the powerful Senate majority leader, got Congress to deliver almost everything he wanted. Then the Vietnam War, with its rising costs and acrimony, seemed to cut down the War on Poverty in its infancy. There wasn't enough money for the growing programs, and the Great Society became discredited. Many of its programs were substantially dismantled or left to die on the vine. Some say the Great Society was never given a chance. Conservatives hold that the undertaking was inherently infeasible, a waste of money that often did more harm than good, locking recipients into **welfare dependency** and encouraging a subculture of drugs and crime. Some poverty specialists, however, say the Great Society programs generally did succeed and lowered the U.S. poverty rate. Conservatives, they say, have exaggerated the inefficiency and misuses that accompany any welfare program and have understated the very real accomplishments.

The Costs of Welfare

Food Stamps Begun as a modest trial program under Kennedy in 1961, the Food Stamp program was implemented nationwide under Johnson in 1964. It has grown significantly, and now more than 40 million Americans (13 percent) benefit. One does not dine well on food stamps; cost per meal per person is figured at about a dollar. One-third of families headed by women receive food stamps.

The Carter administration simplified the program in 1977 by eliminating the provision that recipients *buy* the stamps at a discount with their own money. This policy had meant that the absolutely destitute, people with no money at all, could get no food stamps. Congress changed the law to eliminate the cash payment, and the number of recipients expanded. Reagan, citing an apocryphal story of a young man who used food stamps to buy vodka, tightened eligibility requirements in an effort to eliminate fraud and misuse.

What should be done? The Food Stamp program became bigger than expected, but fraud and waste have not been major factors. Only a few recipients sold food stamps at 50 cents on the dollar to buy liquor and drugs, and all food stamps are now debit cards, which fixes the fraud problem. Cash grants, considered by Carter as a replacement for food stamps, could easily be misused. Direct delivery of surplus commodities, as was done on a small scale in the 1950s and episodically in the 1980s to get rid of government cheese stocks (the result of price supports for dairy farmers), was clumsy and spotty.

Welfare Reform In 1996, President Clinton signed the Personal Responsibility and Work Opportunity Act to "end welfare as we know it." This major welfare reform ended the old Aid to Families with Dependent Children (AFDC) that had begun as part of the 1935 Social Security Act. AFDC had provided federal matching funds to the states to help the poor; most of it went to single mothers. Many accused AFDC of promoting fatherless children and welfare dependency. Because many recipients were nonwhite, the issue became connected with the struggle for racial equality.

workfare Programs limiting the duration of welfare payments and requiring recipients to work or get job training.

The 1996 reform replaced entitlement-type welfare payments with $16.5 billion a year in block grants to the states to spend fighting poverty as they saw fit. Recipients had five years to get off welfare. Many states developed **workfare** programs that required recipients to either take jobs or training. Workfare, which has been tried for years, does not always work and initially costs more than traditional welfare programs, because it must provide both welfare and training for a while. Some recipients who took jobs were still quite poor, because for every dollar they earned,

KEY CONCEPTS ■ WHAT IS POVERTY?

Defining poverty can be tricky. What's "poor" currently might have been "comfortable" in previous eras. Find out how your great-grandparents fared during the Depression. A U.S. Labor Department statistician came up with a formula in 1963 that became standard, although many argue it is out of date. She found that families spent about one-third of their incomes on food, so a "poverty line" is three times a minimal food budget for nonfarm families of four. Using this definition, the percentage of Americans below the poverty line fell from 17.3 percent in 1965, when President Johnson's War on Poverty started, to 11.7 percent in 1973. In 2009, it was 15.7 percent. Black and Hispanic rates are much higher, and one-fifth of America's children are below the poverty line.

Liberals complain that the poverty line—now about $22,000 for a family of four—is set much too low; it can take two to three times that to just get by in big cities, as rent and child care are now bigger items than food. Washington has considered updating the poverty line to include such items. Conservatives point out that poverty figures do not include *noncash* benefits transferred to the poor by government programs— food stamps, for example. Taking such benefits into account raises some poor families above the poverty line.

Before we conclude that the War on Poverty was a success or failure, we must look at the poverty rate in longer perspective. In 1950, some 30 percent of the U.S. population was classified as below the poverty line, and the rate dropped. One of the fastest decreases occurred between 1960 and 1965, *before* the War on Poverty programs were enacted. The U.S. economy expanded from 1950 to 1965, especially during the early 1960s. Jobs were plentiful, and food became cheaper. It is hard to tell if the further drop in the poverty rate from 1965 to 1973 was the result of government programs or of an economy heated by Vietnam War spending.

By the same token, when the poverty rate began to go up again in the mid-1970s, cutbacks in antipoverty spending were only partly to blame; also responsible were the recessions caused by high oil prices and interest rates discussed earlier. Some blame the increase of poverty and homelessness on outsourcing, making many working-class Americans unemployed and pushing them down into the lower class. With the disappearance of modestly paying factory jobs, they faced either low-paid service jobs ("flipping hamburgers") or unemployment and welfare. Antipoverty programs cannot offset massive unemployment caused by long-term trends in the U.S. economy.

they lost around 40 cents in "ancillary benefits," which include food stamps, child day care, and Medicaid. The federal earned income tax credit (EITC), a Republican idea, helps low-paid workers cut their income taxes and even gives some additional cash. Some analysts call EITC the best welfare program because it encourages people to work their way out of poverty.

The 1996 reform came when the U.S. economy was excellent, and most people bumped off welfare found jobs. The unemployment rate for single mothers fell from around 48 percent during the 1980s and early 1990s to 28 percent in 1999. The total number of welfare recipients dropped from 12.2 million in 1996 to 5.8 million in 2000, a decline that does not necessarily mean they got out of poverty; they just got off welfare. The real test of welfare reform is how it holds up during recession. In the recession following the 2008–2009 financial meltdown, unemployment and welfare expenditures shot back up.

Healthcare Reform   The Democrats' healthcare reform, greatly watered down, barely passed in 2010. It did not go nearly as far as most European and Canadian

KEY CONCEPTS ■ POVERTY AND IDEOLOGY

The U.S. debate about poverty is passionately ideological. Conservatives want to limit anti-poverty programs, liberals expand them. The policy analyst must cast ideology aside and gather factual answers to questions such as the following:

Are we talking about welfare or entitlement?

The two categories overlap, but the essence of a welfare program is that it is "means tested," meaning recipients must demonstrate that they are poor according to certain criteria (typically, how much income and how many children). If the program is a pure entitlement, such as Social Security or Medicare, can it realistically be cut?

Do welfare programs have negative consequences?

The great conservative claim is that welfare programs offer incentives for unemployment, illegitimacy, and drug use. Can this be proved or disproved? New York City, with its extensive welfare programs, has a high incidence of poverty. But so does Mississippi, with its weak and underfunded welfare programs. As usual, causality is terribly difficult to prove. Would a massive, nationwide cessation of all welfare programs force the indolent to work? This raises the next question.

Is poverty an unfortunate circumstance or a character defect?

Are people poor because they cannot find work or because they do not want to work? In other words, are the poor really different from you and me? Do they have a "culture of poverty" that instills a "radical improvidence," an indifference to providing for their families and futures? If poverty is a character defect, as most conservatives maintain, then little can be done. If it is the product of unfortunate circumstances, as most liberals maintain, then programs that change those circumstances might get people out of poverty.

How much poverty is simply a lack of good jobs?

Do the jobs available to poor people pay enough for them to support their families? In most of America, people are willing to take medical insurance and will not take effect for several years. It still lacks a "public" option; instead it will operate through private insurers. Critics, not all of them Republicans, worry that the plan is too long, too complex, and too expensive. And it comes at a time when U.S. budget deficits are already swollen from the Iraq and Afghanistan wars and the financial bailouts.

Some say Medicare and Medicaid, the two giants of entitlements, both enacted in 1965, offer warnings of how medical costs escalate. Medicare, a federally funded program for older people, now costs over $490 billion a year. Medicaid combines federal and state funds for poor people and costs almost $300 billion. Both grew so rapidly that benefits had to be limited and eligibility requirements tightened. As 78 million baby boomers start to reach 65 in 2011, Medicare costs will soon double. Who will pay for it?

At least two factors induce exponential growth in medical assistance: More people become eligible and medical costs soar. Medicare is especially expensive, for all get it upon reaching age 65, even rich people. The proportion of older people in American society is increasing steadily, and they are by far the

jobs not much above minimum wage, even though a single mother earning that falls far below the poverty line. Good factory jobs are hard to find because many have moved overseas. Those who would drastically cut welfare should demonstrate there are sufficient jobs with adequate pay. But are poor people generally qualified for decent-paying jobs, or do they lack the skills?

Can we train people out of poverty?

Job training and retraining have long been part of poverty-fighting programs. But do they work? Some who have completed job training still find no work. Can we take people with poor reading and math skills and in a few months make them into skilled technicians? The deeper, underlying problem is the lack of proper education in K–12, which creates an illiterate and innumerate workforce. But is the lack of proper education in the United States the fault of schools and teachers or of families and attitudes? Liberals like to blame schools, conservatives families. Either way, how do you fix the U.S. education system?

What is the international context of domestic poverty?

How much poverty is due to the export of American jobs to low-wage countries? Note how many of your recent purchases were made in China. While lowering costs to consumers, outsourcing has closed thousands of American factories. Is U.S. poverty, then, the natural result of an open world economy in which many countries have much lower labor costs? Should we close our borders to such commerce in order to boost domestic employment? If we did, Americans would live a little less well—their clothing and electronic gadgets would cost more, so they would buy fewer of them—but other Americans would exit poverty through new factory jobs. Our trading partners in other lands would retaliate by keeping out U.S. products, so other U.S. factories would close. On balance, trade protectionism hurts more than it helps.

These are some of the questions we must ask. Simple ideological approaches, either liberal or conservative, often deal with consequences rather than causes. Where ideology reigns, reason has difficulty making its voice heard.

biggest consumers of medical care. Most Americans consume most of their lifetime medical expenses in the last year of life.

Hospitals and doctors, once they are assured of payment, have no incentive to economize. When in doubt, they put the patient in the hospital—at $1,000 a day—and order expensive tests. Some hospitals expanded into medical palaces, and some physicians got rich from Medicare and Medicaid. (Ironically, the powerful American Medical Association had for years lobbied against such "socialized medicine.") Medical costs consume 16 percent of the U.S. gross domestic product, most of it paid by government and private health insurance. Other advanced countries pay less and have healthier populations. Their laws set maximum fees, something U.S. health providers oppose.

Washington tried various ways of tightening up, but medical costs continued to climb. Recipients were required to contribute bigger "copayments" to hold down overuse. Hospitals and doctors were monitored on costs and on how long they kept patients hospitalized. Hospices—nursing homes for the terminally ill—were made allowable under Medicare, as such care is cheaper than hospital care. Competitive bidding began in some states, and patients were assigned only to low-bid hospitals. Fees for each type of disorder were established, and overruns were not reimbursed. Every time insurers tighten medical assistance, patients, families, doctors, and hospitals complain bitterly, and they form a powerful lobby. Any "end of life" decision—at what point to pull the plug?—raises howls of "death panels." But if you never pull the plug, health costs climb even higher. Even conservatives had to admit that the current patchwork of U.S. medical plans was slowly crashing and that something had to be done. People were being shoved out of their private insurance plans for either having "preexisting conditions" or by big hikes in their premiums. Health care and how to pay for it will likely be a major U.S. political quarrel for decades.

HOW BIG SHOULD GOVERNMENT BE?

Americans have the funniest ideas about where their tax dollars go. Many think most of the federal budget goes for welfare, which is not at all the case. Critics suggest it goes to food-stamp and Medicaid fraudsters, but this percentage too is small. As noted earlier, the bulk of federal spending goes not to welfare for the poor but to entitlements for the middle class; it is impossible to repeal or seriously cut most middle-class programs. A Congress dominated by Republicans had to add an expensive prescription-drug benefit to Medicare; otherwise, they would cede the hot issue to Democrats. The complexity of the 2006 program angered many elderly. Fumed one oldster: "It's like having the IRS run by FEMA!" Few discuss trimming Social Security or Medicare expenditures. It's a sure vote-loser. If you want to cut taxes, just what programs are you prepared to cut?

As noted previously, the American welfare state is small compared with that of other countries. Should it get bigger? The American answer, rooted in its political culture, is to keep government small and to suspect and criticize the expansion of government power. But we also recognize that we need government intervention in the economy, education, energy planning, environmental protection, and health care. We have trouble making up our minds about how much government we want. Americans demand various forms of government intervention, but scarcely is the ink on new laws dry before we begin to criticize government bungling. Not understanding where Medicare comes from, one elderly lady told an interviewer, "Don't let the government get its hands on Medicare!" Europeans and Canadians generally do not suffer from this kind of split personality; they mostly accept that government has a major role to play and do not complain as much about their high taxes.

moral hazard Shielding firms from the risky consequences of their behavior.

Americans were in a quandary over the federal government's role in the 2008–2009 financial crisis. In principle, they disliked rescue packages. Both borrowers and lenders should pay for their mistakes, not taxpayers. If government assumes the **moral hazard** of bad loans, firms will just be encouraged in their risky behavior. But the prospect of national economic collapse sobered many into recognizing that government bailouts are sometimes necessary. Even many conservative economists agreed that some firms are "too big to fail" because they would bring down the rest of the economy with them. Scary circumstances turn conservatives into liberals.

The general reluctance to expand government's role, however, may redound to America's long-term advantage. Government programs tend to expand, bureaucracy is inherently inefficient, and ending an entitlement program is all but impossible. Government programs become so sprawling and complex that officials don't even *know* what is in operation, much less how to control it. As political scientist Ira Sharkansky put it, "All modern states are welfare states, and all welfare states are incoherent." Accordingly, it is probably wise to act with caution in expanding government programs.

 EXERCISES

Apply what you learned in this chapter on MyPoliSciKit (www.mypoliscikit.com).

Assessment   Review this chapter using learning objectives, chapter summaries, practice tests, and more.

Menu

Flashcards   Learn the key terms in this chapter; you can test yourself by term or definition.

Flashcards

Video   Analyze recent world affairs by watching streaming video from major news providers.

Videos

Comparative Exercises   Compare political ideas, behaviors, institutions, and policies worldwide.

Comparative
Exercises

KEY TERMS

austerity (p. 296)
bailout (p. 296)
balance of
   payments (p. 298)
bubble (p. 304)
business cycle (p. 297)
consumption (p. 304)
debt (p. 301)
deficit (p. 300)
entitlement (p. 305)

euro (p. 301)
Federal Reserve
   Board (p. 297)
fixed exchange
   rate (p. 298)
floating exchange
   rate (p. 298)
inflation (p. 297)
manias (p. 304)
moral hazard (p. 311)

outsourcing (p. 304)
panics (p. 304)
political
   economy (p. 296)
public policy (p. 296)
recession (p. 297)
stagflation (p. 299)
welfare dependency
   (p. 306)
workfare (p. 307)

FURTHER REFERENCE

Akerlof, George A., and Robert J. Shiller. *Animal Spirits: How Human Psychology Drives the Economy, and Why It Matters for Global Capitalism*. Princeton, NJ: Princeton University Press, 2009.

Baumol, William J., Robert E. Litan, and Carl J. Schramm. *Good Capitalism, Bad Capitalism, and the Economics of Growth and Prosperity*. New Haven, CT: Yale University Press, 2007.

Cassidy, John. *How Markets Fail: The Logic of Economic Calamities*. New York: Farrar, Straus and Giroux, 2009.

Clarke, Peter. *Keynes: The Rise, Fall, and Return of the Twentieth Century's Most Influential Economist*. New York: Bloomsbury, 2009.

DeParle, Jason. *American Dream: Three Women, Ten Kids, and a Nation's Drive to End Welfare*. New York: Viking, 2005.

Ferguson, Niall. *The Ascent of Money: A Financial History of the World*. New York: Penguin, 2009.

Friedman, Benjamin M. *The Moral Consequences of Economic Growth*. New York: Knopf, 2005.

Garfinkle, Norton. *The American Dream vs. the Gospel of Wealth: The Fight for a Productive Middle-Class Economy*. New Haven, CT: Yale University Press, 2007.

Greenspan, Alan. *The Age of Turbulence: Adventures in a New World*. New York: Penguin, 2008.

Hacker, Jacob, and Paul Pierson. *Winner-Take-All Politics: How Washington Made the Rich Richer—and Turned Its Back on the Middle Class*. New York: Simon & Schuster, 2010.

Johnson, Simon, and James Kwak. *13 Bankers: The Wall Street Takeover and the Next Financial Meltdown*. New York: Pantheon, 2010.

Kaletsky, Anatole. *Capitalism 4.0: The Birth of a New Economy in the Aftermath of Crisis*. New York: Public Affairs, 2010.

Kotlikoff, Laurence J., and Scott Burns. *The Coming Generational Storm: What You Need to Know about America's Economic Future*. Cambridge, MA: MIT Press, 2004.

Krugman, Paul. *The Return of Depression Economics and the Crisis of 2008*. New York: Norton, 2009.

Page, Benjamin I., and Lawrence R. Jacobs. *Class War? What Americans Really Think about Economic Inequality*. Chicago: University of Chicago Press, 2009.

Posner, Richard A. *The Crisis of Capitalist Democracy*. Cambridge, MA: Harvard University Press, 2010.

Rajan, Raghuram G. *Fault Lines: How Hidden Fractures Still Threaten the World Economy*.

Princeton, NJ: Princeton University Press, 2010.

Reinhart, Carmen M., and Kenneth S. Rogoff. *This Time Is Different: Eight Centuries of Financial Folly*. Princeton, NJ: Princeton University Press, 2009.

Samuelson, Robert J. *The Great Inflation and Its Aftermath: The Past and Future of American Affluence*. New York: Random House, 2008.

Shiller, Robert J. *The Subprime Solution: How Today's Global Financial Crisis Happened, and What to Do About It*. Princeton, NJ: Princeton University Press, 2009.

Smick, David M. *The World Is Curved: Hidden Dangers to the Global Economy*. New York: Penguin, 2008.

Stiglitz, Joseph E. *Freefall: America, Free Markets, and the Sinking of the World Economy*. New York: Norton: 2010.

Thaler, Richard H., and Cass R. Sunstein. *Nudge: Improving Decisions About Health, Wealth, and Happiness*. New Haven, CT: Yale University Press, 2008.

Political Violence

Greek protesters, angry at deep budgetary and job cuts, riot in Athens in 2010. (Pascal Rossignol/Corbis)

Political scientists—under the influence of the "systems" approach discussed in Chapter 2—often talked about systems and stability. Some even depicted political systems as well-oiled machines that never broke down. But in the late 1960s, the media showed images of violence and revolution, and political scientists began criticizing the status-quo orientation of their discipline and directed their attention instead to breakdown and upheaval. Some had overlooked the tension and violence in their own backyards. With the inner-city riots of 1965–1968, academics suddenly discovered violence in America. Formerly viewing violence as abnormal, many academics eventually suggested, along with black militant H. Rap Brown, that "violence is as American as cherry pie." By the same token, Europeans were shocked to learn, as the nationalities of ex-Yugoslavia slaughtered each other in the 1990s, that they were not immune to violence either.

QUESTIONS TO CONSIDER

1. What causes political systems to break down?
2. What purposes can violence serve?
3. Which types of violence are most prevalent today?
4. How can modernization lead to unrest?
5. How can you tell if there has been a revolution?
6. Why are intellectuals prominent in revolutions?
7. What are Brinton's stages of revolution?
8. Do all revolutions end badly? Why?
9. Why is revolution no longer fashionable?

SYSTEM BREAKDOWN

Political systems can and do break down. Indeed, most countries have suffered or are suffering from **system breakdown**, marked by major riots, civil wars, terrorism, military **coups**, and authoritarian governments of varying degrees of harshness. Dictatorships are rarely the work of small bands of conspirators alone; they are usually the result of system collapse, which permits small but well-organized groups— usually the military—to take over. This is why it does little good to denounce a cruel military regime. True, some governments commit acts of great evil; military regimes in Argentina, Chile, and Guatemala killed thousands on the slightest suspicion of leftism. But why did these coups happen? Why does system breakdown recur repeatedly in some countries? These are the deeper questions that must be asked if we are to begin to understand these horror stories.

system breakdown Major political malfunction or instability.

coup From the French *coup d'état*, hit at the state; extralegal takeover of government, usually by military.

Breakdown starts when legitimacy erodes. Legitimacy, you may recall from Chapter 1, is citizens' feeling that the regime's rule is rightful and should be obeyed. Where legitimacy is high, governments need few police officers; where it is low, they need many. In England, for example, people are mostly law-abiding; police are few and hardly any carry firearms. In Northern Ireland, until recently, terrorists killed with bombs and bullets, for a portion of the population saw the government as illegitimate. Here, the police are armed, and British troops until recently patrolled with automatic weapons and armored cars. The civil war in Northern Ireland cost some 3,600 lives.

Legitimacy erodes as the regime shows it is unfair and ineffective in running the country. Uncontrollable inflation, blatant corruption, massive unemployment, or defeat in war demonstrate that the government is ineffective.

Violence as a Symptom

Violence—riots, mass strikes, terrorist bombings, and political assassinations—by itself does not indicate that revolution is nigh. Indeed, the most common response to serious domestic unrest is not revolution at all but military takeover. Violence can be seen as symptomatic of the erosion of the government's effectiveness and legitimacy. Perhaps nothing major will come of the unrest; new leadership may calm and encourage the nation and begin to deal with the problems that caused the unrest, as Franklin D. Roosevelt did in the 1930s. But if the government is clumsy, if it tries to simply crush and silence discontent, it can make things worse. In 1932, the "Bonus Army" of World War I veterans seeking benefits to help them in the Depression was dispersed by army troops under General Douglas MacArthur. Public revulsion at the veterans' rough treatment helped turn the country decisively against President Herbert Hoover in that fall's election.

Domestic violence is both deplorable and informative. It tells that not all is going well, that there are certain groups that, out of desperation or conviction, are willing to break the law in order to bring change. A government's first impulse when faced with domestic unrest is to crush it and blame a handful of "radicals and troublemakers." To be sure, instigators may deliberately provoke incidents, but the fact that some people support anti-system groups should tell the authorities that something is wrong. At the 1968 Democratic convention, Chicago police went wild in attacking those who had come to protest the Vietnam War—as well as many who just happened to be passing by. The convention ignored the protesters and nominated President Johnson's vice president, Hubert Humphrey, who lost, largely because of his equivocal position on the war. The riot showed that the Democratic Party had drifted out of touch with important elements of its constituency, which only four years earlier had voted for Johnson because he vowed to keep the country out of war. The Democrats should have been listening to instead of ignoring the protesters.

As much as we deplore violence, we have to admit that in some cases it serves a purpose. The United States as a whole and Congress in particular paid little attention to the plight of inner-city blacks until a series of riots ripped U.S. cities in the late 1960s. The death and destruction were terrible, but there seemed to be no other way to get the media's, the public's, and the government's attention. The rioting in this case "worked"; that is, it brought a major—if not very successful—effort to improve America's decaying cities. When America forgot about its inner cities in the 1980s, new rioting reminded us of the problems still there.

> **primordial** Groups people are born into, such as religions and tribes.

The white minority government of South Africa used to pride itself on the capture or killing of black guerrillas. The South African security forces were proficient, but the fact that thousands of young black South Africans were willing to take up arms against the whites-only regime should have told the Pretoria government something. The ruling whites-only National Party had imagined for decades that Africans (75 percent of the country's population) would simply keep their place (on 13 percent of the land). Pretoria engaged in no dialogue with the country's Africans; it expected them merely to obey. Finally, growing violence persuaded the government to begin a dialogue leading to the release of Nelson Mandela from prison, the political enfranchisement of the black majority, and a government elected by all citizens.

China currently experiences thousands of "mass incidents" a year in which citizens gather to protest corrupt local officials, the seizure of their land, or police cover-up of crimes. The regime tries to handle protests with warnings but sometimes resorts to tear gas and gunfire. The message to Beijing is clear: Institute reforms to clean up the corruption and misuse of power before widespread anger explodes. Instead, the regime figures that rapid economic growth, rising living standards, and nationalism will buy off or deflect discontent. It may be mistaken.

Types of Violence

Not all violence is the same. Violence has been categorized in several ways. One of the best is that of political scientist Fred R. von der Mehden, who sees five general types of violence.

Primordial Primordial violence grows out of conflicts among the basic communities—ethnic, national, or religious—into which people are born. Fighting between Sunni and Shia in Iraq, Arabs and Darfuris in Sudan, Tibetans and Chinese in Tibet, and Hutus and Tutsis in Rwanda (which killed some 800,000 in the mid-1990s) are examples of **primordial** violence. It is not necessarily confined to the developing areas of the world, though, for such antagonisms appear in ex-Yugoslavia, the Basque country of Spain, and Northern Ireland, where Protestants and Catholics conducted a nearly tribal feud.

Separatist Separatist violence, sometimes an outgrowth of primordial conflict, aims at independence for the group in question. Tamils in northern Sri Lanka fought from 1983 to 2009 to break away; more than 60,000 were killed. The Igbos tried to break away from Nigeria with their new state of Biafra in the late 1960s, but they were defeated in a long and costly war. But the Bengalis did break away from Pakistan with their new state of Bangladesh in 1971. Croatia and Bosnia fought Serbia in order to separate from Yugoslavia in the early 1990s. Iraqi Kurds want their own state, which could fuel parallel efforts among the Kurds of Turkey, Syria, and Iran.

KEY CONCEPTS ■ TERRORISM

The attacks of September 11 remind us that terrorism is alive. Basically, terrorism is a strategy to weaken a hated political authority. Related to guerrilla or underground warfare, it is not a new thing. The Irish Republican Army and Internal Macedonian Revolutionary Organization (IMRO) go back more than a century. Political, ethnic, nationalistic, religious, economic, and ideological grudges fuel terrorist activity. **Terrorism** is a strategy of groups with grudges.

The governments that terrorists hate are usually corrupt and repressive, which unfortunately is standard in the Middle East. Muslim terrorists hate the United States for supporting these governments. Because they are fighting a more powerful foe, **jihadis** use tactics calculated to surprise and horrify. They put bombs in cars, trucks, and boats and strap them on their own bodies. Before September 11, few thought of using tons of jet fuel to bring down skyscrapers. The only advice that can be given: "Expect the unexpected."

Terrorists are not insane; they are highly calculating. They aim their acts to panic their enemies, to gain publicity and recruits, and to get the foe to overreact and drive more people to side with the terrorists. Osama bin Laden and his followers were calm and rational in their pursuit of political goals that strike outsiders as mistaken and evil. "One man's terrorist," an old saying goes, "is another man's freedom fighter." Basques, Kurds, Palestinians, and Tamils desire their own state. Spain, Turkey, Israel, and Sri Lanka, respectively, do not want them to have their own state and repress their movements. Thus were born, respectively, ETA, PKK, PLO, and the Tamil Tigers. There's always a reason behind every terrorist movement. In these cases, it's national liberation. Al Qaeda aims not for the liberation of separate peoples but for uniting the whole community of Islam, the *umma*.

Terrorism is group activity, the work of committed believers in political causes. Lone gunmen such as John Hinkley, who shot President Reagan, are deranged. Currently, the Middle East is the breeding ground for much terrorist activity.

The reasons are both material and psychological. High birth rates produce many unemployed youth who are attracted to the simplistic lessons of *Islamism* (see page 55), which has made the United States an object of hate. Al Qaeda recruited Sunni Muslims everywhere and bonded them into a religious goal, to make all Muslim countries fundamentalist, remove U.S. influence from the Middle East, and destroy Israel. Bin Laden called his terrorists "the brothers," as if they were a religious order, which they nearly were. Ultimately, only modernization of Muslim lands—a long and very difficult task—can solve the problem of Islamist terrorism.

Many experts now fear it's only a matter of time before terrorists buy a nuclear device or fissile material from North Korea, Pakistan, or Russia. When they get a nuke, they'll use it. Worldwide, there are already more than 30,000 nuclear warheads plus fissile material (highly enriched uranium or plutonium) for another 240,000. Much of this material, especially in ex-Soviet lands, is poorly secured and easily stolen and smuggled by gangsters in league with crooked officials. A nuclear device would not have to be an advanced or compact model to blow up a major city.

All nations officially denounce terrorism, but some—such as Syria, North Korea, and Iran—engage in "state-sponsored terrorism." Although unproven, the 1981 attempt to kill Pope John Paul II clearly traces back to the Kremlin. The Turkish gunman, an escaped convict, got his money, forged passport, and gun from Bulgarian security police, who were supervised by the Soviet KGB. Terrorists need bases, money, arms, and bombs, usually supplied by the intelligence services of one country that wants to undermine another.

Does terrorism work? Rarely, and seldom alone. A touch of violence on top of massive political and economic pressures persuaded whites to abandon their power monopoly in South Africa in the early 1990s. In most cases, however, especially after civilians have been killed, terrorism just stiffens the resolve of the target country. Israelis, attacked by suicide bombers, grew less willing to compromise with Palestinians. The attacks of September 11 united most Americans behind the elimination of al Qaeda and the invasion of Afghanistan and Iraq. But the U.S. occupation of Iraq fostered more terrorism and taught Washington the difficulties of building stable democracy amid chaos.

U.S. agencies, even with the new Department of Homeland Security, are not well prepared to fight terrorism. The FBI and CIA still have trouble communicating with each other, still less with the cop on the beat. Terrorism is tricky to fight because it falls between war and crime. Like war, it has big stakes, but like crime it is extremely diffuse, more like wisps of fog. Fighting it is often presented as a "war," but that is too simple. Terrorism is not a country and cannot be invaded like one. It requires something between an army and police, such as extremely mobile SWAT teams with language skills.

The good news about Islamist terrorism is that it has already begun to fade. Muslim clerics now denounce its violence, especially for killing Muslims, its chief victims. It is divided: Sunnis despise Shia. Al Qaeda, a strictly Sunni movement, has mostly killed Shia Muslims in Iraq. Islamism has no economic plan for putting food on the table, as Iranians have discovered. Several former activists have turned against and denounced al Qaeda as deceptive and extremist. Time may solve the problem.

On 9/11 in 2001, terrorists crashed jetliners into the twin towers of the World Trade Center in New York City, here seen across the Brooklyn Bridge. (Reuters/Sara K. Schwittek/Landov)

terrorism   Political use of violence to weaken a hated authority.

jihadi   From *jihad* (holy war); Muslim holy warrior.

praetorianism   From the Praetorian Guard in ancient Rome; tendency of military takeovers.

Revolutionary   Revolutionary violence is aimed at overthrowing or replacing an existing regime, such as the Islamists (see Chapter 3) who want to take over Muslim countries and make them fundamentalist. Countries such as Algeria, Egypt, Saudi Arabia, and Pakistan are threatened by violent underground Islamist movements. The Sandinistas' ouster of Somoza in Nicaragua, the fall of the shah of Iran, both in 1979, and guerrilla warfare in Colombia are examples of revolutionary violence. Until recently, Central America and Southern Africa were scenes of revolutionary violence. Von der Mehden includes under this category "counterrevolutionary" violence, the efforts of conservative groups to counteract revolutionary attempts—for instance, the killings carried out by Colombian "self-defense forces." The attempts to crush liberalizing movements in Hungary in 1956, Czechoslovakia in 1968, and Poland in 1970 and 1980 would also come under this heading, with the ironic twist that here the Communists were the counterrevolutionary force.

Coups   Coups are usually aimed against revolution, corruption, and chaos. Coups are almost always military, although the military usually has connections with and support from key civilian groups, as in the Brazilian coup of 1964. Most coups involve little violence, at least initially. Army tanks surround the presidential palace, forcing the president's resignation and usually exile, and a general takes over as president. When the military still senses opposition, though, it can go insane with legalized murder. Some 30,000 Argentines "disappeared" following the military takeover of 1976, many dumped alive at sea for the sharks. The Chilean military killed nearly 3,000 following its 1973 coup. Since the 1954 coup, the military in little Guatemala murdered 200,000 on suspicion of leftism. In Latin America, the counterrevolutionary terror that follows some coups is far bloodier than anything the revolutionaries have done.

Once a country has had one coup, chances are it will have another. Some countries get stuck in **praetorianism**. Since 1932, Thailand has had 18 coup attempts, 11 of them successful. Pakistan has had four coups since independence in 1947, the latest in 1999. Given their current unrest, new coups in both countries are possible. Coups generally occur because the civilian institutions of government—parties, parliaments, and executives—are weak, corrupt, and ineffective, leaving the military the choice of taking over or chaos.

Issues   Some violence does not fit any of these categories. Violence oriented to particular issues is a catchall category and generally less deadly than the other kinds. Protests against globalization, strikes by Greeks and French protesting austerity in 2010, and riots triggered by police beating minority youths are examples of issue-oriented violence. Unemployed and hungry Brazilians have looted supermarkets. Chinese villagers turn riotous at local officials who invent fake "taxes" and put the money in their pockets. In 1976, black students in South Africa's Soweto township protested against having to learn Afrikaans in school; police shot down several hundred of them. There may be a fine line between issue-oriented violence and revolutionary violence, for if the issue is serious and the police repression brutal, protests over an issue can turn revolutionary.

thinkpiece   Essay based on logic rather than on firm evidence.

analogy   Taking one thing as the model for another.

dysanalogy   Showing that one thing is a poor model for another.

All of these categories—and others—are arbitrary. Some situations fit more than one category. Some start in one category and escalate into another. The complaints of ethnic Albanians in Kosovo against their second-class status led successively to Albanian political parties, protests, underground groups, violence, and armed rebellion that broke Kosovo away from Serbia in 1999. No country, even a highly developed one, is totally immune to some kind of violence.

HOW TO . . .   ■   CONSTRUCT A THINKPIECE

Sometimes instructors want you to play with ideas rather than concentrate on theses, evidence, and endnotes. They may want you to consider how logically things might unfold, to anticipate events. This is called a **thinkpiece**, and it is quite useful in political science, where we often lack important data but still need an informed estimate of what is likely to happen.

Thinkpieces are often justifiable because we know that many data are flawed. Statistics from developing countries are mostly estimates. Some data are partly subjective, such as the Corruption Perception Index. Top decisions are made behind closed doors, even in democracies, leaving us with anecdotal evidence about who influenced whom. All data are historical; none come from the future. How then can we discuss the possibilities for democracy in China, for authoritarianism in Russia, or for Iran developing nuclear weapons? Soviet specialists who gathered much evidence failed to anticipate the collapse of the Soviet Union. Why? Because it hadn't happened yet, so there were no data.

To counteract this kind of learned helplessness, we turn to logic and construct an "if-then" (see page 217) essay: If A is repeatedly the case, then logically A will appear in similar situations. For example: Countries that modernize and grow their per capita GDP to over $8,000 mostly turn into democracies, as happened in Taiwan and South Korea. Does this mean China will turn democratic in a few years? We have no firm data for this, just an **analogy** drawn from the pattern of the region.

Reasoning by analogy, of course, is often mistaken, as no two situations are exactly alike. China is quite different from Taiwan and South Korea. We can get into trouble with false analogies. One infamous analogy compared the giveaway of Czechoslovakia to Hitler at Munich in 1938 with the challenge the United States faced in Vietnam in 1965. Intelligent Americans said "No more Munichs" in plunging us into the Vietnam War. But a good thinkpiece corrects for mistaken analogies by pointing out the **dysanalogy** between the two situations.

If political scientists are unwilling to do thinkpieces, what good are we on the great questions of the day, questions for which data are missing, mistaken, or incomplete? Do we have to wait until all the facts are in before making such statements as "Israel and Iran sincerely hate each other, and Iran is building nuclear weapons; nuclear war between them is possible"? A thinkpiece is not wild speculation; it is grounded in evidence but does not shy away from carrying it to a logical outcome. Some of the most interesting political science articles are thinkpieces.

Change as a Cause of Violence

Many writers find the underlying cause of domestic unrest in the changes societies go through as they modernize. Purely traditional societies with old authority patterns and simple economies are relatively untroubled by violence. People live as their ancestors lived and expect little. Likewise, modern, advanced societies with rational types of authority and productive economies have relatively minor types of violence. It is the in-between stage, as modernization is upsetting traditional societies, when violence is most likely. Such societies have left one world, that of traditional stability, but have not yet arrived in the new world of modern stability. Everything is changing in such societies—the economy, religious attitudes, lifestyle, and the political system—leaving people worried, confused, and ripe for violent actions.

KEY CONCEPTS ■ RISING EXPECTATIONS

One way of looking at what economic growth does to a society is to represent it graphically (see pages 262–263). Here the solid line represents actual economic change in a modernizing society—generally upward. The broken line represents people's expectations. In a still traditional society—at the graph's left—both actual performance and expectations are low. As growth takes hold, however, expectations start rising faster than actual improvement. Then may come a situation that produces a downturn in the economy—bad harvests, a drop in the price of the leading export commodity, or too much foreign indebtedness—and expectations are frustrated. A big gap suddenly opens between what people want and what they can get. In the words of Daniel Lerner, the "want:get ratio" becomes unhinged, producing a "revolution of rising frustrations."

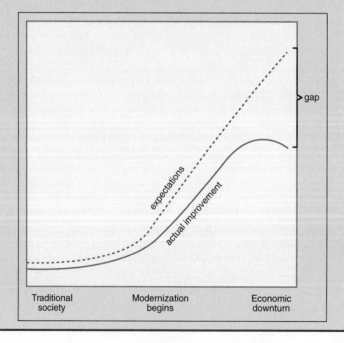

Economic change can be the most unsettling. The curious thing is that improvement can be as dangerous as impoverishment. The great French social scientist Alexis de Tocqueville observed that "though the reign of Louis XVI was the most prosperous period of the monarchy, this very prosperity hastened the outbreak of the Revolution of 1789." Why should this be? When people are permanently poor and beaten down, they have no hope for the future; they are miserable but quiet. When things improve, people start imagining a better future; their aspirations are awakened. No longer content with their lot, they want improvement fast, faster than even a growing economy can deliver. Worse, during times of prosperity, some people get rich faster than others, arousing jealousy. Certain groups feel bypassed by the economic growth and turn especially bitter; the Marxists call this "class antagonisms." Revolutionary feeling, however, typically does not arise among the poor but among what Crane Brinton called the "not unprosperous people who feel restraint, cramp, [and] annoyance" at a government that impedes their right to even faster progress.

> **relative deprivation**   Feeling of some groups that they are missing out on economic growth.
>
> **intellectuals**   Educated people who think deeply about things.

This is an extremely delicate time in the life of a nation. Rebellion and revolution can break out. The underlying problem, as Ted Robert Gurr emphasized, is not poverty itself but **relative deprivation**. The very poor seldom revolt; they're too busy feeding their families. But once people have a full belly they start noticing that others are living much better than they. This sense of relative deprivation may spur them to anger, violence, and occasionally revolution. Gurr's findings match those of Tocqueville and Brinton: Revolutions come when things are generally getting better, not when they're getting worse. China should take careful note.

Other changes can spur unrest. Anthropologist Eric R. Wolf argued that the shift from simple subsistence farming to cash crops dependent on markets, landlords, and bankers impoverishes many peasants and turns them from quietude to revolution. It was precisely the economic modernization of agriculture in Mexico, Russia, China, Vietnam, Algeria, and Cuba that paved the way for successful peasant-based revolutions in those countries, according to Wolf. Rapid population growth is also associated with civil strife. One study found that 80 percent of civil conflicts from 1970 to 2000 came in countries where at least 60 percent of the population was under 30 years of age. Unemployed young males are naturally restless.

The political system may be out of date as well, based on inherited position with no opportunity for mass participation. As the economy improves, educational levels rise. People learn abstract ideas such as "freedom" and "democracy." Especially among intellectuals, there is growing fury at despotic rulers. Peasants may hate the system for squeezing them economically, but urban **intellectuals** hate it for suppressing rights and freedoms. It is the confluence of these two forces, argued Samuel P. Huntington—the "numbers" of the peasants and the "brains" of the intellectuals—that makes revolutions.

REVOLUTIONS

A **revolution** is a quick, dramatic system change that throws out the old system along with its elites. A small or moderate change that essentially leaves the system intact is reform, not revolution. Some regimes, to quiet mass discontent, claim they are going through a revolution, but the changes may be largely cosmetic. One test of a real revolution is to see if it has swept out old elites. If they are still in power, there has been no revolution. In a radical revolution, the new elite gets rid of the old one by guillotine, firing squad, and exile. Revolution is not necessarily bloody, however. In 1989, most East European countries underwent dramatic system change without bloodshed. (Romania was the bloody exception.) South Africa negotiated a revolution in the early 1990s.

---

revolution   Sudden replacement of an old system by a new one.

utopia   An imagined and idealized perfect system.

Frustration is one thing; revolution is something else. People may be unhappy over one thing or another—peasants over crop prices, intellectuals over lack of freedom, businesspeople over corruption, and so on. But if there is no organization to focus their discontents, little will happen. Unrest and discontent by themselves will not bring down a regime; for that, organization is essential. In a study of Brazilian political attitudes under the military dictatorship, Peter McDonough and Antonio Lopez Pina found "a substantial amount of unchanneled dissatisfaction with the authoritarian regime," but it was "free-floating" resentment not especially directed against the government. They suggest that "in the absence of organizational alternatives, resistance is most likely to take the form of apathy and indifference."

The previous factors we have considered may point to violence—rioting and strikes—but without organization, they will not produce a revolution. Who provides the organization? For this, we turn to the role of intellectuals.

Intellectuals and Revolution

Intellectuals are nearly everywhere discontent with the existing state of affairs because they are highly educated and acquainted with a variety of ideas, some of them **utopian**. Preachers, teachers, lawyers, journalists, and others who deal with ideas often have a professional stake in criticizing the system. If everything were fine, there would be little to talk or write about. Intellectuals, although sometimes better off, are seldom wealthy. They may resent people who are richer but not as smart—businesspeople and government officials.

Such factors predispose some intellectuals—but by no means all or even a majority—to develop what James Billington called a "revolutionary faith" that the current system can be replaced with something much better. According to Billington, revolution begins with this "fire in the minds of men." Common folk, ordinary workers and peasants, are seldom interested in abstract ideologies (see Chapter 3); they want improved material conditions. It is the intellectuals' idealistic convictions that provide revolutionary movements with the cement that holds them together, the goals they aim for, and a leadership stratum.

Most twentieth-century revolutionary movements were founded and led by educated people. Lenin, son of a provincial education official, was a brilliant law graduate. Mao Zedong helped found the Chinese Communist Party while a library assistant at Beijing University. Fidel Castro and most of his original guerrilla fighters

KEY CONCEPTS ■ REVOLUTIONARY POLITICAL WARFARE IN VIETNAM

Many people speak of "guerrilla warfare," but this is a misnomer and a redundancy, for *guerrilla* is simply Spanish for "little war," what Spaniards practiced against Napoleon. It is not really about ambushes and booby traps but the accompanying political action. The two combined equal *revolutionary political warfare*, which Bernard Fall described as the struggle "to establish a competitive system of control over the population." Fall, an expert on Vietnam who died when he stepped on a land mine there in 1967, emphasized *administration* as the crux of revolutionary warfare. "When a country is being subverted it is not being outfought; it is being outadministered. Subversion is literally administration with a minus sign in front."

Fall discovered, both under the French in North Vietnam during the early 1950s and under the Americans in South Vietnam during the early 1960s, that the Communists were collecting taxes throughout most of the country under the very noses of the regimes they were overthrowing. The occupying power, whether French or American, deceived itself by being able to drive through villages in armored convoys; this does not indicate administrative control, which may be in the hands of the insurgents. The emphasis on military hardware is a big mistake, argued Fall, for it detracts from the administrative element.

The Vietnamese insurgents were able to outadminister the regime for several reasons. In the first place, they could identify closely with the population, something the French and Americans could never do. Indeed, the fact that the anti-Communist side in both Vietnam wars was connected with white foreigners gave the kiss of death to the effort. There was no political

package the French or Americans could sell to the locals. Even the Saigon rulers lacked legitimacy among their countrymen. The Diem and subsequent Saigon governments were run by Central and North Vietnamese urban Catholics who disliked the largely Buddhist rural South Vietnamese. The Saigon officials were city dwellers who disdained assignments in the provinces and working with the peasants, which was precisely the Communists' strong point.

Terror, to be sure, plays a role in revolutionary political warfare. The Vietcong murdered Saigon officials and government-appointed village headmen. But the villagers were not uniformly horrified at such terror because it was selective and targeted at people who were outsiders anyway. To many peasants, the Vietcong executions seemed like extralegal punishment for collaborators. When the Americans made whole villages disappear, that was terror. There's nothing selective about napalm.

While the insurgent is patiently building a network to supplant the regime, the occupier or government is impatiently trying to substitute firepower for legitimacy. The killing of civilians produces more sympathizers and recruits for the guerrillas. The government's overreliance on firepower erodes its tenuous moral claims to leadership of the nation. Some critics wonder if the American people and leadership ever understood what we were up against in Vietnam and repeated the mistakes in Iraq and Afghanistan. We fought a military war while our opponents fought a political war, and in the end the political mattered more. Said one American officer as he surveyed the smoking ruins of a town, "Unfortunately, we had to destroy the town in order to save it."

were law school graduates. One of them, however—the famous Che Guevara, who was killed in 1967 while trying to foment revolution in Bolivia—was a medical doctor. The leader of Peru's Shining Path guerrillas was a philosophy professor. The leaders of Iran's revolution against the shah were either religious or academically trained intellectuals.

The Stages of Revolution

In his 1938 classic book, *The Anatomy of Revolution*, Harvard historian Crane Brinton (1898–1968) developed a theory that all revolutions pass through similar stages, rather like a human body passing through the stages of an illness. In the English revolution of the 1640s, the American Revolution of 1776, the French Revolution of 1789, and the Russian Revolution of 1917, Brinton found the following rough uniformities.

The Old Regime Decays   Administration breaks down, and taxes rise. People no longer believe in the government; in fact, the government doubts itself. Intellectuals become alienated from the regime and turn to a proposed idealized system. All this is happening while the economy is generally on the upgrade, but this provokes discontent and jealousy.

The First Stage of Revolution   Committees, networks, cells, or conspiracies form, dedicated to overthrowing the old regime. People refuse to pay taxes. A political impasse arises that cannot be solved because the lines are too deeply drawn. The government calls in troops, which backfires because the troops desert and the people are further enraged. The initial takeover is easy, for the old regime has effectively put itself out of business. Popular exultation breaks out.

At First, Moderates Take Over   People who opposed the old regime but were still connected with it by dint of background or training assume command. They initiate moderate, nonradical reforms, which are not enough for extremists among the revolutionaries; they accuse the moderates of cowardice and of compromising with the forces of the old regime. The moderates are "nice guys" and not ruthless enough to crush the radicals, who exist side by side with the moderates in a sort of parallel government.

The Extremists Take Over   More ruthless and better organized than the moderates and knowing exactly what they want, the extremists overthrow the moderates and drive the revolution to a frenzied high point. Everything old is thrown out. People are required to be "good" and obey the new, idealistic society the extremists construct. "Bad" people are punished in a reign of terror. Even revolutionary comrades who are deemed to have strayed from the true path are executed. As French revolutionary Danton reflected at his trial: "The revolution devours its children." The entire society appears to go mad in what Brinton likened to a high fever during an illness.

A "Thermidor" Ends the Reign of Terror   Eventually, the society can take no more revolution. People, even revolutionaries, become exhausted from the frenzy and want to settle down, get the economy working again, and enjoy some personal security and pleasure. Then comes a **Thermidor**—so named after the French revolutionary month during which the extremist Robespierre was guillotined—which Brinton described as a convalescence after a fever. Often a dictator, who ends up resembling the tyrants of the old regime, takes over to restore order, something most people welcome.

Thermidor   Summer month of French revolutionary calendar that marked end of revolutionary extremism.

shah   Persian for king.

ayatollah   Top cleric in Shia Islam.

Another Harvard scholar, sociologist Theda Skocpol, produced a more recent classic on revolution, emphasizing the role of the state. Revolutions do not simply bubble up from below but start at the top, from governments caught in situations they cannot manage, "state crises." International pressures such as war and fiscal

COMPARING ■ THE IRANIAN REVOLUTIONARY CYCLE

The Iranian revolution closely followed Brinton's pattern of previous revolutions. The Iranian economy boomed, especially with the quadrupling of oil prices in 1973–1974, but economic growth was uneven. Some people got rich fast, provoking jealousy. Corruption and inflation soared. Many educated Iranians opposed the shah's dictatorship; students especially hated the **shah** for his repression of freedoms.

Networks of conspirators formed, rallying around the figure of exiled **Ayatollah** Khomeini and using mosques as their meeting places. Major riots broke out in 1978, but the use of troops to quell riots simply enraged more Iranians. Soldiers began to desert. Always disdainful of democracy and mass participation in politics, the shah had relied on his dreaded SAVAK secret police, but even they could no longer contain the revolution. In January 1979, the shah left and Khomeini returned to Iran.

Before he left, the shah named a moderate revolutionary, Bakhtiar, to head the government. But the very fact of being chosen by the shah ruined Bakhtiar, and the newly returned ayatollah, who instantly became the de facto power in Iran, replaced him with Bazargan, another moderate, but one never connected with the shah. Bazargan's government didn't count for much,

though, because real power resided with Khomeini's Revolutionary Council. In November 1979, radical Islamic students, angered over the shah's admission into the United States, seized the U.S. Embassy and began the famous "hostage crisis" that lasted more than a year. Bazargan, realizing he was powerless, resigned.

Muslim extremists devoted to Khomeini took over and purged anyone they did not control. Firing squads worked overtime to eliminate suspected "bad" people, including fellow revolutionaries who had deviated. Tens of thousands of young Iranians, promised instant admission to heaven, threw their lives away in repelling Iraqi invaders.

Strict Islamic standards of morality were enforced—no alcohol or drugs, veils for women, and suppression of non-Islamic religions. After Khomeini died in 1989, the Iranian revolution gradually calmed and stabilized. There was not one single event to mark a Thermidor, but in 1997 a moderate, Mohammed Khatami, won the presidency in a landslide with promises of greater freedom and economic improvement. Khatami's reforms were blocked because real power stayed in the hands of the religious elite, which many Iranians now hate. We may not have seen the last upheaval in Iran.

strain can lead to *elite* (see Chapter 6) divisions and mass mobilization. As Russia was losing to Germany in World War I, the tsarist state collapsed, giving Lenin's small Bolshevik party a chance to grab power. Japan's conquest of China in World War II ruined the effectiveness of the Nationalists and let the Communists win the Chinese Civil War. Without war, it is doubtful that Communism would have taken over Russia or China.

AFTER THE REVOLUTION

Revolutions show a persistent tendency to overthrow one form of tyranny only to replace it with another. In little more than a decade, the French kings had been replaced by Napoleon, who crowned himself emperor and supervised a police state far more thorough than anything previous. The partial despotism of the tsars was replaced by the perfect despotism of Stalin. Russian life was freer and economic growth faster at the turn of the twentieth century under the inefficient tsarist system than under the Communists. Fidel Castro threw out the crooked Batista regime, and Cuban freedom and economic growth declined abruptly.

What good are revolutions? One is tempted to despair with Simon Bolivar, the liberator of South America, who said, "He who aids a revolution plows the sea." In general, revolutions end badly. (As soon as you can accept that statement, you have become to some degree a conservative.)

But what about the United States? We call our 1776–1781 struggle with Britain the Revolutionary War. Some say it was not really a revolution, for it did not remake American society. Indeed, some of its greatest leaders were wealthy and prominent figures in colonial society. They wanted simply to get rid of British rule but keep their elite positions. The American struggle was more a war of independence than a revolution, some argue, and extremists never seized control. Others point out that there was a great deal of revolutionary violence, directed especially at America's Tories, colonials who remained pro-British. Some 100,000 fled in fear to Canada.

Hannah Arendt (1906–1975) also believed the American struggle was indeed a revolution, perhaps history's only complete revolution, for it alone ended with a new foundation of liberty instead of the tyranny that came with other revolutions. According to Arendt, American revolutionaries were fortunate in that they did not have to wrestle with the difficult "social question" that obsessed the French revolutionaries. America was prosperous, and wealth was distributed rather equally. The American struggle was not sidetracked by the poverty problem, so it could focus on establishing a just and durable constitution with balanced powers and political freedom. It was the genius—or, in part, luck—of the American Revolution that it was a purely *political* and not a social matter. America needed no guillotine, for there was no aristocratic class to behead. It needed no demagogues of the Robespierre stripe because there was no rabble to rouse. The French Revolution, trying to correct social injustice, became a bloody mess that ended in dictatorship. In Arendt's terms, it was not a successful revolution because it did not end with the constituting of liberty, as the American Revolution did.

In France, the Revolution is controversial more than two centuries after it occurred. Few celebrate it uncritically, and many French conservatives hate it. Most French people are proud of its original idealistic impulses—"liberty, equality, fraternity"—but many admit that it went wrong, that it turned to bloodshed and dictatorship. The big question here is whether this was an accident—the Revolution fell into the hands of extremists and fanatics—or whether there was something built into the revolutionary process that made breakdown inevitable. Most serious scholars now argue for the inevitability thesis.

In Russia, this question is asked about the 1917 Bolshevik Revolution. Lenin, an intelligent and sophisticated man, died in 1924. Had he lived, would communism have taken a more humane and less brutal path? Stalin, in the view of some diehard Marxists, was the culprit who betrayed the revolution by turning it into his personal dictatorship. More recent scholarship has shown that Lenin was ruthless and willing to exterminate all opposition; there was nothing moderate or humane about him. Some Russian thinkers are now willing to admit that Lenin was wrong from the start.

Revolution, although popular in the 1960s, developed a bad reputation in the 1970s. By the 1980s, many radical countries were trying to back out of their revolutionary systems. There were simply no positive examples of revolutions that had worked out well. The Soviet Union and China, earlier the models for many revolutionaries, admitted that they were in economic difficulty and tried to change to a more open, market system. In 1989, the Communist lands of Eastern Europe simply walked away from communism. Then communism collapsed in the Soviet Union in late 1991. In Africa, the revolutionary Communist lands of Angola, Mozambique, and Ethiopia liberalized and begged for aid from the capitalist West.

The worst revolutionary horror was Cambodia. In the late 1970s, the Khmer Rouge (Red Cambodia) murdered an estimated 1.7 million of their fellow citizens. The nonfiction movie about this bloodbath, *The Killing Fields*, shocked the world. And Vietnam, united by the Communists in 1975 after its fierce war with the United States, turned itself into one of the poorest countries in the world. Tens of thousands of Vietnamese "boat people" risked the open sea and Thai pirates to leave their starving land. Sadly, few countries wanted them. In 1995, Vietnam and the United States established diplomatic relations, and the Vietnamese economy turned to the world market with rapid growth. In Cuba, the Castro brothers continued to proclaim their regime revolutionary, but most Cubans were tired of the shortages and restrictions. And in Nicaragua, a free election in 1990 voted out the revolutionary Sandinistas and replaced them with a democratic coalition.

Currently, there are few major revolutionary movements in operation. In Colombia, Marxist armies, funded by the cocaine trade, wage guerrilla warfare and terrorism but are now in decline. Most Colombians hate them. In Pakistan, Egypt, and Saudi Arabia, Islamists bomb and assassinate in an effort to overthrow corrupt governments. Islamists are motivated by great passion and a burning sense of injustice but have only illusions about what is to come next.

Notice the difference between countries before and after revolutions. Before, revolutionary movements are still idealistic and convinced they will bring a better society. Revolutions are based on the belief that, by seizing state power, a truly

velvet revolution Relatively non-violent mass uprisings that oust Communist and other repressive regimes.

committed regime can redo society, making it just, fair, and prosperous. This feeling grows in societies that are unjust and miserable. But after seizing power, the revolutionary regime discovers it's a lot harder to make an economy work than it thought. Disillusionment and bitterness set in; many people would like to get rid of the revolutionary regime, which stays in power by blaming capitalist holdouts and imperialist saboteurs. To control these alleged plotters, regime leaders give themselves draconian police powers to stamp out private industry and criticism.

But things get worse. Farmers do not plant unless they get a decent price for their crops. Workers do not work without something to buy. Unable to admit it is mistaken after having killed so many people, the revolutionary regime locks itself into power through police controls. After some time of hardship and poor growth, a new generation may come to power and admit that the system needs to loosen up. Embarrassment may be a factor here. Comparing

COMPARING ■ VIOLENT VS. VELVET REVOLUTIONS

Historically, most revolutions have been violent and bitter, as enraged sectors of the population rose up against hated regimes. They swept clean, leaving none of the old elites with power or wealth. But scholars note that recently a new "velvet" revolution has become common, starting with the overthrow of Communist regimes in Eastern Europe in 1989 and the Soviet Union in 1991. These revolutions are largely nonviolent mass outpourings that reject corrupt, bungling regimes that promised much but delivered less and less. The old elites lose power but are not executed or exiled. Communist parties, for example, broadened themselves into Socialist parties and ran in free elections, although seldom winning.

Some scholars say these **velvet revolutions** are not revolutions at all because they lack the ferocious qualities of violent revolutions. But if, as we argued, revolution means sweeping system change, especially the ouster of the ruling elite, the overthrow of Communist regimes was also revolutionary. The impulses are the same as in other systems: injustice and corruption,. Promised a socialist utopia for generations, citizens tired of the failure to deliver. Actually, Soviets generally enjoyed rising living

standards, but their expectations, fanned by the party propaganda line, rose faster. Soviets were aware that the privileged party elite enjoyed special apartments, food shops, medical care, and vacation cottages. Much of the consumer economy ran on the basis of special deals. Desirable products never made it to the store shelf; they were sold through the back door for big profits. Intellectuals deplored the repression of critical views. The same resentments that smoldered in non-Communist countries smoldered in Communist countries.

As in earlier revolutions, the most dangerous time in the life of a Communist regime is when it tries to reform itself, which is as difficult as in traditionalist countries, for Communist elites also have a lot to lose in terms of power and privilege. In their system, the Communist Party elite becomes the conservatives who live well and block reforms. When conditions so deteriorate that reforms have to come, it is too late. Things were bad in the Soviet Union under Brezhnev, but mass unrest came only when Gorbachev instituted major reforms. By admitting that things were wrong, he gave the green light to restive workers, intellectuals, and nationalities to demand more than any had itself with free countries, the revolutionary country sees itself falling behind. Chinese in the 1970s could note with regret that on China's rim—in Singapore, Hong Kong, and Taiwan—Chinese were prosperous, but not in China. Under Deng Xiaoping, China turned to capitalist industry and foreign investment, and the economy set growth records, suggesting that the great Communist revolution had been a colossal mistake.

It takes large-scale revolutionary experiences to demonstrate that revolutions end badly. The revolutionary promise is golden; the revolutionary results are mud. If you don't live through it, you don't believe it. With several revolutionary experiences to ponder, many would-be revolutionaries turned away from revolution. This helps explain why the 1980s was a conservative decade: It could look back and survey the results of the 1960s. Now only holdout Maoists in India and Peru and al Qaeda want revolution.

The crux of revolutionary thinking is that it is possible to remake society. Without that, few would make revolutions. With the discovery that remaking society

dared mention a few years earlier. By asking for support and patience, Gorbachev also showed he was running scared, a further incitement to revolution. By letting in more Western media, he showed the Soviets how well Americans and West Europeans lived. Soon the pressure for massive change became explosive.

Halfway reform does not suffice and often makes things worse. The Communist regimes of Eastern Europe promised reforms and brought in fresh, new leadership. But few were fooled; they recognized that the reforms basically left defective systems intact and that the new leaders were still party bigshots. In Czechoslovakia in 1989, for example, the rapidly growing Civic Forum movement hooted down a new cabinet that the frightened Communist regime presented. The "new" cabinet, still dominated by Communists, looked pretty much like the old one. After massive street protest, Civic Forum won a cabinet of non-Communists, some of whom had been in jail only two weeks earlier. Czech President Vaclav Havel, using a phrase coined earlier, called it the "velvet revolution," and the term stuck. When an unpopular regime begins by offering "reforms," it may end by putting itself out of business.

Faced with this prospect, some regimes attempt to crush mass demands with military force. An example is the bloody 1989 crackdown in China. Hundreds of protesting students were gunned down in Beijing's Tiananmen Square because the elderly party elite feared what they called a "counterrevolutionary revolt." Deng Xiaoping had attempted economic reform only to find that it awoke demands for democracy. Partial reform of a corrupt dictatorship is difficult, because, as soon as you let people criticize it, they demand to replace it. Give them a free speech inch, and they want a democratic mile. That, of course, would mean ousting the Communist elite, which then fights tenaciously for its power and privileges. But by digging in their heels and refusing to institute major reform, the rulers just build up a head of steam for a later and greater explosion. The party can crush political opponents, but it cannot produce the economic growth necessary to feed and house the people, who just get angrier. Ironically, Communist countries, who always claimed to be "revolutionary," indeed led the way to revolution. Other countries may be ripe for velvet revolutions.

leads to terrible difficulties and poor results, the revolutionary dream dies. Does this mean that we will not see another major wave of revolutions? Not necessarily. There is plenty of injustice in the world, and this brings rage. Rage, as Hannah Arendt pointed out, leads to revolution. The greatest cause of rage is the massive corruption now found in the developing lands. Corrupt regimes gain little legitimacy, as the Americans who tried to transform Iraq and Afghanistan painfully discovered.

What can be done to head off revolutions? The answer is simple but difficult to carry out: reforms to end the injustices and corruption that revolutions feed on. Land reform in Peru and the Philippines, elected parliaments in Persian Gulf lands, and jobs in Algeria and Egypt could curb corruption and dampen revolutionary movements in these countries. The Middle East has the world's highest unemployment rates, and unemployed young males are the eager soldiers of Islamic revolution. Persian Gulf sheikhs fear the loss of their wealth and power if they democratize, and they have a good argument that liberalizing at this time would just let radicals take over. If Saudi Arabia held free and fair elections, someone like Osama bin Laden could win. The solution: slow and gradual reform that eliminates corruption.

The statist governments of much of the Third World hate to admit that their corrupt officials siphon economic growth—especially petroleum revenues—directly into their own pockets while mass resentment grows. In practice, reforms are hard to apply because the class in power that has much to lose strongly resists. In South Vietnam, for example, the United States urged the Saigon regime to carry out sweeping land reform to win the peasants away from the Communist guerrillas. But landowners, many of whom collected exorbitant rents from tenant farmers, blocked land-reform bills. If they had given up their land, they might have saved their country; instead, they lost both. The message is to institute reforms before revolutionary feeling is implanted, to head off the problem before it becomes dangerous.

 EXERCISES

Apply what you learned in this chapter on MyPoliSciKit (www.mypoliscikit.com).

 Assessment   Review this chapter using learning objectives, chapter summaries, practice tests, and more.

 Flashcards   Learn the key terms in this chapter; you can test yourself by term or definition.

Video   Analyze recent world affairs by watching streaming video from major news providers.

Comparative Exercises   Compare political ideas, behaviors, institutions, and policies worldwide.

KEY TERMS

analogy (p. 321)
ayatollah (p. 327)
coup (p. 316)
dysanalogy (p. 321)
intellectuals (p. 323)
jihadi (p. 320)
praetorianism (p. 320)

primordial (p. 317)
relative deprivation (p. 323)
revolution (p. 324)
shah (p. 327)
system breakdown (p. 316)
terrorism (p. 320)

Thermidor (p. 327)
thinkpiece (p. 321)
utopia (p. 324)
velvet revolution (p. 330)

FURTHER REFERENCE

Bell-Fialkoff, Andrew. *Ethnic Cleansing*, rev. ed. New York: Palgrave, 1999.

Benjamin, Daniel, and Steven Simon. *The Next Attack: The Failure of the War on Terror and a Strategy for Getting It Right*. New York: Henry Holt, 2006.

Goldstone, Jack A., ed. *Revolutions: Theoretical, Comparative, and Historical Studies*, 3rd ed. Belmont, CA: Wadsworth, 2002.

Greene, Thomas H. *Comparative Revolutionary Movements*, 3rd ed. Englewood Cliffs, NJ: Prentice Hall, 1990.

Halliday, Fred. *Revolution and World Politics: The Rise and Fall of the Sixth Great Power*. Durham, NC: Duke University Press, 1999.

Heymann, Philip B. *Terrorism, Freedom, and Security: Winning Without War*. New York: Cambridge University Press, 2003.

Katz, Mark N., ed. *Revolution: International Dimensions*. Washington, DC: CQ Press, 2000.

Laqueur, Walter. *No End to War: Terrorism in the Twenty-First Century*. New York: Continuum, 2004.

Parsa, Misagh. *States, Ideologies, and Social Revolutions: A Comparative Analysis of Iran, Nicaragua, and the Philippines*. New York: Cambridge University Press, 2000.

Rapoport, David C., and Leonard Weinberg, eds. *The Democratic Experience and Political Violence*. Portland, OR: Frank Cass, 2001.

Skocpol, Theda. *States and Social Revolutions: A Comparative Analysis of France, Russia and China*. New York: Cambridge University Press, 1979.

Snow, Donald M. *Distant Thunder: Patterns of Conflict in the Developing World*, 2nd ed. Armonk, NY: M. E. Sharpe, 1997.

Whittaker, David J. *Terrorism: Understanding the Global Threat*, rev. ed. New York: Longman, 2007.

Wright, Lawrence. *The Looming Tower: Al-Qaeda and the Road to 9/11*. New York: Knopf, 2006.

International Relations

U.S. soldiers from the 3rd Infantry Division return to Fort Benning, Georgia, from Iraq in 2010. (Erik Lesser/Corbis)

International relations differs from the domestic politics we have been studying: There is no world sovereign power over the nations to get them to obey laws and preserve peace. Compared with **domestic politics**, **international relations** (IR) is wilder and more complex. Sovereignty, as considered in Chapter 1, means being boss on your own turf and is the dominant force within a country. Criminals, rebels, and breakaway elements are, in theory, controlled or crushed by the sovereign, who now, of course, is no longer a king or queen but the national government. Sovereignty also means that foreign powers have no business intruding into your country's affairs. Their reach—again in theory—stops at your borders.

So much for theory. In practice, nothing is so clear-cut. Just because a nation is legally sovereign does not necessarily mean it really controls its own turf. Witness Georgia recently: Russia encouraged and armed breakaway regions and even invaded in 2008. Was Georgia still "sovereign"? Europe, on the other hand, peacefully came together first in the Common Market and now the European Union (EU). Its members give up some of their sovereignty to form an economic and political union, which could eventually (but not soon) turn into a United States of Europe. Sovereignty is not a simple yes or no but a question of degree.

Further, the idea that sovereignty precludes outside intervention doesn't hold up. Small, weaker countries are routinely dominated and influenced by larger and more powerful countries. Eastern Europe during the **Cold War** was under Soviet control, and the small countries of Central America were under the watchful eye of the United States. Some Canadians claim that U.S. economic and cultural penetration erodes their sovereignty. What meaning does sovereignty have in a *failed state* (see page 60) that cannot govern anything?

Still, the term has some utility. Where established, national sovereignty does bring internal peace, and most countries can claim to have done this. In dealing with

domestic politics Interactions within states.

international relations Interactions among states.

Cold War Armed tension and mistrust between U.S. and Soviet camps, 1946–1989.

other nations, countries still mostly do what they want. When North Korea tested its first nuclear bomb in 2006, there was nothing that the rest of the world could do to stop it, although many protested. North Korea did what it wished on its territory. When the United States urged the economic isolation of Iran, many countries ignored the call and made trade and oil deals with Tehran. Congress passed laws threatening legal trouble for foreign firms that did business with Cuba and Libya, but the U.S. Congress cannot pass laws for other countries, which ignored the U.S. prohibitions. Most countries signed treaties to combat global warming, land mines, germ warfare, and exporting weapons, but not the United States, which claimed that the treaties were flawed and that it had a sovereign right to ignore them. There was no way for other countries to make the big, powerful United States conform to these treaties.

Within a sovereign entity there is—or at least there is supposed to be—law. If you have a grievance against someone, you do not take the law into your own hands. You take the person to court. In international relations, nearly the opposite applies: Taking the law into your own hands—by the threat or use of force—is quite normal. Often there is no other recourse.

This important difference between domestic and international politics sometimes exasperates skilled practitioners of one when they enter the realm of the other. President Johnson was a master of domestic politics; he got whatever he wanted from Congress. But he could not make skinny little Ho Chi Minh back down, for Ho was boss on *his* own turf, Vietnam. What worked domestically for Johnson—deals, threats, persuasion—flopped internationally. Some suggest that it was Nixon's use of the "dirty tricks" of IR in domestic politics that launched Watergate and his subsequent resignation. Nixon was a clever statesman; he simultaneously improved ties with the Soviet Union and China. But his deviousness tripped him up in a delicate domestic problem. International politics is not just domestic politics writ large.

POWER AND NATIONAL INTEREST

Lacking sovereignty, IR depends a lot on *power*: A gets B to do what A wants. Hans Morgenthau (1904–1980) held that power is the basic element of international politics that idealists ignore at their peril. Without sufficient power, a country cannot survive, let alone prevail, in a tumultuous world. Power is not necessarily evil or aggressive; it may be simply persuading an aggressor to "Leave me alone!"

Power is not the same as force. Force is the specific application of military might; power (recalling our definition from Chapter 1) is a country's more general ability to get its way. Power includes military, economic, political, cultural, and psychological factors. The best kind of power: rational persuasion. Power is tricky to calculate. Whole departments of the CIA spend millions trying to figure out how much power various countries have. Some elements of power—such as a country's geography, natural resources, population, and economy—are tangible or calculable. Some of the most important factors, however—such as a country's military capability, the quality of its political system, and its determination—cannot be learned until it is involved in a war. The war then provides, at a terrible price, the answer about which side had more power.

> **national interest**   What's good for the nation as a whole in world affairs.

In this situation, countries generally pursue their **national interest**, and this makes IR partly intelligible. If you know a country's national interest—from its history, geography, economy, and current politics—you can understand much of its behavior. Russia held the Caucasus region for two centuries as a security belt and hated when it broke away in 1991. Accordingly, Moscow saw its national interest in using military force to control Chechnya and Georgia even though the outside world protested. When it comes to their national interests, nations rarely behave like saints.

Countries see their national interests through different eyes. Most of the world sided with the United States after 9/11 and supported the U.S. overthrow of the Taliban regime in Afghanistan. NATO forces help to try to stabilize the country because many European countries have a national interest in fighting al Qaeda, which had headquarters in Afghanistan. With Iraq in 2003, however, few saw a

KEY CONCEPTS ■ TYPES OF NATIONAL INTEREST

National interests may be divided into four categories:

1. Vital versus secondary
2. Temporary versus permanent
3. Specific versus general
4. Complementary versus conflicting

A vital interest is one that potentially threatens the life of your nation, such as Soviet missiles in Cuba. When a country perceives a threat to its vital interests, it may go to war. A secondary interest is usually more distant and less urgent. The United States, for example, has an interest in an open world oil supply, with no nation restricting or controlling it. Nations are more inclined to negotiate and compromise over their secondary interests.

A temporary interest is one of fixed duration, as in U.S. support for Iraq during its 1980s war with Iran. U.S. diplomacy had trouble understanding that, as soon as that war was over, their complementary interests vanished. A permanent interest lasts over centuries, as in the U.S. interest in keeping hostile powers out of the Western Hemisphere.

A specific interest focuses on a single problem, such as Japanese trade barriers to U.S. goods. A general interest might be universal respect for human rights.

When nations have some important goals in common, their interests are *complementary*, which happened in the 1991 Gulf War; several Arab countries sided with the West. Complementary interests are what make alliances. When interests conflict, as when a new Madrid government saw no Spanish national interest in keeping its small peacekeeping force in Iraq in 2004, countries pull apart.

Two countries, even allies, seldom have identical national interests. The best one can hope for is that their interests will be complementary. The United States and Iraqi Kurds, for instance, had a common interest in opposing Saddam's genocidal campaign (which included poison gas) against Kurds, but the U.S. interest is a general, temporary, and secondary one concerning human rights and regional stability. The Kurdish interest is a specific, permanent, and possibly vital one of forming an independent Kurdistan that includes oil-rich Mosul and Kirkuk. Our interests may run parallel for a time, but we must never mistake Kurdish interests for U.S. interests.

micro theories Focus on individuals.

macro theories Focus on nations and history.

balance of power System in which major nations form and reform alliances to protect themselves.

national interest, and several countries warned against destabilizing Iraq. These were different situations and different perceptions of national interest.

The diplomat's work is in finding and developing complementary interests so that two or more countries can work together. (Listening to diplomats' warnings against invading Iraq could have saved the United States much grief.) Often, countries have some interests that are complementary and others that are conflicting, as when NATO members cooperated to block the Soviet

KEY CONCEPTS ■ WHY WAR?

Very broadly, theories on the cause of war divide into two general camps, the *micro* and the *macro*—the little, close-up picture as opposed to the big, panoramic picture.

Micro Theories

Micro theories are rooted in biology and psychology. They might explain war as the result of genetic human aggressiveness that makes people fighters. In this, humans are no different from other mammals. Most anthropologists reject such biological determinism, arguing that primitive peoples exhibit a wide variety of behavior—some are aggressive and some not—that can be explained only by culture, learned behavior. Psychologists explore leaders' personalities, what made them that way, and how they obtained their hold over the masses and brought them to war.

Biological and psychological theories offer some insights but fall far short of explaining wars. If humans are naturally aggressive, why aren't all nations constantly at war? How is it that countries fight a long series of wars—the Russian–Turkish struggle or the Arab–Israeli wars—under different leaders? Under what circumstances do humans become aggressive? When they think they are being attacked. For that, we turn to politics.

Macro Theories

Macro theories are rooted in history and political science and concentrate on the power and

ambitions of states. States, not individuals, are the key actors, argue macro theorists. Where they can, states expand, as in the Russian's push into the Caucasus, the Americans' "manifest destiny," and the growth of the British Empire. Only countervailing power may stop the drive to expand. One country, fearing the growing power of a neighbor, will strengthen its defenses or form alliances to offset the neighbor's power. Much international behavior can be explained by the aphorisms *Si vis pacem para bellum* ("If you want peace, prepare for war") and "The enemy of my enemy is my friend." Political leaders have an almost automatic feel for national interest and power and move to enhance them, argue IR theorists. Does the pursuit of power lead to war or peace? Again, there are two broad theories.

Balance of Power The oldest and most commonly held theory is that peace results when several states use national power and alliances to balance one another. Would-be expansionists are blocked. According to **balance-of-power** theorists, the great periods of relative peace—between the Peace of Westphalia in 1648 and the wars that grew out of the French Revolution (1792–1814), and again from 1815 to the start of World War I in 1914—have been times when the European powers balanced each other. When the balances broke down, there was war. Fighting in Bosnia calmed in 1995 only after power there roughly balanced. When the threat but clashed over who was to lead the alliance. The French–U.S. relationship can be described in this way. Where interests totally conflict, of course, there can be no cooperation. Here it is the diplomat's duty to say so and find ways to minimize the damage. Do not despair in this situation; national interests shift, and today's adversary may be tomorrow's ally. Few would have guessed in the 1960s that China would be a U.S. friend in the 1970s, a condition that did not last into the 1990s.

Defining the national interest in any given situation may be difficult. Intelligent, well-informed people may come up with opposite definitions of the national interest. Hawks in the 1960s, for example, claimed a Communist victory in Southeast Asia would harm U.S. interests. Others claimed Vietnam was of little importance to us. Neoconservatives in the Bush 43 administration claimed taking out Saddam Hussein in

Serbs were ahead, they had no motive to settle; when they were on the defensive, they decided to settle. Many thinkers consider the Cold War a big and durable balance-of-power system that explains why there was relative peace—at least no World War III—for more than four decades.

Hierarchy of Power   Other scholars reject the balance-of-power theory. Calculations of power are problematic, so it is impossible to know when power balances. Often periods of peace occurred when power was *out* of balance, when states were ranked hierarchically in terms of power. Then every nation knew where it stood on a ladder of relative power. In transitional times, when the power hierarchy is blurred, countries are tempted to go to war. A big war with a definitive outcome brings peace because then relative power is clearly known.

Misperception

Weaving micro and macro approaches together, some thinkers focus on "image" or "perception" as the key to war. It's not the real situation (which is hard to know) but what leaders perceive that makes them decide for war or peace. They often misperceive, seeing hostility and threats from another country, which sees itself as merely defensive. JFK portrayed a Soviet "missile gap" over the United States and increased the U.S. missile program. It turned out that the Soviets were actually behind the United States, and they perceived the American effort as a threat that they had to match. The misperceptions led to the 1962 Cuban Missile Crisis, the closest we came to World War III. Iraq's weapons of mass destruction (WMD) were dismantled under UN supervision in the 1990s, but Bush 43 was convinced Iraq had revived its WMD programs and went to war in 2003 to remove a nonexistent threat. In the emotional and patriotic climate after 9/11, America was angry and suspicious. Intelligence data were skewed to show what the administration wanted to show. Misperception can count for more than reality.

In misperception or image theory, the psychological and real worlds bounce against each other in the minds of political leaders. They think they are acting defensively, but their picture of the situation may be distorted. In our time, it is interesting to note, no country ever calls its actions anything but defensive. The Americans in Vietnam and Iraq saw themselves as defending freedom; the Russians in Georgia saw themselves as defending their country.

Leaders often use ideology and mass media to work citizens into anger and then march to war. Under rabidly nationalistic leadership, most Germans and Japanese in World War II saw themselves as defending their countries against hostile powers. Once convinced that they are being attacked, peaceful people will commit atrocities.

weapons of mass destruction (WMD) Nuclear, chemical, and bacteriological weapons.

collective security An agreement among all nations to automatically counter an aggressor.

Iraq was urgent, to prevent him from building **weapons of mass destruction (WMD)**. Critics countered that it was an unnecessary war. How can you tell when a genuine national interest is at stake? One way is feasibility; power is the connecting link. An infeasible strategy—where your power is insufficient to carry out your designs—is a mistake. If the type of power is wrong for the setting (for example, helicopters and artillery against terrorists; air power to stop a civil war), you are undertaking an infeasible strategy.

Foreign policy is inherently an elite (see pages 104–105) game, and elites usually define the national interest. Unless facing a war or major threat, most people pay little or no attention to foreign policy, which, until 9/11, was nearly absent in U.S. elections. In a democracy, the masses may influence foreign policy—as angry Americans did over the Vietnam and Iraq wars—but only long after the basic decisions have been made in secrecy. Foreign policy decisions, even in democracies, are made by perhaps a dozen people. Notice how even in the United States, presidents and a few advisors make foreign policy and then announce it to the American people and to Congress, which usually goes along with it. In late 2001, President Bush decided to invade Iraq, but only a few knew. Only years later did the United States get a real debate on the wisdom of the Iraq War.

KEEPING PEACE

Whatever its causes, what can be done to prevent or limit war? Many proposals have been advanced; none has really worked.

World Government

The real culprit, many claim, is sovereignty itself. States should give up some of their sovereignty—the ability to go to war—to an international entity that would prevent war much as an individual country keeps the peace within its borders. But what country would give up its sovereignty? Certainly not the United States. Does Iran heed UN calls to open its nuclear sites to international inspection? Without the teeth of sovereignty, the United Nations becomes a debating society, useful for diplomatic contact but little more.

Collective Security

The United Nations' predecessor, the League of Nations, tried **collective security**. Members of the League (which did not include the United States) pledged to join in economic and military action against any aggressor. If Japan, for example, invaded China, every other power would break trade relations and send forces to defend China. Aggressors would back down. It was a great idea on paper, but when Japan conquered Manchuria in 1931, the League merely studied the situation. Japan claimed the Chinese started it (a lie), and the other powers saw no point in entering a distant conflict where they had no interests. The League had no mechanism to make the other countries respond, and the same happened when Italy invaded Ethiopia in 1935. Japan, Italy, and Germany withdrew from the League to practice more aggression, and the League collapsed with World War II.

> **functionalism** Theory that cooperation in specialized areas will encourage overall cooperation among nations.

Functionalism

Another idea related to world organizations is to have countries work together first in specialized or "functional" areas so they see that they accomplish more by cooperation than by conflict. Increasingly able to trust each other, gradually they will work up to a stable peace. **Functionalism** will produce a "spillover" effect. Dozens of UN-related agencies now promote international cooperation in disease control, food production, weather forecasting, civil aviation, nuclear energy, and other areas. Even hostile countries are sometimes able to sit together to solve a mutual problem in specialized areas.

But there is no spillover effect; they remain hostile. Sometimes the specialized organization becomes a scene of conflict, as when the developing nations group expelled Israel and South Africa from the UN Educational, Scientific, and Cultural Organization (UNESCO) and the United States quit UNESCO over alleged Soviet dominance. Even offers of the UN-related International Monetary Fund (IMF) to bail out distressed economies generates controversy, as the recipient country often

KEY CONCEPTS ■ THE DEMOCRATIC PEACE

No two democracies have ever gone to war with each other. Can you name any cases where two democracies have fought each other? Some say the U.S. Civil War, but the South was not really a democracy. Argentina against Britain over the Falklands in 1982? But Argentina was then a military dictatorship. India against Pakistan seems a likely candidate, but Pakistan has been mostly ruled by generals. The theory of the democratic peace is robust.

Why, logically, should democracy bring peace? Democracy renders leaders accountable, so they tend to be cautious and follow Friedrich's famous "rule of anticipated reactions" (page 123). They think, "If I take the country to war, how will voters react? Hmm, I guess I better not." When President Johnson ignored such caution in Vietnam—because he thought voters would hold it against him if the Communists won—he lost support and could not stand for a second term. Bush 43 and the Republicans suffered similarly from the Iraq War. Dictators have no such inhibitions and may be inclined to reckless misadventures, as when Brezhnev invaded Afghanistan in 1979 or Saddam Hussein invaded Kuwait in 1990.

Democracies, because they are better informed through free media, cannot easily demonize other democracies. (They do demonize non-democracies.) The French and Americans are periodically irritated at one another, but neither portrays the other as an enemy. Dictatorships, through their control of the media, can convince their people that hostile powers threaten. North Korea tells its hungry citizens that they have a high standard of living that the Americans want to take away. With little outside information, many North Koreans believe it. The cause of peace is served by the spread of democracy.

third party   A nation not involved in a dispute helping to settle it.

treaty   A contract between nations.

peacekeeping   Outside military forces stabilizing a cease-fire agreement.

UNPROFOR   UN Protective Force; ineffective peacekeeping effort in Bosnia in early 1990s.

IFOR   Implementation Force; effective NATO-sponsored peacekeeping effort in Bosnia following 1995 Dayton Accords.

claims that economic reforms mandated by the IMF interfere with its sovereignty. The functionalist approach has brought some help in world problems but has not touched the biggest problem, war.

Third-Party Assistance

One way to settle a dispute is to have a **third party** not involved in the conflict mediate between the contending parties to try to find a middle ground. Third parties carry messages back and forth, clarify the issues, and suggest compromises, as the UN's Ralph Bunche did between Arabs and Israelis in 1949, President Carter did with Begin and Sadat at Camp David in 1978, and Richard Holbrooke did at Dayton over Bosnia in 1995. Third parties can help calm a tense situation and find compromise solutions, but the contenders have to *want* to find a solution. If not, third-party help is futile.

Diplomacy

The oldest approach to preserving peace is through diplomatic contact, with envoys sent from one state to another. A good diplomat knows all the power factors and interests of the countries involved and has suggestions for compromise that leave both parties at least partly satisfied. This is crucial: There must be willingness to compromise. This can be hard because countries often define their vital, nonnegotiable interests grandly and are unwilling to cut them down to compromisable size. After years of intensive negotiations, presided over by the United States, Israelis and Palestinians could not compromise on what they saw as their vital interests.

If successful, diplomats draw up **treaties**, which must be ratified and observed. If one country feels a treaty harms it, there is nothing to stop it from opting out, as Bush did in 2002 with the 1972 Anti-Ballistic Missile Treaty with Russia. Countries enter into and observe treaties because it suits them. Some observers say the United States and Soviet Union, both relative newcomers to the world of great-power politics, were unskilled at diplomacy, too unwilling to compromise. The climate of mistrust between them was one of the hallmarks of the Cold War.

Peacekeeping

Related to diplomacy is the idea of using third-party military forces to support a cease-fire or truce to end fighting. Wearing the blue berets of the UN, they helped calm and stabilize truces between Israel and its Arab neighbors and between Greeks and Turks on Cyprus. Such forces cannot "enforce peace" by stopping a conflict that is still in progress. The only way to do that would be to take sides in the war, and that would be the opposite of **peacekeeping**. It was therefore inherently unrealistic to expect **UNPROFOR** (the UN Protective Force) to separate and calm the warring parties in Bosnia. UNPROFOR, given an impossible mission, covered itself with shame. The **IFOR** (Implementation Force) that took over from

A UN helicopter delivers aid to a Congo refugee camp in 2008 amid civil war. The UN's resources are far too few for the huge Democratic Republic of Congo. (Uriel Sinai/Getty Images)

UNPROFOR was different and successful because it came after the three sides—Bosnia, Croatia, and Serbia—agreed to a U.S.-brokered peace in Dayton. IFOR was also equipped and instructed to destroy attackers; these robust **rules of engagement** dissuaded rambunctious elements, something UNPROFOR was unable to do. Some propose the IFOR model for future peacekeeping, but such actions work only if a peace agreement has been reached beforehand.

> **rules of engagement** Specify when peacekeeping forces can shoot back.

BEYOND SOVEREIGNTY?

The end of the Cold War and of the most violent century in history brought into question the basic point of international politics, sovereignty—namely, is sovereignty slipping? Increasingly, the world community is acting in ways that infringe on the internal workings of sovereign states. For some decades, the International Monetary Fund has been able to tell countries that wanted loans to stop their inflationary economic policies. The recipients of such advice often fume that the IMF is infringing on their sovereignty, but if they want the loan, they take the advice, as Greece had to do in 2010. With the end of the Cold War, now even former Communist countries are going along with this sort of infringement on their sovereignty.

Starting with the Nuremberg War Crimes Trials in 1945–1946, international law increasingly discounts sovereignty as a cover for mass murder. The Tokyo war

supranational A governing body above individual nations (such as the UN).

crimes trials and 1961 Eichmann trial in Israel reinforced the Nuremburg precedent. Mass murderers in Bosnia and Rwanda were tried before international tribunals. (Saddam Hussein was tried before an Iraqi court but with strong international support.) Nothing like this happened before World War II. International law is slowly eating into sovereignty.

After a broad, U.S.-led coalition booted Iraq out of Kuwait in 1991, UN inspectors combed through Iraq looking for the capacity to build WMD. The Baghdad dictatorship screamed that Iraq's sovereignty was being infringed upon. Indeed it was, and most of the world was glad of it. Should the international community stand back while a tyrant develops the power to annihilate neighboring countries? By the same token, should the civilized world stand by while the Sudanese government sponsors genocide against its own people? Should the rest of Europe act as if Balkan massacres were none of its concern? A new doctrine, the "responsibility to protect" (R2P), is growing and could someday override sovereignty.

The world seems to be changing, willing to move beyond sovereignty and toward some kind of order. The trouble is no one knows what kind of order. Bush 41 used the term "new world order" in building a coalition against Iraq, but he dropped the expression just as debate on it was starting. What to do in the face of the disorder unleashed by the dissolution of Soviet power? Paradoxically, the world was more orderly during the Cold War, because the two superpowers controlled and restrained their respective allies and spheres of influence.

Few wanted the United States to play world cop, but most understood that if there was to be leadership, only America could provide it. Could **supranational** (above-national) entities be getting ready to take on some of the responsibilities previously

HOW TO... ■ AVOID "THEY"

Beware of collective pronouns like "they," which often paint with too broad a brush. When you use "they," always ask who it represents. Grammatically, "they" refers to the previous plural noun. Many new students of international relations use "they" as if an entire national population is carrying out decisions and actions when in reality only a handful of top decision makers are. The leaders of France are often critical of U.S. policy. Some Americans then say that "the French" are against us. Actually, 99.99 percent of French people either have no interest in or no input into foreign policy. And many like the United States.

To guard against the overgeneralization that comes with "they," either specify who is taking the action—the president of France, the foreign minister, or the Quai d'Orsay (French foreign ministry)—or use the name of the capital to stand for the top decision makers—"Paris" for France's foreign policy elite, "Moscow" for Russia's, and "Beijing" for China's.

There isn't even much of a "we" in U.S. foreign policy. Most Americans have no views or weak views on foreign affairs, and few have any input into foreign policy decisions. Many do not support administration policies. Even "inside the beltway" (around the District of Columbia), every policy provokes conflicting views. In such situations, instead of the term "Washington," use the person's name and/or organization espousing the viewpoint: "Secretary of State Hillary Clinton sometimes found herself at odds with Secretary of Defense Robert Gates." Specific is better.

associated with individual nations' sovereignty? A new class of "world-order" issues has emerged, such as climate change, that no country can handle on its own. Are any organizations able to play such a role?

> **bipolar**   System of two large, hostile blocs, each led by a superpower, as in the Cold War.
>
> **multipolar**   System divided among several power centers.

The United Nations

The United Nations comes quickly to mind, and indeed the UN functioned better after the Cold War than during it. But it still has problems. As permanent members of the Security Council, Russia and China have the power to veto anything they dislike, such as leaning on Iran to allow nuclear inspections. Russia did nothing against Serbia, long regarded as a Slavic little brother. The UN has sent many peacekeepers to observe truces, as in the Middle East and Balkans, but these few and lightly armed forces from small countries were in no position to enforce peace. The bloodthirsty Khmer Rouge in Cambodia repeatedly kidnapped UN peacekeepers, knowing they would do nothing. Without enforcement powers and fragmented into blocs, the UN remained largely a "talking shop."

The North Atlantic Treaty Organization

NATO was arguably the best defensive alliance ever devised. The former Communist countries of Eastern Europe were happy to join, as NATO assured their freedom and security. Since 1949, NATO coordinated Western Europe and North America to act as a single defender under unified command in the event of Soviet attack. But the North Atlantic Treaty is limited in scope—that an attack on one member in Europe or North America be treated as an attack on all—and does not apply anywhere else, not in the Middle East, the Balkans, or the Caucasus, which are "out of area." NATO members can, to be sure, volunteer to keep peace in Bosnia and Afghanistan, but they cannot be counted on.

There is no organization that can seriously calm and stabilize world trouble spots. Should there be one, or should the civilized world put together a series of ad hoc arrangements, as the United States did in Afghanistan in 2001? Either way, the United States will have to take a leading role if anything is to be done effectively.

U.S. FOREIGN POLICY: INVOLVED OR ISOLATED?

The Cold War created a **bipolar** system that was clear but dangerous: us against the Soviets. Many describe the current system as **multipolar**, a more complicated system and one that reawakened an old question: Should the United States defend its interests on the near or far side of the oceans? For most of America's history, it was assumed that we should generally stay on our own shores, that little overseas really concerned us. Americans, some say, are natural-born isolationists. With Pearl Harbor in 1941, however, isolationism was rejected in favor of massive involvement in world affairs, first in winning World War II and then the Cold War. Isolationism was not an option. Is it one now?

foreign policy Interface of domestic and world politics; in Lippmann's phrase, "the shield of the Republic."

interventionism Policy of using military force overseas.

isolationism U.S. tendency to minimize importance of outside world.

tariff A tax on an import.

quota A numerical limit on an import.

With the Cold War over and with budgetary constraints, U.S. armed forces shrank. Presidents Bush 41 and Clinton used them little overseas. After 9/11, Bush 43 plunged U.S. forces into Afghanistan and Iraq until they were stretched thin. Few suggest returning to a draft, which would take an act of Congress. More than 70 percent of Americans supported the 2003 Iraq War, but by 2006 the same percentage thought it had been a mistake. Public opinion, as we saw in Chapter 8, is volatile.

Cycles of U.S. Foreign Policy

U.S. **foreign policy** tends to swing between **interventionism** and **isolationism**. Can we find a stable and moderate middle ground? Many scholars think not; they see a pendulum swing between overinvolvement and underinvolvement. Stanley Hoffmann discerned "the two *tempi* of America's foreign relations," alternating "from phases of withdrawal (or, when complete withdrawal

KEY CONCEPTS ■ THE IMPORTANCE OF ECONOMICS

Economics now looms large in IR, perhaps the biggest single factor. The big flaw in the Cold War bipolar model was that it all but left out economics, the very factor that brought down the Soviet Union. In the words of Columbia economist Jeffrey Sachs, "Markets won." But will markets stay the winner? Historically, countries tend to control, regulate, or own their industries. Perhaps the most free-market economy is that of the United States. The Europeans construct large and expensive welfare states whose controls and taxes work against starting new enterprises. In East Asia the state guides key industries aimed at rapid growth and dominance of certain markets. Many say Adam Smith's ideas on a free economy are just theories, and few totally practice them.

Controlled economies got a jolt from British Prime Minister Margaret Thatcher's attack on the welfare state and her promotion of capitalism. "Thatcherism" spread to many countries, leading to freer markets. Some countries—in large part because domestic interest groups strongly objected—resisted the encroachments of free markets; they tended to hide behind

tariffs or **quotas**. And a few countries simply prohibit certain foreign imports; Japan, for example, for decades allowed no imported rice. Many domestic interest groups have sufficient clout to block foreign goods.

Keeping world trade open by cutting tariffs and other barriers is the task of the World Trade Organization (WTO), aimed at freer trade and having some powers of judicial settlement of disputes. Its predecessor before 1995, the General Agreement on Tariffs and Trade (GATT), did the same thing but without enforcement powers. GATT and WTO have done much good. Tariffs are at an all-time low, and most goods flow unhindered over the globe, but now nontariff barriers increasingly irritate international economic relations, many of them concerning nonindustrial products. Several countries (including Canada and France) limit U.S. movies and TV shows, arguing that they replace local productions and endanger cultural and national identities. Some countries (including Japan and China) keep out U.S. banks and search engines, arguing that such vital areas belong under national control. Americans argue that if TV and online is impossible, priority to domestic concerns) to phases of dynamic, almost messianic romping on the world stage." Hans Morgenthau saw U.S. policy moving "back and forth between extremes of indiscriminate isolationism and an equally indiscriminate internationalism or globalism." Getting more specific, historian Dexter Perkins divided American foreign relations in cycles of "relatively pacific feeling," followed by "rising bellicosity and war," followed by "postwar nationalism," and then back to "relatively pacific feeling." If Perkins is right, in which phase of the cycle are we now?

unilateralism Doing things our way against the wishes of allies.

protectionism Policy of keeping out foreign goods to protect domestic producers.

globalization Free flow of commerce across borders, making the world one big market.

Some argue that under Bush 43 we practiced **unilateralism**, ignoring allies and rejecting treaties that most countries want (against global warming, germ warfare, land mines, and other issues). The neoconservatives prominent in the Bush 43 administration despised most of our European allies as cowardly. Unilateralism, however, alienated allies and isolated us. Exercising too much U.S. power can actually lose us the power to influence others. Remember that power is the ability of one country to get another to do something.

technology are what we do best, our products should flow wherever there are customers. Keeping world trade open is a never-ending task, for new industries are always developing, and countries continually come up with excuses to keep out the new foreign products. The 2008–2009 global financial meltdown brought a new wave of **protectionism**, as one country after another worried about keeping jobs at home.

If the WTO system breaks down and the world goes back to protected markets, we could see another depression. The very high Hawley-Smoot tariff, which the United States introduced in 1930 to protect U.S. manufacturers from foreign competition as the Great Depression began, brought retaliation from our trading partners and made the Depression deeper and longer and worldwide. The Depression was the biggest factor that led to the rise of Hitler and World War II.

Some argue that **globalization** is the big trend. Most countries play in the world market, a largely capitalistic competition where goods, money, and ideas flow easily to wherever there are customers. The motto of a globalized system:

"Make money, not war." The few countries that don't play, such as Cuba and North Korea, live in isolation and poverty. But there are problems with globalization. Is it a cause or a consequence of peace? Are the two intertwined? If so, what happens to one when the other is disrupted? Predictions that economic interdependency would prevent war (widely believed before World War I) have proved false. The British-led globalization of the nineteenth century collapsed with World War I. It revived, led by the United States, after World War II. Now some say globalization is reversing: "de-globalization."

Prosperity does not necessarily bring peace. Indeed, newly affluent countries often demand respect, resources, and sometimes territory. As China got richer, for example, it combed the globe for oil and mineral deals and defined its borders more grandly, reaching far out into the South and East China Seas to include Taiwan. And globalization creates resentments, especially in Muslim and other lands with proud and different cultures, at the American and capitalist culture of a globalized system: "McWorld." The whole world does not wish to become America.

CLASSIC WORKS ■ KLINGBERG'S ALTERNATION THEORY

A *behavioral* (see page 29) political scientist, Frank L. Klingberg, using such indicators as naval expenditures, annexations, armed expeditions, diplomatic pressures, and attention paid to foreign matters in presidential speeches and party platforms, discovered alternating phases of "introversion" (averaging 21 years) and "extroversion" (averaging 27 years). Klingberg added: "If America's fourth phase of extroversion (which began around 1940) should last as long as the previous extrovert phases, it would not end until well into the 1960s." Writing about 1950 and making no reference to Vietnam, Klingberg virtually predicted the impact of the Vietnam War, for it was precisely in the late 1960s (1940 plus 27 years) that the U.S. public and Congress tired of the Vietnam War and intervention in general, an amazingly accurate prediction. Are we now in a new period of extroversion, or are Americans again cautious about sending troops overseas?

---

noninterventionism A policy of not sending troops abroad.

Because isolationism connotes ignorance, some prefer the term **noninterventionism**, a reluctance to use U.S. forces overseas. From the birth of the Republic until the 1898 war with Spain, the United States rarely intervened overseas, focusing instead on its own continent. World War II and the Cold War brought massive U.S. overseas intervention. For two decades after Vietnam, we used few U.S. forces abroad and with caution, a "risk-averse" strategy. This suggested that the United States was not completely happy about a world leadership role. 9/11 changed that, but with the Iraq and Afghanistan wars—the two longest wars in U.S. history—Americans shied away from further world involvement. Should the United States intervene overseas to stop horrors that do not directly affect U.S. national interests?

The United States in a Dangerous World

Foreign policy is one of the most difficult areas of governance, because we have to take into account not only our own abilities and preferences but those of dozens of

CLASSIC WORKS ■ KENNAN'S DINOSAUR ANALOGY

In a famous and oft-reprinted 1950 speech, diplomat-historian George F. Kennan (1904–2005) compared American democracy to a pea-brained dinosaur sitting contentedly in a swamp, unmindful of threats around him. Once harmed by an adversary, though, he erupts into a violent rage that not only destroys the foe but wrecks his own habitat. "You wonder whether it would not have been wiser for him to have taken a little more interest in what was going on at an earlier date and to have seen whether he could not have prevented some of these situations from arising instead of proceeding from an undiscriminating indifference to a holy wrath equally undiscriminating." Kennan had U.S. entrance into World War I in mind, but his advice fits many more recent instances of blind American rage. Pay attention earlier. In 2002 at age 98, Kennan warned that the U.S. conquest of Iraq would leave a difficult and chaotic aftermath.

other states. We can make two opposite errors (and often do), both related to the problem of *misperception* (discussed on page 339). First, we can underestimate the dangers we face. In the late 1930s, as the clouds of World War II gathered, we supposed the oceans would serve as two great moats, shielding us from the war. It took the shock of Pearl Harbor to make Americans realize they could not stay isolated.

During the Cold War, however, we often overestimated the importance of a region, supposing that all areas of the globe were of equal and urgent importance to our national security. On this basis we plunged into Vietnam, with unhappy results. Ironically, a decade and a half after the Communists took over South Vietnam, we won the Cold War largely due to the economic inefficiency of communism. American firms, taking advantage of low Vietnamese wages, now manufacture athletic clothing and footwear there.

Thus U.S. foreign policy faces a twin problem: (1) a messy outside world that often defies our influence and (2) an American people and government little interested in or equipped for putting this world in order. There is no simple solution. Wise practitioners of foreign policy such as George Kennan (see box on page 348) urge calm, reason, and patience. Avoid emotion and extremes. Military power is sometimes necessary but should be used sparingly, as the aftermath of wars is often a power vacuum.

We have recently been in a time of emotion and anger in our foreign affairs. This has led to oversimplifications and unanticipated consequences. Whichever side you take in a foreign policy debate, panic or despair are seldom justified. Our generation lived through the fears of the Cold War and sometimes overreacted. We now realize that we were always going to win, that communism was an unworkable system that was eventually going to collapse. Current threats are not trivial, but we must not panic over Islamist extremism, which is likely to fade because, like communism, it cannot put food on the table.

The big problem is how to handle a rapidly rising China. Already the world's largest exporter and second-largest economy, China demands respect. Some IR

CLASSIC WORKS ■ THUCYDIDES ON WAR

The terrible Peloponnesian War (431–404 B.C.) destroyed Athens. A cashiered Athenian general, Thucydides, turned into a historian who reflected on what had gone wrong. "War became inevitable," he wrote, "with the growth of Athenian power and the fear this caused in Sparta." The long and brutal war deranged both sides. Greek civilization took a big step backward and never fully recovered. Political discourse became debased:

> What used to be described as a thoughtless act of aggression was now regarded as courage...; to think

of the future and wait was merely another way of saying one was a coward; any idea of moderation was just an attempt to disguise one's unmanly character; ability to understand a question from all sides meant that one was totally unfitted for action. Fanatical enthusiasm was the mark of a real man.... Anyone who held violent opinions could always be trusted.... Society became divided into camps in which no man trusted his fellow.

Any resemblance to current situations?

theorists argue that rising powers must collide with other powers, usually resulting in war. That is true of the Athenian, Roman, Arab, British, Japanese, and several other empires. The United States too emerged on the world stage through a series of wars. The rising Portuguese and Spanish empires, though, never fought each other; they agreed to let Spain dominate in Latin America and Portugal in Asia. The trick seems to be to make an agreement in advance as to who has what.

China historically never expanded overseas, although it easily could have. Currently Beijing defines its national interest as economic growth and will not likely do anything that disrupts it. This insight explains why China claims Taiwan but has not invaded it, why it is reluctant to let its currency rise, and why it lines up energy and raw materials deals around the globe. Things could go wrong, however. Strong nationalism smolders just beneath the surface in China. The Chinese military is constructing a major fleet and itches to take over Taiwan. Border claims trouble relations with India. And China's rapid economic growth may not always be smooth.

The great task for your generation will be to define U.S. and Chinese national interests in compatible ways. Beware of misleading *analogies* (see page 321) that equate China to Imperial Japan or the Soviet Union. China is neither of these. Handled with calm and reason, the world can live in peace with a rising China. We made it through the Cold War; you will make it through the twenty-first century, which, with the spread of democracy, may turn out to be a relatively peaceful one.

mypoliscikit EXERCISES

Apply what you learned in this chapter on MyPoliSciKit (www.mypoliscikit.com).

Assessment   Review this chapter using learning objectives, chapter summaries, practice tests, and more.

Flashcards   Learn the key terms in this chapter; you can test yourself by term or definition.

Video   Analyze recent world affairs by watching streaming video from major news providers.

Comparative Exercises   Compare political ideas, behaviors, institutions, and policies worldwide.

KEY TERMS

balance of power (p. 338)
bipolar (p. 345)
Cold War (p. 336)
collective security (p. 340)
domestic politics (p. 336)

foreign policy (p. 346)
functionalism (p. 341)
globalization (p. 347)
IFOR (p. 342)
international relations (p. 336)

interventionism (p. 346)
isolationism (p. 346)
macro theories (p. 338)
micro theories (p. 338)
multipolar (p. 345)

national interest (p. 337)

nonimterventionism
    (p. 348)

peacekeeping (p. 342)

protectionism (p. 347)

quota (p. 346)

rules of engagement (p. 343)

supranational (p. 344)

tariff (p. 346)

third party (p. 342)

treaty (p. 342)

unilateralism (p. 347)

UNPROFOR (p. 342)

weapons of mass
    destruction (p. 340)

FURTHER REFERENCE

Bacevich, Andrew J. *Washington Rules: America's Path to Permanent War*. New York: Metropolitan Books, 2010.

Bobbit, Philip. *The Shield of Achilles: War, Peace, and the Course of History*. New York: Knopf, 2002.

Brzezinski, Zbigniew. *Second Chance: Three Presidents and the Crisis of American Superpower*. New York: Basic Books, 2008.

Calvocoressi, Peter. *World Politics Since 1945*, 9th ed. New York: Longman, 2009.

Cashman, Greg, and Leonard C. Robinson. *An Introduction to the Causes of War: Patterns of Interstate Conflict from World War I to Iraq*. Lanham, MD: Rowman & Littlefield, 2007.

Chua, Amy. *Day of Empire: How Hyperpowers Rise to Global Dominance—and Why They Fall*. New York: Knopf, 2009.

Dunne, Tim, Milya Kurki, and Steve Smith, eds. *Theories of International Relations: Discipline and Diversity*. New York: Oxford University Press, 2007.

Gallarotti, Giulio M. *The Power Curse: Influence and Illusion in World Politics*. Boulder, CO: Lynne Rienner, 2010.

Ikenberry, G. John, ed. *American Foreign Policy*, 6th ed. Belmont, CA: Wadsworth, 2011.

Kennedy, Paul. *Parliament of Man: The Past, Present, and Future of the United Nations*. New York: Random House, 2006.

Kissinger, Henry. *Does America Need a Foreign Policy?* New York: Simon & Schuster, 2001.

Little, Richard. *The Balance of Power in International Relations: Metaphors, Myths, and Models*. New York: Cambridge University Press, 2007.

Mahbubani, Kishore. *The New Asian Hemisphere: The Irresistible Shift of Global Power*. New York: PublicAffairs, 2008.

McWilliams, Wayne C., and Harry Piotrowski. *The World Since 1945: A History of International Relations*, 7th ed. Boulder, CO: Lynne Rienner, 2009.

Morgenthau, Hans J., Kenneth W. Thompson, and David Clinton. *Politics Among Nations: The Struggle for Power and Peace*, 7th ed. Burr Ridge, IL: McGraw-Hill, 2005.

Sachs, Jeffrey D. *Common Wealth: Economics for a Crowded Planet*. New York: Penguin, 2008.

Zakaria, Fareed. *The Post-American World*. New York: Norton, 2008.

Glossary

absolutism Post-feudal concentration of power in monarch.

accusatorial Like adversarial but with a prosecutor accusing a defendant of crimes.

administration Executives appointed by U.S. president, equivalent to European "government."

adversarial System based on two opposing parties to a dispute.

adversarial Inclined to criticize and oppose, to treat with enmity.

AFL-CIO American Federation of Labor-Congress of Industrial Organizations, the largest U.S. union federation.

aggregate Thing or population considered as a whole.

amicus curiae Statement to a court by persons not party to a case.

anachronism Something out of the past.

analogy Taking one thing as the model for another.

anecdotal Recounting the views of a few respondents.

anglophone An English speaker.

anticlericalism Movement in Catholic countries to get Church out of politics.

apartheid System of strict racial segregation formerly practiced in South Africa.

apolitical Not interested or participating in politics.

apparatchik Russian for "person of the apparatus"; full-time Communist party functionary.

appeal Taking a case to a higher court.

appropriation Government funds voted by legislature.

attentive public Those citizens who follow politics, especially national and international affairs.

austerity Drastically cutting government spending.

authoritarian Nondemocratic government but not necessarily totalitarian.

authority Political leaders' ability to command respect and exercise power.

autonomías Spanish regions with devolved powers.

ayatollah Top cleric in Shia Islam.

backbencher Ordinary member of parliament with no leadership or executive responsibilities.

bailout Emergency government loan to save firm from collapse.

balance of payments The value of what a country exports compared with what it imports.

balance of power System in which major nations form and reform alliances to protect themselves.

bandwagon Tendency of front-runners to gain additional supporters.

bar graph   Stand-alone data points comparing categories.

Basic Law   German *Grundgesetz.* Germany's constitution since 1949.

behavioralism   The empirical study of actual human behavior rather than abstract or speculative theories.

bench   The office of judgeship.

bicameral   Parliament having two chambers, upper and lower.

bimodal   A distribution with two large clusters at the extremes and a small center.

bipolar   System of two large, hostile blocs, each led by a superpower, as in the Cold War.

blog   Short for "Web log"; online free magazine, often partisan and idiosyncratic.

bourgeois   Adjective, originally French for city dweller; later and current, middle class in general. Noun: *bourgeoisie.*

brief   Written summary submitted by one side giving relevant facts, laws, and precedents.

bubble   Market that has gone too high.

Bundesrat   Upper, weaker chamber of German parliament.

Bundestag   Lower, more important chamber of German parliament.

bureaucracy   The *career* civil service that staffs government executive agencies.

bureaucratic politics   Infighting among and within agencies to set policy.

business cycle   Tendency of economy to alternate between growth and *recession* over several years.

cabinet   Top executives who head major ministries or departments.

cadre party   One run by a few political professionals and only intermittently active.

canon law   Laws of the Roman Catholic Church, based on Roman law.

Capitol Hill   Home of U.S. Congress. (Note spelling: -ol.)

career   Professional civil servant, not political appointee.

caste   Rigid, hereditary social class or group.

catchall   Large, ideologically loose parties that welcome all.

center   Nation's capital and its powers.

center-fleeing   Parties become extremist, ignoring voters in center.

center–periphery tension   Resentment of outlying areas at rule by nation's capital.

center-seeking   Parties become moderate, aiming for large block of votes in center of political spectrum.

centralization   Degree of control exercised by national headquarters.

centrifugal   Pulling apart.

chancellor   Germany's prime minister.

charismatic   Having strong personal drawing power.

civil disobedience   The nonviolent breaking of an unjust law to serve a higher law.

civil law   Noncriminal disputes among individuals.

civil rights   Ability to participate in politics and society, such as voting and free speech; sometimes confused with but at a higher level than human rights.

civil society   Humans after becoming civilized. Modern usage: associations between family and government.

class action   Lawsuit on behalf of a group.

class voting   Tendency of a given social class to vote for a party that promotes its economic interests.

classic liberalism   Ideology founded by Adam Smith to keep government out of economy; became U.S. conservatism.

coalition   Multiparty alliance to form a government.

code law   Laws arranged in books, originally updated Roman law.

coherence   Sticking together to make a rational whole.

Cold War   Armed tension and mistrust between U.S. and Soviet camps, 1946–1989.

collective security   An agreement among all nations to automatically counter an aggressor.

common law   "Judge-made law," old decisions built up over the centuries.

communism   Marxist theory merged with Leninist organization into a totalitarian party.

confederation   Political system in which components override *center*.

conservatism   Ideology of keeping systems largely unchanged.

consistency   Applying the same standards to all.

constituency   The people or district that elects an official.

constituency casework   Attention legislators pay to complaints of people who elect them.

constituent assembly   Legislature convened to draft new constitution.

constitution   Basic rules that structure a government, usually written.

constitutional law   That which grows out of a country's basic documents.

constitutionalism   Degree to which government limits its powers.

constructed   Something widely believed as old and hallowed but actually recent and artificial.

consumption   Buying things.

corporatism   The direct participation of interest groups in government.

corruption   Use of public office for private gain.

coup   From the French *coup d'état*, hit at the state; extralegal takeover of government, usually by military.

covariance   How much two factors change together, indicating how strongly they are related.

critical election   One showing a realignment.

cross-pressured   Pulled between opposing political forces; said to produce apathy.

culture   Human behavior that is learned as opposed to inherited.

cynical   Untrusting and suspicious, especially of government.

deadlock   In presidential systems, executive and legislative branches blocking each other.

dealignment   Major, long-term decline in party ID.

debt   The sum total of deficits over many years.

decentralization   Shifting some administrative functions from central government to lower levels; less than *devolution*.

deficit   Spending more in a given year than you take in.

demagogue   Politician who whips up masses with extreme and misleading issues.

democracy   Political system of mass participation, competitive elections, and human and civil rights.

democratic peace   Theory that democracies do not fight each other.

department   French first-order civil division.

dependent variable   The factor that changes under the impact of the *independent variable*.

descriptive   Explaining what is.

devolution   Shifting some powers from central government to component units.

devotee party   One based on a single personality.

Diet   Japan's national legislature.

discipline   A field of study, often represented by an academic department or major.

dissolve   Send a parliament home for new elections.

domestic politics   Interactions within states.

dysanalogy   Showing that one thing is a poor model for another.

economic issues   Questions relating to jobs, income, taxes, and welfare benefits.

economic rights   Guarantees of adequate material standards of living; the newest and most controversial rights.

Electoral College   U.S. system of weighting popular presidential vote to favor smaller states.

electoral system   Laws for running elections; two general types: single-member district and proportional.

electromagnetic spectrum   The airwaves over which signals are broadcast.

elite media   Highly influential newspapers and magazines read by elites and the attentive public.

elites   The "top" or most influential people in a political system.

empirical   Based on observable evidence.

entitlement   U.S. federal expenditure mandated by law, such as Social Security and Medicare.

environmentalism   Ideology that environment is endangered and must be preserved through regulation and lifestyle changes.

Estates General   Old, unused French parliament.

euro   Since 2002, common EU currency used in most of West Europe; value fluctuates but in 2010 worth $1.40.

face-to-face   Communication by personal contact.

failed state   One incapable of even minimal governance, with essentially no national government.

fall   In parliamentary system, a cabinet is voted out or resigns.

fascism   Extreme form of nationalism with elements of socialism and militarism.

Federal Reserve Board   "The Fed"—U.S. central bank that controls interest rates and money supply.

federalism   Balancing of power between a nation's capital and autonomous subdivisions, such as U.S. states.

feminism   Ideology of psychological, political, and economic equality for women.

feudalism   System of political power dispersed among layers.

first-order civil divisions   Countries' main territorial components, such as U.S. states or Spanish provinces.

Five-Year Plans   Stalin's plans for rapid, centrally administered Soviet industrial growth.

fixed exchange rate   Dollar buys set amounts of foreign currencies.

floating exchange rate   Dollar buys varying amounts of foreign currencies, depending on market for them.

foreign policy   Interface of domestic and world politics; in Lippmann's phrase, "the shield of the Republic."

framing   A news story's basic direction and interpretation.

franchise   The right to vote.

francophone   A French speaker.

functionalism   Theory that cooperation in specialized areas will encourage overall cooperation among nations.

fusion of power   Executive as an offshoot of the legislature.

gender gap   Tendency of American women to vote more Democratic than do men.

general will Rousseau's theory of what the whole community wants.

glasnost Gorbachev's policy of media openness.

globalization Free flow of commerce across borders, making the world one big market.

government In Europe, a given cabinet, equivalent to U.S. "administration."

Great Society President Johnson's ambitious program of social reforms.

gross domestic product (GDP) Sum total of goods and services produced in a given country in one year, often expressed per capita (GDPpc) by dividing population into GDP.

habeas corpus Detainee may protest innocence before judge.

hierarchy Organized in a ranking of power from top to bottom, as if on a ladder.

higher law That which comes from God.

honeymoon High support for presidents early in their terms.

human rights Freedom from government mistreatment such as arrest, torture, jail, and death without due process.

hypothesis An initial theory a researcher starts with, to be proved by evidence.

ideologue Someone who believes passionately in an ideology.

ideology Belief system that society can be improved by following certain doctrines; usually ends in -*ism*.

if-then statement Says that two variables are linked: Where X happens, so does Y.

IFOR Implementation Force; effective NATO-sponsored peacekeeping effort in Bosnia following 1995 Dayton Accords.

illiberal democracy Regimes that are elected but lack democratic qualities such as civil rights and limits on government.

immobilism Getting stuck over a major political issue.

impeachment Indictment by the House for the Senate to try the president.

imperialism Amassing of colonial empires, mostly by European powers; pejorative in Marxist terms.

inchoate Not yet formed.

incumbent Official who already occupies the office.

independent variable The factor you think influences or causes something to happen.

indict Pronounced *in-dite*; to formally charge someone with a crime.

indigent Having no money.

inflation A general, overall rise in prices.

instability Frequent changes of cabinet.

institutionalize To make a political relationship permanent.

institutions The formal structures of government, such as the U.S. Congress.

integration Merging subcultures into the *mainstream* culture.

intellectuals Educated people who think deeply about things.

intensity The firmness and enthusiasm with which an opinion is held.

interest aggregation Melding separate interests into general platforms put forward by a political party.

interest group An association that pressures government for policies it favors.

international relations Interactions among states.

interventionism Policy of using military force overseas.

introspective Looking within oneself.

investigating judge In European legal systems, judicial officer who both gathers evidence and issues indictments.

irrational Based on the power to use fear and myth to cloud reason.

Islamism Muslim religion turned into a political ideology.

isolationism U.S. tendency to minimize importance of outside world.

jihadi From *jihad* (holy war); Muslim holy warrior.

Jim Crow System of segregationist laws in the U.S. South.

judicial activism Willingness of some judges to override legislatures by declaring certain statutes unconstitutional.

judicial restraint Unwillingness of some judges to overturn statutes passed by legislatures.

judicial review Ability of courts to decide if laws are constitutional; not present in all countries.

Junker (Pronounced: YOON-care) Prussian state nobility.

KGB Soviet Committee on State Security, powerful intelligence and security agency.

kleptocracy Rule by thieves, used in derision and jest.

Knesset Israel's 120-member unicameral parliament.

laissez-faire French for "let it be"; economic system of minimal government interference and supervision; capitalism.

Land German federal first-order civil division; plural *Länder.*

law That which must be obeyed under penalties.

leftist Favors social and economic change to uplift poor.

legitimacy Mass feeling that the government's rule is rightful and should be obeyed.

libertarianism U.S. ideology in favor of shrinking all government power in favor of individual freedom.

life cycle Theory that opinions change as people age.

life peer Distinguished Briton named to House of Lords for his or her life, not hereditary.

line graph Connection of data points showing change over time.

lobbying Interest-group contact with legislators.

log rolling Legislators mutually supporting each other to get pork-barrel bills passed.

longitudinal Studying how something changes over time.

Lords Upper, weaker chamber of British parliament.

macro theories Focus on nations and history.

mainstream Sharing the average or standard political culture.

majoritarian Electoral system that gives more than half of seats to one party.

majority More than half.

mandate A representative carrying out the specific wishes of the public.

manias Periods of market boom in which greed trumps fear.

Maoism Extreme form of communism, featuring guerrilla warfare and periodic upheavals.

marginalized Pushed to the edge of society and the economy, often said of the poor and of subcultures.

mass media Modern means of communication that quickly reach very wide audiences. (The word *media* is plural; *medium* is the singular form.)

mass party One that attempts to gain committed adherents; usually has formal membership.

media event News incident planned to get media coverage.

merit civil service One based on competitive exams rather than patronage.

methodology The techniques for studying questions objectively.

METI Japan's Ministry of Economy, Trade, and Industry; formerly MITI, Ministry of International Trade and Industry.

micro theories Focus on individuals.

minister Head of ministry, equivalent to U.S. departmental secretary.

ministry Major division of executive branch; equivalent to U.S. *department*.

minority Subgroup distinct by background, viewpoint, or practice within the larger society.

minority government Cabinet lacking firm majority in parliament.

MITI Japan's Ministry of International Trade and Industry.

mixed-member Hybrid electoral system that uses both single-member districts and proportional representation.

mobilization Rousing people to participate in politics.

modern liberalism Ideology favoring government intervention to correct economic and social ills; U.S. liberalism today.

monarchy Hereditary rule by one person.

moral hazard Shielding firms from the risky consequences of their behavior.

MP British member of Parliament, namely, the House of Commons.

multicausal Several factors making something happen.

multipolar System divided among several power centers.

NAM National Association of Manufacturers, a major federation of U.S. industrial executives.

nation Population with a historic sense of self.

National Assembly Lower, more important chamber of French parliament.

national interest What's good for the nation as a whole in world affairs.

nationalism A people's heightened sense of cultural, historical, and territorial identity, unity, and sometimes greatness.

nationalization Putting major industries under government ownership.

natural law That which comes from nature, understood by reasoning.

neoinstitutional theory Institutions take on lives of their own, sometimes disconnected from electorates.

neoconservatism U.S. ideology of former liberals turning to conservative causes and methods.

nomenklatura Lists of top Soviet positions and those eligible to fill them, the Soviet elite.

noneconomic issues Questions relating to patriotism, religion, race, sexuality, and personal choice.

noninterventionism A policy of not sending troops abroad.

nonpaternalism Not taking a supervisory or guiding role.

normative Explaining what ought to be.

oligopoly A few big firms dominate a market.

ombudsman Swedish for "agent"; lawyer employed by parliament to help citizens wronged by government.

opinion leaders Locally respected people who influence the views of others.

opportunists Persons out for themselves.

opposition Those parties in parliament not supporting the government.

outlier Item that deviates from its expected position.

outsourcing U.S. firms producing overseas.

overt socialization Deliberate government policy to teach culture.

panics Periods of market collapse in which fear trumps greed.

paradigm A model or way of doing research accepted by a discipline.

parliament National legislature; when capitalized, British Parliament, specifically House of Commons.

parliamentary systems Those with election of parliament only, which in turn elects the prime minister.

parochial Narrow; having little or no interest in politics.

participatory Interest or willingness to take part in politics.

party identification Long-term voter attachment to a given party.

party system How parties interact with each other.

peacekeeping Outside military forces stabilizing a cease-fire agreement.

personalistic Based on personality of strong ruler.

petrostate Country based on oil exports, such as Saudi Arabia.

plaintiff The person who complains in a law case.

pluralism Theory that politics is the interaction of many groups.

plurality The most, even if less than half.

polarization Opinion fleeing the center to form two hostile camps.

polarize To drive opinion into a *bimodal* distribution.

polarized pluralism System in which parties become more extremist.

Politburo Russian for "political bureau"; the ruling committee of a Communist party.

political action committee (PAC) U.S. interest group set up specifically to contribute money to election campaigns.

political appointment Government job given to non–civil servant, often as reward for support.

political competence Knowing how to accomplish something politically.

political culture The psychology of the nation in regard to politics.

political economy Influence of politics and economy on each other; what government should do in the economy.

political efficacy Feeling that one has at least a little political input (opposite: feeling powerless).

political generations Theory that great events of young adulthood permanently color political views.

political institution Established and durable pattern of authority.

political party Group seeking to elect officeholders under a given label.

political power Ability of one person to get another to do something.

pork barrel Government projects aimed at legislators' constituencies, also called earmarks.

portfolio Minister's assigned ministry.

positive law That which is written by humans and accepted over time—the opposite of natural law.

positivism Theory that society can be studied scientifically and incrementally improved with the knowledge gained.

postbehavioral Synthesis of traditional, behavioral, and other techniques in the study of politics.

postmaterialism Theory that modern culture has moved beyond getting and spending.

praetorianism From the Praetorian Guard in ancient Rome; tendency of military takeovers.

pragmatic Using whatever works without theory or ideology.

precedent Legal decisions based on earlier decisions.

prefect Administrator of a French department.

prefecture Japanese first-order civil division.

premier France's and Italy's prime ministers.

president In U.S.-type systems, the chief political official; in many other systems, a symbolic official.

presidential systems Those with separate election of executive (as opposed to symbolic) president.

prime minister Chief political official in parliamentary systems.

primordial Groups people are born into, such as religions and tribes.

productivity The efficiency with which goods or services are produced.

proletariat Marx's name for the industrial working class.

proportional representation Elects representatives by party's percent of vote.

protectionism Policy of keeping out foreign goods to protect domestic producers.

public financing Using tax dollars to fund something, such as election-campaign expenses.

public opinion Citizens' reactions to current, specific issues and events.

public policy What a government tries to do; the choices it makes among alternatives.

quantify To measure with numbers.

quasi- Nearly or almost.

Question Hour Time reserved in Commons for opposition to challenge cabinet.

quota A numerical limit on an import.

quota Drawing a sample to match categories of the population.

rally event Occurrence that temporarily boosts presidents' support.

randomization Drawing a sample at random, with everyone having an equal chance of inclusion.

rational Based on the ability to reason.

realignment Major, long-term shift in party ID.

realism Working with the world as it is and not as we wish it to be; usually focused on power.

recession Period of economic decline; a shrinking GDP.

reciprocity Mutual application of legal standards.

red scare Exaggerated fear of Communist subversion, as in World War I and McCarthy periods.

referendum A mass vote on an issue rather than for a candidate; a type of direct democracy.

regionalism Feeling of regional differences and sometimes breakaway tendencies.

regions Portions of a country with a sense of self and sometimes subcultural differences.

relative deprivation Feeling of some groups that they are missing out on economic growth.

religiosity Depth of religious conviction (not same as choice of denomination).

representative democracy One in which the people do not rule directly but through elected and accountable representatives.

republic A political system without a monarch.

republic In Communist Soviet Union and Yugoslavia, federal first-order civil division.

retrospective voting Voters choosing based on overall incumbent performance.

revisionist Changing an ideology or view of history.

revolution Sudden replacement of an old system by a new one.

Riksdag Sweden's parliament.

Roman law System based on codes of ancient Rome.

rule of anticipated reactions Politicians form policies based on how they think the public will react.

rules of engagement   Specify when peacekeeping forces can shoot back.

salience   Literally, that which jumps out; the importance of given issues in public opinion or the characteristics of the public holding various opinions.

sample   Those persons to be interviewed in a survey, a small fraction of a population.

scandal   Corruption made public.

scattergram   Graph showing position of items on two axes.

scholarship   Intellectual arguments supported by reason and evidence.

secular   Not connected to religion.

sedition   Incitement to public disorder or to overthrow the state.

separation of powers   Legislative and executive branches checking and balancing each other.

separation of powers   U.S. doctrine that branches of government should be distinct and should check and balance each other, found in few other governments.

shah   Persian for king.

single-issue group   Interest association devoted to one cause only.

single-member district   Electoral system that elects one person per district, as in the United States and Britain.

sit-in   Tactic of overturning local laws by deliberately breaking them, as at segregated lunch counters.

skewed   A distribution with its peak well to one side.

social class   A broad layer of society, usually based on income and often labeled lower, middle, and upper.

social contract   Theory that individuals join and stay in civil society as if they had signed a contract.

social democracy   Mildest form of socialism, stressing welfare measures but not state ownership of industry.

socialism   Economic system of government ownership of industry, allegedly for good of whole society; opposite of capitalism.

socialization   The learning of culture.

socioeconomic status   Combination of income and prestige criteria in the ranking of groups.

soft money   Campaign contributions to parties and issue groups so as to skirt federal limits on contributions to candidates.

source   Who or where a news reporter gets information from.

sovereignty   A national government's being boss on its own turf, the last word in law in that country.

stagflation   Combination of slow growth plus inflation in the U.S. economy in the 1970s.

Standing Committee   Top leadership of Chinese Communist Party, China's ruling elite.

state   In Europe, all branches of the national political system; what Americans call "the government."

state   Government structures of a nation.

State Duma   Russia's national legislature.

state of nature   Humans before civilization.

statism   Economic system of state ownership of major industries to enhance power and prestige of state; a precapitalist system.

status quo   Keeping the present situation.

statute   An ordinary law passed by a legislature, not part of the constitution.

strong state   Modern form of government, able to administer and tax entire nation.

structured access   Long-term friendly connection of interest group to officials.

stump Verb, to campaign by personally speaking to audiences.

subculture A minority culture within the *mainstream* culture.

subject Feeling among citizens that they should obey authority but not participate much in politics.

subprime Risky mortgage made to unqualified borrower.

suffrage The right to vote.

Sullivan Short for *New York Times v. Sullivan*, 1964 Supreme Court decision protecting media against public officials' libel suits.

superstructure Marx's term for everything that is built on top of the economy (laws, art, politics, etc.).

supranational A governing body above individual nations (such as the UN).

survey A public opinion poll.

swing Percentage of voters switching parties from one election to the next.

system breakdown Major political malfunction or instability.

tariff A tax on an import.

tendency Finding that two variables are linked but not perfectly.

terrorism Political use of violence to weaken a hated authority.

Thermidor Summer month of French revolutionary calendar that marked end of revolutionary extremism.

thesis A main idea or claim, to be proved by evidence.

thinkpiece Essay based on logic rather than on firm evidence.

third party A nation not involved in a dispute helping to settle it.

Third World The developing areas: parts of Asia, Africa, and Latin America.

Titoism Mild, decentralized form of communism.

Tory Nickname for British Conservative.

totalitarian Political system in which the state attempts total control of its citizens.

transparency Political money and transactions open to public scrutiny.

treaty A contract between nations.

trustee A representative deciding what is the public good without a specific mandate.

turnout Percent of eligible voters who vote in a given election.

two-plus party system Country having two big and one or more small parties.

unforeseen consequence Bad or counterproductive result when laws or policies do not work as expected.

unicameral Parliament with one chamber.

unilateralism Doing things our way against the wishes of allies.

unimodal A single, center-peaked distribution; a bell-shaped curve.

unitary system Centralization of power in a nation's capital with little autonomy for subdivisions.

UNPROFOR UN Protective Force; ineffective peacekeeping effort in Bosnia in early 1990s.

utopia An imagined and idealized perfect system.

values Deeply held views; key component of political culture.

velvet revolution Relatively non-violent mass uprisings that oust Communist and other repressive regimes.

vice minister Top bureaucrat in a Japanese ministry.

volatility Tendency of public opinion to change quickly.

vote of confidence Vote in parliament to support or oust government.

voting bloc Group with a marked tendency.

Warren Court The liberal, activist U.S. Supreme Court under Chief Justice Earl Warren, 1953–1969.

WASP White, Anglo-Saxon, Protestant.

weak state One unable to govern effectively, corrupt and penetrated by crime.

weapons of mass destruction (WMD) Nuclear, chemical, and bacteriological weapons.

welfare dependency Stuck on welfare with no incentive to get off.

welfare state Economic system of major government redistribution of income to poorer citizens.

Weltanschauung German for "worldview"; parties that attempt to sell a particular ideology.

whig democracy Democracy for the few, typical of early stages of democracy.

whip Legislator who instructs other party members when and how to vote.

wire service News agency that sells to all media.

workfare Programs limiting the duration of welfare payments and requiring recipients to work or get job training.

X axis The horizontal leg of a graph.

Y axis The vertical leg of a graph.

Zeitgeist German for "spirit of the times"; Hegel's theory that each epoch has a distinctive spirit, which moves history along.

References

Acemoglu, Daron, and James A. Robinson. *Economic Origins of Dictatorship and Democracy.* New York: Cambridge University Press, 2005.

Ackerman, Bruce. *The Decline and Fall of the American Republic.* Cambridge, MA: Harvard University Press, 2010.

Ackerman, Bruce. *The Failure of the Founding Fathers: Jefferson, Marshall, and the Rise of Presidential Democracy.* Cambridge, MA: Harvard University Press, 2005.

Akerlof, George A., and Robert J. Shiller. *Animal Spirits: How Human Psychology Drives the Economy, and Why It Matters for Global Capitalism.* Princeton, NJ: Princeton University Press, 2009.

Alexander, Jeffrey C. *The Civil Sphere.* New York: Oxford University Press, 2007.

Almond, Gabriel A. *Ventures in Political Science: Narratives and Reflections.* Boulder, CO: Lynne Rienner, 2002.

Almond, Gabriel A., and James S. Coleman. *Politics of Developing Areas.* Princeton, NJ: Princeton University Press, 1960.

Alterman, Eric. *What Liberal Media? The Truth About Bias and the News.* New York: Basic Books, 2004.

Alvarez, R. Michael, and John Brehm. *Hard Choices, Easy Answers: Values, Information, and American Public Opinion.* Princeton, NJ: Princeton University Press, 2002.

Amar, Akhil Reed. *America's Constitution: A Biography.* New York: Random House, 2006.

Arkes, Hadley. *Natural Rights and the Right to Choose.* New York: Cambridge University Press, 2002.

Aronowitz, Stanley. *How Class Works: Power and Social Movement.* New Haven, CT: Yale University Press, 2003.

Asher, Herbert. *Polling and the Public: What Every Citizen Should Know*, 8th ed. Washington, DC: CQ Press, 2010.

Axelrod, Alan. *Minority Rights in America.* Washington, DC: CQ Press, 2002.

Bacevich, Andrew J. *Washington Rules: America's Path to Permanent War.* New York: Metropolitan Books, 2010.

Bach, Amy. *Ordinary Justice: How America Holds Court.* New York: Holt, 2010.

Baradat, Leon P. *Political Ideologies: Their Origins and Impact*, 11th ed. New York: Longman, 2012.

Barber, Sotirios A., and James E. Fleming. *Constitutional Interpretation: The Basic Questions.* New York: Oxford University Press, 2007.

Bartels, Larry M. *Unequal Democracy: The Political Economy of the New Gilded Age.* Princeton, NJ: Princeton University Press, 2008.

Baum, Lawrence. *Judges and Their Audiences.* Princeton, NJ: Princeton University Press, 2008.

Baumol, William J., Robert E. Litan, and Carl J. Schramm. *Good Capitalism, Bad Capitalism, and the Economics of Growth and Prosperity.* New Haven, CT: Yale University Press, 2007.

Beer, Jeremy, Bruce Frohnen, and Jeffrey O. Nelson, eds. *American Conservatism: An Encyclopedia.* Wilmington, DE: ISI Books, 2006.

Bell-Fialkoff, Andrew. *Ethnic Cleansing*, rev. ed. New York: Palgrave, 1999.

Belsky, Martin H., ed. *The Rehnquist Court: A Retrospective.* New York: Oxford University Press, 2002.

Benjamin, Daniel, and Steven Simon. *The Next Attack: The Failure of the War on Terror and a Strategy for Getting It Right.* New York: Henry Holt, 2006.

Bennett, W. Lance, Regina G. Lawrence, and Steven Livingston. *When the Press Fails: Political Power and the News Media from Iraq to Katrina.* Chicago: University of Chicago Press, 2008.

Berinsky, Adam J. *In Time of War: Understanding American Public Opinion from World War II to Iraq.* Chicago: University of Chicago Press, 2009.

Bernstein, Andrew. *The Capitalist Manifesto: The Historic, Economic, and Philosophic Case for Laissez-Faire.* Lanham, MD: University Press of America, 2005.

Berry, Jeffrey M. *The New Liberalism: The Rising Power of Citizen Groups.* Washington, DC: Brookings, 2000.

Bibby, John F., and L. Sandy Maisel. *Two Parties—Or More? The American Party System.* Boulder, CO: Westview, 1998.

Biersack, Robert, Paul S. Herrnson, and Clyde Wilcox, eds. *After the Revolution: PACs, Lobbies, and the Republican Congress.* Needham Heights, MA: Allyn & Bacon, 1999.

Bingham, Tom. *The Rule of Law.* London: Allen Lane, 2010.

Birnir, Johanna Kristin. *Ethnicity and Electoral Politics.* New York: Cambridge University Press, 2007.

Bishop, Bill, and Robert G. Cushing. *The Big Sort: Why the Clustering of Like-Minded America Is Tearing Us Apart.* Boston: Houghton Mifflin, 2008.

Blondel, Jean, and Takashi Inoguchi. *Political Cultures in Asia and Europe: Citizens, States and Societal Values.* New York: Routledge, 2006.

Blumenthal, Max. *Republican Gomorrah: Inside the Movement That Shattered the Party.* New York: Basic Books, 2009.

Bobbit, Philip. *The Shield of Achilles: War, Peace, and the Course of History.* New York: Knopf, 2002.

Boehlert, Eric. *Bloggers on the Bus: How the Internet Changes Politics and the Press.* New York: Simon & Schuster, 2010.

Boesche, Roger. *The First Great Political Realist: Kautilya and His Arthashastra.* Lanham, MD: Lexington, 2003.

Boulding, Kenneth E. *Three Faces of Power.* Newbury Park, CA: Sage, 1989.

Brader, Ted. *Campaigning for Hearts and Minds: How Emotional Appeals in Political Ads Work.* Chicago: University of Chicago Press, 2006.

Brady, W. David, and Craig Volden. *Revolving Gridlock: Politics and Policy from Jimmy Carter to George W. Bush*, 2nd ed. Boulder, CO: Westview, 2005.

Brewer, Mark D., and Jeffrey M. Stonecash. *Split: Class and Cultural Divides in American Politics.* Washington, DC: CQ Press, 2007.

Breyer, Stephen. *Making Our Democracy Work: A Judge's View.* New York: Knopf, 2010.

Brisbin, Richard, and John Kilwein. *Real Law Stories: Inside the American Judicial Process.* New York: Oxford University Press, 2010.

Brogan, Hugh. *Alexis de Tocqueville: A Life.* New Haven, CT: Yale University Press, 2007.

Browne, William P. *Groups, Interests, and U.S. Public Policy.* Washington, DC: Georgetown University Press, 1998.

Brzezinski, Zbigniew. *Second Chance: Three Presidents and the Crisis of American Superpower.* New York: Basic Books, 2008.

Buell, Emmett H. Jr., and Lee Sigelman. *Attack Politics: Negativity in Presidential Campaigns since 1960.* Lawrence, KS: University Press of Kansas, 2008.

Burgess, Michael. *Comparative Federalism: Theory and Practice.* New York: Routledge, 2006.

Burke, John P. *The Institutional Presidency: Organizing and Managing the White House from FDR to Clinton*, 2nd ed. Baltimore, MD: Johns Hopkins University Press, 2000.

Burns, James MacGregor. *Packing the Court: The Rise of Judicial Power and the Coming Crisis of the Supreme Court.* New York: Penguin, 2009.

Buruma, Ian. *Taming the Gods: Religion and Democracy on Three Continents.* Princeton, NJ: Princeton University Press, 2010.

Calvi, James V., and Susan Coleman. *American Law and Legal Systems*, 6th ed. Upper Saddle River, NJ: Prentice Hall, 2007.

Calvocoressi, Peter. *World Politics Since 1945*, 9th ed. New York: Longman, 2009.

Campbell, David E., ed. *A Matter of Faith: Religion in the 2004 Presidential Election.* Washington, DC: Brookings, 2007.

Campbell, W. Joseph. *Getting It Wrong: Ten of the Greatest Misreported Stories in American Journalism.* Berkeley, CA: University of California Press, 2010.

Caplan, Bryan. *The Myth of the Rational Voter.* Princeton, NJ: Princeton University Press, 2007.

Carp, Robert A., Ronald Stidham, and Kenneth Manning. *Judicial Process in America*, 7th ed. Washington, DC: CQ Press, 2007.

Carr, Craig L. *Polity: Political Culture and the Nature of Politics.* Lanham, MD: Rowman & Littlefield, 2007.

Carter, Lief H., and Thomas F. Burke. *Reason in Law*, 8th ed. New York: Longman, 2009.

Carty, R. Kenneth, William Cross, and Lisa Young. *Rebuilding Canadian Party Politics.* Vancouver, BC: University of British Columbia Press, 2000.

Cashman, Greg, and Leonard C. Robinson. *An Introduction to the Causes of War: Patterns of Interstate Conflict from World War I to Iraq.* Lanham, MD: Rowman & Littlefield, 2007.

Cassidy, John. *How Markets Fail: The Logic of Economic Calamities.* New York: Farrar, Straus and Giroux, 2009.

Ceaser, James W., and Andrew E. Busch. *Red Over Blue: The 2004 Elections and American Politics.* Lanham, MD: Rowman & Littlefield, 2005.

Cheibub, José Antonio. *Presidentialism, Parliamentarianism, and Democracy.* New York: Cambridge University Press, 2007.

Chua, Amy. *Day of Empire: How Hyperpowers Rise to Global Dominance—and Why They Fall.* New York: Knopf, 2009.

Cigler, Allan J., and Burdett A. Loomis, eds. *Interest Group Politics*, 7th ed. Washington, DC: CQ Press, 2006.

Claggett, William J. M., and Byron E. Shafer. *The American Public Mind: The Issues Structure of Mass Politics in the Postwar United States.* New York: Cambridge University Press, 2010.

Clarke, Peter. *Keynes: The Rise, Fall, and Return of the Twentieth Century's Most Influential Economist.* New York: Bloomsbury, 2009.

Cohen, G. A. *Why Not Socialism?* Princeton, NJ: Princeton University Press, 2009.

Cohen, Jeffrey E. *The Presidency in the Era of 24-Hour News.* Princeton, NJ: Princeton University Press, 2008.

Cohen, Jeffrey E., Richard Fleisher, and Paul Kantor, eds. *American Political Parties: Decline or Resurgence?* Washington, DC: CQ Press, 2001.

Collier, Paul. *Wars, Guns, and Votes: Democracy in Dangerous Places.* New York: Harper, 2010.

Colomer, Josep M. *The Science of Politics: An Introduction.* New York: Oxford University Press, 2010.

Copeland, Gary W., and Samuel C. Patterson, eds. *Parliaments in the Modern World: Changing Institutions.* Ann Arbor, MI: University of Michigan Press, 1994.

Cornell, Saul. *A Well-Regulated Militia: The Founding Fathers and the Origins of Gun Control in America.* New York: Oxford, 2006.

Cushman, Clare, and Melvin I. Urofsky, eds. *Black, White and Brown: The Landmark School Desegregation Case in Retrospect.* Washington, DC: CQ Press, 2004.

Dahl, Robert A. *How Democratic Is the American Constitution?* 2nd ed. New Haven, CT: Yale University Press, 2003.

Dahl, Robert A. *On Political Equality.* New Haven, CT: Yale University Press, 2006.

Dahl, Robert A., and Bruce Stinebrickner. *Modern Political Analysis*, 6th ed. Upper Saddle River, NJ: Prentice Hall, 2003.

Dalton, Russell J. *Citizen Politics: Public Opinion and Political Parties in Advanced Industrial Democracies*, 5th ed. Washington, DC: CQ Press, 2008.

Dalton, Russell J., and Martin P. Wattenberg, eds. *Parties without Partisans: Political Change in Advanced Industrial Democracies*. New York: Oxford University Press, 2001.

Damrosch, Leo. *Tocqueville's Discovery of America*. New York: Farrar, Straus & Giroux, 2010.

Deering, Christopher J., and Steven S. Smith. *Committees in Congress*, 3rd ed. Washington, DC: CQ Press, 1997.

DeParle, Jason. *American Dream: Three Women, Ten Kids, and a Nation's Drive to End Welfare*. New York: Viking, 2005.

Diamond, Larry, and Marc F. Plattner, eds. *How People View Democracy*. Baltimore, MD: Johns Hopkins University Press, 2008.

Diamond, Larry. *The Spirit of Democracy*. New York: Holt, 2009.

Dodd, Lawrence C., and Bruce I. Oppenheimer, eds. *Congress Reconsidered*, 9th ed. Washington, DC: CQ Press, 2008.

Doran, Charles. *Why Canadian Unity Matters and Why Americans Care: Democratic Pluralism at Risk*. Toronto: University of Toronto Press, 2001.

Douthat, Ross, and Reihan Salam. *Grand New Party: How Republicans Can Win the Working Class and Save the American Dream*. New York: Doubleday, 2008.

Dunne, Tim, Milya Kurki, and Steve Smith, eds. *Theories of International Relations: Discipline and Diversity*. New York: Oxford University Press, 2007.

Duverger, Maurice. *Political Parties: Their Organization and Activities in the Modern State*, 3rd ed. London: Methuen, 1964.

Dworkin, Ronald. *Is Democracy Possible Here? Principles for a New Political Debate*. Princeton, NJ: Princeton University Press, 2009.

Dworkin, Ronald. *The Supreme Court Phalanx: The Court's New Right-Wing Bloc.* New York: New York Review of Books, 2008.

Easton, David. *A Framework for Political Analysis*. Englewood Cliffs, NJ: Prentice Hall, 1965.

Edwards, Mickey. *Reclaiming Conservatism: How a Great American Political Movement Got Lost—and How It Can Find Its Way Back*. New York: Oxford University Press, 2008.

Eisgruber, Christopher L., and Lawrence G. Sager. *Religious Freedom and the Constitution*. Cambridge, MA: Harvard University Press, 2007.

Elazar, Daniel J. *The American Mosaic: The Impact of Space, Time, and Culture on American Politics*. Boulder, CO: Westview Press, 1994.

Eldersveld, Samuel J., and Hanes Walton Jr. *Political Parties in American Society*, 2nd ed. New York: Palgrave, 2000.

Elster, Jon. *Alexis de Tocqueville: The First Social Scientist*. New York: Cambridge University Press, 2009.

Exoo, Calvin F. *The Pen and the Sword: Press, War, and Terror in the 21st Century*. Thousand Oaks, CA: Sage, 2010.

Fagan, Andrew. *The Atlas of Human Rights: Mapping Violations of Freedom Around the Globe*. Berkeley, CA: University of California Press, 2010.

Farber, David. *The Rise and Fall of Modern American Conservatism: A Short History*. Princeton, NJ: Princeton University Press, 2010.

Farrell, David M. *Electoral Systems: A Comparative Introduction*. New York: Palgrave, 2001.

Ferguson, Niall. *The Ascent of Money: A Financial History of the World*. New York: Penguin, 2009.

Fisher, Louis. *The Constitution and 9/11: Recurring Threats to America's Freedoms*. Lawrence, KS: University Press of Kansas, 2008.

Flanigan, William H., and Nancy H. Zingale. *Political Behavior of the American Electorate*, 12th ed. Washington, DC: CQ Press, 2009.

Flathman, Richard E. *Pluralism and Liberal Democracy*. Baltimore, MD: Johns Hopkins University Press, 2005.

Flynn, James R. *Where Have All the Liberals Gone? Race, Class, and Ideals in America.* New York: Cambridge University Press, 2008.

Frank, Thomas. *The Wrecking Crew: How Conservatives Rule.* New York: Metropolitan, 2008.

Freeberg, Ernest. *Democracy's Prisoner: Eugene V. Debs, the Great War, and the Right to Dissent.* Cambridge, MA: Harvard University Press, 2009.

Friedman, Benjamin M. *The Moral Consequences of Economic Growth.* New York: Knopf, 2005.

Friedrich, Carl J., ed. *Authority.* Cambridge, MA: Harvard University Press, 1958.

Frum, David. *Comeback: Conservatism That Can Win Again.* New York: Doubleday, 2009.

Fuller, Jack. *What Is Happening to News: The Information Explosion and the Crisis in Journalism.* Chicago: University of Chicago Press, 2010.

Gallagher, Michael, and Paul Mitchell, eds. *The Politics of Electoral Systems.* New York: Oxford University Press, 2006.

Gallarotti, Giulio M. *The Power Curse: Influence and Illusion in World Politics.* Boulder, CO: Lynne Rienner, 2010.

Gant, Scott. *We're All Journalists Now: The Transformation of the Press and Reshaping of the Law in the Internet Age.* New York: Simon & Schuster, 2007.

Garfinkle, Norton. *The American Dream vs. the Gospel of Wealth: The Fight for a Productive Middle-Class Economy.* New Haven, CT: Yale University Press, 2007.

Geer, John G. *In Defense of Negativity: Attack Ads in Presidential Campaigns.* Chicago: University of Chicago Press, 2006.

Gelman, Andrew. *Red State, Blue State, Rich State, Poor State: Why Americans Vote the Way They Do.* Princeton, NJ: Princeton University Press, 2008.

Gerken, Heather K. *The Democracy Index: Why Our Election System Is Failing and How to Fix It.* Princeton, NJ: Princeton University Press, 2009.

Goldsmith, Jack. *The Terror Presidency: Law and Judgment Inside the Bush Administration.* New York: Norton, 2007.

Goldstone, Jack A., ed. *Revolutions: Theoretical, Comparative, and Historical Studies,* 3rd ed. Belmont, CA: Wadsworth, 2002.

Goldwag, Arthur. *'Isms and 'Ologies: All the Movements, Ideologies, & Doctrines That Have Shaped Our World.* New York: Vintage, 2007.

Graber, Doris A. *Mass Media and American Politics,* 8th ed. Washington, DC: CQ Press, 2009.

Graziano, Luigi. *Lobbying, Pluralism and Democracy.* New York: Palgrave, 2001.

Greene, Thomas H. *Comparative Revolutionary Movements,* 3rd ed. Englewood Cliffs, NJ: Prentice Hall, 1990.

Greenhouse, Linda. *Becoming Justice Blackmun: Harry Blackmun's Supreme Court Journey.* New York: Times Books, 2005.

Greenspan, Alan. *The Age of Turbulence: Adventures in a New World.* New York: Penguin, 2008.

Greenstein, Fred. *Inventing the Job of President: Leadership Style from George Washington to Andrew Jackson.* Princeton, NJ: Princeton University Press, 2009.

Grosby, Steven. *Nationalism: A Very Short Introduction.* New York: Oxford University Press, 2005.

Grossman, Gene M., and Elhanan Helpman. *Special Interest Politics.* Cambridge, MA: MIT Press, 2002.

Hacker, Jacob, and Paul Pierson. *Winner-Take-All Politics: How Washington Made the Rich Richer—and Turned Its Back on the Middle Class.* New York: Simon & Schuster, 2010.

Halliday, Fred. *Revolution and World Politics: The Rise and Fall of the Sixth Great Power.* Durham, NC: Duke University Press, 1999.

Halper, Stefan. *The Beijing Consensus: How China's Authoritarian Model Will Dominate the Twenty-First Century.* New York: Basic Books, 2010.

Hamilton, Nigel. *American Caesars: Lives of the Presidents from Franklin D. Roosevelt to George W. Bush.* New Haven, CT: Yale University Press, 2010.

Hardt, Michael, and Antonio Negri. *Commonwealth.* Cambridge, MA: Harvard University Press, 2009.

Hayes, Michael T., and Lou Frey Jr., eds. *Inside the House: Former Members Reveal How Congress Really Works*. Lanham, MD: University Press of America, 2001.

Heilbrunn, Jacob. *They Knew They Were Right: The Rise of the Neocons*. New York: Doubleday, 2008.

Heilmann, John, and Mark Halperin. *Game Change: Obama and the Clintons, McCain and Palin, and the Race of a Lifetime*. New York: HarperCollins, 2010.

Helms, Ludger. *Presidents, Prime Ministers and Chancellors: Executive Leadership in Western Democracies*. New York: Palgrave, 2005.

Hershey, Marjorie Randon. *Party Politics in America*, 14th ed. New York: Longman, 2010.

Hetherington, Marc J., and William J. Keefe. *Parties, Politics, and Public Policy in America*, 11th ed. Washington, DC: CQ Press, 2009.

Heymann, Philip B. *Terrorism, Freedom, and Security: Winning Without War*. New York: Cambridge University Press, 2003.

Hill, Steven. *Fixing Elections: The Failure of America's Winner Take All Politics*. New York: Routledge, 2003.

Howard, John. *Concentration Camps on the Home Front: Japanese Americans in the House of Jim Crow*. Chicago: University of Chicago Press, 2008.

Howard, Philip K. *Life Without Lawyers: Liberating Americans from Too Much Law*. New York: Norton, 2009.

Hueglin, Thomas O., and Alan Fenna. *Comparative Federalism: A Systematic Inquiry*. Decorah, IA: Broadview, 2006.

Hunt, Lynn. *Inventing Human Rights: A History*. New York: Norton, 2007.

Hunter, James Davison, and Alan Wolfe. *Is There a Culture War?: A Dialogue on Values and American Public Life*. Washington, DC: Brookings, 2006.

Huntington, Samuel P. *Who Are We?: The Challenge to America's National Identity*. New York: Simon & Schuster, 2004.

Huysmans, Jeff. *What Is Politics? A Short Introduction*. New York: Columbia University Press, 2004.

Ifill, Gwen. *The Breakthrough: Politics and Race in the Age of Obama*. New York: Doubleday, 2009.

Ikenberry, G. John, ed. *American Foreign Policy*, 6th ed. Belmont, CA: Wadsworth, 2011.

Janis, Irving L. *Victims of Groupthink: A Psychological Study of Foreign-Policy Decisions and Fiascoes*. Boston: Houghton Mifflin, 1972.

Johnson, Dennis W. *No Place for Amateurs: How Political Consultants Are Reshaping America*. New York: Routledge, 2007.

Johnson, Haynes, and David S. Broder. *The System: The American Way of Politics at the Breaking Point*. Boston: Little, Brown, 1996.

Johnson, Simon, and James Kwak. *13 Bankers: The Wall Street Takeover and the Next Financial Meltdown*. New York: Pantheon, 2010.

Jones, Alex S. *Losing the News: The Future of the News That Feeds Democracy*. New York: Oxford University Press, 2009.

Jones, Charles O. *The American Presidency*. New York: Sterling, 2009.

Jreisat, Jamil E. *Comparative Public Administration and Policy*. Boulder, CO: Westview, 2002.

Kagan, Jerome. *Galen's Prophecy: Temperament and Human Nature*. New York: Basic Books, 1994.

Kaiser, Robert G. *So Damn Much Money: The Triumph of Lobbying and the Corrosion of American Government*. New York: Knopf, 2009.

Kaletsky, Anatole. *Capitalism 4.0: The Birth of a New Economy in the Aftermath of Crisis*. New York: Public Affairs, 2010.

Karvonen, Lauri, and Stein Kuhnle, eds. *Party Systems and Voter Alignments Revisited*. New York: Routledge, 2001.

Katz, Mark N., ed. *Revolution: International Dimensions*. Washington, DC: CQ Press, 2000.

Kennedy, Paul. *Parliament of Man: The Past, Present, and Future of the United Nations*. New York: Random House, 2006.

Kenski, Kate, Bruce W. Hardy, and Kathleen Hall Jamieson. *The Obama Victory: How Media, Money, and Message Shaped* the 2008 Election. New York: Oxford University Press, 2010.

Kerwin, Cornelius M., and Scott R. Furlong. *Rulemaking: How Government Agencies Write Law and Make Policy*, 4th ed. Washington, DC: CQ Press, 2010.

King, Anthony. *Running Scared: Why America's Politicians Campaign Too Much and Govern Too Little*. New York: Free Press, 1997.

Kissinger, Henry. *Does America Need a Foreign Policy?* New York: Simon & Schuster, 2001.

Kotlikoff, Laurence J., and Scott Burns. *The Coming Generational Storm: What You Need to Know about America's Economic Future*. Cambridge, MA: MIT Press, 2004.

Krugman, Paul. *The Conscience of a Liberal*. New York: Norton, 2007.

Krugman, Paul. *The Return of Depression Economics and the Crisis of 2008*. New York: Norton, 2009.

Kumar, Martha Joynt. *Managing the President's Message: The White House Communications Operation*. Baltimore, MD: Johns Hopkins University Press, 2009.

LaCroix, Alison L. *The Ideological Origins of American Federalism*. Cambridge, MA: Harvard University Press, 2010.

Lane, Jan-Erik, and Svante Ersson. *Culture and Politics: A Competitive Approach*, 2nd ed. Williston, VT: Ashgate, 2005.

Lane, Ruth. *Political Science in Theory and Practice: The "Politics" Model*. Armonk, NY: M. E. Sharpe, 1997.

Laqueur, Walter. *No End to War: Terrorism in the Twenty-First Century*. New York: Continuum, 2004.

Lardner, James, and David A. Smith, eds. *Inequality Matters: The Growing Economic Divide in America and Its Poisonous Consequences*. New York: New Press, 2005.

Lasswell, Harold. *Politics: Who Gets What, When, How*. New York: McGraw-Hill, 1936.

Laver, Michael, and Norman Schofield. *Multiparty Government: The Politics of Coalition in Europe*. New York: Oxford University Press, 1990.

Laver, Michael. *Private Desires, Political Action: An Invitation to the Politics of Rational Choice*. Thousand Oaks, CA: Sage, 1997.

Lawson, Kay, and Peter H. Merkl, eds. *When Parties Prosper: The Uses of Electoral Success*. Boulder, CO: Lynne Rienner, 2007.

Lewellen, Ted C. *Political Anthropology: An Introduction*, 3rd ed. Westport, CT: Greenwood, 2003.

Lewis, Anthony. *Freedom for the Thought That We Hate: A Biography of the First Amendment*. New York: Basic Books, 2008.

Lewis, Charles. *The Buying of the President 2004*. New York: HarperCollins, 2004.

Lichtblau, Eric. *Bush's Law: The Remaking of American Justice*. New York: Pantheon, 2008.

Lijphart, Arend, ed. *Parliamentary Versus Presidential Government*. New York: Oxford University Press, 1992.

Lijphart, Arend. *Patterns of Democracy: Government Forms and Performance in Thirty-Six Countries*. New Haven, CT: Yale University Press, 1999.

Lindblom, Charles E. *The Market System: What It Is, How It Works, and What to Make of It*. New Haven, CT: Yale University Press, 2001.

Lindblom, Charles E. *The Policy-Making Process*, 3rd ed. Englewood Cliffs, NJ: Prentice Hall, 1992.

Lindsay, D. Michael. *Faith in the Halls of Power: How Evangelicals Joined the American Elite*. New York: Oxford University Press, 2007.

Linz, Juan. *Totalitarian and Authoritarian Regimes*. Boulder, CO: Lynne Rienner, 2000.

Lipset, Seymour Martin, and Jason M. Lakin. *The Democratic Century*. Norman, OK: University of Oklahoma Press, 2004.

Lipset, Seymour Martin. *Political Man: The Social Bases of Politics*, rev. ed. Baltimore, MD: Johns Hopkins University Press, 1981.

Lipset, Seymour Martin, ed. *Political Philosophy: Theories, Thinkers, and Concepts*. Washington, DC: CQ Press, 2001.

Little, Richard. *The Balance of Power in International Relations: Metaphors, Myths, and*

Models. New York: Cambridge University Press, 2007.

Losco, Joseph, and Leonard Williams, eds. *Political Theory: Classic and Contemporary Readings*, 2nd ed., 2 vols. Los Angeles: Roxbury, 2002.

Luther, Kurt, and Ferdinand Müller-Rommel, eds. *Political Parties in the New Europe: Political and Analytical Challenges.* New York: Oxford University Press, 2005

Luyendijk, Joris. *People Like Us: Misrepresenting the Middle East.* Berkeley, CA: Soft Skull, 2009.

Maddex, Robert L., Jr. *Constitutions of the World*, 3rd ed. Washington, DC: CQ Press, 2007.

Mahbubani, Kishore. *The New Asian Hemisphere: The Irresistible Shift of Global Power.* New York: Public Affairs, 2008.

Mair, Peter. *Party System Change: Approaches and Interpretations.* New York: Oxford University Press, 1997.

Mann, Thomas E., and Norman J. Orenstein. *The Broken Branch: How Congress Is Failing America and How to Get It Back on Track.* New York: Oxford University Press, 2006.

Maranto, Robert, Tom Lansford, and Jeremy Johnson, eds. *Judging Bush.* Stanford, CA: Stanford University Press, 2009.

Mark, David. *Going Dirty: The Art of Negative Campaigning.* Lanham, MD: Rowman & Littlefield, 2006.

Mayer, Jane. *The Dark Side: The Inside Story of How the War on Terror Turned into a War on American Ideals.* New York: Doubleday, 2008.

Mayer, William G. *The Making of Presidential Candidates, 2008.* Lanham, MD: Rowman & Littlefield, 2008.

Mayhew, David R. *Congress: The Electoral Connection*, 2nd ed. New Haven, CT: Yale University Press, 2004.

McCabe, Neil Colman, ed. *Comparative Federalism in the Devolution Era.* Lanham, MD: Lexington, 2002.

McCarty, Nolan, Keith Poole, and Howard Rosenthal. *Polarized America: The Dance of Ideology and Unequal Riches.* Cambridge, MA: MIT Press, 2006.

McDonald, Michael D., and Ian Budge. *Elections, Parties, Democracy: Conferring the Median Mandate.* New York: Oxford University Press, 2005.

McFaul, Michael. *Advancing Democracy Abroad: Why We Should and How We Can.* Lanham, MD: Rowman & Littlefield, 2010.

McWilliams, Wayne C., and Harry Piotrowski. *The World Since 1945: A History of International Relations*, 7th ed. Boulder, CO: Lynne Rienner, 2009.

Micklethwait, John, and Adrian Wooldridge. *The Right Nation: Conservative Power in America.* New York: Penguin, 2004.

Miklis, Sidney M., and Michael Nelson. *The American Presidency: Origins and Development*, 5th ed. Washington, DC: CQ Press, 2007.

Milgram, Stanley. *Obedience to Authority: An Experimental View.* New York: Harper & Row, 1974.

Mindich, David T. Z. *Tuned Out: Why Americans Under 40 Don't Follow the News.* New York: Oxford University Press, 2004.

Minogue, Kenneth. *Politics: A Very Short Introduction.* New York: Oxford University Press, 1995.

Minow, Newton N., and Craig L. LaMay. *Inside the Presidential Debates: Their Improbable Past and Promising Future.* Chicago: University of Chicago Press, 2008.

Moreno, Luis. *The Federalization of Spain.* Portland, OR: F. Cass, 2001.

Morgenthau, Hans J., Kenneth W. Thompson, and David Clinton. *Politics Among Nations: The Struggle for Power and Peace*, 7th ed. Burr Ridge, IL: McGraw-Hill, 2005.

Morris, Ian. *Why the West Rules—For Now: The Patterns of History, and What They Reveal About the Future.* New York: Farrar, Straus & Giroux, 2010.

Morris, Irwin L. *The American Presidency.* New York: Cambridge University Press, 2010.

Mueller, John. *Overblown: How Politicians and the Terrorism Industry Inflate National Security Threats and Why We Believe Them.* New York: Simon & Schuster, 2006.

Mueller, John. *War, Presidents and Public Opinion.* New York: Wiley, 1973.

Murphy, Walter F. *Constitutional Democracy: Creating and Maintaining a Just Political Order.* Baltimore, MD: Johns Hopkins University Press, 2007.

Nelson, Michael, ed. *The Elections of 2008.* Washington DC: CQ Press, 2009.

Nelson, Samuel P. *Beyond the First Amendment: The Politics of Free Speech and Pluralism.* Baltimore, MD: Johns Hopkins University Press, 2005.

Neustadt, Richard E. *Presidential Power and the Modern Presidents: The Politics of Leadership from Roosevelt to Reagan.* New York: Free Press, 1991.

Nivola, Pietro S., and David W. Brady, eds. *Red and Blue Nation?: Characteristics and Causes of America's Polarized Politics.* Washington, DC: Brookings, 2007.

Page, Benjamin I., and Lawrence R. Jacobs. *Class War? What Americans Really Think about Economic Inequality.* Chicago: University of Chicago Press, 2009.

Parsa, Misagh. *States, Ideologies, and Social Revolutions: A Comparative Analysis of Iran, Nicaragua, and the Philippines.* New York: Cambridge University Press, 2000.

Patterson, Thomas E. *The Vanishing Voter: Public Involvement in an Age of Uncertainty.* New York: Knopf, 2003.

Peleg, Ilan. *Democratizing the Hegemonic State: Political Transformation in the Age of Identity.* New York: Cambridge University Press, 2007.

Perlmutter, David D. *Blogwars.* New York: Oxford University Press, 2008.

Perlstein, Rick. *Nixonland: The Rise of a President and the Fracturing of America.* New York: Simon & Schuster, 2007.

Peters, Guy. *Politics of Bureaucracy: An Introduction to Comparative Public Administration,* 6th ed. New York: Routledge, 2009.

Pfau, Michael, J. Brian Houston, and Shane M. Semmler. *Mediating the Vote: The Changing Media Landscape in U.S. Presidential Campaigns.* Lanham, MD: Rowman & Littlefield, 2007.

Phares, Walid. *The War of Ideas: Jihadism against Democracy.* New York: Palgrave, 2007.

Pika, Joseph A., and John Anthony Maltese. *The Politics of the Presidency.* 7th ed. Washington, DC: CQ Press, 2009.

Poguntke, Thomas, and Paul Webb, eds. *The Presidentialization of Politics: A Comparative Study of Modern Democracies.* New York: Oxford University Press, 2005.

Polsby, Nelson W. *How Congress Evolves: Social Bases of Institutional Change.* New York: Oxford University Press, 2003.

Polsby, Nelson W., and Aaron Wildavsky. *Presidential Elections: Strategies and Structures of American Politics,* 12th ed. Lanham, MD: Rowman & Littlefield, 2007.

Posner, Richard. *Not a Suicide Pact: The Constitution in a Time of National Emergency.* New York: Oxford University Press, 2006.

Posner, Richard A. *The Crisis of Capitalist Democracy.* Cambridge, MA: Harvard University Press, 2010.

Prior, Markus. *Post-Broadcast Democracy: How Media Choice Increases Inequality in Political Involvement and Polarizes Elections.* New York: Cambridge, 2007.

Przeworski, Adam. *Democracy and the Limits of Self-Government.* New York: Cambridge University Press, 2010.

Putnam, Robert D., and David E. Campbell. *American Grace: How Religion Divides and Unites Us.* New York: Simon & Schuster, 2010.

Rajan, Raghuram G. *Fault Lines: How Hidden Fractures Still Threaten the World Economy.* Princeton, NJ: Princeton University Press, 2010.

Rapoport, David C., and Leonard Weinberg, eds. *The Democratic Experience and Political Violence.* Portland, OR: Frank Cass, 2001.

Raskin, Marcus, and Robert Spero. *The Four Freedoms Under Siege: The Clear and Present Danger from Our National Security State.* Westport, CT: Praeger, 2007.

Rauch, Jonathan. *Government's End: Why Washington Stopped Working.* New York: PublicAffairs, 1999.

Rawls, W. Lee. *In Praise of Deadlock: How Partisan Struggle Makes Better Laws.* Baltimore, MD: Johns Hopkins University Press, 2009.

Reinhart, Carmen M., and Kenneth S. Rogoff. *This Time Is Different: Eight Centuries of Financial Folly.* Princeton, NJ: Princeton University Press, 2009.

Riley-Smith, Tristram. *The Cracked Bell: America and the Afflictions of Liberty.* New York: Skyhorse, 2010.

Rimmerman, Craig A. *The New Citizenship: Unconventional Politics, Activism, and Service,* 3rd ed. Boulder, CO: Westview, 2005.

Rosen, Jeffrey. *The Supreme Court: The Personalities and Rivalries That Defined America.* New York: Times Books, 2007.

Rosenblum, Nancy. *On the Side of the Angels: An Appreciation of Parties and Partisanship.* Princeton, NJ: Princeton University Press, 2008.

Rosenstone, Steven J., and John Mark Hansen. *Mobilization, Participation, and Democracy in America.* White Plains, NY: Longman, 2002.

Rudalevige, Andrew. *The New Imperial Presidency.* Ann Arbor, MI: University of Michigan Press, 2005.

Sabato, Larry J. *A More Perfect Constitution: 23 Proposals to Revitalize Our Constitution and Make America a Fairer Country.* New York: Walker, 2007.

Sabato, Larry J., and Glenn R. Simpson. *Dirty Little Secrets: The Persistence of Corruption in American Politics.* New York: Times Books/Random House, 1996.

Sachs, Jeffrey D. *Common Wealth: Economics for a Crowded Planet.* New York: Penguin, 2008.

Samuelson, Robert J. *The Great Inflation and Its Aftermath: The Past and Future of American Affluence.* New York: Random House, 2008.

Sandle, Mark. *Communism.* New York: Longman, 2006.

Savage, Charlie. *Takeover: The Return of the Imperial Presidency and the Subversion of American Democracy.* New York: Little, Brown, 2007.

Savoie, Donald J. *Power: Where Is It?* Montreal: McGill-Queen's University Press, 2010.

Schaller, Thomas F. *Whistling Past Dixie: How Democrats Can Win Without the South.* New York: Simon & Schuster, 2008.

Schedler, Andreas, ed. *Electoral Authoritarianism: The Dynamics of Unfree Competition.* Boulder, CO: Lynne Rienner, 2006.

Schier, Steven E. *You Call This an Election?: America's Peculiar Democracy.* Washington, DC: Georgetown University Press, 2003.

Schmitt, Richard, ed. *Toward a New Socialism.* Lanham, MD: Lexington, 2007.

Schumpeter, Joseph A. *Can Capitalism Survive? Creative Destruction and the Future of the Global Economy.* New York: HarperCollins, 2009.

Seabright, Paul. *Company of Strangers: A Natural History of Economic Life.* Princeton, NJ: Princeton University Press, 2004.

Seib, Philip. *Beyond the Front Lines: How the News Media Cover a World Shaped by War.* New York: Palgrave, 2004.

Sen, Amartya. *The Idea of Justice.* Cambridge, MA: Harvard University Press, 2009.

Shiller, Robert J. *The Subprime Solution: How Today's Global Financial Crisis Happened, and What to Do About It.* Princeton, NJ: Princeton University Press, 2009.

Shively, W. Phillips. *The Craft of Political Research,* 8th ed. Upper Saddle River, NJ: Prentice Hall, 2010.

Skocpol, Theda. *States and Social Revolutions: A Comparative Analysis of France, Russia and China.* New York: Cambridge University Press, 1979.

Smick, David M. *The World Is Curved: Hidden Dangers to the Global Economy.* New York: Penguin, 2008.

Smith, Bradley A. *Unfree Speech: The Folly of Campaign Finance Reform.* Princeton, NJ: Princeton University Press, 2001.

Snow, Donald M. *Distant Thunder: Patterns of Conflict in the Developing World,* 2nd ed. Armonk, NY: M. E. Sharpe, 1997.

Snyder, Louis L. *The New Nationalism.* New Brunswick, NJ: Transaction, 2003.

Snyder, Timothy. *Bloodlands: Europe Between Hitler and Stalin.* New York: Basic Books, 2010.

Starr, Paul. *Freedom's Power: The True Force of Liberalism.* New York: Basic Books, 2008.

Starr, Paul. *The Creation of the Media: Political Origins of Modern Communications.* New York: Basic Books, 2004.

Stepan, Alfred. *Democracies in Danger,* Baltimore, MD: Johns Hopkins University Press, 2009.

Stephens, G. Ross, and Nelson Wikstrom. *American Intergovernmental Relations: A Fragmented Federal Polity.* New York: Oxford University Press, 2006.

Stiglitz, Joseph E. *Freefall: America, Free Markets, and the Sinking of the World Economy.* New York: Norton: 2010.

Stone, Geoffrey R. *Perilous Times: Free Speech in Wartime from the Sedition Act of 1798 to the War on Terrorism.* New York: Norton, 2004.

Stonecash, Jeffrey M. *Class and Party in American Politics.* Boulder, CO: Westview, 2000.

Suleiman, Ezra N., ed. *Parliaments and Parliamentarians in Democratic Politics.* New York: Holmes & Meier, 1986.

Sullivan, Andrew. *The Conservative Soul: How We Lost It, How to Get It Back.* New York: HarperCollins, 2007.

Sunstein, Cass R. *A Constitution of Many Minds: Why the Founding Document Doesn't Mean What It Meant Before.* Princeton, NJ: Princeton University Press, 2009.

Tanenhaus, Sam. *The Death of Conservatism.* New York: Random House, 2009.

Tannenbaum, Donald, and David Schultz. *Inventors of Ideas: An Introduction to Western Political Philosophy,* 2nd ed. Belmont, CA: Wadsworth, 2003.

Tate, C. Neal. *Comparative Judicial Systems.* Washington, DC: CQ Press, 2005.

Thaler, Richard H., and Cass R. Sunstein. *Nudge: Improving Decisions About Health, Wealth, and Happiness.* New Haven, CT: Yale University Press, 2008.

Theodoulou, Stella, and Rory O'Brien, eds. *Methods for Political Inquiry: The Discipline, Philosophy, and Analysis of Politics.* Upper Saddle River, NJ: Prentice Hall, 1999.

Thomas, Clive S., ed. *Political Parties and Interest Groups: Shaping Democratic Governance.* Boulder, CO: Lynne Rienner, 2001.

Tilly, Charles, and Sidney Tarrow. *Contentious Politics.* Boulder, CO: Paradigm, 2006.

Tilly, Charles. *Democracy.* New York: Cambridge University Press, 2007.

Tinder, Glenn. *Political Thinking: The Perennial Questions,* 6th ed. New York: Longman, 2003.

Todd, Chuck, and Sheldon Gawiser. *How Barack Obama Won: A State-by-State Guide to the Historic 2008 Presidential Election.* New York: Vintage, 2009.

Toobin, Jeffrey. *The Nine: Inside the Secret World of the Supreme Court.* New York: Doubleday, 2007.

Traugott, Michael W., and Paul J. Lavrakas. *The Voter's Guide to Election Polls,* 4th ed. Lanham, MD: Rowman & Littlefield, 2008.

Tushnet, Mark. *Why the Constitution Matters.* New Haven, CT: Yale University Press, 2010.

Urofsky, Melvin I. *Louis D. Brandeis: A Life.* New York: Pantheon, 2009.

Van Creveld, Martin. *The Rise and Decline of the State.* New York: Cambridge University Press, 1999.

Wald, Kenneth D., and Allison Calhoun-Brown. *Religion and Politics in the United States,* 5th ed. Lanham, MD: Rowman & Littlefield, 2006.

Walzer, Michael. *Politics and Passion: Toward a More Egalitarian Liberalism.* New Haven, CT: Yale University Press, 2004.

Ware, Alan. *Political Parties and Party Systems.* New York: Oxford University Press, 1996.

Warren, Mark E., ed. *Democracy and Trust.* New York: Cambridge University Press, 1999.

Wasik, Bill. *And Then There's This: How Stories Live and Die in Viral Culture.* New York: Penguin, 2010.

Wedel, Janine R. *Shadow Elite: How the World's New Power Brokers Undermine Democracy, Government and the Free Market.* New York: Basic Books, 2009.

Weissberg, Robert. *Polling, Policy, and Public Opinion: The Case Against Heeding the "Voice of the People."* New York: Palgrave, 2002.

West, Darrell M. *Air Wars: Television Advertising in Election Campaigns, 1952–2008,* 5th ed. Washington, DC: CQ Press, 2009.

Westen, Drew. *The Political Brain: The Role of Emotion in Deciding the Fate of the Nation.* New York: PublicAffairs, 2008.

White, John Kenneth. *Barack Obama's America: How New Conceptions of Race, Family, and Religion Ended the Reagan Era.* Ann Arbor, MI: University of Michigan Press, 2009.

White, Stephen K., and J. Donald Moon, eds. *What Is Political Theory?* Thousand Oaks, CA: Sage, 2004.

Whittaker, David J. *Terrorism: Understanding the Global Threat,* rev. ed. New York: Longman, 2007.

Wilcox, Clyde, and Carin Larson. *Onward Christian Soldiers? The Religious Right in American Politics.* Boulder, CO: Westview, 2006.

Wills, Gary. *Bomb Power: The Modern Presidency and the National Security State.* New York: Penguin, 2010.

Wilson, Edward O. *Sociobiology: The New Synthesis.* Cambridge, MA: Harvard University Press, 1975.

Wilson, James Q. *Bureaucracy: What Government Agencies Do and Why They Do It.* New York: Basic Books, 1990.

Wiseman, Nelson. *In Search of Canadian Political Culture.* Vancouver, BC: University of British Colombia Press, 2007.

Wittes, Benjamin. *Law and the Long War: The Future of Justice in the Age of Terror.* New York: Penguin, 2008.

Wolfe, Alan. *The Future of Liberalism.* New York: Knopf Doubleday, 2010.

Wolfensberger, Donald R. *Congress and the People: Deliberative Democracy on Trial.* Baltimore, MD: Johns Hopkins University Press, 2000.

Wright, Lawrence. *The Looming Tower: Al-Qaeda and the Road to 9/11.* New York: Knopf, 2006.

Zakaria, Fareed. *The Post-American World.* New York: Norton, 2008.

Zelizer, Julian E., ed. *The Presidency of George W. Bush: A First Historical Assessment.* Princeton, NJ: Princeton University Press, 2010.

Zijderveld, Anton C. *The Waning of the Welfare State: The End of Comprehensive State Succor.* Piscataway, NJ: Transaction, 1999.

Zimbardo, Philip. *The Lucifer Effect: Understanding How Good People Turn Evil.* New York: Random House, 2007.

Photo Credits

Index